AF757414

Unsound Empire

Unsound Empire

CIVILIZATION AND MADNESS IN LATE-VICTORIAN LAW

Catherine L. Evans

Yale UNIVERSITY PRESS

New Haven & London

Published with assistance from the Louis Stern Memorial Fund.

Copyright © 2021 by Catherine L. Evans. All rights reserved. This book may not be reproduced, in whole or in part, including illustrations, in any form (beyond that copying permitted by Sections 107 and 108 of the U.S. Copyright Law and except by reviewers for the public press), without written permission from the publishers.

Yale University Press books may be purchased in quantity for educational, business, or promotional use. For information, please email sales.press@yale.edu (U.S. office) or sales@yaleup.co.uk (U.K. office).

Set in Adobe Garamond type by IDS Infotech Ltd., Chandigarh, India.
Printed in the United States of America.

Library of Congress Control Number: 2021932166
ISBN 978-0-300-24274-4 (hardcover : alk. paper)

A catalogue record for this book is available from the British Library.

This paper meets the requirements of ANSI/NISO Z39.48-1992 (Permanence of Paper).

10 9 8 7 6 5 4 3 2 1

For Padraic

Contents

Introduction

On the afternoon of 28 November 1885, Lakshman Dagdu was home sick with fever. He and his family lived in Nasik, a bustling town popular with European tourists and Hindu pilgrims on the banks of the Godavari River in present-day Maharashtra, in peninsular India.[1] Dagdu had been ill for five days, and his temper was short. His two young daughters began to cry soon after their mother left the house. Dagdu took the baby out of her cradle and slit her throat with a hatchet. He killed his elder girl, only three, near the door. In the silence, he slept. Later, he surrendered himself to the police and confessed. His wife would soon testify that he was fond of his children.[2]

At his trial for murder at the Nasik Court of Session, an English judge—an alumnus of the elite Winchester School and Pembroke College, Oxford, who had arrived in India in 1864—found Dagdu guilty of murder over the objections of two Indian "assessors," or legal advisers, who argued for his acquittal on the ground that "no one but a lunatic would kill his own young children."[3] His sentence was death. In accordance with procedure, the case was forwarded to the Bombay High Court of Judicature for review. Dagdu's lawyer argued that his client was delirious at the time of the killings, and that this made him "incapable of knowing the nature of his act, or that he [was] doing anything wrong."[4]

Two Cambridge-educated judges, Herbert Mills Birdwood and John Jardine, heard the case at the high court. Although his apparently motiveless attack, for which Dagdu showed no "sorrow or remorse," seemed to indicate insanity, Birdwood argued that the court was bound to find him responsible for his children's deaths. Fever and confusion were not enough. Without conclusive evidence that Dagdu's delirium had destroyed his ability to understand what he had done, Birdwood explained, "it would be impossible for us to acquit the accused." A doctor might find the defendant insane, but the court could not. And so, the judges affirmed Dagdu's conviction. Still, there was hope. Instead of the original capital sentence, the high court recommended transportation to a penal colony. Perhaps, Birdwood and Jardine mused in a note to the Bombay government, the true nature of the prisoner's mental disorder would become clear in time. If he lived long enough, and were sick enough, Dagdu might one day be free.[5]

Seven years later, in an office in Melbourne, Australia, Alfred Deakin, a barrister and future prime minister of Australia, prepared notes for a trial. His client was Frederick Bailey Deeming, an Englishman accused of killing his wife and children in Lancashire. The discovery of his second wife's body under their living room floor in suburban Melbourne precipitated an international manhunt. When Deeming was captured and tried, the evidence against him was strong. A murder conviction carried a mandatory sentence of death in the colony of Victoria, as it did elsewhere in the British world. Only a successful insanity defense seemed to offer any chance of reprieve. The notes Deakin scrawled in pencil on scraps of thin paper outlined the speech he would give to try to save Deeming's life. In the top margin of one page, he wrote "Savage, p. 462"—a reference to *Insanity and Allied Neuroses* (1884) by George H. Savage, an English physician who spent most of his career at Bethlem Hospital (often called Bedlam) in London. "Just as we have seen," Savage wrote in the passage Deakin picked out, "that there is no clear distinction between sanity and insanity, so we must admit that there is no possibility of drawing by definition any clear distinction between liability for acts done, and irresponsibility."[6]

Unsound Empire is about nineteenth-century debates over who was mentally fit enough—in legal language, sufficiently *responsible*—to be convicted in British criminal courts.[7] Judges, lawyers, and physicians in cases like Lakshman Dagdu's and Frederick Deeming's acknowledged the difficulty, even the impossibility, of crafting categories that effectively distinguished the sane and responsible from the insane and irresponsible. Long-standing disputes over the meaning and legal consequences of insanity intensified from the early 1840s to the end of the nineteenth century. These disputes were about more than the technical problem of diagnosing mental disease. Politicians, physicians, and lawyers understood that defining legal insanity, and its implied legal irresponsibility, meant defining its opposite: responsible subjecthood.

Political subjecthood and the relationship between subject and sovereign acquired new importance in the last decades of the eighteenth century, knitting an expanded and increasingly diverse empire together after the upheavals of the Seven Years' War.[8] A century later, subjecthood remained central to imperial governance, but its focus had shifted decisively inward. As Britain's colonial strategy turned away from military conquest and indirect rule toward settlement and governance through anglicized legal institutions, administrators were more confident in asserting British jurisdiction over colonial populations. As the administration of law in the empire became more standardized, professional, bureaucratic, and ostentatiously "English," however, officials faced new challenges. If defendants were to be judged according to Anglo legal principles, they had to be cognitively and morally capable of responsible action. Otherwise, British law would be unmasked as hypocritical, inconstant, and cruel. It was relatively easy for British officials to claim sovereignty over foreign lands and peoples. Delivering British justice was another matter.

Legal, medical, and political officials struggled to differentiate the mental and moral symptoms of brain disease—itself difficult to detect—from the alleged constitutional weaknesses of the empire's "primitive" peoples. In fact, Victorian evolutionary theories led some to argue that many forms of mental illness were caused by civilizational decline, and the atavistic reversion of sufferers to a more primitive state. And so the bare assertion that a person was a British subject could not answer the question of his or her mental competence. Determining whom officials could govern through law required an intimate, psychological inquiry, often bolstered by expert medical and ethnological testimony. Mapping territory was not enough; the problem of responsibility focused the resources of the imperial state on the plotting of subjects' inner lives. The mind emerged as the Victorian Empire's vast internal frontier.

Since the British Empire's mid-twentieth-century collapse, scholars have abandoned triumphalist narratives in favor of analyses of imperial weakness. These postimperial studies show that in the late-nineteenth century, the empire was overstretched and decentralized, dogged by scandal and incompetence. Its long survival now seems to demand more scholarly explanation than its demise. Historians have offered several reasons for the empire's longevity, from capitalism to bureaucracy to Anglo settler solidarity.[9] *Unsound Empire* instead looks to law as the premier organizing instrument and ideological core of British imperialism. Responsibility was, and is, a central precept of common-law jurisprudence. By extension, this book argues, responsibility controversies had clear ramifications for imperial governance. Cases in which a defendant's sanity was at issue (what I call "responsibility cases") brought new medical and anthropological theories into courtrooms across the empire and into imperial jurisprudence. These cases, and their remarkable similarities across colonial jurisdictions, show the robust circulation of legal concepts in the empire. They also lay bare the vulnerability of an empire committed equally to an exclusionary, hierarchical cult of British "civilization" and to a legal order premised on the presumption that most people, most of the time, are sane.

"An unwarrantable act without a vicious will," wrote English jurist William Blackstone in his *Commentaries on the Laws of England* (1769), "is no crime at all."[10] The Latin maxim "actus non facit reum, nisi mens sit rea," usually translated as "an act does not make [the doer of it] guilty, unless the mind be guilty," expresses the same principle.[11] The common law distinguishes accidents from intentional harm. In the words of American lawyer and judge Oliver Wendell Holmes Jr., "Even a dog distinguishes between being stumbled over and being kicked."[12] The idea that only intentional, sane, blameworthy acts deserve punishment has powerful appeal. This model of responsibility gained traction in the Victorian era, when the liberal vision of individuals as autonomous agents, free to choose and to reap the consequences of their choices, was ascendant in many domains, from politics and economics to literature.[13]

How can we know what someone else is thinking or feeling, let alone prove it in court? In his 1863 book, *A General View of the Criminal Law of England*, James Fitzjames Stephen, among the most celebrated legal thinkers of his generation, was of the opinion that the assessment of a person's mental state was an inference made with "little consciousness." In a criminal case, jurors, doctors, and lawyers could watch defendants—scrutinizing clothing, mannerisms, tone of voice—but the best they could hope for were clues.[14] Rounding these clues up to a judgment about a defendant's guilt, or a defendant's life, was an act of empathy and imagination.[15] The closer the resemblance between defendants and their judges, the easier it was to overlook the gap that inference filled. Conversely, when a defendant struck officials as unlike themselves, whether by dint of disease, gender, confession, or race, the precariousness of judgments about mental state was exposed.

In the nineteenth century, physicians who specialized in the study of madness and the care of the insane held themselves out as experts in the new field of mental science. Often called alienists or mad doctors, they were the predecessors of modern psychiatrists, neurologists, and psychologists.[16] The opinions of family and neighbors had once been sufficient to sift the sane from the insane, but a growing belief that insanity was a subtle condition that required expert, medical diagnosis pushed physicians into the witness box.[17] Lawyers for both prosecution and defense began to recruit alienists to assess defendants' sanity and to testify to it in court.

Irresponsibility and insanity were not identical, however. Criminal responsibility was a legal concept and not, fundamentally, a medical one. Stephen explained: "The question 'What are the mental elements of responsibility?' is, and must be, a legal question. It cannot be anything else, for the meaning of responsibility is liability to punishment."[18] Nonetheless, medical and legal accounts of what it meant to be mentally sound became entangled and mutually referential throughout the nineteenth century. Lawyers relied on medical knowledge to inform their opinions and arguments about the sanity of their clients. Doctors commented on the legal responsibility of their patients. Ultimately, the fields of criminal law and mental science were both invested in constructing an image of the broken and damaged psyche that could be contrasted with the whole and healthy one. This shared interest, and the shared space of the criminal courtroom, made it nearly impossible to consider responsibility without medicine, or insanity without law.[19]

Physicians and lawyers shared more than just concern for the mind. Class, race, and gender bound these middle-class, white, professional men together, as did family ties, patriotism, Protestantism, business ventures, the alumni networks of elite schools and universities, and structures of political patronage. But for all their affinities, men of medicine and law were divided by contests over the borders of criminal responsibility, as much within each profession as between them. Alienists steadily pushed the boundaries of their field, developing increasingly complex and capacious definitions of insanity. Eccentricity and aggression came to be classified as symptoms of mental disease, at least by some. Meanwhile, new fields, especially ethnology informed by what George Stocking calls "sociocultural evolutionism" and criminal anthropology (later, criminology), began to argue that tendencies toward deviant behavior, including insanity and certain types of criminality, were inherited.[20] Inspired by mid-nineteenth-century evolutionary theories, these early social scientists also claimed that the supposedly "primitive" peoples of the world suffered from physical and, most important, mental weaknesses that made them more prone to crime and less able to comply with British law. By the late-nineteenth century, primitivism, insanity, and criminality had bled into the concept of the irresponsible subject, which it was up to British criminal jurisprudence to define, detect, and manage.

How could British criminal law, premised on the idea that mens rea was essential to responsibility and that insanity could obviate it, function in the world Victorian science was slowly unveiling? The proportion of Britain's subjects within an expanding empire who seemed fully capable of choosing their actions and suffering the consequences was, at least according to mental science, ethnology, and related disciplines, shrinking. Physicians tried to save defendants from punishment; lawyers tried to save the common law from the presumption of defendants' impunity.

Birdwood, the Bombay judge, was a well-heeled lawyer and devoted amateur naturalist with roots in the subcontinent. All five of his children served in the Indian Army. At the time of Dagdu's trial, one of Birdwood's sons, who had attended the exclusive Rugby School in England, was at work building railways in Sind.[21] Birdwood's colleague Jardine, meanwhile, belonged to a powerful Scottish family of colonial administrators and opium traders. Jardine retired from an illustrious career in the Bombay Civil Service to enter parliamentary politics in England, eventually becoming a baronet. Deakin, the barrister, was a fixture of Melbourne civic life. The city, and the colony of Victoria, attracted ambitious professionals and entrepreneurs from across the British world. These men were part of a network of politicians, lawyers, and physicians with a common investment in the fate of the mad in British criminal justice.

As they well knew, law and lawyering held special places in the ideological and practical operation of the empire. It was a Victorian commonplace, if not precisely accurate, that where Britons went the common law followed.[22] "The British people have an instinctive love of 'law and order,'" one Australian journalist commented in the early-twentieth century. "Where seventy or eighty persons are settled in a British community, the policeman is sure to appear, and there will never be difficulty in obtaining the services of a local tradesman or local orator as a justice of the peace."[23] For law-loving Britons, criminal law was a symbol of good government and was a core technology of British rule at home and in the colonies. In a 1932 speech before the House of Commons, Edward Marjoribanks hailed law as the source of Britain's "magnificent" global power, and as "one of the things of which we are most proud in this country."[24]

But what was "law" in the British Empire? There was no unitary legal system, no linear hierarchy of courts where British subjects could seek justice. The highest court of the empire, the Judicial Committee of the Privy Council, sat in London and exercised pan-imperial jurisdiction, but it heard only select cases, almost none of them criminal appeals, and those by application rather than by right.[25] Even criminal law in the empire, which was most "British" in both form and content, was not British. In 1900, Arthur Balfour, then First Lord of the Treasury, declared, "The circumstances of the various parts of the Empire are so different that a universal criminal law applicable to all is almost illusory."[26] Imperial legislation, colonial statutes, Privy Council recommendations, common-law principles and case law, and the jurisprudence of particular colonies together formed an intricate and variegated body of law.

Law in the British Empire was changeable and ornate, but it had an organizing logic. Although statutes varied from colony to colony, as did divisions among intracolonial legal jurisdictions, British lawyers remained ideologically committed to the core of common-law jurisprudence. Most lawyers of the empire had strong cultural and professional attachments to British legal theory and practice. Before the mid-nineteenth century, colonial authorities tended to give Indigenous polities a wide berth in the management of their own legal affairs, particularly in matters inter se or on civil-law questions.[27] But this tolerance for pluralism, motivated largely by a desire to extract revenue from colonial possessions with a minimum of hassle, waned as the infrastructure and personnel of colonial states grew. Homicide, though, had long been an exception to the empire's pragmatic approach to jurisdiction. Even before the aggressive expansion of colonial courts' powers in the later nineteenth century, criminal law, especially homicide, was generally reserved for British-style courts and British jurisprudence.[28] Responsibility debates, then, happened in colonial courtrooms across the globe, wherever common-law criminal jurisprudence was practiced. Whether in Victoria or Bombay, on the shores of Hudson Bay or the South China Sea, many lawyers and doctors involved in homicide cases read the same medical and legal texts, cited the same precedents, and drew on a shared cultural patrimony.

Law justified and organized the British Empire. Although British courts did not claim exclusive jurisdiction over every facet of life in the colonies, British law was the moral heart of the imperial project. After spending fifteen years as a successful advocate on the Midland circuit, James Fitzjames Stephen traveled to India in 1869 to serve as Law Member of the Viceroy's Council, a high-level legal advisory position. He wrote to his wife, Mary, about his plans to codify and reform colonial Indian law and to make himself the "Indian Blackstone." At first, the work was electrifying. "All the people are wide awake, fiercely hard at work—full of zeal & vigour, & there is the strange subtle feeling of pride in one's name & nation, that runs through every part of every day," he wrote. "It is something to be proud of when one takes one of the first places in the very boldest & most successful enterprise ever tried by mortal man." Stephen was delighted by the gunfire that woke him every day at 5:30 A.M. while he lived at Fort William in Calcutta. He felt that he was on the frontlines of empire, leading the charge against backwardness. He thought it was a noble enterprise. He missed his wife and children but believed "that to have made a great sacrifice for such objects, will be a lesson to all our children, which nothing else could be."[29]

At home or abroad, many of the men, and some women, who made, interpreted, and contested British law shared Stephen's belief in the world-historical importance of the common law. In consequence, any threat to the integrity of the law seemed to be a threat to the ideological foundations of British government, in the United Kingdom and in the rest of the world—an attack on what was considered the best and most powerful aspect of British civilization. Armies could conquer territories, but the law consolidated British rule. If those who had committed crimes could not be held responsible and punished, then the law was useless. As Stephen put it, "If criminal law does not determine who are to be punished under given circumstances, it determines nothing."[30]

The responsibility contests of the late-nineteenth century were not unique to the British Empire. In France, for example, alienists and jurists had been embroiled in debates about the implications of determinism and new scientific theories for criminal justice since the 1820s, including the concern that humans might degenerate, reversing evolutionary gains.[31] Similar clashes among lawyers and experts, the subject of Charles Rosenberg's influential book *The Trial of the Assassin Guiteau* (1968), rocked the United States in the wake of President James A. Garfield's assassination by a man whom advocates claimed was mad.[32] The politics of responsibility varied, however, even when the general parameters of the controversy and many of the key scientific texts stayed the same. While themes in the global history of the late-nineteenth-century responsibility debates recurred across jurisdictions—including race, gender, class, free will, capitalism, degeneration, and morality—different emphases emerged. In the United States, for example, the implications of insanity for democratic self-governance preoccupied the new republic.[33] In France, the psychic consequences of revolutionary politics provoked concern.[34] In the British world, responsibility was, in many ways, about empire.

Homicide trials were what one might call "typical exceptions." They made up a tiny minority of the legal business of British rule. Only some murder cases raised questions about the sanity of a defendant, or the limits of responsibility. In this sense, the cases in this book were all exceptional, representing breaks in the rhythm of everyday legal and social life. Responsibility cases were symbolically and jurisprudentially important, however. Lindsay Farmer describes homicide as the "'metaphysical' centre of the modern law," shaping the interpretation of legal rules and practices—perhaps to ill effect—despite the crime's relative rarity.[35] Homicides also attracted attention. The crueler the killing, the more legal, medical, and journalistic commentary it inspired, and the more press and paperwork it generated. Ordinary people knew about these cases, even when they happened far away. Each one was a unique scandal, but together responsibility cases were a familiar, regular feature of British legal administration.

Moreover, legal and medical experts consistently described homicide cases as central to the mission of criminal law. These cases were subject to heightened scrutiny by the senior judges and political officials generally tasked with reviewing and confirming death sentences, as the High Court of Judicature did in Dagdu's case. Decisions were likely to be recorded in law reports and to establish precedents that would influence the rulings and reasoning of future courts. Because responsibility was a foundational principle of common-law jurisprudence, changes in how lawyers defined and proved it could ripple out from homicide to lap at other areas of law. So, although homicide cases involving insanity pleas were statistically infrequent, they were part of the landscape of British justice, with clear implications for the legal system.

Because homicide cases tested the underlying conceptual and procedural integrity of British justice, doctors and lawyers who sparred openly about the definition of insanity or criticized the law could pose political risks to the British state, at home and abroad. One way to mitigate that damage was to shunt responsibility controversies away from the courtroom. Even conservatives who favored a legalistic definition of insanity acknowledged how difficult it often was to distinguish sanity from insanity, especially in court. After a conviction, jurors, judges, lawyers, physicians, chaplains, and others regularly appealed to executive authority to calibrate the prisoner's punishment to match his or her "true" guilt.[36] Despite the mandatory capital sentence for murder, many more murderers were convicted than were hanged. In the colonies, governors had to decide whether to uphold a death sentence. In Britain, this task fell to the Home Office, which wielded the prerogative of mercy on the Queen's behalf. In 1875, the Earl of Kimberley declared, before the House of Lords, that the prerogative "involve[d] the exercise of one of the most delicate functions of the machinery of Colonial Government." This technological metaphor notwithstanding, Kimberley's account of the operation of the prerogative privileged human intuition over mechanical precision. Colonial governors enjoyed considerable discretion in how they decided who deserved death and who did not. This was, in Kimberley's view, as it should be. "In matters of this kind," Kimberley continued, "we ought not to be too logical. Constitutional Government in this country has not grown up by means of a rigorous application of the principles of logic, but rather by a happy application of good sense on the part of men who proved themselves equal to deal with emergencies."[37]

As the prerogative of mercy shows, the ambiguities of a defendant's responsibility were hardly fatal to the operation of the British criminal justice system. In a criminal trial, though, apparent deviations from legal principles could look suspiciously arbitrary. Mental science and ethnology, similarly, took on new valences in legal contexts. Among physicians or social scientists, or even in public discourse, ideas about the social and biological determinants of human behavior provoked responses from indifference to outrage. When expert witnesses or lawyers insisted on a defendant's irresponsibility in court, their arguments could quickly shift in scale from a defense specific to a given case to broader claims against a legal order premised on free choice. Victorians who held a narrow interpretation of insanity, or who argued for a low mental threshold for criminal responsibility, did not necessarily reject the insights of the new sciences or the "good sense" of the prerogative. Rather, they sought to keep these uncertainties, political calculations, and radical reinterpretations of the human condition in hospitals and government offices safely apart from criminal courts.[38]

The responsibility debates of the latter half of the nineteenth century took place against the backdrop of Victorian penal reform campaigns. By the late-eighteenth century, corporal punishment was in decline in England. In the early-nineteenth century, a movement for national penal reform gathered momentum, taking aim at public floggings, executions, and dueling. Reformers' primary concern was the noxious effect that spectacular violence had on those who witnessed or participated in it, rather than the prisoner's suffering.[39]

Whereas exemplary, bloody punishment had once seemed an edifying deterrent against crime, it now struck reformers as brutalizing. To guard against savagery, the law would have to be less savage. Reformers argued that "civilization" required that people submit themselves to government by predictable, rational, impartial rules. "Only such an authority," writes historian Martin Wiener, "itself restrained, could nurture self-mastery in the people."[40] A series of legislative victories followed: the pillory was abolished in 1837; the use of public whipping, in 1862; transportation, in 1867; public hanging, in 1868. Carceral institutions, from penitentiaries to asylums, workhouses, and residential schools, claimed to substitute reform for cruelty. Their superintendents hoped to bolster inmates' character, including the ability to resist primitive impulses to drink, steal, brawl, fornicate, and kill.[41] Prisons were particularly appealing to reformers because punishments measured in time, in contrast to specific acts of violence or banishment, could be tailored more precisely to the severity of the offense. This satisfied reformers' calls for proportionality and for rational, even scientific, punishment. By the middle of the nineteenth century, uniformity, certainty, and predictability had become the guiding principles of British penal administration.[42]

Efforts to shore up civilization in Britain had obvious imperial implications. Reformers argued that violent, public punishment undercut the "civilizing mission," exposing Britons to accusations of hypocrisy and of corrupting the moral sentiments of settlers and Indigenous people alike. The anti-flogging campaigns of the 1830s and 1840s, for instance, drew British humanitarians to the Cape Colony, Mauritius, and the Australian colonies. They continued the work of antislavery activists who had fixated on the whip as a symbol of slavery's barbarism.[43] Reformers pushed the idea of punishment as a barometer of civilization outward from Britain, using it to assess the civilization of colonial populations. In India from the 1830s, the East India Company and, after 1857, the Crown used humanitarian rhetoric to justify British paramountcy and to undermine the authority of Indian rulers by prohibiting punishments they considered cruel.[44] Radhika Singha argues that penal reform and humanitarianism in India were linked to strategies of colonial rule, including increasing the legitimacy of law as a tool of governance. The same is true, she observes, with respect to governance in England and in the wider empire.[45]

Less successful were efforts to abolish less visible forms of corporal and capital punishment in the United Kingdom, or even to radically restrict their ambit. Wiener notes that executions in England continued at the steady rate of roughly fifteen per year from 1850 to 1914. Capital punishment was abolished only in 1965, and corporal punishment persisted, behind closed doors, until 1948.[46] Moreover, the predictability and uniformity that liberal Britons prized so highly in imprisonment eluded capital punishment. Kimberley's 1875 admonition against being "too logical" in weighing petitions for mercy captured the general feeling that death was a punishment apart. While a capital *sentence* was subject to the strict rule-of-law aspirations of later Victorian criminal justice, execution was a moral, political matter that demanded the discretion of executive authority. Many were content with the flexibility of capital punishment, but others continued to see its arbitrariness and violence as remnants of a bygone and more primitive penal regime.

Criticism of the death penalty converged with the problem of responsibility and insanity. One of the chief complaints of death-penalty critics was that insane prisoners were being hanged. Most commentators, even those who supported capital punishment, conceded that mistakes were possible. In the late 1870s and 1880s, lobbyists associated with the Howard Association, a British penal reform society, and reform-minded politicians attempted to pass legislation abolishing capital punishment. During an 1881 Commons debate that ended with the defeat of the abolition bill he had championed, Joseph Whitwell Pease, a Quaker and Liberal member of Parliament, argued that insanity affected "the whole subject" of capital punishment, as "between madness and badness the distinction was difficult."[47] The Howard Association also used insanity to focus a general attack on the death penalty. One report argued that murderers were more likely than other offenders to suffer from mental illness, claiming that 17 percent of those tried for murder in England were found insane, versus only 0.25 percent of defendants in other criminal trials. Even so, British law related to insanity was "so contrary to medical science, and to *common-sense*" that it compounded the "admittedly extreme difficulty" of determining criminal responsibility.[48] Homicide cases therefore placed jurors in the uncomfortable position of perhaps voting to hang a "lunatic for the results of the pitiable calamity of mental disease."[49]

Responsibility and capital punishment were distinct questions. Nevertheless, death lurked behind contests over the definition of insanity and the limits of culpability. A mistaken or unfair assessment of the sanity of a defendant could mean his or her execution. An unjust execution was not only an individual tragedy but also an indictment of the legal system. Those who criticized the legal definition of insanity argued that the doctrine poisoned everything it touched, including capital punishment and the penal regime that countenanced it. Liberal reformers seized upon this argument, reinforcing the idea that a corrupt doctrine of responsibility implied systemic legal rot and uncivilized, antiscientific government.

In Britain as in the colonies, a death sentence was, therefore, an everyday emergency of government.[50] The gap between the conviction of a defendant and his or her date of execution was measured in weeks, or at best a month or two. As soon as the judge donned his black cap and pronounced the sentence, those with an interest in keeping the prisoner alive went to work, drafting letters and petitions. A colonial governor might find his desk buried in correspondence. In such instances, as Kimberley said, there was little call for strict adherence to rules. Those empowered to dispense the Queen's mercy were encouraged to follow their intuitions about the prisoner's blameworthiness and the public mood. When capital convictions reached executive review, the borders between legal responsibility and medical insanity, and between these concepts and the overarching question of the morality of punishment, broke down. Law, medicine, religion, and science were subsumed under a Victorian understanding of "good sense," which government officials relied on to determine, with very little oversight or guidance, who deserved to die.

The responsibility debates of the late-nineteenth century coincided with a period of reconstitution in the British Empire. Scholars have tried to explain how a North Atlantic archipelago came to assert sovereignty over a quarter of the world—to color so much of the globe the notorious, dusty pink of nineteenth-century maps. From *why* many have turned to *how*, focusing on the histories of techniques of rule and organizing logics, searching for patterns in the diversity of the empire's places and peoples. In the past several decades, historians have argued that centralized, metropolitan control over the empire was an illusion. Power devolved onto colonial governors or petty administrators who made decisions in response to colonial circumstances, sometimes in conformity with instructions from London, but often according to their own whims or in response to local crises.[51] By these lights, the ideology and governance of the British Empire were epiphenomena of many local decisions, something like a flock of starlings, in which thousands of individuals making simple calculations and adjustments acquire a surprising unity.

In the mid-1800s Britain turned its attention to Africa, acquiring new territories that it was ambivalent about governing.[52] The settler colonies of Canada, Australia, New Zealand, and South Africa tightened their grip on Indigenous lands and people, insisting that a sovereignty that had once been mostly notional become devastatingly real.[53] Thousands of miles of telegraph wires and train tracks collapsed physical and metaphorical distance, allowing people, products, and information to circulate more quickly and widely than ever before. The empire had never been bigger or richer.

Technology, commerce, and growing cities promised to bring the natural world to heel, allowing human beings to live faster, grander lives—perhaps too fast and too grand. As early as 1796, magistrate, statistician, and author Patrick Colquhoun wrote that moral turpitude in London increased in tandem with "the unparalleled extent and opulence of the metropolis, and . . . the vast amount of moving property which exhibits London not only as the grand magazine of the British Empire, but also as the general receptacle for the idle and depraved of almost every Country."[54]

As in London, so in the empire. The concentration of people and resources in increasingly wealthy imperial cities sparked fears of criminality and chaos, including organized unrest among the poor and the colonized. Closer imperial connections also fed concerns about international crime and contagion, as people, goods, knowledge, and pathogens traveled from colony to colony, and from the colonies to Britain, especially to London.[55] Some physicians theorized that Europeans' bodies and minds could not adapt to the frenetic pace of modern life. Train travel could jangle delicate nerves, smog could corrode sensitive lungs, and stress could upset finely balanced minds. To many, insanity, like criminality, seemed to keep pace with civilization; the success of the British way of life seemed to contain the seeds of its own destruction. Alcoholism, prostitution, and other vices were identified as both cause and consequence of mental weakness, signs—especially among the poor—of what certain thinkers called "degeneration."[56] They posited that modern living and contact with colonial populations were hurtling Europeans backward in biological time. As "degenerates" multiplied, they gave birth to successively weaker and less civilized generations. Isolated instances of atavistic savagery among individuals were troubling; the prospect of population-level decline accelerated by compounding heritable weakness was even more so. Degeneration had mental and moral consequences. Some argued that it made its victims more impulsive, violent, covetous, and dull, and less able to resist the primitive nature that stalked even the most civilized person.

These anxieties about modernization, degeneration, and imperialism raised the stakes of responsibility contests still higher. If Britons were becoming less capable of the foresight, self-control, and understanding that criminal jurisprudence presumed, the basic premises of criminal responsibility were at risk. Worse, perhaps, were the implications of this pessimistic introspection for colonial governance. The "civilizing mission" of the nineteenth century proposed that societies could be improved through judicious governance undergirded by just, rational laws. Law was, as Farmer writes, "both an index and instrument of the civilizing process."[57] How could Britons subject colonized people to the criminal law if the law could fairly judge only the "civilized"? Contempt among Britons for the putatively uncivilized peoples of the world was not a Victorian invention. Mental science, ethnology, and imperial ideology's commitment to law, however, made the integrity of criminal jurisprudence sharply salient, and newly assailed.

In this book, I focus on cases from England, Canada, Australia, and India. These jurisdictions were legally sophisticated and politically and economically important in the late-nineteenth century, an importance evident in the depth of their archives. For example, most Privy Council appeals in the late-nineteenth century were Indian, and the India Office in London kept voluminous records. The Australian and Canadian judicial archives are also comprehensive, replete with correspondence, depositions, notes of evidence, and other documents. Within those jurisdictions, some places—London, Melbourne, Agra, Battleford—host clusters of cases that illuminate particular institutions, networks of professionals, or crises.

I have ignored the usual scholarly separation between the colonies of settlement and India.[58] Historians Ronald Robinson and John Gallagher wrote in 1961 that the Indian Empire "to all Victorians was the exception to every rule."[59] Many nineteenth-century British judges, including Birdwood, might have disagreed. Reading Indian cases alongside Australian, Canadian, and English ones shows that, at least insofar as responsibility was concerned, India was distinct but not entirely different. In this book, British and colonial cases are arranged in counterpoint, to illustrate the striking consonances between responsibility contests across the empire. Ideas about insanity, civilization, and responsibility did not emanate from London to be uncritically applied in the rest of the British world. Judges and jurors in the metropolis and abroad interpreted the law and the defendant's state of mind through the lens of their own experiences, including their knowledge of local conditions, and in response to what they heard in court. And yet, while much divided these jurisdictions, responsibility controversies touched them all, revealing in the process how important common-law jurisprudence was to British governance everywhere.

Unsound Empire describes responsibility largely through the eyes of the administrators involved in the management of madness through criminal law: lawyers, judges, physicians, coroners, and political officials. Imperial historians have lately revalued administrative and bureaucratic histories of empire—or, more precisely, the histories of administrators and bureaucrats.

Lauren Benton and Lisa Ford have called these officials "men in the middle" who wielded, in a phrase borrowed from Maitland, "middle power."[60] Petty administrators of various stripes thought of themselves as subjects, and agents, of the British Empire, tied by training, patronage, pay, and inclination to Britain. Their identity shaped their participation in a global legal-bureaucratic order. Although they created much of the surviving colonial archive, especially on matters related to law and the daily operation of imperial governance, they have at times been overlooked by historians of the empire. Through their neat handwriting and fastidious record keeping, magistrates, justices of the peace, and other middling officials slowly remade imperial law in the nineteenth century. And they did not do it alone. Medical men, including the coroners, medical officers, asylum superintendents, and prison surgeons of Britain and the empire shaped how defendants and prisoners fared under the law. These men, like the lawyers with whom they collaborated and clashed, had loyalties to an international professional fraternity as well as to the project of British rule.

Histories that follow private individuals and groups of officials and other professionals across the empire capture the size and diversity of the British world while preserving its human scale.[61] Transportation and communication networks structure these stories, explaining where, why, and how people moved, lived, and thought. Scholarship on the "paper empire" complements histories of "imperial careering," emphasizing how official paperwork, private correspondence, fiction, news, the missionary press, and scientific and social scientific literature guided imperial ideology and practice.[62] These histories, like *Unsound Empire*, often aim to build an account of how officials understood the empire and their place in it. The emphasis, therefore, is not only on administrative practices or on imperial administration as a system but also on administrators as individuals and as a class.[63]

Fealty to the common law and a vague but dearly held liberalism, deeply troubled by advances in medicine and social science, connected Britain's imperial officials to one another and to the United Kingdom. As I use the term, the "official" class includes lawyers and physicians who were essential to the elaboration of British criminal law, in Britain and beyond, but who were not directly, or exclusively, employees of the state. Imperial decision making was fractured and decentralized, often driven by "crises" in the colonies rather than by metropolitan directives.[64] The officials who ran the empire were as heterogeneous as its colonies. And yet, acknowledging difference should not mute similarity. Officials worked together to build what they hoped would be a civilized empire. This project united them, even when they disagreed vehemently about the parameters of legal insanity or the result in an individual case.[65]

When judges and other officials were scattered across the British world, they brought their legal knowledge and habits of mind with them. They applied principles gleaned from cases tried in England and in other British colonial jurisdictions in new places, making the changes they thought that context required while preserving what they interpreted as the basic principles of British justice and fair play. The analogical reasoning of the common law allowed officials to make compromises without feeling that they had compromised their integrity, or the integrity of British rule. They were skilled at the lawyer's trick of dividing particularity from general principle; within superficially isolated episodes, British-trained lawyers found, created, or amplified connections.

The common law maintains an impressive degree of coherence even as it adapts in response to new cases and the reinterpretation of the old. A. W. B. Simpson, the English legal historian, cautioned against trying to discover the alchemical formula that transformed the "muddle" of the common law into something that we often experience, perhaps incorrectly, as a system. "The explanation," he wrote, "for the degree of consensus which exists at any one time will be very complex, and no *general* explanation will be possible."[66] Looking closely at cases, he warned, would only make the common law more baffling.[67]

Perhaps sharing the view that cases are unlikely to provide satisfying explanations of large-scale historical phenomena, historians have tended to privilege colonial or imperial statutes over case law in their legal histories of the British Empire. Cases might appear to be too small, specific, and idiosyncratic to say much about law in general. Also, from a practical standpoint, cases can be more difficult for scholars to locate in the archives, particularly in comparison with published collections of statutes. The assumption, however, that legislation was the primary tool of colonial governance, what Mitra Sharafi calls the "codification fallacy," obscures the importance of case law as a preeminent form of legal ordering in the empire, both before and after statutes were promulgated.[68]

Case histories open up the relationship between the common law and the British Empire while capturing individual experiences. The level of detail in criminal case files can be arresting, allowing a reconstruction of a crime or court scene that can seem to border on fiction.[69] Case records preserve accounts that witnesses gave during inquests or trials, and show how lawyers refined them through cross-examination and in speeches before the jury. Medical doctors were also storytellers, relying on legal records, interviews, and family histories to describe their patients' pathologies and the contents of their minds. People across the British Empire used legal and medical narratives to make sense of who they were and how they could be governed.

The case files now housed in the archives and libraries of the former British Empire are the fruits of bureaucratic and administrative practices. Michel Foucault famously cast the "case" as a means through which scientific, legal, and religious authorities transformed individuals into objects of knowledge, to be catalogued, dissected, and controlled. The "turning of real lives into writing," he argues, made inscrutable, troublesome people intelligible and manageable. The case, then, is not "a monument for future memory, but a document for possible use."[70] Case records preserve glimmers of the lives of patients and prisoners, as well as the lives of their families, neighbors, and victims. Asylum casebooks and criminal dossiers have as much, or more, to tell us about their authors—medical superintendents, judges, and state officials—and their host institutions as they do about their ostensible subjects.[71]

Cases had many uses. Among other functions, asylum case files tracked a patient's progress, satisfied government oversight regulations, and justified the patient's continued confinement or release. A legal case file generally digested courtroom events and testimony, and referred important questions to experts and branches of government. Foucault made much of the differences between how lawyers and doctors use cases. Case-based reasoning and documentary techniques have, however, long been common to both medicine and law, traded between domains along with ways of knowing and organizing individuals.[72] Responsibility cases, in addition, naturally transgressed traditional disciplinary and professional boundaries. For instance, defendants often acquired two files: one medical, which included personal correspondence and doctors' notes, and one legal, collecting documents from arrest warrants to trial transcripts. But even though these files were housed separately and had different audiences, they were conjoined. In Britain, for example, physicians regularly forwarded copies of medical documents to the Home Office, where they were tucked into prisoners' legal dossiers. Legal records sent to the India Office might contain physicians' opinions on a defendant's sanity. Asylum casebooks still flutter with newspaper clippings describing patients' trials. The issue of the patient-cum-prisoner's responsibility was at once medical, legal, and political. Starting with the case and considering its institutional context and uses shows that efforts to define responsible subjecthood extended beyond courtrooms and hospitals, engaging the apparatus of the wider imperial state.

The stories cases tell are twinned: the story of the defendant or the patient coexists with, and is constituted by, the story of the case's compilers. For a book like *Unsound Empire*, both matter. Despite the characteristic restraint of Victorian official correspondence, the drama and emotion of homicide cases shaped officials' responses to responsibility questions. I temper my focus on officials and their foibles with an emphasis on the humanity of defendants and the tragedy of their crimes. Still, as John Forrester writes, "The act of building a theory out of a well-examined life only makes more evident the deafening silence that constitutes that life's secret truths."[73] This is true of defendants in responsibility cases, and even truer of their victims, whose presence is light in the official documentary record. The people drawn into contact with British officials following a violent death doubtless had their own understandings of madness, violence, and justice. *Unsound Empire* marks moments where imperial and local perspectives likely differed, but it is not a cultural or social history of madness or criminal justice across the empire. Instead, the book seeks to describe responsibility's place in the nineteenth-century imperial imagination. Committed as they were to case histories and case files, British officials often acknowledged that "life's secret truths" were beyond their ken. *Unsound Empire* explores how they grappled with their own ignorance even as they rushed to palliate it with bold racial and medical theories.

The risk of a case-based approach is that digging into the history of any case will obscure broad patterns in favor of the granular details of a conflict, or even a life. The same might be said, in reverse, of attempting to write about the "British Empire" instead of individual colonies. In gesturing at "imperial law," colonial histories might be lost, flattened, and distorted. *Unsound Empire* mediates between individual and imperial scales by juxtaposing cases from disparate jurisdictions. Situating each story in its context and linking it to others builds a history of imperial law in sedimentary layers. This book does not attempt to describe trends in the disposition of homicide cases. While it narrates dozens of cases and cites many more, it is not comprehensive. Responsibility cases are a predictable presence in late-nineteenth-century legal archives, and I argue that they cannot be dismissed as mere curiosities. The book's micro-historical method, especially when coupled with a multi-sited approach, is necessarily uneven. Folding the imperial map to bring together London and Melbourne, or Agra and Ottawa, can, however, reveal trends otherwise hidden by distance and difference.

"All crime is local," declared the Judicial Committee of the Privy Council in its judgment in *John McLeod v The Attorney General New South Wales*, an 1891 bigamy case.[74] The judges were explaining the committee's long-standing reluctance to hear appeals in criminal cases. But criminal responsibility, like the rest of British criminal law in the colonies, was emphatically *not* local—it was a self-consciously European export and a tool for colonial transformation, not an outgrowth of Indigenous or even settler tradition. Even in English port cities and country towns, common-law doctrine and procedure could compete with regional customs, illuminating a separation between "local" law and the law of the centralizing British state.[75] The jurisprudence of criminal law claimed to derive universal principles from centuries of British life, but it was never perfectly attuned to the moment or place of its application. If society changed gradually, the law could keep up or, depending on one's perspective, could offer standards toward which to strive. A ballooning empire and the stresses and discoveries of the late-nineteenth century seemed, however, to be driving Britons away from their law. If they lost sight of it altogether—if it, like they, were unfit for modernity—what then?

Criminal responsibility is an often unseen but always present aspect of common-law jurisprudence, which Britons unspooled as they moved across the imperial world. Responsibility debates connected the empire's courtrooms to one another and to London, both ideologically and as a heuristic for organizing and justifying criminal punishment. The common law was flexible, but it had a breaking point. Responsibility cases asked judges in England and elsewhere to determine where that point was—how much of the new scientific ideas about criminality, race, and the mind the law could accommodate before its connection to the past, and to its own principles, snapped.

Unsound Empire begins with medical or psychiatric ways of understanding irresponsibility and moves toward explanations that centered civilizational or racial rationales. Early chapters draw out ways that internal, biological processes like mental disease and degeneration threatened the presumption of liberal subjecthood at the heart of common-law jurisprudence. These were conditions that could strike almost anyone, even the propertied white men who considered themselves paragons of responsible self-government. Later chapters, in contrast, consider those on the margins of responsibility: white women and racialized colonial populations. Strategies for governing and judging these presumptively "less responsible" subjects were more flexible but also more confused. When, if ever, did a less responsible subject become an irresponsible subject? Were less responsible people more prone to mental illness, or was their difference somehow protective?

Sanity, gender, and race were axes along which Victorians plotted responsible subjecthood; perceived deficiencies along any or all three could plunge a person into irresponsibility. The distinctions among the qualities that defined responsible subjecthood also often dissolved as Victorians analogized mental disease, innate psychological immaturity, and "primitivism." Thus, disputes over the meaning of legal insanity distilled nineteenth-century debates over human nature, competence, and civilization, forcing British officials to consider the implications of these ideas for the empire of law they had built.

CHAPTER I

Guilt and the Gallows

On 2 March 1898, James Shaw begged Queen Victoria to spare his life. He wrote from his cell at Northampton Prison, where he had been awaiting his execution for the four months since his trial. "I saw My Mother die I was the youngest of the seven I left school when I passed the fourth standard," Shaw wrote in a careful hand. As a teenager, he suffered an attack of "the Brain fever." Later, after seven years in the Scots Guards, he returned home to find his father, sister, and brother dead. Shaw omitted the reason for his conviction. The previous July, he had lured his nine-year-old niece, Alice, and thirteen-year-old nephew, Albert, into an oat field. Two days later, a police officer found a bloody razor, some string, a button, a sweet, and, eventually, Albert's body. The child's severed head rested in the grass nearby.[1]

Murder was a capital offense in Britain and its empire throughout the nineteenth century. Once a jury foreman declared a verdict of willful murder, the judge donned his black cap and pronounced the inevitable sentence: death. The gallows drew the eyes and ears of the press and the public to homicide cases. Under this scrutiny, British authorities at home and in the colonies worked to ensure that death sentences comported with "civilized," liberal values. A government body—the Home Secretary's Office in Britain or, in many colonies, the Governor-General-in-Council—reviewed each capital case. The prerogative of mercy allowed these authorities to substitute terms of imprisonment or transportation to Britain's penal colonies for death, or even to grant prisoners full pardons. As Douglas Hay argued in his study of eighteenth-century capital punishment, executive mercy and judicial terror worked in tandem in the administration of British criminal justice.[2] Statutes that mandated a murderer's execution proclaimed the impartiality and moral clarity of British law and governance. Commutations and pardons, meanwhile, gave authorities politically valuable flexibility and the opportunity to display their humanity and compassion. Historians have long understood what Hay's intervention underscored: that judicial executions, whether they happen or not, are opportunities for statecraft.[3] In the first half of the twentieth century, approximately half of prisoners convicted of murder in Britain received commutations. Nineteenth-century commutation rates varied in Britain and the empire across time and place but sometimes reached as high as 70 percent.[4]

Jurors and judges knew that a guilty verdict meant a death sentence, not necessarily a death. The mandatory capital sentence for murder gave defendants and their lawyers impetus to make bold arguments against narrow understandings of fault. The insanity defense became their proving ground. Responsibility was central to the logic of mercy. When executive authorities reviewed capital cases, they often focused on questions of desert. Did the prisoner deserve to die? Was there a chance of remorse and redemption? These inquiries turned on evaluations of the character and capacity of the prisoner, including the critical issue of his or her sanity. Officials usually had only files to guide them. Their most intimate access to the prisoner's person was through the reports of prison surgeons and expert witnesses, supplemented by judges' summaries and the occasional petition.

In 1892, English physician Daniel Hack Tuke argued that insanity was an ancient problem. "The madman," he wrote, "was a recognised character, a felt anomaly, among his fellows. Although so frequently regarded as possessed, or as simply criminal, cruel, and bloodthirsty, a certain number were seen to be what is vulgarly understood as 'mad,' and more or less irresponsible."[5] But while mentally ill defendants were certainly familiar characters on the British legal scene, nineteenth-century developments in medicine and ethnology suggested that they were becoming, and perhaps had always been, difficult to recognize. Alienists were part of a robust administrative system dedicated to the management of the criminally insane. The legislative innovations of the nineteenth century meant that patients could be safely, and legally, confined in state-run asylums for the rest of their natural lives. As British criminal justice became less bloody, jurists and politicians were expected to offer more fulsome justifications for the state's application of its lethal power. These justifications rested, in part, on physicians' ability to divide the sane from the insane. The problem was that there was little agreement about how to do it.

James Shaw was tried for the murder of Albert Smith on 18 November 1897.[6] Alice Sarah Smith, Shaw's niece and Albert's younger sister, testified that the children and their uncle had lingered in an oat field while out walking. As Albert ate sweets some distance away, Alice and her uncle were "together 'ever so long.' She did not cry out, although her uncle hurt her." Alice left the field alone; she could not see her brother in the tall grass. Shaw was arrested two days later.[7]

Robert Hammond-Chambers, an Eton- and Oxford-educated barrister, defended Shaw in court.[8] The killing was cruel and motiveless, Hammond-Chambers told the jury; Shaw could not have been sane.[9] Despite pleas for caution from medico-legal authorities, most jurists considered absence of motive to be the hallmark of an insane act.[10] Hammond-Chambers called two expert witnesses: Lee Cogan, a prison doctor who supervised Shaw during his pretrial detention, and Joseph Bayley, a physician at St. Andrew's Hospital for Mental Diseases in Northampton. At trial, Cogan testified that Shaw seemed "confused and unnatural" when addressed and viewed his crime with "levity." He declared Shaw's sanity "questionable."[11] Bayley had been the resident physician at a private lunatic asylum for thirty-three years, where he had little contact with the criminally insane.[12] Nevertheless, he was confident that Shaw suffered from homicidal monomania, a condition marked by superficial rationality and random, uncontrollable outbursts of extreme violence. Bayley testified that Shaw could not have refrained from violence even "if a policeman were standing by."[13]

To strengthen Bayley's diagnosis, Hammond-Chambers recounted a lurid version of Shaw's family history. Shaw's father, John, had attempted suicide three times, once "by trying to hang himself to [*sic*] the bedstead with a pocket handkerchief."[14] Shaw himself had suffered fits as a child, culminating in the case of "brain fever" that left him unconscious for weeks. As an adult, he was often erratic and violent. In prison, he had attempted to "mutilate himself by cutting off his private parts with a piece of broken glass."[15] The members of the jury deliberated into the night, while a crowd waited outside the courthouse for news. At ten o'clock they emerged and declared Shaw guilty of murder.[16]

Hammond-Chambers would have known that his odds of winning the case were slim. Homicidal monomania had a long and troubled association

Daniel McNaughten, as photographed by Henry Hering at Bethlem Royal Hospital c. 1857–1859. The original caption reads: "D.M. Mania. Homicide." Credit: © Bethlem Museum of the Mind, HPA-34.

with the modern English definition of legal insanity, established in the most famous insanity case in the history of the common law, *R v M'Naghten* (1843).

Daniel McNaughten, a Glaswegian cabinetmaker, shot Prime Minister Sir Robert Peel's secretary, Edward Drummond, in January of 1843, as Drummond left Whitehall. A porter watched McNaughten take the gun from his breast pocket and aim it at Drummond. When a watchful police officer tackled him, the pistol discharged and Drummond fell. Although a surgeon was able to extract the ball from his back, he died the next morning. The chief inspector of police visited McNaughten in his cell on the evening of the killing, anxious to know "under such revolting circumstances, who and what the man was."[17] The men talked for a long time, swapping stories of McNaughten's native Scotland. The prisoner explained that his true target had been Peel, whose Conservative Party he believed was persecuting him.

Daniel McNaughten never spelled his name M'Naghten, although this is its most common rendering among legal writers. Witnesses at trial described him as penurious, hardworking, shy, and sickly. One neighbor testified that McNaughten liked to fill his pockets with crumbs for the birds. His father, also named Daniel McNaughten, had tried to convince his son that there was no conspiracy against him. McNaughten believed that spies followed him, sometimes shaking bundles of sticks or straws, which he took as a sign that they would soon reduce him to beggary. When his father asked why he had never seen these spies for himself, McNaughten replied, "Oh, no . . . it is only when I am alone they follow me."[18]

The main medical witness for the defense was Edward Monroe, an alienist with legal training. McNaughten, Monroe wrote, said he had been "tossed like a cork on the sea, that wherever he went, whether in town or country, or by the sea shore, he was perpetually watched, and followed." The physician had not "the remotest doubt of his insanity." Monroe explained that it was an established principle of mental science that a person could experience a condition called partial insanity or monomania. In this type of madness, the reason and self-control of sufferers were overborne by a single, specific delusion, leaving their faculties otherwise intact. Monroe also believed that monomania could affect a person's moral sense. McNaughten was so tormented by fantasies of persecution "that he did not distinguish between right and wrong." Two Scottish doctors agreed with Monroe's assessment, as did Forbes Winslow, another physician who appeared as an expert witness in many mid-Victorian murder trials.[19]

The jury held that McNaughten was not guilty on the ground of insanity. He was delivered to Bethlem asylum on 13 March 1843, at the age of twenty-nine.[20] On the same day, the House of Lords discussed criminal insanity. "The public mind," reflected Lord Campbell, "was in considerable alarm on this subject. The public had been inundated by medical books calculated very much to mislead juries in the case of future trials of a similar kind." According to Campbell, medical books promoted the dangerous idea that many murderers experienced a "homicidal propensity" that made them irresponsible for their criminal acts. Henry Peter Brougham, First Baron Brougham and Vaux, a judge and the architect of the modern Judicial Committee of the Privy Council, also felt that legal insanity required official clarification. In his view, lay persons were liable to misconstrue a guilty verdict as a moral indictment, leading to excessive lenience in cases where a defendant seemed mentally abnormal or otherwise sympathetic. In reality, responsibility was a lawyer's tool for meting out punishment and deterring future crime, nothing more. He thought it wise to make the technical, dispassionate nature of legal insanity clear.[21]

To dispel any confusion, the House of Lords, including Brougham and Campbell, formally responded to several questions put to them about insanity. Their answers quickly became known as the *M'Naghten* rules. Lord Chief

Justice Tindal's summary of the Lords' responses to the questions McNaughten inspired, delivered in June of 1843, became the core of the common law's modern approach to insanity: "To establish a defence on the ground of insanity, it must be clearly proved that, at the time of the committing of the act, the party accused was labouring under such a defect of reason, from disease of the mind, as not to know the nature and quality of the act he was doing; or, if he did know it, that he did not know he was doing what was wrong."[22]

From then on, the *M'Naghten* rules dominated insanity cases in Britain and the British Empire. They emphasized cognition over any other aspect of mental function. In principle, defendants could only succeed under the rules if their insanity prevented them from appreciating that their actions were wrong, or from understanding them at all. Joel Eigen has described the rules as a "defensive move" on the part of members of the judiciary who worried that the expanding medical definition of insanity would swallow responsibility whole.[23] Monroe and many of the other doctors who testified at the trial emphasized the inability of McNaughten to control himself. The *M'Naghten* rules, however, gave no quarter to definitions of insanity that included purely volitional or moral (noncognitive) impairment. Thus, *M'Naghten* came under immediate attack. Critics felt that it was cruelly restrictive and out of touch with medical science. Many would continue to decry the unfairness of *M'Naghten* throughout the century.

As the *M'Naghten* rules became notorious, Daniel McNaughten himself was slowly forgotten. Following his acquittal, he was confined, like most English criminal lunatics at the time, in a special wing at Bethlem Hospital. Founded in the thirteenth century, Bethlem had endured wars, fires, neglect, ignominy, and three relocations by the time its criminal lunatic ward was closed in 1863. The hospital slouched into the nineteenth century infamous for violence and misery. Daniel Hack Tuke, reflecting on the state of Bethlem before 1815, rued "the absurdly antiquated medical treatment and the actual inhumanity practised there." Asylum reformers Philippe Pinel and Tuke's great-grandfather, William Tuke, had advocated "moral management"—nonrestraint and nonviolence in the treatment of the insane—in the early-nineteenth century. Tuke was sure that "before that good men and true must . . . [have] shuddered in their secret souls at the cruelties practiced upon the insane." Conditions at the hospital only began to improve, at last, in the 1820s.[24]

The steady bettering of living standards at Bethlem did not extend to its criminal ward. "It is not a modern prison," wrote alienist John Charles Bucknill in 1854, "for there is no corrective discipline; it is not an hospital, for suitable treatment is impossible; it is not an asylum for the relief and protection of the unfortunate, for it is one of the most gloomy abodes to be found in the metropolis. It is simply a *receptacle*; into which the waifs of criminal law are swept, out of sight and out of mind."[25] For years, Parliament debated what to do about the overcrowded and understaffed criminal ward. Criminal lunatics were considered too dangerous to be released and too disruptive to be housed in ordinary asylums. Finally, the Criminal Lunatics Asylum Act (1860) established a new institution: Broadmoor Criminal Lunatic Asylum. Convict laborers built the hospital, an imposing redbrick pile, amid the tall pines of the Crown Estate of Windsor Forest.[26] When the new asylum opened, the criminal lunatics of Bethlem, including McNaughten, were bustled from London to their new home in the Berkshire woods.

Like many deemed criminally insane, McNaughten was never released.[27] His doctors at Bethlem described him as timorous and secretive. Even after he had spent eleven years on the ward, McNaughten's attendants could only glean that he believed that he was being harassed by someone or something, real or imagined. "If a Stranger walks through the Gallery," wrote one physician, "he at once hides in the Water Closet or in a Bed room [*sic*] and at other times he chooses some darkish corner where he reads or knits."[28] Near the end of March 1864, shortly after McNaughten arrived at Broadmoor, his chief doctor considered his new patient. McNaughten believed "that he must have done something very bad or they would not have sent him to Bethlem. . . . When asked whether he now thinks that he must have been out of his mind—he replies 'Such was the Verdict—the opinion of the Jury after hearing the Evidence.'" His health faded quickly, and he was beset by heart and kidney disease, rheumatism, and anemia. McNaughten spent his last months bedridden, pale and puffy. He "gradually sank and died" in the middle of the night in the spring of 1865, at the age of fifty-two.[29]

By the time James Shaw's lawyers pleaded for mercy after his trial, physicians had argued for decades that the *M'Naghten* definition of insanity lagged behind developments in mental science. Shaw, who was literate, spoke coherently, and seemed to have no extravagantly false beliefs, was not an ideal candidate for *M'Naghten*. Hammond-Chambers knew, however, that insanity defenses in such instances could still succeed. Savvy defense lawyers had no trouble finding physicians willing to diagnose apparently rational defendants with brain diseases, and to speak powerfully against their responsibility in court. When faced with contradictory expert testimony, juries and judges frequently departed from strict interpretations of the *M'Naghten* rules, returning unpredictable and inconsistent verdicts. This created an opening for lawyers like Hammond-Chambers to present textured portraits of their clients, introducing medical and circumstantial evidence of insanity that did not directly address the *M'Naghten* criteria but might still sway decision makers. For example, Hammond-Chambers emphasized Shaw's history of seizures. Epilepsy had long been associated with madness, and according to some physicians the condition could manifest itself in fits of non-delusional insanity.[30] The lawyer also tried to establish that Shaw had killed without motive—another stamp of madness in Victorian mental science. Here, he encountered some difficulty.

The prosecution, led by George Sills, rejected Hammond-Chambers's argument that Albert's killing was a random act of violence. The prosecutor argued that Shaw was strange and sinister but sane enough to satisfy the *M'Naghten* rules. The crime was calculated: he had killed Albert to conceal his assault on the boy's sister, Alice.[31] In support of this theory, the local surgeon testified that Alice had suffered redness and inflammation of her "private parts" as well as a suspicious discharge, which were consistent with "friction" and "with a man having tampered with her." Under cross-examination by Hammond-Chambers, though, the surgeon admitted that Alice's hymen was intact and that she had no bruises, making the cause of her injuries uncertain. The defense then speculated that Alice's redness might be due to her own sexual impropriety. If Hammond-Chambers could discredit Alice's testimony and suggest that her assault never happened, then Shaw's putative motive would evaporate.[32] For both the prosecution and the defense, Alice's assault was a secondary concern, relevant only insofar as it related to Shaw's intentions. Indeed, Shaw was never formally charged with sexual assault. He had certainly killed Albert, but the truth of what happened to Alice remained, in the eyes of many, ambiguous. Without Albert, there were no witnesses beyond Alice and Shaw, and the physical evidence was inconclusive. Alice's word was not enough; her testimony was vulnerable to the skepticism with which Victorians regarded most evidence of sexual assault given by women and children.[33]

Sills, the prosecutor, mentioned sex only to elucidate Shaw's motives. Hammond-Chambers, for the defense, never went further. Even though the circumstances seemed to call for it, the lawyer declined to describe Shaw's mental disorder as sexual. This was a strategic elision. Early sexologists, beginning in the mid-nineteenth century, insisted that physicians remain alert to sexual pathology, including sexual psychosis.[34] Sexual dysfunction and violence were widely acknowledged symptoms of mental illness. If he had portrayed Shaw as a sexual psychopath, not a homicidal monomaniac, Hammond-Chambers might have been able to persuade at least some members of the jury that his client had a brain disease. Mental illness alone, however, did not guarantee acquittal. The *M'Naghten* rules' insistence on cognitive disturbance, rather than defects of will or perversions of desire, was designed to exclude those whose crimes could be attributed to immorality or a failure to exercise appropriate self-control. The alternative, some thought, was unacceptable: a legal system in which the vilest, wildest subjects of the British Crown could escape punishment by claiming that the evil of their crimes was, in itself, excusatory. If Hammond-Chambers had tried to portray Shaw as sexually compulsive, he might have unwittingly galvanized the court against him. The defense sought to prove that Shaw had a sick brain; to do this, Shaw could not plead a sick soul.

Alfred Wills, the judge in Shaw's case, was a popular and affable figure and an acquaintance of the influential lawyer James Fitzjames Stephen.[35] When the two served together on the Midland Circuit in the 1850s, Wills could not fathom how Stephen could spend his evenings reading Hobbes, which struck him as dreadfully dull.[36] Wills's lack of interest in philosophy showed in Shaw's case. He was more concerned about managing dangerous men, sane or insane, and avoiding political scandal than he was about abstruse concepts of responsibility. Stephen was different. As a young lawyer, he contemplated abandoning his practice to write a "book of high importance & permanent value," possibly "on the fundamental problems of religion & morals."[37] He had published his *General View of the Criminal Law of England* in 1863 and thought about experimenting with more theoretical work.[38] In a letter, John Stuart Mill counseled Stephen against giving up his profession—and generous income—to take up moral philosophy.[39]

In the end, Stephen stuck with law and became increasingly convinced of its importance to political and social life. He was especially interested in how law and legal institutions contributed to just governance in the empire. In 1866 and 1867, he appeared twice in court on behalf of the Jamaica Committee, a group chaired by Mill that lobbied for the criminal prosecution of Governor Edward John Eyre, who had ordered the brutal suppression of protests in Morant Bay, Jamaica, in 1865. In 1869, Stephen struck out for Calcutta, where he succeeded Henry Maine as Law Member of the Viceroy's Council, the highest-ranking legal office in the colony. His job was to draft legislation in response to proposals from London and to revise bills in response to the council's suggestions.[40] Stephen worked with energy and focus, pushing through a number of acts regulating the law of contract, evidence, criminal procedure, and infanticide. He relished the efficiency of lawmaking in India, unencumbered by the party politics and endless consultations of parliamentary democracy.[41]

Stephen advocated the rapid anglicization of Indian law on the ground that British rule in India could not claim to be enlightened or liberal unless it were also uncompromisingly "Western." He clashed with British authorities in India who sought to protect their executive powers against government by rule-of-law principles. Indian law should be British in spirit and content, he argued, although collected in the clear, portable codes that many legal thinkers judged best suited to the colonies.[42] In his 1872 "Minute on the Administration of Justice in British India," Stephen wrote, "The establishment of a system of law which regulates the most important part of the daily life of the people, constitutes in itself a moral conquest more striking, more durable, and far more solid, than the physical conquest which renders it possible."[43]

On his return to England from India in 1872, Stephen was made a high-court judge. For the rest of his life, he remained engaged in Indian affairs. In the 1870s, India became a touchstone in British domestic politics as members of Parliament sparred over the future of colonial rule. Should Britain prepare India for eventual self-government? Could British despotism be benevolent even if it were permanent? Stephen was clear-eyed about the reality of conquest. He understood that British rule in India might be—must be, in his view—civilizing, but that Britain's liberal reformism rested on force. This comfort with the violence of law, and with the codependence of benevolence and despotism, colored his legal philosophy. He was an advocate of legal reform in England, but his greatest legislative successes—including the 1892 Criminal Code of Canada, based on his draft code—were colonial, not metropolitan.[44]

In 1883, Stephen published his comprehensive three-volume *History of the Criminal Law of England.* The *History* reflected his experiences as a legislator and judge, and his formative years in India. Stephen argued that the doctrine of mens rea was deceptively simple, concealing a multiplicity of meanings. Mens rea referred to the mental element—that is, the culpable state of mind, knowledge, intention, or even emotion—that was a necessary feature of most criminal offenses. The precise nature of the mental element varied based on the crime. Murder, for instance, required "malice aforethought," while the law of theft stipulated that the defendant must have intended to deprive the owner of his or her property permanently or fraudulently.[45] Any theorizing about mens rea meant little, according to Stephen, unless it took account of how particular doctrines and cases fractured the concept.

More broadly, Stephen saw responsibility as chiefly a technical legal matter, rather than a philosophical or medical one. He adopted an approach to responsibility that has led at least one scholar to describe him as a "compatibilist": an advocate of the idea that legal responsibility remains coherent even in a universe where human behavior is determined by forces outside our control. According to this view, a person's actions can be meaningfully classified as either intentional or unintentional, and the person as either legally sane or insane, regardless of whether "free will" exists in the abstract.[46] In keeping with this generally practical orientation, Stephen described criminal responsibility as "nothing more than actual liability to legal punishment." "It is common," he wrote, "to discuss this subject as if the law itself depended upon the result of discussions as to the freedom of the will," but this was a mistake.[47] Instead, he argued that criminal law expressed society's right to punish wrongdoers, which depended not on "free will" or "conscience" but on utilitarian calculations of the best means to maximize the public good.[48] Metaphysical discussions were perhaps inevitable, but beside the point.

Like Stephen, Wills, the judge in Shaw's case, questioned the value of philosophy to the life of the law. He was especially critical of the medical and philosophical handwringing about insanity and responsibility that followed *M'Naghten*. Juries made decisions on the circumstances of the case, Wills argued. Theory was unlikely to sway the man on the street, confronted with the drama of a killing and the unique mind of a killer.[49] *M'Naghten* provided adequate guidance on a complex issue about which jurors were likely to vote with their guts, regardless of what an alienist said on the witness stand. Wills understood and accepted this. He encouraged the jurors in Shaw's case "not to be too nice about the rule as laid down [in *M'Naghten*] . . . if they thought the whole circumstances looked like the act of a man under the influence of homicidal mania."[50]

His mention of homicidal mania shows that Wills was out of step with contemporary mental science. Joseph Bayley, the physician from St. Andrew's private lunatic asylum, had introduced the term during the trial.[51] Bayley, hardly an expert in criminal lunacy, spent more time worrying about his patients' access to amusements and trips to the sea (and diarrheal illness, in the asylum's earlier years) than he did about homicidal maniacs. By the time he appeared in Shaw's trial, "homicidal mania" and "monomania" had become almost as unpopular among alienists as the *M'Naghten* rules.

Étienne-Jean Georget coined the term "monomania" in 1817. He described it as a motiveless need to destroy living things, including human beings. Sufferers committed crimes with "all the refinements of the most execrable cruelty."[52] Another French physician, Étienne Esquirol, popularized the diagnosis. He believed that there was a type of insanity characterized by "a partial lesion of the intelligence, affections or will." Sufferers "seize[d] upon a false principle, which they pursue[d] without deviating from logical reasonings." Esquirol's account of monomania was clinical yet harrowing. A monomaniac might feel compelled to kill even if his conscience rebelled. He might be rational and yet so impaired that he could offer "very reasonable explanations" for his disturbing behavior. On all subjects but the one at the center of their delusions, patients could "think, reason and act, like other men."[53] Esquirol, like many French alienists, relied heavily on the concept of the lesion, a physical injury or a wound. But where in the body might one look for a "lesion of the will"?[54] Nineteenth-century physicians considered the question and offered a variety of answers—the brain, the nerves, the skull. The suggestion by Esquirol of the existence of a lesion somewhere in the body of the monomaniac reinforced his argument that insanity was a physical disorder, as urgent and real as a broken leg.

Homicidal monomania was controversial. Joel Eigen describes how the disorder "propelled its victims into murder and its proponents into turbulent border wars," especially between lawyers and physicians.[55] Debates over the existence and potential consequences of non-delusional definitions of mental illness extended across national borders. British physicians drew from the work and experience of their French, German, and American colleagues, who faced similar challenges in their efforts to induce courts to recognize monomania and related disorders. For instance, in 1840 Charles Chrétien Henri Marc, physician to Louis Philippe I of France, published *De la folie, considérée dans ses rapports avec les questions médico-judiciaires*.[56] During Daniel McNaughten's 1843 trial, the expert witness and alienist Edward Monroe was asked if he had ever read the works of "Monsieur Marcs [*sic*]." Monroe recalled that Marc had described "an insanity which irresistibly compels a person to commit particular crimes."[57] Marc argued that Georget had been too fervent in his evangelism. Rampant overdiagnosis of monomania among defendants in criminal cases had made criminal lawyers and judges suspicious, even leading them to deny the existence of the disease.[58] Marc wished to restore the credibility of monomania and its proponents, especially in France. While German courts had rightly taken pity on monomania sufferers, the French had executed them.[59] Marc thought this was a national disgrace.

Thanks in part to his book, monomania surged in popularity in the early 1840s, just in time for *M'Naghten.*

By the end of the nineteenth century, however, monomania had once again fallen out of favor among physicians. William Orange, the longtime superintendent of Broadmoor, was critical of the court's reliance on "partial insanity" (of which monomania was a subtype) in the *M'Naghten* case. "It is difficult to understand," complained Orange, "what is meant by a person being deprived of *all* self-control, while the *other* faculties are sound."[60] He dismissed monomania as a voguish diagnosis inspired by French aristocratic science, with minimal clinical support. The diagnosis, like the *M'Naghten* rules, was dated and in need of renovation. Orange wrote that the "rules so given to the world were scarcely likely to be of a character to be binding upon all posterity." In its place, he called for an individualized approach to responsibility, in which doctors described defendants' particular impairments and jurists determined whether they were "punishable." While a discrete psychiatric diagnosis could be a useful medical shorthand, it was not a substitute for the careful assessment of a patient's symptoms. Mental illness could be unpredictable, and it was always specific to a person's experiences and circumstances. Disease classifications were of limited utility, in Orange's view, and did not bear directly on responsibility attribution in court. "There may be both criminality and insanity co-existing, and combined in an infinite variety of proportions," he concluded.[61]

Orange was not alone in his skepticism. For example, the two French authors of the entry on homicidal monomania in Tuke's *Dictionary of Psychological Medicine* (1892) distanced themselves from mid-century French mental science. Monomania now belonged to the category of terms "which are more or less sacred by reason of long use . . . although it is recognised that they no longer correspond to the actual state of science."[62] One English alienist writing in 1874 believed that the clinical prevalence of monomania had been exaggerated, and that jurists in cases like *M'Naghten* had given it "a more rigid definition than [was] conformable with nature."[63]

Although some alienists regarded it with scorn, monomania retained its purchase in homicide cases and in popular writing about insanity. Many Victorian novels, like Mary Elizabeth Braddon's popular *Lady Audley's Secret* (1862), used monomania as a literary device. In one scene, Lucy Audley, the title character, expresses the conventional wisdom that excessive reading, smoking, or dwelling on a single idea can trigger monomania. Monomaniacs, she warns, "know that they are mad, but they know how to keep their secret," at least until a "paroxysm seizes them" and they yield to "the frightful, passionate, hungry craving for violence and horror."[64] Even after monomania largely faded from mental science, it remained a well-worn narrative trope. In Arthur Conan Doyle's 1904 Sherlock Holmes story "The Six Napoleons," Watson proposes that monomania might explain a suspect's apparent compulsion to smash busts of Napoleon. "There are no limits to the possibilities of monomania," he tells Holmes.[65]

As alienists argued among themselves over the existence of partial insanities like homicidal monomania, judges, lawyers, and jurors tried to apply contested medical understandings of insanity in the courtroom. Psychiatric knowledge changed quickly over the course of the century, not necessarily in tandem with shifts in popular understandings of mental illness. Jurists had to navigate legal, medical, and lay definitions of insanity that were often irreconcilable. Daniel McNaughten's monomania diagnosis, supported by Monroe and many of the other medical witnesses in the trial, was no longer fashionable among alienists working fifty years later. And yet, *M'Naghten* had preserved it as the archetypical diagnosis for insane criminals. Worse, the definition of legal insanity in the *M'Naghten* rules was a caricature of monomania, far more limited and inflexible than the condition Monroe had described in court in 1843. Given the medical uncertainty about the scientific validity of *M'Naghten*, Wills can be forgiven for encouraging the jury "not to be too nice about the rule as laid down," in deciding whether Shaw was insane.[66]

Hammond-Chambers thought that he could exploit the controversy over *M'Naghten* to save Shaw. Wills agreed. Both judge and lawyer were surprised when the jury announced its decision to convict. It soon emerged, however, that there had been a terrible misunderstanding. In a letter from the foreman that he received the morning after the trial, Wills learned that the jury had intended to pronounce Shaw guilty of murder but legally insane. The jurors agreed that Shaw killed Albert but were split on the issue of his responsibility. That, the foreman argued, "no jury *could* possibly determine. . . . [S]uch a point must be one for medical skill alone."[67]

The jurors expected Wills to ask two questions, one about Shaw's guilt and the other about Shaw's responsibility. On its face, this might seem absurd. If a man were not responsible for his crimes, then he could not be considered guilty under the common-law definition of murder. The history of the insanity defense in the nineteenth century shows, however, that the Shaw jurors were justifiably confused: by 1897, it was not at all clear that guilt and irresponsibility were incompatible under Anglo law.

Although the insanity defense had an ancient common-law history, it was formalized in legislation in 1800. The 1800 Criminal Lunatics Act was passed in the aftermath of the trial of James Hadfield, who shot at King George III at the Drury Lane Theatre. The jury found Hadfield not guilty by reason of insanity. The 1800 act passed as legislators scrambled to prevent Hadfield from being released. It stipulated that in cases of high treason, murder, or felony, persons acquitted on the ground of insanity or found incompetent to stand trial were to be detained until "His Majesty's pleasure shall be known."[68] The 1800 act troubled the connection between insanity and irresponsibility. Although defendants could still be found not guilty by reason of insanity, the act imposed a custodial sentence on people who were technically innocent. For some, especially those whose crimes were not capital, the consequences of becoming "pleasure men" were worse than a guilty verdict.[69] One nineteenth-century lawyer wrote, "The confinement was so protracted that counsel are said to have frequently withdrawn a plea of insanity because punishment was less severe than a committal to an asylum."[70]

From 1800 to 1883, the statutory special verdict of acquittal by reason of insanity chipped away at the idea that insanity obviated guilt, and irresponsibility barred punishment. The primary and crucial material difference between responsibility and irresponsibility was that irresponsible killers could not be hanged. Still, under Victorian law irresponsibility did not connote innocence. In 1883, the Trial of Criminal Lunatics Act further confused the issue.[71] In 1882, Roderick McLean shot at Queen Victoria. He was found not guilty by reason of insanity and sent to Broadmoor. The Queen, who had been the target of several assassination attempts, pressured Parliament to change the special verdict to reflect the seriousness of crimes committed by the insane, and the opprobrium that she felt they deserved.[72] The 1883 act duly reworded the verdict from "not guilty by reason of insanity" to "guilty, but insane." The drafters of the act acknowledged, in its first section, that the new special verdict was "open to the objection that it declares a man to be at once *guilty* of an offence and not responsible for it." They hoped, however, that the word "guilty" might have a "deterrent effect on the partially insane," thereby justifying the act's conceptual "anomaly." Moreover, they continued, "the whole law as to criminal lunatics proceeds on the assumption that a man may be a criminal and a lunatic at the same time."[73]

By the time of Shaw's trial, then, it was not unthinkable for a man to be declared both guilty and irresponsible. Indeed, Wills had expected the foreman to announce that Shaw was "guilty, but insane," and was surprised when the foreman declared, simply, that Shaw was guilty. The foreman waited for a chance to add "but insane" to the verdict, but the question he expected about Shaw's sanity never came. The debacle over the wording of the verdict in Shaw's trial shows how distant the insanity defense had become from the jurisprudential and philosophical concepts at the core of the doctrine of responsibility. The Shaw jurymen misunderstood courtroom procedure, but they did not really misunderstand the law. In many ways, and precisely as they had assumed, a defendant's guilt and a defendant's sanity had become two separate questions. Upon receiving the foreman's note, Wills wrote frantically to Sir Matthew White Ridley, the Home Secretary, hoping to avoid the embarrassment and expense of a retrial. The two men resolved to send Shaw to a lunatic asylum as quickly and discreetly as possible.[74] For Shaw to become an official criminal lunatic, however, Ridley needed certificates signed by two physicians affirming that he was insane.

Two weeks after the trial, Shaw wrote the first of several petitions to the Queen. He proclaimed his innocence. "I wouldn't like to leave this life so soon," he pleaded.[75] He told a different story to Dr. David Nicolson and Dr. Richard Brayn, who came from Broadmoor to interview him. Shaw said that he had been drinking on the day of the murder. He slipped a razor into his pocket and lured Alice and Albert into the field.[76] Then he led Albert, alone, into the grass. There, he forced Albert, as Nicolson and Brayn reported, to "handle his (prisoner's) private parts and that when this had brought about a seminal emission, he thereafter took out the razor and cut off the boy's head." Shaw then returned to Alice and attempted to rape her. Nicolson and Brayn were horrified. They reported that Shaw's crime was an instance of "lust-murder developed out of an excessive indulgence in drink."[77] Throughout their interview, Shaw was calm, and "expressed no sorrow or regret in the matter." He did not suffer from "an insane condition such as would imply . . . irresponsibility."[78]

"Lust murder" was a disorder described by Austro-German sexologist Richard von Krafft-Ebing in his popular *Psychopathia Sexualis* (1886). Although Krafft-Ebing held that "psychopathic conditions" were probable in cases of lust-murder, Nicolson and Brayn argued that Shaw was sane. This might have surprised Krafft-Ebing, who complained, "Law and Jurisprudence have thus far given but little attention to the facts resulting from investigations in psycho-pathology," arguing that many serious sexual crimes were the product of a "psychopathic state."[79] But in England, at the end of the nineteenth century, the problem was not too little contact between mental science and jurisprudence but too much. The lines between medical and legal understandings of sanity blurred as medical experts' presence in the criminal justice system increased. It became common for alienists, especially those with professional ties to the courts or the government, to adjust their assessment of a patient's mind in order to speak more clearly to their legal interlocutors. In such instances, physicians might divorce their medical judgment about patients' insanity from their recommendation as to how the court or political authorities should view their responsibility. And so, experts might conclude that a prisoner was mentally unwell but legally sane, as Nicolson and Brayn did in Shaw's case.

Nicolson and Brayn appreciated the dilemma faced by their colleagues, Cogan and Bayley, who had testified at Shaw's trial. Given the brutality of the crime, they conceded, "it not unnaturally follows that the medical opinion as given at the trial should be in favour of the existence of insanity in the prisoner." But Cogan and Bayley had been duped. Nicolson and Brayn saw Shaw's crime and his subsequent behavior as calculating, not compulsive. Shaw had denied his crime until a confession and a performance of remorse might benefit him. Nicolson and Brayn even dismissed his mutilation of his genitals as "pretended mental aberration in the presence of a sufficient motive." Nicolson and Brayn were no doubt aware of the association between lust murder and Krafft-Ebing's account of sexual psychopathy, but they adapted their conclusion that Shaw did not suffer from a condition that implied "irresponsibility in the individual" to the legal question at hand. Cogan, the prison surgeon, and Bayley, the private asylum superintendent, could not match the experience of Nicolson and Brayn with the criminally insane or, crucially, their appreciation of the gap between medical and legal approaches to insanity.[80]

Brayn and Nicolson's refusal to find Shaw insane was a problem for those who wanted to see him immured at Broadmoor. "I do not suppose," remarked Wills in a letter to the Home Secretary, "that any one will care whether he is at Broadmoor or Dartmoor [Prison], though those of the jury who may share the foreman's views . . . would of course raise their voices if he were to be hung."[81] Ultimately, Wills and Ridley engineered Shaw's commutation, ignoring Nicolson and Brayn's post-conviction report in favor of Cogan and Bayley's courtroom testimony. Nicolson and Brayn and their successors became Shaw's caretakers over the next several decades. At Broadmoor, in Shaw's yearly medical reports, doctors did not name their patient's specific disorder or do more than hint at its sexual character, but they did surmise its cause: syphilis.[82] James Shaw never left Broadmoor. His Home Office medical file is filled with stamps, one for every year that he spent there. Each stamp described his bodily condition as "poor" and his mental condition as "demented." After suffering from severe dementia and declining health for years, he died of heart disease in 1947 at the age of seventy-five, having spent fifty years at the asylum.[83]

The saturation of responsibility contests with the language and concepts of mental science did not transform cases like Shaw's into purely medical inquests. Rather, conflicting medical expertise drove many lawyers, jurors, and lay commentators to seek answers in common sense and gut feeling. If they deployed medical categories, they often did so eccentrically, picking and choosing from among scientific texts to create medical narratives that aligned with their intuitions. "I find it increasingly necessary," wrote Wills as he ruminated on Shaw's case, "to trust a good deal to my own impressions on these constantly recurring questions of lunacy, as to which some of the 'mad doctors' are scarcely sane themselves."[84]

The case of the Reverend Henry John Dodwell takes us behind the Broadmoor gates. Dodwell was arrested in the winter of 1878 for firing a pistol at Sir George Jessell, the Master of the Rolls, the highest-ranking civil-law judge on the Court of Appeal, as he stepped out of a cab. Jessell recognized him immediately. Dodwell had been, until recently, the master of an elite school in Devonshire. He was dismissed in 1876 on allegations of misconduct. When the school's trustees tried to force him to give up the master's residence, Dodwell went to court and insisted on defending himself. Jessell was the judge. "Like most persons who plead their own cause," Jessell reflected, "he had not quite understood the legal points, but he made a very long harangue." A year later, Dodwell was back in court. He had managed to find work as a chaplain at an industrial school in Brighton but had quickly been fired. Dodwell, again, represented himself in a civil suit and, again, tried Jessell's patience. "He recounted to us his diverse grievances," the judge wrote, "and . . . the way in which the world in general had conspired against him." The next time Jessell saw him, Dodwell was in the Rolls Yard in Chancery Lane, holding a gun.[85]

Dodwell, true to form, represented himself at his trial for attempted murder. He blustered and proclaimed himself a victim of lies and incompetence. "I have come to the most unwelcome conclusion," wrote Dodwell in a letter read aloud at trial, "that I can gain a hearing, not a grand thing for any man in any country, only by breaking the law." The jury found him not guilty of attempted murder (there was some dispute over whether the pistol was even loaded) and not guilty by reason of insanity on the charge of common assault.

Despite the absence of any medical testimony, and over his protestations, Dodwell was declared insane.[86]

When Dodwell was admitted to Broadmoor on 23 February 1878, he was fifty-two years old. On his intake form, under "Chief Delusions or Indications of Insanity," one physician wrote, "*None.*"[87] Dodwell's friends urged more doctors to interview him to establish his sanity and secure his release.[88] One alienist who answered the call, Lyttelton Stewart Forbes Winslow, was known for his bold theories about the identity of Jack the Ripper. He held degrees from Oxford and Cambridge and lectured on insanity at Charing Cross Hospital Medical School. In a report submitted to the Home Office, Winslow described Dodwell as "most rational in every respect."[89]

In the 1880 edition of his *Manual of Medical Jurisprudence*, Alfred Swaine Taylor, England's premier expert in medical jurisprudence, accused Winslow of bias in his evaluation of Dodwell. Taylor also praised the court for finding Dodwell insane without hearing expert medical evidence. Otherwise, Taylor wrote, "there would have been the usual conflict of opinion. Some physicians would have pronounced him sane, and others insane and irresponsible. This would only have confused the jury."[90] Although Dodwell's case predated Shaw's by twenty years, efforts to adapt evolving medical understandings of insanity for use in criminal courts had already produced widespread confusion and frustration. Taylor shared many of his colleagues' concerns that by airing their professional squabbles in court, alienists had compromised the credibility of their field and estranged lawyers and jurors from mental science. Alienists could save more defendants and improve the public profile of their profession by rationing their expertise, particularly in cases like Dodwell's where the jury had independently preferred insanity over the noose.

Winslow would not be deterred, defending himself in the pages of the *British Medical Journal.* "Every Englishman has a perfect right to bring forward his grievance in any way, and as often as he sees proper," Winslow wrote. "If all the unfortunate individuals who continue to pin their faith on hopeless causes were to be considered as lunatics our asylums would not be large enough to contain them. Many industrious lawyers, who make [a] harvest out of these persons, would have to beg for their bread." In his opinion, Dodwell was a patriot who justly refused to surrender his right to a fair trial despite judicial persecution.[91] Others concurred.[92] Another physician, who believed that Dodwell was a brilliant man laid low by professional misfortune, reported that Dodwell said "that if he must go to the workhouse, he preferred that it should be through the criminal dock." Both favorable reports appeared in the *Journal of Psychological Medicine*, of which Winslow was the editor.[93]

Some physicians were unimpressed. In a joint report, Orange, then superintendent of Broadmoor, and Dr. Robert Mundy Gover, who had recently been the medical inspector of prisons for the Home Office, acknowledged that it was important for medical men not to mistake idiosyncrasy for insanity. Yet, their position on Dodwell was unambiguous. Where Winslow had seen perseverance and devotion to truth and justice, Orange and Gover diagnosed pathological obsession. To them, Dodwell's calm rationality was actually sick self-regard. Dodwell, they wrote, "does not regret having wasted six years in endeavouring to prove that he was in the right. . . . His first duty, in short, is to himself." Orange and Gover warned that Dodwell was a "dangerous lunatic" who should not be allowed to leave their custody.[94]

An active and fractious body of medical professionals consulted in cases of criminal insanity in the late-nineteenth century. Contrary to some scholars' accounts, Victorian mad doctors were not universally eager to seek professional acclaim through the courts.[95] The threat of judicial execution that allegedly insane defendants faced weighed heavily on the physicians called to defend them. Perhaps heavier still was the duty alienists felt to care for the criminal lunatics who were too dangerous to be released, and too mad to hang.

The Association of Medical Officers of Asylums and Hospitals for the Insane was founded in 1841. Membership in the association was at first restricted to medical officers who worked in asylums. In some years, as few as three or four members attended the annual meeting, which was always held at an asylum. In other years, no meeting was held at all. But by the early 1850s, membership rates and interest had grown. In 1853, the association published the first issue of the *Asylum Journal*. Within two years, it was rebranded as the *Asylum Journal of Mental Science*. In 1858, the journal became the *Journal of Mental Science*.[96] Over this period, the association evolved from a loose collective of asylum managers to a modern professional association for physicians with expertise in mental illness. The organization officially became the Medico-Psychological Association in 1865.

Members of the Medico-Psychological Association generally began their careers in public or private lunatic asylums. Asylum superintendents spent their days visiting patients, supervising orderlies, ordering autopsies, corresponding with government officials and distraught relatives, and traveling the country to evaluate purportedly insane prisoners as they awaited trial. They knew how hard it was to diagnose a person after a brief interview. For them,

Broadmoor asylum male staff, 1885. Dr. William Orange, then medical superintendent, sits fifth from the left in the first row, wearing a top hat, white handkerchief, and watch chain. Dr. David Nicolson, then deputy medical superintendent, is to Orange's immediate left, sporting his signature bushy moustache. Credit: Berkshire Record Office and the West London Mental NHS Trust, D/H14/B6/1.

criminal insanity was more than just a philosophical or scientific conundrum; it was their livelihood. To preserve their professional standing, alienists sometimes deferred to legal definitions of insanity that departed from cutting-edge mental science.

William Orange, the superintendent of Broadmoor who oversaw Dodwell's care, had spent many years living among criminal lunatics. He was confident that his patient belonged at the asylum. Orange, upright and resolute, was descended from an old Huguenot family. Nicolson wrote that Orange's reserve and calm, level stare "rather gave strangers the impression that they were 'psychologized.'"[97] Orange came to Berkshire as deputy superintendent in 1862, just before the first patients were transferred there from Bethlem. His supervisor, Dr. John Meyer, was the institution's first medical superintendent. In the spring of 1863, Broadmoor's first residents arrived—ninety-five women transferred from other lunatic asylums. Male patients, including Daniel McNaughten, were brought to Broadmoor from Bethlem and its overflow unit, Fisherton House, in February of 1864. By the end of the year, there were 309 patient-prisoners at Broadmoor.[98]

The asylum could be chaotic. Before its high perimeter walls were finished, patients routinely hopped fences and hedges to freedom. While most were eventually recaptured after days or weeks on the lam, a few disappeared into the countryside. Broadmoor was also violent. More than half of its inmates were killers or attempted killers who had been confined indefinitely at Her Majesty's pleasure.[99] One Sunday in 1866, while Meyer kneeled to receive Communion in the Broadmoor chapel, a patient struck him on the head with a stone slung in a handkerchief. He never fully recovered. Orange replaced Meyer as superintendent in 1870. He reached out to doctors around Britain and France in his efforts to develop standards of patient care and guidelines for professional conduct in relation to questions of insanity and law. In 1876, Nicolson joined Orange as deputy superintendent. Nicolson admired his friend's capacity for "penetrating the intimate workings of the mind of accused persons," especially in the context of criminal justice.[100]

Orange might have been skilled and experienced in his dealings with the criminally insane, but Broadmoor—as Meyer had discovered before him—was a dangerous place. On 6 June 1882, four years after his admission to the asylum, Dodwell exacted his revenge. While Orange looked over a stack of letters, Dodwell crept up beside him and swung a heavy stone, wrapped in a handkerchief, into the doctor's skull.[101] Like Meyer, Orange never recovered. A colleague wrote that the attack had "produced such effects as to make it in the highest degree improbable that [Orange] will ever be able to practice his profession again in any mode whatsoever."[102] Even after a year's sick leave, Orange struggled. In addition to running the asylum, he was summoned to jails across the country to evaluate defendants in criminal cases. In his last full year at Broadmoor, 1885, he advised in thirty-three capital cases.[103] Despite the efforts of the Home Office to persuade him to stay on, he retired in 1886, at the age of fifty-two. Nicolson assumed his position as medical superintendent.[104]

Dodwell loathed Broadmoor. In one of many letters to his solicitor, he wrote, "Dr. Orange is crafty, polished, oily, able to lie with consummate grace and neatness without moving a muscle but still has the unsteady eye and the feigned hollow voice of the untrustworthy." Nicolson, meanwhile, was simply "an uncouth Scotch man [*sic*]." Twenty years later, at the time of his interview with Shaw, David Nicolson would be an old hand at managing an asylum. But in 1878, when he first encountered Dodwell, he was relatively new to Broadmoor.[105]

Nicolson was born on Christmas Day in Aberdeenshire.[106] He had a thick Scottish accent and a disarming forthrightness that even Dodwell could not entirely resist. Nicolson received his medical degree from the University of Aberdeen in 1866, when he was twenty-two. He then spent several years working as an assistant surgeon in prisons before coming to Broadmoor. Nicolson did his best to liven up the place. He formed an asylum choral society and performed in a staff-patient joint production of *H.M.S. Pinafore*.[107] While Dodwell saw Orange as his equal and his nemesis, he grudgingly appreciated Nicolson's rougher charms. "He is blunter in his nature and has had to deal with Convicts (I believe)," wrote Dodwell, who was pleased that Nicolson occasionally apologized when accused of inadvertent slights.[108]

Nicolson did not escape Broadmoor unscathed, either. In the fall of 1884, a patient injured him so severely that he was forced to take a three-month leave.[109] He was attacked again in November 1889, requiring a six-week absence.[110] Nicolson persisted as superintendent until 1896, when he was appointed Lord Chancellor's Visitor in Lunacy. His obituary in the *Lancet*, after his death in 1932 at the age of eighty-seven, described him as "the first authority in the country on the way to deal with the insane subject when breaking the law."[111]

Dodwell and his supporters complained that Orange and Gover's report, in which they had described him as "selfish," was not independent, and he demanded a third set of medical opinions. Henry Maudsley and a colleague, both members of the Medico-Psychological Association, were called to Broadmoor.[112] Maudsley was a leading light among London alienists. He wrote often and at length about the philosophical and medical dimensions of insanity and was among the most vocal critics of *M'Naghten*. The joint editor of the *Journal of Mental Science* from 1863 to 1878, he lectured on insanity at St. Mary's Hospital from 1868 to 1881 and was appointed professor of medical jurisprudence at University College London from 1869 to 1879.[113] Maudsley was rich and well connected. The author of eleven books, he also maintained a successful private practice. His wife, Caroline, was the youngest daughter of John Conolly, the famous alienist and a leader of the movement to abandon restraint and other violence in the treatment of the insane.[114]

In their report, the consulting alienists declared that Dodwell was insane, and that he suffered from delusions of persecution. Given his "incapacity to

Henry Maudsley.
Photograph by G. Jerrard, 1881.
Credit: Wellcome Collection.
Attribution 4.0 International
(CC BY 4.0).

see either the folly or the wrong of what he has done," they recommended that he remain at Broadmoor.[115] As a lifelong opponent of *M'Naghten* who never shied from controversy, Maudsley believed that subtle eccentricities and perversions could be evidence of profound mental disease. He was especially interested in patients whose insanity was perceptible only by experts. These were the people whose lives were threatened by the otiose, unfair *M'Naghten* rules. "It is of great importance," wrote Maudsley, "to recognise a borderland between sanity and insanity, and of greater importance still . . . to study carefully the doubtful cases with which it is peopled."[116] For him, the problem of distinguishing between sanity and insanity was technological, not metaphysical. Maudsley was certain that, someday, the physiological causes of insanity would be revealed.[117] Madness was as much a bodily disease as smallpox; it was just harder to diagnose.

After Dodwell attacked Orange in 1882, he was removed from his relatively comfortable room in block 2, where well-behaved patients could see visitors, to a cell in block 1, one of Broadmoor's "back blocks" reserved for those with violent tendencies. Dodwell continued his letter-writing campaign undaunted, and his paranoia only grew. Slowly, his friends and family fell away. He grew old and sick, and on 15 June 1900 he died of heart failure in the Broadmoor infirmary.[118]

There was little agreement among alienists about the relationship between sanity and irresponsibility, or the nature of mental illness. The judge and jury in his case considered Dodwell manifestly mad. Winslow, however, thought that Dodwell was sane, abused by a legal system that would not hear his grievances. Orange thought that he was insane and dangerous. So did Maudsley. In the end, Dodwell's vicious attack on Orange confirmed suspicions that he was volatile, conniving, and deluded. His removal to block 1 dashed any possibility of his release—although it seems he never realized it.

The contact medico-psychological specialists had with patients shaped how they understood their mission as physicians and their relationship to the justice system. Men and women passed through the courts, from arrest to indictment to trial, in a matter of weeks or months, but their time in criminal lunatic asylums was measured in years and decades. People who had terrified their communities and perplexed judges and jurors seemed to shrink in the monotony and pettiness of daily life at Broadmoor. Patients spent their days reading and complaining, while managing physicians attended to their casebooks and correspondence.

Doctors at Broadmoor lived and worked with the most notorious offenders in Britain. This intimacy bred empathy and pragmatism among asylum staff. They delved into the particularities of their patients' delusions, catalogued what patients read, ate, and said, and worried about their health. Physicians were inclined to believe that their charges were insane, and they tended to have a flexible understanding of what might constitute insanity. They also knew, however, that the residents of Broadmoor could be unpredictable, and they were often pessimistic about their chances of recovery and discharge. Medical superintendents like Nicolson and Orange were state officials, with a responsibility to protect the public from the men and women in their care. Still, and unlike many of the lawyers who wrote about and who were involved in the trials of criminal lunatics, the physicians of Bethlem and Broadmoor saw their charges as patients rather than as sources, or subjects, of legal doctrine. Although the Medico-Psychological Association had moved concertedly toward academic medicine, science, and professional prestige, men like Orange and Nicolson had less time for writing and theorizing than their peers. Both did write scholarly essays, as Orange had for Tuke's

1892 *Dictionary of Psychological Medicine*, but they were usually too busy dodging rocks, recapturing escapees, and filling out forms to produce major medical texts.

Several medico-psychological specialists approached the debate over moral insanity from a different, more scholarly perspective. Maudsley best represents this strand of mental science, although even he admitted that grand theories were of limited value in clinical settings. In his *Body and Will: Being an Essay Concerning Will in Its Metaphysical, Psychological, and Pathological Aspects* (1883), amid meditations on dualism, causation, and God, Maudsley wrote, "I have been engaged all my life in dealing with the mind in its concrete human embodiments. . . . I have had no choice but to leave the barren heights of speculation for the plains on which men live and move and have their being."[119]

In considering the history of criminal responsibility, Maudsley's thoughts on "the mind in its concrete human embodiments" are helpful. Shaw's and Dodwell's cases both show how the question of responsibility functioned as a philosophical, doctrinal, and procedural matter in the British legal system. The doctors, lawyers, politicians, and jurors who assessed a defendant's responsibility could not do so purely in the abstract. Their task was not just to decide whether, for example, homicidal mania existed but also to determine whether the person standing before them was a homicidal maniac. They assessed a patient's or a prisoner's sanity knowing that their decision could tip the scales toward life or death, indefinite confinement or freedom.

For many doctors and lawyers, capital punishment animated the debate over criminal insanity. James Fitzjames Stephen and Henry Maudsley, each among the most outspoken members of his profession in the late-nineteenth century, both acknowledged that the mandatory death sentence for murder spurred arguments about insanity and responsibility. Defendants found not guilty by reason of insanity rarely left the asylum, and no one pretended that daily life was much different at Broadmoor or Newgate. But a murder conviction meant death, barring the intercession of the Crown, and a finding of insanity did not. "Abolish capital punishment," Maudsley wrote, "and the dispute between lawyers and doctors ceases to be of practical importance."[120]

Stephen did little to contradict him. As far as he was concerned, insanity and responsibility were only so combustible because British society had become uncomfortable with capital punishment. Stephen supported the systematic execution of habitual criminals, even nonviolent ones. "If society could make up its mind to the destruction of really bad offenders," he wrote, breezily, "they might, in a very few years, be made as rare as wolves."[121] Although Maudsley and Stephen had opposing views of the justice and usefulness of executing criminals, they agreed that anxiety about the death sentence made responsibility especially fraught. If execution were reserved for only the very worst offenders, then it was essential that the legal system differentiate between the mad and the bad, the evil and the ill.

CHAPTER 2

A Criminal Lunatic in Search of a Trial

On Christmas Eve night in 1879, Thomas James Maltby of the Madras Civil Service was en route from Vizianagrum to Chicacole in the Madras Presidency of British India.[1] After three or four hours the men hired to carry him were tired and footsore. They placed the heavy palanquin on the ground under a tree in the village of Sattivada. Maltby was impatient and eager to press on.[2] Latchmi Nayudu, the village *munsif* or local judge, and two other villagers sat with Maltby while the bearers warmed themselves around a fire. Suddenly, three gunshots pierced the night and the munsif fell, dead. Another man, wounded in the cheek, fled into the village. Maltby ran off, clutching the Colt .38 revolver that had been hidden in his clothes. The next morning, authorities apprehended him and brought him back to Vizianagrum.[3]

Shortly after his arrest, the Madras government declared Maltby a criminal lunatic and shipped him back to his native England. In response, Maltby, a consummate bureaucrat, embarked on a zealous letter-writing campaign demanding a trial. Almost six months after Latchmi Nayudu's death, Sir Louis Mallet forwarded a sheaf of printed papers to the Home Office in London. Mallet, the permanent undersecretary of the India Office, had recently received the documents from the government of Madras. In his cover letter, Mallet promised that William Orange, then superintendent of Broadmoor, would be given due warning of his new patient's arrival.[4] The day before the papers arrived at the Home Office, Maltby boarded the S.S. *Stelvio.*[5] Although his days as a traveler were not yet over, he would never return to India.

The British Empire's vast bureaucracy—the endless drafts, petitions, memorials, reports, and warrants—formed the terrain upon which Maltby fought for his rights, identity, and sanity. His file was transferred from the India Office to the Home Office, which occupied opposite ends of Whitehall, while a ship bore Maltby himself across the ocean. Responsibility for Maltby, and legal authority to confine him as a "criminal lunatic," would also shift, from the government of India to the Queen.[6] The journey from India to England was measured in thousands of miles; from the India Office to the Home Office, in feet. The British Empire operated on both scales. Imperial authorities could be remarkably attentive to small matters and small men, perhaps because they knew that the decisions they made and the policies they adopted could move, like Maltby, across the globe.

Men like Maltby reveal the human dimensions of the imperial legal system. Dense connections linked the professionals and institutions involved in the management of the British legal world. Responsibility was a matter of common-law jurisprudence but also of British and imperial policy. When officials committed acts of public, unprovoked violence, they undermined British claims to benevolent governance in the colonies. The trial and punishment of unruly officials could vindicate the colonial justice system but also risked transforming a local embarrassment into an imperial scandal. Lunacy offered a tidy solution. The designation of accused criminals as insane excused their violence and gave administrators access to a set of procedures and institutions that sanctioned their removal from the colony and indefinite detention in a metropolitan asylum. The ambiguities of responsibility complicated decision making in homicide trials and in commutation hearings, pushing public institutions like prisons, hospitals, and government ministries to cooperate in new ways. While responsibility controversies could be vexing, they could also make space for discretion and creativity in policy making and in the management of the allegedly insane. Once a person had been declared a criminal lunatic, he or she entered a complex regulatory system where the focus shifted from judgment to cure, and from justice to political and fiscal expediency.

Many people in Britain and the empire were drawn into the criminal justice system, but not all of their cases were heard in court, and even fewer culminated in a judicial execution. At every point in the legal process, there were paths that led away from the gallows and toward freedom, the asylum, or jail. Peter King has imagined eighteenth and early-nineteenth-century British criminal justice as a series of rooms along a corridor. Each room is a stage, from accusation to execution, and each contains people who open doors and reveal tunnels through which the accused might escape to freedom. Only some unfortunates proceed to the end of the corridor and walk through the final, fatal door.[7]

If we focus only on criminal cases that went to trial, or only on those that ended in execution, we miss those that did not and come away with an incomplete view of the justice system. Concerns about his or her responsibility could change the fate of a prisoner at any moment. Maltby was never tried. And yet doctors and government officials classified him, from 1879 until his death in 1921, as a "criminal lunatic."[8] Orange, in his first address as president of the Medico-Psychological Association in 1883, acknowledged the strangeness of the phrase. He mused, "What is a criminal lunatic? . . . The name appears, at first sight, to imply a contradiction of terms, inasmuch as a person who is a lunatic may be said to be incapable of committing what, in the strictest sense of the word, can be called a crime." Despite this, "criminal lunatic" had been in use in Britain for eighty years, since the creation of the special verdict in 1800. Although the category of the criminal lunatic could not "claim for itself mathematical precision," Orange hailed it as "really descriptive of the class of persons to whom it is applied."[9]

The British criminal justice system, in England and across the empire, relied on administrators as much as it did on lawyers, judges, jurors, and medical experts. The prerogative of mercy and executive review of capital sentences allowed political authorities to adjust the punishment of a convicted prisoner to reflect what they saw as his or her moral culpability, or to avoid scandal. But the prerogative was not their only tool. There were many places along the corridor where the madness of a defendant could divert him or her from the gallows to prison, a hospital, or freedom. Maltby's case reveals one important avenue for the management of troublesome subjects, both in the colonies and in Britain itself: denying their fitness to plead.

Nigel Walker, in his study of crime and insanity in England, estimates that in the period from 1884 to 1893 approximately 11 percent of those indicted for murder in English courts were acquitted on the ground of insanity. Among killers, meanwhile, 11.4 percent were found unfit to plead and were transferred to asylums as criminal lunatics without trial.[10] Although the prisoner's trial was technically only postponed in such cases, in reality defendants labeled unfit were almost never tried. Usually, they remained in the asylum until their deaths, or else were quietly released once their doctors, and the government, agreed that they had regained their sanity. Although consigning prisoners to Broadmoor without trial occasionally attracted criticism, it was undeniably efficient.[11]

Maltby was appalled that Englishmen could lose their liberty, sometimes forever, without a trial. The practice continued through the century. In 1899, William Norris, another Broadmoor inmate confined without trial, would plead for an "Engelishmum['s] Right Eather a triale [or] my Liberty."[12] The "rights of Englishmen" did not, however, always trump administrators' and jurists' desire for quick, quiet solutions in cases where a violent defendant's responsibility seemed to them to be compromised. Incentives for officials to whisk troublesome prisoners away from public scrutiny multiplied in the colonies, where a trial risked exposing conflicts among colonial authorities and Europeans' abuse of Indigenous populations.

Maltby was born on 16 December 1844 in London. His father, also Thomas James Maltby, was a solicitor who would later become the British vice-consul in Belgium. The young Maltby passed his Civil Service examinations in 1865. His performance was undistinguished.[13] He went to Madras and was stationed in and around the Ganjam district in present-day Andhra Pradesh. In 1874, five years before he killed Latchmi Nayudu, Maltby published his first book, *A Practical Handbook of the Uriya or O'di'ya Language*.[14] Maltby argued that European officials should acquire at least basic facility in "native" languages. How could magistrates record statements in the vernacular without even a "slight acquaintance" with the language? This was essential if the colonial government "wish[ed] their officers to possess any real influence with the people."[15] Maltby was fluent in at least Telugu and Uriya. Interestingly, he distinguished carefully in his *Handbook* between "the native style of conversation" and the European one.[16] He believed that language was a matter of dialect and of social convention, and that knowledge of both was necessary for cultural fluency.

Three days before Christmas, Maltby arrived in Vizianagrum from his usual station at Parvatipur. He stayed with Major James William Smith Butler, a twenty-year veteran of the Madras Army.[17] Maltby behaved strangely. He had an inappropriate conversation with the local rajah at the racket court; was baffled by telegram procedures; and paced and muttered to himself all night while handling a revolver.[18] He was also obsessed with the Rampa Rebellion. In 1879, members of tribal groups in the mountains of Vizagapatam district had rebelled against British rule, protesting administrative corruption and restrictions on toddy tapping. The rebels were from Telugu- and Uriya-speaking areas, and witnesses testified that Maltby "harangued his bearers in Telugu" about a notorious rebel named Chendrayya.[19]

Maltby was convinced that his language skills would help him to catch the rebel Chendrayya and pacify the district. This would bring him the recognition he felt he deserved, but had been denied, in the Civil Service. During a visit with an agent of a major imperial bank, Maltby complained that the Duke of Buckingham, then governor of Madras, had treated him terribly, moving him around the presidency five times in the previous year.[20] After eating half a pound of jam while declaiming on the ill-treatment of "American Indians," Maltby declared that he would soon settle the Rampa Rebellion by "speaking to the people in their own tongue."[21]

On 23 December 1879, the day before he left for Chicacole, Maltby met with an acquaintance whom he had come to see about booking his passage on a steamer to Calcutta to bring his grievances to the attention of the Indian government. Maltby accused Buckingham of "ruining the service" through the "intolerable" treatment of "Civilians," as members of the Indian Civil Service were called. In the same breath, Maltby said "the [Rampa] business was being mismanaged by the Duke. He said his [Maltby's] whole service had been among the hillmen, and that he understood them thoroughly."[22] Maltby saw Buckingham's bungling of the Rampa Rebellion as proof of the governor's incompetence and failure to value experienced civil servants. Maltby's vernacular facility was integral to his identity as a competent official, not just a career ornament.

Maltby's linguistic expertise also led, in part, to the tragedy at Sattivada. Many witnesses remarked on the suddenness of Maltby's violence. One of the bearers, Bandi Paidi Gadu, testified, "There were no high words, quarrel or anything of the sort before the shooting."[23] Maltby wrote that he first became suspicious when he discovered that one of the bearers was called Chendrá, and that his name was pronounced in "a low peculiar tone." He was further unsettled by his bearers' silence, as they failed to make their "*usual Ojo! Ojo! noise, which is invariably the custom* in the north." Worse yet, Maltby claimed that he heard one of the bearers say "*(Kottandi! Kottandi!)* strike! strike!" Piecing together other snatches of overheard conversations in Telugu, Maltby became convinced that Chendrá was in fact the rebel leader Chendrayya, and that "*his gang intended to murder* [him]." Maltby argued that he killed the munsif in self-defense. There had been no angry confrontation, because he had cleverly lulled his would-be attackers into complacency.[24]

In his official statement, Maltby wrote that he was "in a position to realize the state of affairs in the north," where the rebels had wreaked havoc and remained "unpunished" by police.[25] The statement was peppered with Telugu words, with his translations written next to them. Maltby claimed that he was so attuned to Indian ways that his perception of the threat to his life had been obvious to him, where it would have been invisible to most Englishmen. In a letter written during his confinement in Madras, Maltby relied on both British and Indian conventional wisdom to press his case that he had acted reasonably. "We have the authority of Shakespeare," he wrote, "that 'treason and murder ever kept together.' Legally speaking, moreover, I was not the assailer, but the assaulted."[26] Maltby's understanding of Indian culture allowed him to see the bearers' apparently innocuous behavior as "openly treacherous." Shakespeare allowed him to see their treachery and conspiracy as a prelude to murder.

Maltby argued that he had killed Latchmi Nayudu in self-defense based on a reasonable assessment of the threat to his life. A common-law claim of self-defense could succeed despite a defendant's mistake as long as the mistaken belief was both genuine and reasonable.[27] "Where a man acts . . . under a mistake of fact . . . in what he supposes, on reasonable grounds, to be the defence of his person . . . against serious instant danger," explained James Fitzjames Stephen, "his position is, generally speaking, the same as it would have been if the facts which he supposed to exist had really existed."[28]

Like most Civilians, Maltby had no formal legal training.[29] And yet, he leaned heavily on his experiences as a magistrate to position himself in his correspondence as a man of the law. His father's active legal career likely also contributed to Maltby's facility with legal concepts and legal language. As a result, Maltby understood that he did not have to prove that Chandrayya's men really *had* tried to kill him in Sattivada. Rather, he needed to prove that his perception of the threat posed to his life was reasonable. He also knew, however, that most Englishmen would not have felt that they were in "serious, instant danger," in Stephen's phrase, that night in Sattivada. To the casual British observer, the villagers appeared to have done nothing suspicious. In fact, Maltby's behavior struck his fellow civil servants as not only unreasonable but insane.

When Maltby was arrested, he had recently been appointed acting senior assistant magistrate of Vizagapatam. He had been in Madras for approximately twelve years.[30] From the moment he was captured in Sattivada, allegedly after a night spent hiding in the bushes and begging a local "fortune teller" (also described as a "mad woman") to shelter him, he became concerned about his legal position.[31] He seems to have experienced great shock, and probably remorse, when first confronted with his crime. He quickly began, however, consciously or unconsciously, to reshape the night's events into a narrative that not only painted his actions as heroic but also, and more important, as legally justifiable.

Early in the morning on 25 December, a group of villagers brought Maltby back to the foot of the tree. There, the corpse of the munsif still lay, surrounded by the dead man's crying widow and four children. One older man testified that the crowd took Maltby to the body, and that he "fell upon the corpse and cried when he saw it," crying out in Telugu.[32] Another villager chastised Maltby for his hypocrisy—how could one judge slay another for no reason? He reported asking Maltby, "You are a type of justice; is it proper to kill the Nayudu?" To which Maltby replied, "I did not know I killed him."[33] Maltby had not yet, in the immediate aftermath of the killing, settled upon the elaborate story of conspiracy and betrayal that he would tell in his official statement. The villagers' and bearers' testimony suggest that Maltby was bewildered, chagrined, and ashamed. He grieved, perhaps for Latchmi Nayudu, and perhaps for himself. Whatever the truth of the killing, his identity as a conscientious civil servant and as an "insider" with special access to Madras's Telugu-speaking people was crumbling.

On the afternoon of 25 December, J. Sunder Siva Row Pantulu, the police inspector of Vizianagrum, and the sub-magistrate, Chendica Raghnayakulu Nayudu, arrived in Sattivada. They found Maltby lingering near the corpse, surrounded by a crowd of three hundred people. It had been more than twelve hours since Maltby had killed the munsif, and by now his narrative of a surprise attack by Chendrayya and his gang had taken shape. He told the inspector that "he had done a dreadful deed, but he was right in doing so, as the deceased was a member of Chendrayya's party."[34] Maltby was excited and impulsive on the ride back to Vizianagrum. He galloped his pony too fast, flitted in conversation from one subject to another, spoke at length of his fears of reprisal by Chendrayya's henchmen, and insisted that the inspector hold him around the waist to comfort him.[35]

On arriving in Vizianagrum, Maltby was confined in a guesthouse to await the arrival of O. B. Irvine, acting head magistrate of the district and Maltby's direct superior. On 26 December, Irvine decided to "hold [his] Court" immediately.[36] Maltby realized he was in trouble. He had killed a fellow justice of the peace in what appeared, at least, to have been a senseless attack. There were dozens of witnesses. He was under arrest and in disgrace. Although he first argued that he had killed in self-defense, the arguments he turned to most often in the wake of the crime were procedural and technical: lawyerly arguments about jurisdiction, rules of evidence, and the interpretation of statutes. Ultimately, his ability to negotiate the colonial legal system did not change his fate. Still, his constant objections moved government officials and lawyers to respond uncharacteristically to the grievances of a criminal lunatic.

When Irvine first examined his prisoner, Maltby "got very excited and said he would not allow the witnesses for the prosecution to be examined as in reality he was the prosecutor and had several charges to bring against the witnesses."[37] Irvine left the guesthouse convinced that Maltby was insane. He decided to suspend proceedings and begin a formal inquiry into his prisoner's mental state, under section 423 of the Code of Indian Criminal Procedure (1872).[38] Once Irvine suspected that Maltby was insane, Maltby ceased to be the subject of the law's judgment and became the object of its scrutiny, to be managed but not tried or formally punished. Within a week, he had been assigned a bungalow at the local Waltair Asylum, with a full police guard. His horses and dogs were auctioned off, and the government prepared to send him to the presidency asylum in Madras pending his deportation to England.[39] During Maltby's first week at Waltair, a civil surgeon reported, "As regards the crime of which he has been guilty, he is quite irrational and so far from appreciating the gravity of the act he either treats the subject with indifference or expresses his satisfaction with what he has done."[40]

Maltby was an exceptionally prolific correspondent but otherwise quite ordinary. Indian civil servants were known to break under the pressure of their posts, at times slipping into violent paranoia. Many Victorian physicians believed that sunstroke, which French alienists called *coup de soleil*, could result in madness that produced erratic behavior and an extreme susceptibility to the effects of alcohol.[41] Although no one officially diagnosed Maltby with sunstroke-induced madness, his carers might well have interpreted his pomposity, suspiciousness, and violence as proof that he was afflicted. "A European is, from the heat, in greater danger of ailment of brain than he would be in this country," declared a British judge when he considered Maltby's predicament in 1881.[42] Maltby maintained that his years in India and his careful study of Indian culture made him an especially competent civil servant, but his judges and doctors assumed his long service in the Indian heat made him mentally and legally incompetent.

It is tempting to dismiss Victorian evocations of "brain fever" as excrescences of their fear of, and fascination with, the tropics.[43] Some scholars have suggested, though, that there might have been something to the idea that nineteenth-century Britons could come mentally undone in the colonies. In his work on nineteenth-century colonial expeditions in Central Africa, Johannes Fabian argues that European explorers experienced states of "ecstasis"—a sense of being "out of their minds." Explorers guzzled laudanum, a tincture of opium and alcohol, and dosed themselves with quinine and arsenic in desperate attempts to ward off insomnia, fevers, and dysentery. They were hot, lonely, sick, frightened, tired, and obsessed with hiding these weaknesses from the "natives."[44] Maltby's twelve years in India were almost certainly more comfortable than the months that Fabian's explorers spent trekking through equatorial jungles. Still, he was a long way from home. The decorum and control that colonial officials were expected to maintain came at a psychic cost. Sometimes colonial Britons lost their minds, and when they did, colonial subjects usually paid the price.

When Britons in the colonial service became paranoid and violent, their superiors ordered them back to Europe. The Criminal Lunatic Acts of 1849 and 1851 gave colonial Indian authorities the right to detain defendants indefinitely after they had been acquitted on the ground of insanity, in the same way that the 1800 Criminal Lunatics Act had created England's "pleasure men." The 1851 act made it easier for regional authorities to transfer criminal lunatics among Indian asylums and, importantly, to ship them to institutions in England. By the 1870s, Indian asylums, perpetually overcrowded and underfunded, had long served as what Waltraud Ernst describes as "a depot for Europeans *en route* to repatriation."[45]

Maltby arrived in Madras on 7 January 1880 and was placed under the care of the superintendent of the Madras Asylum. On 31 January, Maltby wrote a statement describing in detail his version of the events of 24 and 25 December.[46] The superintendent forwarded the document to the Indian government, explaining that the first half of the statement was in Maltby's handwriting but that he himself had copied the second half because his patient refused to part with the original.[47] The statement was among the legal documents Maltby diligently prepared in anticipation of his criminal trial. He would not accept that, as a criminal lunatic, his trial might be years away, or might never come at all. A few weeks later, the Official Visitors of the Madras Lunatic Asylum found Maltby to be rational—except about Chendrayya. When they mentioned the rebel leader, Maltby became agitated and grandiose. They declared him "of unsound mind and unable to make a defence of his actions before a judicial tribunal."[48] Maltby was stuck. A self-defense claim was his best chance at acquittal. But *because* Maltby insisted that he had acted in self-defense, which officials found implausible and outlandish, they assumed that he was insane and could not stand trial.

There seemed to be no way out. Maltby was neither guilty nor innocent, neither a prisoner nor a patient. At the age of thirty-five, his career, even his liberty, had been snatched away. Maltby believed that the tragedy was not his alone. His desperate desire for a trial reflected not only his hope for acquittal and release but also his commitment to what he saw as the "proper administration of justice in this vast country." Maltby accused the Madras government of abusing its executive authority by usurping the power of the courts. The government, "having . . . assumed the extraordinary and anomalous role of Master and Guardian, accuser and judge, all rolled into one," risked making "English magistrates . . . more liable than ever to the danger of outrage and intimidation" at the hands of the colonial state.[49] Patients in metropolitan asylums leveled similar charges against executive and legal authorities who confined them without trial. What Maltby saw as colonial corruption was in fact a regular feature of British efforts to manage the criminally insane.

While in the asylum, Maltby wrote a satirical essay entitled "How to Make a Government Lunatic," which he sent to the *Madras Mail* (it is unclear whether it was ever published). In the essay, Maltby provided instructions for how to drive a sane man mad. He exhorted his imagined "Government," "Irritate [him] by treating him neither as a fool, or a criminal, or a knave, or a lunatic. If you can, allow him to imagine himself to be an amalgamated compound of all four. Continue above treatment for 10 days. . . . Heap up the agony, add to the suspense, and by general uncertainty harass not only his life, but the very soul out of him as well."[50] In May of 1880, after nearly five months in Madras, Maltby was sent back to London. A surgeon who accompanied him on the voyage foiled his attempt to escape when the ship docked in Malta.[51]

Maltby was admitted to Broadmoor on 10 June 1880. His doctors, Orange and Nicolson, reported that he continued to profess his innocence and his sanity. Maltby claimed that "the Government ha[d] kept him from the Court because they were afraid of the disclosures that he would make" and that "his great insight into the Native mind was a source of prejudice and jealousy to the authorities."[52] As became the norm where Maltby was concerned, the exact terms of his confinement were left undefined.[53] Weeks after his arrival at Broadmoor, he was transferred to the private Moorcroft House Asylum in

Hillingdon at his family's request.[54] Beginning in 1828, the public Commission in Lunacy, supported by a staff of medical experts known as Commissioners in Lunacy, had overseen the licensing and operation of British asylums.[55] In November, the Commissioners in Lunacy visited Moorcroft. They concluded that Maltby was now sufficiently sane to plead and to be transported to India to stand trial.[56]

Despite the commissioners' recommendations, the seasons passed, and Maltby remained at Moorcroft. His wife, Maud, repeatedly wrote to the Home Office and the India Office, demanding her husband's release and financial support for herself and their two children.[57] On 8 September, Maltby was formally discharged from the Civil Service, on the pension he would have received had he been invalided after twelve years' service. The total, before deductions, came to £310 per year.[58] The money helped the family but did not signal any softening in the government's position.[59] The officials involved in his case clearly thought that sending Maltby back to Madras for trial would only result in his return to England either as a convicted murderer or, once again, as a criminal lunatic. The trial was not a good investment of the government's money and time.[60]

It is not clear that officials in England could have returned Maltby to India even if they had wanted to. Maltby was repatriated under the Act to Authorize the Removal from India of Insane Persons (1851).[61] The law allowed the repatriation to England of insane persons charged with offenses in India, and their indefinite detention in British asylums. William Macpherson, secretary of the Judicial Department of the India Office from 1879 to 1882, believed that the act did not allow for the patient's return to the colonies. He wrote of Maltby, "Probably when the Madras Government sent him to England, they never intended that he should be returned to them for trial."[62]

In frustration, Maltby hired lawyers and petitioned for a writ of habeas corpus against the Home Secretary and the superintendent of Moorcroft House. The Court of Queen's Bench heard the case, reported as *In re Maltby*, on 25 March 1881.[63] Maltby's barristers argued that the 1851 act applied only to those who had been formally charged with a crime. Since in India a British subject had to be tried for murder before a jury, Maltby could only properly be charged before a jury. His interview with Irvine in the guesthouse was, by this reasoning, insufficient to constitute either a "court" or a "charge," and so Maltby's deportation under the act was illegal. Counsel for the Home Office argued that Irvine had successfully brought the "court" to Maltby out of kindness on that day in December, and that he had, in fact, been "charged" with murder. Doubts about Maltby's sanity overshadowed these legalistic arguments over the proper meanings of "court" and "charge." Even if there had been procedural irregularities in his case, the government's lawyers insisted that returning Maltby to India could change nothing: "If . . . he must be sent back for trial to India . . . he will be acquitted on the ground of insanity and again sent here to be detained."[64]

Maltby lost. His campaign was compromised by his alleged insanity and because the court agreed that colonial circumstances could excuse—even require—deviations from metropolitan criminal procedure. Justice Denman in his speech in Maltby's case described the 1851 act as designed to remove "Europeans from the hot climate to their native air. . . . I do not think," he continued, "we are bound to hold that the words [of the statute] are to be limited to the exact meaning which they would bear if we were dealing with a matter wholly arising in the United Kingdom, the circumstances being so different."[65] Maltby was bitterly disappointed. In a petition to the Queen, he accused the two judges in the case of falsely alleging that he was a danger to the public.[66] His lawyers advised against an appeal.

In the wake of the killing, imperial authorities had been eager to remove Maltby from Madras expeditiously. Partly, this helped to preserve the Indian colonial government's prestige by hiding the weakness and cruelty of its officers. However, the imperative to conceal cases of criminal insanity by avoiding the courtroom, and a high-profile and inevitably divisive trial, was not only colonial. British authorities, whether at home or abroad, struggled to manage criminal lunatics. The asylum seemed to jurists and government officials to represent, simultaneously, a threat to traditional penal institutions and the principles that underpinned judicial punishment, and a boon to officials who needed somewhere to send the mad. Once Maltby had been safely secured (or so officials believed) in the asylum, there was little incentive to risk scandal by allowing him to stand trial for murder.

On 23 May 1881, Maltby took "advantage of an opportunity that offered itself," as he put it, and escaped from Moorcroft.[67] The staff at the asylum, which catered principally to paying clients, were unaccustomed to men like Thomas Maltby. That day, an attendant had accompanied Maltby to the station to collect Maud for her regular visit. Maud claimed that she had hurt her foot and asked for a carriage. When the attendant returned, they were gone.[68]

Reactions to Maltby's escape were mixed. "Nothing can be done," remarked one Home Office official, "his family must take the consequences of any fresh development of his insanity."[69] William Harcourt, the Home Secretary, was less blasé. He called Maltby a "dangerous lunatic" and demanded an inquiry.[70] Recapturing Maltby presented major difficulties, however. The first of these was the ambiguity of his legal status. There was no precedent for a case like his.[71] Maltby was a criminal lunatic held under warrant. And yet, the fact that he had been housed at a private asylum, rather than at Broadmoor, had the unexpected consequence of shielding him from the authority of either of the two major statutes governing escaped lunatics.

The first of these, the 1853 Lunatic Asylums Act, stipulated that escaped lunatics could be retaken within fourteen days under the authority of their existing medical certificates and committing documents.[72] The Commissioners in Lunacy did not, though, think it applied to criminal lunatics. The act dealt with lunatics who were found not to be under proper "care and control" in their local communities; it offered no guidance for how to handle men who absconded overseas with the connivance of their friends. A second statute, the 1860 Criminal Lunatic Asylums Act, stated that any person who escaped from "any Asylum for Criminal Lunatics" could be "retaken at any Time."[73] But although Maltby was a criminal lunatic, Moorcroft was not an "Asylum for Criminal Lunatics." His recapture remained possible. Maltby and Maud had fled to his father's home in Brussels. Home Office staff thought that Belgian officials could be persuaded to arrest and deport him if they were shown the depositions from the Madras inquiry and the Home Office warrant.[74] Still, having no clear law giving the British government authority to assert its jurisdiction over their erstwhile prisoner was inconvenient. The Home Office set about remedying the legal "defect" Maltby's situation had revealed.[75] In the meantime, Maltby was in legal limbo.

Maltby's escape to Belgium also raised political difficulties. Initiating formal extradition proceedings and involving the Belgian police would embarrass the government and chance a diplomatic incident. Beyond asking Thomas Maltby Sr., the vice-consul, to surrender his son, Scotland Yard recommended that the Home Office take no action to retrieve their prisoner.[76] Some were relieved to have Maltby safely out of their hands. The Indian government and the Home Secretary might prefer, guessed one official, not to apply for his extradition, even if Belgium were to oblige.[77] By July of 1881, the British government had retreated from pursuing Maltby across international borders. The superintendent of Moorcroft wrote that summer, barely containing his jubilation, to ask if he could officially strike Maltby's name from his list of patients. The Home Office agreed.[78]

Maltby continued his campaign for exoneration as a fugitive. He finished his petition to the Queen on 21 October 1881, and noted his address as 63,

Avenue Louise, Brussels. The petition was professionally printed in a neat booklet on glossy paper, with each of twenty-one key points duly enumerated.[79] Like almost all Maltby's writings, the petition respected the formalities of official correspondence. He provided a full account of the legal and bureaucratic missteps and abuses, as he saw them, which had led him to his desperate situation. He demanded compensation for all that he had lost: his property, his "personal status," his pay, and, most of all, "for the wrongful, cruel and unjust loss of liberty which your Petitioner endured in India and in England between the 27th December 1879, and the 23rd May 1881."[80] The petition was Maltby's talisman. He sent copies, often multiple copies, to almost everyone with whom he had official contact from 1881 on.

Maltby's petition to the Queen is discomfiting to read. For a man deemed incapable of making his defense in court, Maltby was distressingly lucid. His account of his departure from India and his experiences in England was accurate, when checked against official correspondence, and his grasp of the machinations of the government bodies involved in his case—the Madras High Court, the Madras government, the Home Office, the India Office—was impressive. No doubt the bureaucrats and lawyers with whom Maltby corresponded thought so, too. Shortly after arriving in Brussels, Maltby wrote to request the arrears of his pension, which Maud had not drawn for months. Maltby was so prompt in requesting the proper paperwork that he was the first to inform the India Office of his escape from Moorcroft. A Judicial Department minute from that August hints at the alarm Maltby's correspondence could produce: "Mr. Maltby, writing from *Brussels*, asks to be supplied with the necessary papers in order to draw his pension. . . . [T]his Office has received no information of Mr. Maltby's departure from the Asylum in England in which he was detained by order of the Home Office."[81]

This was the first of many official letters that Maltby would send to the India Office from Brussels. In another, Maltby described his surprise that the permanent undersecretary, Louis Mallet, refused to communicate officially with him while he was a "fugitive from justice (?)."[82] The bracketed question mark was in Maltby's original letter, which he wrote in an elegant hand from the English Club, Brussels, using its monogrammed stationery. Maltby enclosed a copy of his petition to the Queen. Mallet was a man known for his discipline and enthusiasm for protocol.[83] He must have been nonplussed by this extended, semiprivate correspondence with a criminal lunatic who demanded, in the most proper bureaucratic register, that his pension be dispensed while he gallivanted around Belgium. Maltby went unpaid.

The next three years of Maltby's life are mysterious. At some time in 1882, he left Brussels for Colorado and New Mexico in the United States, where he may have owned property.[84] The superintendent of the Madras Asylum reported that Maltby believed that he had only survived Chendrayya's attack thanks to "dodges he had learned in America."[85] Maud had given birth to the couple's third child, a girl, in Topeka, Kansas, in 1878.[86] In 1882, Maltby and Maud had their fourth.[87]

Meanwhile, Maltby kept writing. In 1883, he sent a petition to the High Court of Madras from somewhere in Chicago, although his permanent address was in Idaho Springs. True to form, he carefully described his case and numerous statutes he thought relevant. As usual, he rejected the claim that he had ever been legally "charged" and begged to "reassert that old maxim of English law *falsus in uno, falsus in omnibus*, which openly proclaims that fraud is in itself sufficient to vitiate all judicial or *quasi*-judicial proceedings founded thereon."[88] Maltby's petition was sufficiently credible to prompt the high court to initiate proceedings in the matter. The court, however, merely found that it could not entertain Maltby's objections unless a pleader, a lawyer, presented them in person, through the superintendent of a jail where he, Maltby, was confined.[89] It is unclear exactly where Maltby went and what he did in America. In an 1897 letter, he remembered appearing in North American courts "on more than one occasion in connection with law-suits in that country."[90] The contrast between his freedom and access to the courts in America and his experiences in England was not lost on him.

British authorities had given him up, and Maltby was free to travel the world, sue his neighbors, and expand his family, but he could not resist the temptation to return to England. Neither time nor liberty could blunt his determination to stand trial. On 25 October 1884, two Scottish officers apprehended Maltby while he was sitting in the waiting room of the India Office in London.[91] He was indignant, protesting the humiliating public arrest and the roughness with which he was bundled into a cab and taken back to Moorcroft.

It is difficult to believe that Maltby would return to the India Office after three years abroad. It seems that he took the Madras High Court's 1883 proceedings in response to his petition as an invitation to plead his case and not what it really was: a refusal to deal with a fugitive. He wrote, "Having received the permission of the Madras High Court to appear in person . . . , I returned to England from North America, and, whilst attending to my private affairs at the India Office, I was suddenly seized . . . and brought down to this private prison, called by some a Lunatic Asylum."[92]

The police report on Maltby's recapture fills in the details. Maltby arrived in London on 15 October. He and Maud had had a falling out in America, and she had returned to London alone, to the Waterloo Hotel, in late September. Apparently, Maltby's appearance at the hotel had caused "great astonishment and consternation to his wife," and a "violent scene" ensued. The two stayed together, but Maud was always careful to keep the door to their adjoining rooms locked.[93] It is unclear who first alerted the authorities to Maltby's return. Perhaps it was Maud, so overwhelmed by her husband's behavior that she had fled to England, where he was sure to be arrested if he followed. Maud "now wishe[d] him to be in an asylum" and, Home Office staff believed, would never again conspire to help her husband escape.[94]

A London Metropolitan Police inspector went to the Waterloo Hotel on 24 October and interviewed guests about Maltby. The inspector proceeded to the India Office the next morning to ask what they thought should be done with him. As it happened, Maltby was already there, having come to apply for his pension in person. While Maltby waited at the India Office, the policeman walked through the building to Home Office headquarters. Eventually, he and another inspector arrested him. Maltby "struggled violently" and "refused to walk quietly," and he was dragged from Whitehall as officials and messengers poured into the corridor to watch. The police took Maltby to Scotland Yard. While he waited to be transferred to Moorcroft, he wrote four letters: two to politicians, one to his wife, and one to a sergeant of the City Police. As Maltby was being hauled, struggling and screaming, to the carriage, he turned to his captors and asked, "Do you think I have let [Home Secretary] Harcourt have enough of it?" to which one replied, "I certainly think you have and us too." Maltby burst out laughing and decided to "leave off," walking calmly the rest of the way. He had returned to England and would never leave or live outside an asylum again.[95]

During Maltby's absence from London, the law had changed. Earlier in 1884, the Colonial Prisoners Removal Act came into effect.[96] During the second reading of the bill in the House of Lords, in March of that year, the Earl of Derby argued that the new act would make it easier to transfer criminals, including criminal lunatics, from the colonies back to England. The justifications for this practice echoed those expressed by the Court of Queen's Bench in Maltby's habeas suit. Derby explained, "If you are to deal with an English sailor imprisoned on the West Coast of Africa as you would at Portland, you would probably kill him—if his confinement has to be relaxed and mitigated, to avoid the danger from climate, it ceases in a great measure to be penal, and introduces irregularity in the discipline of the prison, if Natives are also confined there."[97] Section 9 of the act dealt specifically with the case of escaped criminals, including criminal lunatics, who had been deported to England from the colonies. The first part of the section stipulated that if a prisoner escaped, "by breach of prison or otherwise, out of custody, he may be retaken in the same manner as a person convicted of a crime against the law of the place to which he escapes may be retaken upon an escape." The second subsection made both the escapee and anyone who helped him subject to criminal punishment.[98]

Another act, also passed in 1884, enhanced the authority of officials and doctors to retrieve escaped criminal lunatics and to punish their accomplices. Section 11 of the Criminal Lunatics Act (1884) resolved the uncertainties of the Criminal Lunatics Asylums Act (1860), which had caused so much confusion after Maltby's escape. The 1884 act specified that sections 11 and 12 of the 1860 act applied to "every asylum or place in which criminal lunatics are confined so far as regards those lunatics, and to the criminal lunatics in such asylum or place, in all respects as if such asylum or place were an asylum for criminal lunatics."[99]

Maltby did not take recapture well. The long-suffering medical superintendent of Moorcroft House complained, "[Maltby] was represented as being quiet and harmless and not requiring constant attention. After his return here . . . he was so excitable and bent upon escaping, that it became necessary to place an attendant with him constantly."[100] Desperate to be rid of his bothersome patient, the physician even wrote directly to Harcourt, the Home Secretary, informing him that Maltby had made violent attempts to escape since his return and had threatened the lives of his attendants and anyone else complicit in what he called his "illegal detention."[101] And so, Maltby found himself back at Broadmoor in March 1885.

Orange's and Nicolson's letters and reports suggest a precipitous decline following Maltby's readmission to Broadmoor. In one note to the India Office, Nicolson wrote that Maltby experienced bouts of mania marked by incoherent rambling, interrupted by periods of lucidity "found to end in a profusion of letter-writing to various people in connection with what he regards as his grievances."[102] Maltby even attempted to revive his 1883 petition to the Madras High Court, the official response to which had lured him back to London in 1884.[103] Always a careful observer of procedure, he ensured that Nicolson, who succeeded Orange as superintendent in 1886, signed the covering letter.[104] He hired new lawyers in Madras. Even though his doctors at Broadmoor considered him virtually incapable of coherent conversation, the high court agreed to hear his objections again. In November, the judges decided that Irvine's inquiry in Vizianagrum had been conducted according to law, that Maltby's deportation to England was therefore also lawful, and that "the High Court has no jurisdiction over persons confined in jails or asylums in England, and therefore cannot interfere in the matter of the present petition."[105] They directed copies of Maltby's petition to the government of Madras, which sent copies to the India Office and to the secretary of state for India in London, which shared them with the Home Office.[106] Thereafter, asylum staff forwarded Maltby's legal correspondence straight to the Home Office.[107] Staff summarized his condition on the back of one such letter, addressed to the member of Parliament Randolph Churchill: "Body indifferent, mind unsound."[108]

Maltby fades from the archives after 1886. Fewer and fewer avenues for reopening his case remained. His only prospect rested in proving to his doctors that he was sane. Most of his letters mentioned nothing about his sanity, however, but were focused on procedural issues and reconstructions of the night of the killing. On Christmas Eve in 1879, just before Maltby set out for Chicacole, one witness remembered him handing her a pistol and saying, "This is a thing I dare not trust myself with in one of my insane moments." She also reported that he asked her anxiously over dinner whether she thought him insane.[109] As the ten-year anniversary of his crime approached, his doctors gave up hope of any improvement. In an 1887 report, Nicolson put it bluntly, "[Maltby] is quite unfit by reason of his insanity to stand his trial or to be sent to India with that view; and I am of opinion that his mind will never be sufficiently restored to make him fit to do so."[110]

Maltby's friends and enemies were disappearing—Irvine and Maltby's father, the vice-consul, were dead by the late 1880s. In the margin of one letter in which Maltby announced his father's recent death in words uncharacteristically ill formed, Nicolson scribbled, "Mr. Maltby's mental condition is at present much decayed and unsettled."[111] As the years passed, Maltby made overtures to new government officials in both Madras and London, but the longer he stayed at Broadmoor, the less likely he was to receive answers. One of his last archived letters was addressed to Sir Philip Hutchins, who had once been a judge on the Madras High Court and was, by 1897, a member of the Imperial Legislative Council of India.[112] Instead of writing back to Maltby, Hutchins wrote to his doctors. Richard Brayn, who had become medical superintendent in 1896 after Nicolson retired, warned Hutchins, "If you reply to his letter, it will only encourage him to write again, and annoy you with a further correspondence."[113] In February of 1898, Maltby made a final plea. "There is an old legal maxim," he wrote, "which says 'falsus in uno falsus in omnibus,' and I feel sure that as a just man, you must regret in any way being a party to a miscarriage of justice, which has consigned me to prison for more *than fourteen years without a trial*. . . . I am likely to remain here the rest of my life."[114] Maltby's correspondents stopped writing back. After 1898, Maltby vanished from the records of the Judicial Department of the India Office. He remained at Broadmoor until his death, at the age of seventy-six, in 1921.[115] By the time he died, he had spent thirty-eight years in custody and forty-one as a criminal lunatic in the eyes of the British and Indian governments.

The heavy bound volumes of the public and judicial files among the India Office Records are replete with letters by and about Maltby. He has his own dedicated file in the archives of the Home Office, in the British National Archives, and in the archives of Broadmoor Hospital.[116] In addition to printed records of the evidence collected in Madras in the wake of his trial, Maltby's appeal to the Court of Queen's Bench made it into the English law reports.[117] Compared to similar cases, Maltby's case generated an extraordinary quantity of writing.

Maltby's ability to communicate with the officials, lawyers, and administrators handling his case in their own register, respecting the formalities of bureaucratic prose and written self-presentation, piqued their interest in his predicament. The European insane in India included some who were educated and relatively genteel, as Maltby was.[118] He enjoyed the additional advantage of fluency in the two languages that were most pertinent to his circumstances: that of the Indian Civil Service and that of the law. Even after many years at Broadmoor, he followed epistolary conventions in his official correspondence and publications. Maltby tapped into the empire's bureaucratic networks. His case placed him in ambiguous jurisdictional territory—he killed the munsif in Madras, was under the custody of the Home Office, and drew his financial support from the India Office—which provided a wide catchment area of potential official correspondents. The fact that Maltby's flurries of writing, apparently produced in and among moments of mania, were received as formal petitions, legal instructions, and official memoranda should not be overlooked. Despite his status as a criminal lunatic, Maltby continued to speak in the voice of a civil servant and magistrate; he was too intelligible to his interlocutors to be summarily dismissed. His correspondents also wrote to him and about him because his case raised important legal and administrative issues. The two 1884 statutes that would have governed his 1880 transportation to England and his 1881 escape if they had been in force, the Criminal Lunatics Act and the Colonial Prisoners Removal Act, might well have been conceived with Maltby in mind.

Homicide cases were risky for colonial authorities. None of Maltby's correspondents, even the exasperated superintendent of Moorcroft, argued that he should die for killing the munsif Latchmi Nayudu (no one asked Nayudu's widow what she thought her husband's killer deserved). Maltby might have been dangerous, but he did not strike fear into the hearts of most who met him. Colonial administrators did not seem to think that sparing his life would encourage others to commit violent acts, or that it would be immoral to let him live. The officials who managed his case and his care seem genuinely to have believed that he was insane, but their assertions that he would satisfy the *M'Naghten* conditions strain credulity. It was often easier to ship patients halfway across the world than to confront their ambiguous criminal responsibility in court.

Men and women like Maltby circulated around the British world, in search of their fortunes and their freedom. When they committed crimes, they were sucked into a criminal justice system that regularly crossed continents. Just as lawyers in Indian courts cited British precedent, men who had killed their victims in London and in Madras could find themselves stalking Broadmoor's halls side by side, eking out lives on the same wards, petitioning the same authorities for their release.

CHAPTER 3

Lovers, Monsters, and the Problem of Evil

The farmlands of Ontario, for which William Bigg had traded the smokestacks and slag heaps of Swansea, held a temptation he could not resist: horses.[1] He crept into pastures at night to cut their throats. When police finally caught him, he confessed to torturing the horses and to twisting the necks of farm birds and hiding their bodies in woodpiles.[2] He was then twelve years old.[3] After a year in jail, Bigg returned to his family. His father and stepmother locked him in a separate room at night. He had once attempted to strangle his brother and had pressed a pile of clothes against his infant sister's face. When police captured him with money stolen from his father's desk, Bigg was sentenced to seven years' imprisonment in the local penitentiary. He spent time in the criminal asylum connected to the prison but was discharged at the end of his sentence.

One night, after his son's second release, Bigg's father cut himself while paring apples. Bigg, according to doctors who would later record his history, "was observed to become restless, nervous, pale, and to have undergone a peculiar change of demeanour."[4] In the hubbub, he slipped into a neighbor's yard and cut a horse's throat. He fled to the woods, where he raped a young girl who stumbled upon his hiding place. He was arrested, tried, and sentenced to death for the assault but after ten years was pardoned and released.[5] On his way home from prison, Bigg captured yet another horse, cutting off parts of its tongue and slashing its belly and neck.[6] He was arrested and transferred to

Rockwood Asylum in Kingston, Ontario, in late September 1879. Bigg's doctors described him as intelligent, well dressed, and pleasant but also volatile, manipulative, and cruel. He tortured and killed any animal that wandered into the ward. He "literally crushed" an attendant's terrier in a bucket. He "split up" a cat, "from the throat to the tail." Bigg's fellow inmates fared little better. He was notorious for leading severely disabled patients into the dark recesses of the asylum in order to mutilate them.[7]

Five years later, Bigg absconded from an asylum picnic and was narrowly prevented from raping another girl. At his trial, neither the prosecution nor the defense mentioned insanity, even though Bigg had escaped from an asylum. The only ambiguous reference to his history was the judge's declaration at sentencing that he "must be lenient under the circumstances."[8] The jury found Bigg guilty, and he received a six-month prison sentence. During Bigg's final trial, Dr. Daniel Hack Tuke, hailed by his Canadian hosts as "the celebrated English alienist," visited Rockwood.[9] Tuke later described Bigg's case at the 1885 annual meeting of the Medico-Psychological Association in Cork. Even for men accustomed to working with the criminally insane, Bigg's behavior was shocking.[10] Tuke hoped that Bigg's combination of perversion and superficial rationality would convince the assembled of the existence of a disturbing mental illness: moral insanity.

For nineteenth-century physicians, "moral" had many meanings. Doctors rarely used it as a simple synonym for "ethical." The mind's "moral" facets could include every quality and function that was not purely cognitive.[11] The morally insane patient was, one historian has argued, "distinguished by the *absence* of what is otherwise considered to be the core phenomenon of mental illness: mental derangement."[12] The ambiguity and capaciousness of moral insanity made it controversial. How could the will and desires of a person be diseased while his or her cognition remained unscathed? Worse, moral insanity was never able to shake its prima facie association with evil. Moral insanity was not, by definition, a disease of the conscience or the soul. And yet, patients who seemed most obviously morally insane were those who committed horrific violence without apparent motive. To some physicians, moral insanity provided an explanation for senseless cruelty. The diagnosis, however, brought alienists into direct conflict with the lawyers and judges who also made violence, and the punishment of the violent, their business.

Moral insanity challenged traditional, legal understandings of criminal responsibility. It seemed to erase any distinction between criminality and insanity, suggesting in essence that those who were the most depraved were the least responsible for their actions. Most types of insanity, including monomania and puerperal insanity, which afflicted women during and after pregnancy, raised significant questions about where to draw the line between responsibility and irresponsibility. But moral insanity, more than any other diagnosis, forced lawyers and doctors to consider what they knew and could ever know about the human condition, and to interrogate their beliefs about how a just society should operate.

Moral insanity dramatized a clash between competing visions of British civilization. One faction saw most deviance as the result of disease or biological destiny, which called for medical treatment, not legal punishment. Some argued that humane governance required the recognition of the frailty of human minds and the diversion of unfit populations into therapeutic institutions. An opposing faction saw the presumption that most people were sane and responsible as an axiom of just governance, and judgment under criminal law as an affirmation of the accused's status as an autonomous subject.[13] Should British civilization be humane, or should it be just? Could it be either without being both? Mental science, theories of degeneration, and emerging understandings of race and heredity were refashioning how Victorians saw human nature. In this shifting intellectual landscape, moral insanity seemed to challenge jurists, physicians, and others to declare themselves: to embrace a new world in which most accused criminals were unfit and subject to scientific management; or to defend the old, in which most criminals acted freely and deserved—even were entitled to—punishment.

English physician and ethnologist James Cowles Prichard credited himself with coining the phrase "moral insanity" in an essay in the *Cyclopaedia of Practical Medicine* (1833).[14] There was always some dispute about the novelty of the notion that a person could be insane without suffering from delusions or hallucinations. One phrenologist commented, in a footnote added to one of Prichard's papers, that "to phrenologists, moral insanity ha[d] long been familiar."[15] Still, Prichard popularized the diagnosis and became its most eminent British advocate. In his *On the Different Forms of Insanity in Relation to Jurisprudence* (1842), Prichard described moral insanity as "a disorder which affects only the feelings and affections, or what are termed the moral powers of the mind, in contradistinction to the powers of the understanding or intellect."[16] He distinguished moral insanity from monomania, the older and better-known category of mental disorder marked by delusion.[17] At times, he also differentiated between moral insanity and "instinctive insanity," which attacked a sufferer's self-control.[18] However, especially in his early works, this separation of "moral sense" from will or self-control was obscure. Prichard wrote, for instance, that what the French called "homicidal monomania," with its "sudden and often irresistible impulse . . . to commit acts which under a sane condition of mind would be accounted atrocious crimes," was moral insanity.[19]

The persistent difficulty of distinguishing between moral insanity as perversion and moral insanity as lack of self-control is important. Moral insanity was so broad that it was difficult for nineteenth-century physicians to debate coherently because each physician and lawyer had his own esoteric understanding of its borders.[20] Most agreed that it did not involve cognitive or intellectual disturbance. Beyond that, little was clear. Physicians and lawyers spilled much ink in the effort to describe the differences—if any—among moral insanity, instinctive insanity, homicidal monomania, and Philippe Pinel's *manie sans délire*. As one physician explained after his own attempt to pick apart these diagnoses: "The above disquisition may appear a trifling with words; not so when it is considered that the words involve doctrines on which formidable consequences hang, both moral and judicial."[21]

A lawyer first used moral insanity as a defense in a British court in 1844, in the Australian colony of New South Wales.[22] John Knatchbull, a thief, fraudster, convict, and sea captain, had killed a shopkeeper named Ellen Jamieson, splitting her head open with a tomahawk. Jamieson lived for twelve days after the attack.[23] British lawyer Robert Lowe defended Knatchbull. Lowe had come to Sydney to make his fortune in 1842 after his doctors said that his albinism would cause him to go blind within seven years. A great orator, he was famously erudite and uncompromising.[24] At trial, Lowe accepted the prosecution's version of events but argued that the prisoner was "one of those persons for whom laws had not been made, and who, although for the peace and welfare of society he ought to be placed under the most severe restraint, ought not to be held responsible for his actions." Lowe told the jury that the brain could be divided into distinct faculties, and that any one faculty could be diseased without affecting the others. Insanity could also infect the will. A person suffering from a disease might feel "irresistibly compelled . . . to crimes which if a perfectly free agent he would be the last to commit." No sane man would have murdered Ellen Jamieson so brutally, especially with no chance of escaping detection. Stranger still, Knatchbull belonged to a wealthy English family. He had grown up in Kent with every material advantage. In a final absurdity, he had murdered Jamieson on the night before his own wedding.

Lowe called no expert witnesses to support his argument, protesting that he had not been given enough time to prepare the case. The judge, Sir William Burton, was openly skeptical. He told the jury that the law protected lunatics but did not "extend itself to those whose will was so depraved as to lead them to the commission of crimes for which no other excuse than their depraved will could be found." Burton worried that accepting a will-based insanity defense would reward weakness with impunity. Whatever its philosophical purchase, Burton declared, "it had no place in the law of England, nor . . . had it a place either in common sense or morality."[25] Although one magazine would later describe this statement of Burton's as "a perfect piece of absurdity—full of twaddle," it was persuasive.[26] The jury returned a guilty verdict without even leaving the box.

From the beginning of its career in British courtrooms, many lawyers, agreeing with Judge Burton, cast moral insanity as a threat to the entire edifice of the common law. To some commentators, Knatchbull was a "monster in human form."[27] Burton spoke for many in his profession when he argued that the law could not recognize moral insanity as exculpatory without offering legal immunity to those who committed the most depraved crimes.[28]

On the other hand, Lowe's advocacy shows that not all lawyers were hostile to moral insanity. In October of 1844, *The Zoist: A Quarterly Journal of Cerebral Physiology and Mesmerism* featured an article, "The Punishment of Death," commenting on Knatchbull's case and decrying the execution of the insane.[29] The journal reprinted the entire account of the trial from the *Sydney Morning Herald*. Lowe, who in addition to his legal work edited the Sydney *Atlas*, republished the article.[30] The *Zoist* praised Lowe, mocked Burton, and accused the government of ignoring the clear signs of Knatchbull's disease. "Is it right," the author asked, "to take revenge upon a being who . . . has acted in accordance with the promptings of his organism, over the formation of which organism he exercised no control[?]" Knatchbull's crime had been inevitable and biologically determined. British judges were wrong to "act upon the assumption that a man can be a moral or immoral character just as he pleases."[31]

Knatchbull remained convinced almost to the last that his sentence would be commuted, especially given that the governor of New South Wales was a family friend. The Executive Council, however, refused to grant him clemency. He was hanged on 13 February 1844, before a crowd of more than five thousand who had assembled outside Sydney's new Darlinghurst jail.[32] As was standard practice at major Australian prisons, a cast of Knatchbull's head was taken for phrenological research.[33] Lowe and his wife, Georgiana, adopted Ellen Jamieson's orphaned children. The family returned to England in 1850. Lowe had a long and illustrious political career in Britain, including a stint as Home Secretary, and was elevated to the House of Lords as Viscount Sherbrooke in 1880.[34] Although his eyesight remained poor, he never went blind.

Moral insanity was also making incursions into murder cases in England in the 1840s. William Newton Allnutt was a slight boy of twelve when he poisoned his grandfather, Samuel Nelme, with arsenic in 1847. Nelme was fond of sprinkling powdered sugar, which he spooned from the family's sugar bowl with his one remaining arm, onto the fruit that he ate most evenings. A week before Nelme's death, Allnutt had asked his mother, Maria Louisa, "what arsenic was like; [she] said it was like flour." At trial, Maria Louisa said that she had had "a good deal of trouble" with her young son. As an infant, Allnutt had fallen and knocked himself unconscious on the blade of a plough. The year before the killing, he had slipped on some ice and returned home "as pale as possible, and very queer and bewildered." From then on, he had become willful and weirdly silent. Maria Louisa said, "He has told me that . . . somebody seemed to say to him, 'Do it, do it, you will not be found out'; that they talked to him in his head." In a letter from Newgate Prison, Allnutt confessed to poisoning his grandfather in revenge after a quarrel. "I know I have sinned against God," he wrote, "and I deserve to be cast into hell." Still, he begged for mercy.[35]

In the 1840s, Allnutt's lawyer, William Ballantine, was the most celebrated barrister at the Old Bailey.[36] Even for him, it would not be easy to convince the jury to accept that his client satisfied the *M'Naghten* criteria. Allnutt's keepers at Newgate said that he seemed completely sane. In response, Ballantine enumerated his young client's symptoms: he heard voices and was prone to sleepwalking, scrofula, and chronic ringworm. His physical ailments, which also included a history of head injuries, were both signs of mental disease and potential causes of it. A family history of mental weakness, the lawyer added, might also have contributed to Allnutt's troubles.

Ballantine referred in court to the published work of alienist Dr. Forbes Benignus Winslow (the father of Dr. Lyttelton Stewart Forbes Winslow, who would pronounce Dodwell sane in 1878). The senior Winslow wrote that a sufferer from moral insanity "struggles for a considerable time against the diseased impulse, till at last it overpowers him."[37] But the coroners agreed that it had taken at least a week of steady poisoning for the arsenic in Nelme's system to reach fatal levels. Moreover, Allnutt had a motive. The Newgate Prison surgeon pronounced Forbes "not of very great authority" anyway. Ballantine examined several medical witnesses in person, but only one was an expert in insanity. This was Dr. John Connolly, Henry Maudsley's father-in-law, the director of the Hanwell Lunatic Asylum, and a pioneer of the moral treatment movement. Connolly testified that Allnutt was "imperfectly organized." He was unwilling to diagnose the boy with moral insanity outright but speculated that "the future character of his insanity would be more in the derangement of his conduct than in the confusion of his intellect."[38] The jury found William Allnutt guilty of willful murder. He was sentenced to death, commuted to transportation for life. He died of consumption in Western Australia in 1853, at the age of eighteen.[39]

Ballantine offered ample evidence that something was wrong with Allnutt but could not meet the high bar set by *M'Naghten*. No one paid much attention to the voices the boy heard, perhaps because they were not overwhelming enough to cloud his understanding. Ballantine, in his memoirs, took no explicit position on moral insanity. He doubted the soundness of the *M'Naghten* rules, however, and was critical of efforts to restrict legal insanity to a narrow set of cognitive deficiencies.[40] The rules, in principle if not in practice, limited the protections of legal insanity to defendants whose delusions or lack of understanding seemed to untether them from reality. They had moral intuitions but so misperceived the world that they could not use their intuitions to guide their actions. These defendants could be understood as well-intentioned blunderers, not calculating villains. Those whom some physicians diagnosed with moral insanity were different. They saw the world as it was and committed antisocial acts anyway. Legal insanity and moral insanity were, in these ways, opposites. While the type of insanity described in *M'Naghten* implied diseased understanding and intact moral sense, moral insanity implied diseased moral sense and intact understanding. Many physicians and lawyers believed that most defendants' mental disorders lay somewhere between these extremes, involving degrees of both cognitive and moral debility. Even those who denied the existence of moral insanity often agreed with Ballantine that *M'Naghten* was unrealistic and unfair.

The cases of John Knatchbull and William Allnutt were not only about the fate of a dissolute sea captain or a troubled child. Moral insanity cases also expose an important but underexamined element of Victorian understandings of responsibility: the link between madness and civilization. Britons' growing suspicion that civilization, both individual and collective, was fragile shaped their understanding of moral insanity cases. Primitivism was no longer the exclusive preserve of colonized peoples. Instead, ethnologists and alienists inspired by evolutionary theories entertained the possibility that even bourgeois Britons might be subject to savage impulses.[41] Thomas Mayo, a physician, wrote in 1854 that moral insanity was "the sudden outbreaks [*sic*] of the brutal character—a character under rapid development at present in the lower orders of the country."[42] The discourse of civilization in responsibility cases was not confined to medical matters or individual minds. Institutions, too, were subject to civilizational analysis. Was it more civilized for a justice system to excuse an allegedly insane killer and ferry him to hospital, or more civilized to hang him, thereby vindicating his victims and deterring future violence? Britons keen to avoid an unpalatable choice between the barbarism of executing the mad and the anarchy implicit in a low threshold for irresponsibility sought a third option: one that could deliver the humane, effective justice that animated the idea of British civilization.

The case of George Victor Townley, a middle-class dreamer who killed his paramour in 1863, shows how questions of criminal responsibility drew alienists, lawyers, and government officials into debates about human nature and the integrity of the legal system. Townley was admitted to Bethlem Hospital's criminal ward on 11 January 1864. He was highly educated, fastidious, with a "pleasing expression of countenance." His doctors glued newspaper clippings about his trial into the asylum's casebook. "This case," they noted, "is one that has been exciting much attention lately, there being great diversity of opinion regarding his mental condition."[43]

When Townley was tried at the Derby Assizes for murder in December 1863, municipal authorities erected barriers around the courthouse. Although the event was scheduled to begin at ten o'clock, eager spectators—mostly women—poured into the courthouse gallery early that morning. The decision to admit only those lucky enough to secure tickets had kept the crowd, according to the *Mercury*, "much smaller than upon the occasions of recent trials for murder." Many seats had been reserved for journalists from local and metropolitan newspapers. Townley, dressed in black, stared intently at the judge as he entered the courtroom. A reporter observed that he looked older than he had at his committal hearing, and that he had trimmed back his large beard. Townley hardly spoke to his lawyers and stood only once, to hear the court's final judgment on the last day of the trial.[44]

Townley, the son of a respectable family of Manchester merchants, had fallen in love with Bessie Goodwin, a military captain's granddaughter, four or five years earlier. Soon, they were engaged to be married. But in the summer of 1863, Goodwin called off the engagement. Townley had few prospects. Still, he begged Goodwin for a final meeting. "We shall both be happier and better in mind, as well as body, after this last interview," he assured her. "I do not wish to see you," she replied, "if it can possibly be avoided."[45] There were rumors that she was in love with a clergyman.[46]

On 21 August 1863, Townley rushed to Goodwin's family home at Wigwell Hall in Wirksworth, near Derby. He and Goodwin talked in the library, and then in the garden. Shortly after Townley started down the lane toward the train station, a passerby heard a woman moan. He found Goodwin leaning against the garden wall, covered in blood. He tried to help her to the house, but she collapsed. She had been stabbed four or five times behind her ears, and one deep strike had severed her carotid artery. Townley helped the good Samaritan to carry Goodwin's body into the house, where she died in Townley's arms. He admitted openly to the killing: "The woman that deceives me dies." Captain Goodwin, Bessie's grandfather, a frail man of eighty, brought Townley, covered in blood, into the library. The pair drank brandy until the police and the doctor arrived.[47]

Townley's counsel accepted these facts but argued that their client was insane.[48] Kenneth Macaulay, one of Townley's barristers and the cousin of lawyer and colonial official Thomas Babington Macaulay, learned that nearly a dozen of his client's close relatives had died by suicide or in lunatic asylums. Macaulay argued that Goodwin's rejection of the gentle, fragile Townley roused the madness to which he was susceptible. Macaulay was confident that he could satisfy the *M'Naghten* rules. The defense called Forbes Winslow, whose work Ballantine had quoted in William Allnutt's trial. Winslow met with Townley twice in jail while he awaited his trial, for a total of just over two hours. The mad doctor was sure the prisoner was insane. Townley refused to accept that killing Goodwin was wrong. She was his property, he said, and he believed he had "as perfect a right to deal with her life as he had to deal with any other description of property." Townley "very insanely argued" that the killing was righteous, and that he was the victim of a conspiracy. What sane murderer, asked Winslow, would not only turn himself in but even cradle his victim's head as she died? Who but a madman would have calmly sat down to drink with Captain Goodwin? Winslow diagnosed his patient with "general moral derangement." He found Townley's "moral sense more vitiated than in any man [he] ever saw."[49]

The judge, Baron Martin, was skeptical. "I have watched very carefully for proof of any delusion under which he has laboured," he said to Macaulay.

"Can you tell me where to find it?" There was no requirement in the *M'Naghten* rules that the defendant experience a distinct delusion. Still, Townley's lack of one hurt his case. Martin had done his own research into the law of insanity, which he shared with the jury. He said he had read about a man who believed that he was made of glass. If he had killed someone to avoid shattering, then he would have been legally irresponsible. However, anything short of this type of spectacular delusion was not enough, in Martin's opinion, to shield a defendant from responsibility.

The judge's views likely struck the medical witnesses as hopelessly wrongheaded. The jury, however, was convinced. They took only six minutes to return a guilty verdict. Martin delivered Townley's death sentence in dramatic tones, sobbing in the middle of his judgment.[50] James Fitzjames Stephen, who participated in Townley's defense, was more equivocal. In letters to his wife, he argued that Townley's intellect was "very defective," but that Forbes Winslow's evidence of his insanity was "legally speaking, no defence at all."[51] Stephen suspected that the stress of the killing and the trial had damaged Townley's psyche, but he was not convinced that Townley was legally irresponsible for his actions. Stephen fulfilled his responsibilities as defense counsel, arguing vigorously on his client's behalf. But once the trial ended, he criticized every aspect of the case except for the result. The entire defense had been, in his opinion, "the most deplorable failure." Macaulay had been misguided and ineffectual.[52] Forbes Winslow had been unpersuasive on the stand.[53] The judge had adopted an extreme definition of legal insanity; Martin seemed "determined to take the narrowest view of the law, a view so narrow that if it were true, madness would really make no difference at all."[54] Consistent with the stance he would take two decades later in his 1883 *History*, however, Stephen would not embrace a definition of legal insanity that included moral insanity. The trial had been an embarrassment, but Townley had rightly been found guilty. Townley, he wrote, "was no more mad than I."[55]

A writer for the *Liverpool Mercury* summed up the public hostility to the interference of mad doctors in murder trials. Their theories would, if accepted by judges and juries, "ensure absolute impunity to the worst crimes of the worst criminals" and "be utterly destructive of human life." Winslow's testimony in the Townley case was especially galling. To make an absence of remorse proof of irresponsibility was a "revolting paradox," in which the most ruthless were the least culpable.[56] If all "men who commit monstrous crimes are mad," wrote a journalist for the *Western Times*, "the occupation of judges and juries would be gone and penal laws a dead letter."[57]

James Fitzjames Stephen. Portrait for his carte-de-visite taken in the 1870s. Credit: © National Portrait Gallery, London.

Even so, Townley would be spared. Days after the trial, Martin wrote to the Home Secretary to recommend that a commission be constituted to inquire into Townley's state of mind. Martin still supported the jury's guilty verdict but worried that Townley might currently be insane and not fit to be executed.[58] Friends of Townley filed a petition begging for his life. The mayor of Derby was the first signatory; Stephen refused to sign at all.[59] In Manchester, a second petition circulated near the end of December that garnered ten thousand signatures. Townley's father declared to the Home Office that there were eleven "known and well authenticated cases of actual insanity" on his wife's side, but that this evidence had not been presented at his son's trial for "obvious family reasons."[60] Christmas came and went, and Townley's sentence was not commuted. The local hangman was informed that his services would be needed at ten o'clock on New Year's Eve.[61]

On Boxing Day, two local doctors—Henry Goode and Thomas Harwood—interviewed Townley in the condemned cell. Goode boasted only an M.B., a junior medical qualification, and Harwood, although he had worked as a surgeon and physician in Derby for more than forty years, had trained as an apothecary.[62] Townley repeatedly asserted that he was perfectly sane, and that he did not believe that he had done anything wrong in killing Goodwin. "I believe myself to be of perfectly sound mind . . . and," he said, "perfectly easy on the point of what I did."[63] The doctors forwarded the transcripts of their interviews to London for review. A letter from the Commissioners in Lunacy arrived in Derby on 29 December, two days before Townley's execution date, postponing the hanging on the ground that he was insane.[64]

Townley was transferred to Bethlem in mid-January. He would not stay long. There were rumblings in the press to the effect that Townley, with his powerful friends and ample means, had bought a reprieve. "I hear all the people in Derby are furious about Townley," wrote Stephen, "& I am inclined to think they are not wrong."[65] Before the suspension of Townley's capital sentence, the lawyer had praised his family for their grace and bravery. Once Townley had been spared, Stephen felt "a horrible disgust for the whole family . . . as if the girl's blood lay between me and them."[66] The Derbyshire magistrates also protested. "If Townley and his friends had been poor," they wrote in a public letter, "he would have been executed."[67] One reporter was less outraged than puzzled. His headline read, "'Killing No Murder!' Or the Strange Efforts to Save Townley."[68] The controversy reached such a pitch that the Home Office released copies of official correspondence regarding the case.[69] There was a general feeling that Townley's respite would be temporary. Some argued that only Townley's death could restore the dignity of the court and the government.[70]

In late January, a new Lunacy Commission was sent to Bethlem to evaluate Townley. This time, four high-profile alienists conducted the investigation.[71] The commissioners met with Townley and reviewed all the documents related to his case, including accounts of his family's history of insanity. They unanimously found Townley sane and ordered his removal from Bethlem to Pentonville Prison.[72] The Home Office felt it would be distasteful to push for Townley's execution and satisfied itself with a commutation of his capital sentence to a lifetime of penal servitude.[73] Like his stay at Bethlem, though, Townley's time at Pentonville would be short. Townley usually sat silently in chapel. In February of 1865, however, he belted out the last verses of a hymn—"Where is death's sting? Where, grave, thy victory?"—in a bass so booming that the men in his pew all noticed. As the prisoners filed out, Townley clambered over the balcony railing and jumped, headfirst, onto the concrete twenty-four feet below.[74]

The anonymous author in *Mental Science* crowed that Townley's suicide "was, perhaps, the last small act of justice which he could do to [an] outraged society." Townley's case had "mercilessly dragged" the whole medical profession, including its medico-psychological specialists, into "foul disgrace." The physicians and humanitarians who argued for Townley's insanity had indulged in "a disgusting aping of science" with the cynical aim of perverting the course of justice. The author held moral insanity in special contempt. He accused physicians who believed in the condition of peddling bogus theories that were irreconcilable with social life. Alienists were "incapable of rising from a narrow view of the individual as a subject of medical science to the larger view of him as an element in the social system,—of the man as a citizen, and of the relations of his crime to society."[75]

The same issue of *Mental Science* included another anonymous article on Townley. The author wrote, "In the gabble of medical science, irresponsibility is proved by the mere fact of extraordinary immorality. . . . Henceforth, the greater the knave, the less his guilt." After Townley's death, an autopsy had found nothing amiss—no lesions, no wasting, no damage beyond that caused by the fall. The author had little patience for the claim that there was no necessary correlation between insanity and organic disease of the brain. Moral insanity was merely a "mischievous juggle of words" that harmed the reputation of the medical profession and the integrity of the law.[76] The editors of the *Lancet*, however, maintained throughout the Townley affair that he was insane. Men like Townley, they argued, suffered from a cruel disease that physicians were duty bound to acknowledge, to treat, and to pity.[77]

By 1885, when Tuke addressed the Medico-Psychological Association about William Bigg, the horse slasher, moral insanity had existed as a distinct diagnostic category for more than fifty years. Many alienists refused to embrace it, however. By the late-nineteenth century, physicians and jurists had become partners in the management of the criminally insane. Joel Eigen estimates that medical witnesses appeared in 10 percent of English criminal insanity trials in the mid-1700s, while by the 1840s they testified in 50 percent of insanity trials involving offenses to property, and 90 percent of insanity trials involving assault and other violent offenses.[78] Neither government statistics nor statistics produced by scholars set out the proportion of criminal trials in which moral insanity was explicitly alleged. This book, certainly, does not attempt a quantitative survey. Anecdotally, however, non-delusional forms of insanity, including moral insanity, were mooted often in trials of defendants who committed acts that seemed motiveless or gratuitously violent. An acquittal in such a case could provoke scandal and indignation. If alienists advocated too stridently for moral insanity and against the criminal responsibility of those who suffered from it, they risked their professional reputations and their ability to sway juries toward acquittals, and away from capital sentences, in other insanity cases.

After Tuke spoke at the association meeting, Dr. David Nicolson took the floor. Nicolson reminded his audience that moral insanity placed the professional credibility of its supporters, the integrity of the legal system, and the safety of the community at stake. He believed in the diagnosis, but cautioned, "If we were to allow the term to be too influential in our minds, we would be thwarting justice, and cutting our own throats as men who were endeavouring to carry out scientific ideas: so that instead of carrying weight in the courts of law we would be laughed at."[79]

Tuke thought that his skeptical colleagues were cowards. He published his account of Bigg's case and more notes on the next six years of his hospitalization in an 1891 book. "We are still, it seems to me," he argued, " . . . under the curse of the law."[80] Tuke accused the legal establishment of interfering in the elaboration of medico-psychological knowledge. In his view, moral insanity was a logical development in mental science.[81] By the middle of the nineteenth century, medical opinion in Britain had coalesced around the idea that insanity could be almost undetectable, except by trained experts. Delusions or outlandish behavior were no longer the only signs of mental illness. And yet, in Tuke's opinion, many physicians refused to name the psychological disorder that was an open secret in their asylums, hospitals, and prisons.[82] Specifically, he accused them of ignoring overwhelming medical evidence of moral insanity because they were afraid of legal controversy and public ridicule. Tuke believed that Bigg's history, and his mutilated horses, would force his colleagues to overcome their hesitations by placing the existence of moral insanity beyond dispute.

William Bigg was held at Rockwood Asylum, where Dr. William Metcalf was the medical superintendent, until August of 1885. Metcalf struggled, often unsuccessfully, to protect the weaker patients from Bigg. One evening, the superintendent rushed to the bedside of a severely epileptic patient. Bigg had stabbed the man in the gut with a pocketknife, pierced him with a fork, and bitten him. Bigg told Metcalf, "There are times when I am impelled to do such things and I have not the power to resist."[83] His violence was gruesome but sporadic, often interspersed with years of amiable docility. Although Bigg spent many nights muzzled and confined to his room, the staff always, eventually, allowed him to return to asylum life. He went to see fireworks in town; he danced at balls; he helped around the wards. "This Institution," Metcalf angrily reminded a lawyer who criticized his handling of Bigg, "is an ordinary *hospital* for the insane."[84] After the stabbing, Metcalf wrote in his journal that he "urged [Bigg] in future to tell the keeper when the impulse to shed blood was strong and to ask to be put into his room until he felt that he had control over himself." Bigg apologized and promised to do better.[85]

Like many of his colleagues at Broadmoor, Metcalf would pay dearly for his efforts. One morning, as he and his staff walked the ward, Patrick Moloney, a paranoid patient whom no one had suspected of having homicidal tendencies, leapt out from a doorway and stabbed Metcalf in the abdomen.[86] Three days later, he died. His assistant, Charles Kirk Clarke, took over the asylum.[87] Clarke, born in 1857 in Elora, Canada West (Ontario), was the son of an England-born liberal journalist and minor politician who was passionately devoted to democratic electoral reform, agricultural improvement, and natural history.[88] Two of Clarke's sisters married alienists. Metcalf was one. The other, Joseph Workman, was the superintendent of the Asylum for the Insane in Toronto. Workman hired Clarke in 1874, when he was only seventeen, as a clinical assistant. Clarke soon completed his medical education at the University of Toronto, assuming positions as assistant medical superintendent at the Hamilton Asylum and, in 1882, at Rockwood. He would remain in Kingston until 1904, when a series of glittering appointments at hospitals in Toronto and a medical deanship at the university drew him to the city.[89] He was proud of Ontario asylum superintendents' commitments to science and the principles of moral treatment, including the rejection of restraints and physical chastisement. Patients at Rockwood learned "bookbinding, tinsmithing, tailoring, blacksmithing, gardening," and other trades, as well as music, gymnastics, and calisthenics. Clarke was especially fond of the hospital's twenty-two-piece brass band.

In an 1893 address, however, originally read at a conference in Chicago and later published in the *American Journal of Insanity*, Clarke argued that Canada, like the United States, trailed behind the United Kingdom in its care of the criminally insane. There were no institutions solely devoted to the treatment of criminal patients, for example. Worse was the Canadian public's

William Bigg. A copy of this photograph was included in Bigg's asylum casebook at Rockwood. It also accompanied Daniel Hack Tuke's article in the *American Journal of Insanity*, vol. 43 (1886–1887). Credit: The image of William Bigg is used by kind permission of the College of Physicians of Philadelphia.

hostility to the idea that insanity could cause crime. The retrograde *M'Naghten* principles continued to dominate understandings of legal insanity, and newspapers encouraged suspicion that defendants who pled insanity were malingering to escape the scaffold. "As long as the legal definition of insanity is so crude and imperfect," wrote Clarke, "and the newspapers hold up the bogy [*sic*] called the 'insanity dodge,' we may look for little or no improvement."[90] While he waited for public opinion on criminal responsibility and insanity to evolve, he worked to extend the benefits of a modern, progressive asylum system "characterized by kindness and gentleness" to men like William Bigg.[91]

Bigg looked ordinary enough. In a photograph taken while he was in prison, he stared dreamily at the camera, the corners of his thin lips haunted by a smile.[92] Once, when he took part in one of the asylum's regular minstrel performances, he "exhibited boyish glee at the prospect . . . but when the performance came off, he sat in the 'charmed circle' like a lump of stone . . . even when he was the 'centre piece' of a joke no smile was provoked—he was quite incapable of understanding the slightest fun."[93] His doctors pronounced Bigg a "remarkable man."[94] One physician described him as suffering from "probably the most extraordinary case of mania for bloodletting known to the Specialist of insanity."[95] Those who cared for Bigg described his "cruel thirst" for violence as compulsive and uncontrollable, especially whenever he saw blood.[96] Though Bigg was cruel, he was also sick. His doctors described his violence in physiological terms: as an addiction, an appetite, an intoxicant that his frail body and weak mind could not resist.

Men like Bigg were born, not made, according to supporters of moral insanity. His doctors made much of his father's "hysterical" concern for the well-being of William and his four brothers.[97] Moral insanity also fitted neatly into Victorian scientific ideas about evolution and the biological causes of behavior. Bigg's brother, Frederic, also seemed to have inherited their father's mental instability. A history of the Bigg family assembled by the doctors at Rockwood described Frederic as a "monster" who "used to gratify the demon in his soul" by holding his wife down and thrusting kitchen knives into the floor around her head.[98] Clarke predicted that Frederic would "probably startle the world by committing some horrible crime."[99] This emphasis on heredity and biological determinism was widespread in Victorian accounts of both crime and insanity. Men like William and Frederic Bigg represented the culmination of both criminal anthropology and hereditarian approaches to mental science.

In the nineteenth-century British world, controversies over insanity and responsibility were not only about the fate of individual people but also about the competence of groups, often delineated by imagined racial characteristics. By the end of the century, ethnologists and criminal anthropologists had proposed theories that explicitly linked criminal propensities to race, and race to heredity. For them, allusions to "savagery" or "primitivism" were not metaphors but references to human biological evolution.[100] While Victorian commentators applied these modifiers freely to the nonwhite peoples of the empire, they also used them to describe Europeans, especially members of the poor and the working classes and those accused of terrible or motiveless violence. When white Britons committed "savage" crimes, they were not acting *like* savages but revealing a genuinely savage nature that evolution had not yet stamped out.

One ethnologist, Edward B. Tylor, enjoyed a wide audience among Victorian alienists. In his *Primitive Culture* (1871), Tylor described the "hideous misery and depravity" of the urban lower classes in Europe. He wrote, "If we have to strike a balance between the Papuans of New Caledonia and the communities of European beggars and thieves, we may sadly acknowledge that we have in our midst something worse than savagery. But it is not savagery; it is broken-down civilization."[101] In Tylor's view, "savage" peoples were, from a moral and intellectual perspective, like children. They lived their lives on the edge of violence, requiring only minor distress or temptation to tip over into brutality. This made "savages" unsuitable for participation in civilized life, where their "natural" inclinations would make them criminals. Tylor was not a lawyer, and he never explored the implications of his ethnology for criminal responsibility. But lawyers and alienists read him, and at least some, like Mayo, took his account of the "broken-down civilization" of the European poor to heart. Mayo and others saw moral insanity as a ready-made defense for European degenerates and took it upon themselves to slam shut the doors of criminal responsibility before "city savages" elbowed their way through.

Charles Darwin's 1859 *Origin of Species* had been quickly taken up by natural and social scientists, some of whom saw Darwinian evolutionary theory as scaffolding for older ideas about, in Nancy Stepan's words, the "fixity, antiquity, and hierarchy of human races."[102] In the late-nineteenth century, accounts of racial difference rooted in evolutionary processes acquired, Roger Smith writes, "mythic stature," "reinterpret[ing] human evil . . . as the unavoidable consequences of an animal descent."[103] Mental science was not immune to evolutionary models in which mental and moral acuity were functions of race. Henry Maudsley, a staunch believer in degeneration, argued that moral insanity and primitivism were sides of the same coin. For him, moral insanity was the clear result of the "degeneration"—the de-evolution—of a civilized brain into a state of atavistic savagery. By the late-nineteenth century, Maudsley's writings on insanity had become increasingly ethnological. Like other physicians of his generation, Maudsley was taken with Herbert Spencer's application of Darwinian evolution to the mind, and with Spencer's promotion of ethnopsychology. Maudsley argued that compulsive violence was a sign of sickness among Europeans. Non-European peoples, whom he and many of his contemporaries arranged on a ladder from debasement to near-civilization, were less susceptible to moral insanity because they had a shorter distance to fall. In one of his later works, *The Pathology of Mind* (1895), Maudsley illustrated his theory of the relationship between race and moral insanity. "The Australian savage," he wrote, " . . . clearly cannot go mad because of a breach of the moral law, nor ever present an example of true moral insanity; before he can undergo moral degeneration he must first be humanized and then civilized."[104]

Maudsley admitted that moral insanity seemed at times to "confound all distinction between vice or crime and madness."[105] Medical experts could, with enough time and information, separate moral insanity from wickedness, but Maudsley accepted that this was difficult in the context of a criminal trial. Moreover, it was impossible for a sane person fully to grasp the workings of an insane mind. "If a sane person could succeed in doing this," Maudsley wrote, "it could be only on one condition—namely, that he should become as insane as the person whose mind he was studying."[106] Maudsley's solution to the limits of mental science was for the law to take a broad and flexible view of insanity and to execute as few defendants as possible. Moral insanity was a difficult diagnosis for doctors to make, and perhaps an impossible one for the common law to accommodate. Maudsley felt, however, that mad doctors were bound to proclaim the fact of the disease's existence, regardless of its practical implications. "As there are persons . . . having what is called colour-blindness," he wrote, "so there are some few who are congenitally deprived of moral sense."

Daniel Hack Tuke also saw a relationship between insanity and primitivism. He echoed Maudsley's theory that moral insanity, and violence generally, were the result of degeneration. Morally insane people lacked the mental control that they should have inherited from their civilized forebears. Either that, or they had lost their civilized mind through vice or misfortune. The morally insane sufferer became, because of his disease, like the primitive peoples of the far reaches of the empire. "Such a man as this," wrote Tuke, "is a reversion to an old savage type, and is born by accident in the wrong century. He would have . . . been in harmony with his environment, in a barbaric age, or at the present day in certain parts of Africa, but he cannot be tolerated now as a member of civilized society. But what is to be done with the man who, from no fault of his own, is born in the nineteenth instead of a long-past century? Are we to punish him for his involuntary anachronism?"[107]

Tuke's account of moral insanity differs slightly from Tylor's. For Tylor, Europeans could never genuinely recapture the primitivism of their evolutionary past.[108] He was most concerned about the urban proletariat and the debauchery that he believed thrived in London slums. In contrast, Tuke had a more literal understanding of European savagery. His morally insane subject was an evolutionary throwback—a type of person he imagined still predominated in remote parts of the empire. The morally insane had not chosen to be born out of step with European civilization. They were not evil, but out of sync. Tuke's rhetorical question as to what ought to be done with a man afflicted with this type of "involuntary anachronism" went to the crux of the problem. If the morally insane were not responsible for their actions, but they posed an intolerable threat to "civilized" society, then how should the government and the law respond?

James Fitzjames Stephen offered one solution to the problem of moral insanity, and to Victorian notions about the diversity of moral and cognitive standards among racial and cultural groups. Stephen saw no reason to doubt the clinical experience of Prichard and Maudsley. The problem, for Stephen, arose when medical men tried to argue that the law should take these differences in moral sensibility into account when it determined responsibility. "The moral sense of an English gentleman, the moral sense of an Irish peasant, the moral sense of a Hindoo, the moral sense of any two individual men, differ profoundly," he wrote. "The criminal law . . . says to all alike, 'Think and feel as you please about morals, but if you do certain things you shall be hanged.'"[109] Why, asked Stephen, should a person who was "bad" due to mental disease or biology receive more lenient treatment than a person whose transgressions were products of character, education, or birth? Stephen, who after all had made his name as the architect of the Indian Evidence Act and as a supporter of codification, embraced a degree of legal authoritarianism that made some of his colleagues uncomfortable.

In late-Victorian Britain, natural and social scientists were increasingly drawn to determinist accounts of the universe, including determinist understandings of the mind and human behavior. These new theories clashed with older visions of human beings as essentially autonomous and self-governing.[110] The resulting "free will problem" played out dramatically in insanity cases.[111] "The *absence* of responsibility" due to insanity, writes Thomas A. Green, inevitably implicated and defined "the *presence* of irresponsibility."[112] Often, moral insanity pitted not only free will against determinism but also agnosticism against Christianity. Some scholars have even described the late-nineteenth century as a time of "war" between determinist scientists and free-will-loving lawyers and religious leaders, with mental diagnoses such as moral insanity, monomania, and dipsomania (alcoholism) as flashpoints.[113] Professional and academic communities never split cleanly along religious or philosophical lines, however.[114]

A famous 1886 debate between Thomas Henry Huxley, a natural scientist and "Darwin's Bulldog," and William Samuel Lilly, a Catholic barrister and former member of the Indian Civil Service, captures the legal implications of the free-will controversy. Lilly argued that materialism, determinism, and atheism, which he used interchangeably, had led Britain into a great "moral crisis" in which traditional religious and moral values were being replaced by faith in a soulless natural law. He was convinced that determinism would make criminal law nothing but *leges sine moribus vanae* (useless laws without morals); that without morality, law would become just the brutish "*ultima ratio* of force." Despite his histrionics, Lilly hit on the central problem of responsibility in the age of scientific determinism: "Poor victims of temperament, of heredity, of environment, they are to be pitied, not blamed."[115]

Huxley, in response, argued that natural science had not invented determinism. Christianity had long wrestled with predetermination and the implications of faith in an omniscient and omnipotent god. Science and even a belief that all human behavior was caused by ineffable forces were not obstacles to belief in the divine or in transcendent human experiences.[116] Huxley's essay might have reassured some readers, but it missed the immediate concerns Lilly raised about criminal justice. As a barrister with experience in the administration of law in the empire, Lilly understood the interdependence of free will and responsibility in common-law jurisprudence. The justification of judicial punishment rested on the presumption that most defendants in criminal cases had chosen to act relatively freely. Controversies about moral insanity, because of the disorder's links to notions of primitivism and self-control, often engaged this much broader nineteenth-century debate about the nature of the self.

Sometimes, conflicts over insanity were more apparent than real. Stephen was untroubled by the prospect of executing an insane criminal. *M'Naghten* separated severe insanity from its more moderate forms, he argued, and so was sound. Stephen would have narrowed the legal definition of insanity even further. "If a special Divine order were given to a man to commit murder," he wrote, "I should certainly hang him for it unless I got a special Divine order not to hang him."[117] And yet, Stephen was preoccupied by responsibility. In his *History*, for example, he argued that a weakened will always accompanied intellectual derangement. It was the madman's duty to struggle against his baser urges. But in the small class of cases where madness destroyed a person's power of self-control, Stephen thought that the sufferer should be excused from responsibility. Stephen and Maudsley adopted opposing and complementary positions. While Stephen thought that an absence of self-control was a rare aberrance, Maudsley assumed that most people—perhaps all—lacked the power to make autonomous choices. "The dogma of free will," argued Maudsley, "has not imbued the regulations made for the conduct of life."[118]

Unlike George Townley, William Bigg met a comfortable end. He died in his bed at the Hamilton Asylum in 1915, at the age of seventy-seven.[119] In an 1886 article about Bigg, Clarke argued that he was a "moral imbecile" of "an absolute type." He distinguished, although not at all clearly, between "moral imbecility" and "moral insanity." He wrote that Bigg was freed by his imbecility "from the trammellings of that hazy definition known as 'moral insanity.'"[120] And yet, Clarke approvingly cited Tuke's article about Bigg, moral insanity, and criminal responsibility in the *Journal of Mental Science*. It seems likely that Clarke simply preferred to leave the squabbling about moral insanity to others. In 1914, the *Bulletin of the Ontario Hospitals for the Insane* published an updated version of Clarke's article, entitled "Notes of a Clinical Case: The Case of Wm. B.—Moral Imbecility."[121] Dr. J. Webster, then the superintendent of the Hamilton Hospital for the Insane, contributed notes on Bigg's medical history after 1886. Every year or two, Bigg would break down and lapse into violence. Every time, he first denied his guilt before confessing. Like Clarke, Webster believed that his patient could not control himself. Bigg "usually showed deep contrition, rightly maintaining that he was not responsible, saying, 'It's a kind of mania, I can't help it.'" Although he denied that he was insane, he told his doctors in 1895 that he did not wish to be free because he feared that he would "again get into trouble" if left to his own devices. As Bigg grew older and feebler, he became a chronic masturbator; he also enjoyed pulling the wings off flies and scalded other patients with hot water in the bathrooms. Webster noted in his last published word on the case, however, that his elderly patient appeared to have more insight into his condition than ever before. In the quiet years between assaults, asylum staff saw the man that Bigg might have been. In these moments, he was, wrote Webster, "a willing, intelligent worker, cheerful and pleasant in conversation, and nothing in his appearance suggested that he was other than a simple, kindly, inoffensive man."[122]

Charles Kirk Clarke's later career underscores the theme of chapters to come: the links between moral insanity and primitivism, and ideas of intellectual and racial incapacity. In the nineteenth century, Clarke—humane, cultured, energetic, optimistic—epitomized the liberal, Victorian alienist. By the early-twentieth century, though, Rockwood had become crowded with patients whose illnesses seemed incurable. Clarke had survived a series of violent assaults, growing disillusioned and tired. He turned increasingly from treatment to prevention. Clarke found a second calling in the field of mental hygiene, which positioned mental illness as a public-health challenge. He became an ardent devotee of eugenics and a vocal anti-immigrationist. In 1918, he would leave his post as medical director of the Toronto General Hospital to become the medical director of the Canadian National Committee for Mental Hygiene. In 1920, he resigned as dean of the Faculty of Medicine at the University of Toronto in order to concentrate on his work for the committee.[123] In 1923, when the British Medico-Psychological Association invited him to deliver its fourth annual honorary Maudsley Lecture, Clarke argued that mental disease could be eradicated if the public could learn to lead "better and saner lives." Outpatient programs targeting vulnerable populations, like delinquent youth or prostitutes, might offer cures; aggressive policing of Canada's borders against "mental defectives" could inoculate the population against hereditary illness. Clarke seemed to address his younger self when he described the asylum-based alienist as "living in a contracted sphere, because, after all, his medical association is largely with terminal cases. . . . [E]ugenics," he argued, "will do more than anything else to solve the problem."[124]

The shift in his professional focus from mental disease to racial contamination reflected Clarke's personal experiences and the changing preoccupations of his time. The apparent ease with which he and many others infused understandings of mental deficiency, and responsibility, with biological racism suggests that these concepts were never utterly divorced, even in the liberal heyday of Victorian mental science. Moral insanity, especially, relied on the civilizational thinking, and the figment of degenerationist threat, that informed later eugenic understandings of the relative incapacity of non-European peoples.[125]

Moral insanity was a medical, legal, philosophical, social, and institutional conundrum. Its definition was so broad that it could describe almost any shade of aberrant or destructive behavior. Disturbed and disturbing people like Bigg embodied the condition. Men like Townley and Knatchbull who committed acts of sudden violence, but who were less theatrically perverse, were more difficult to classify. And yet, moral insanity was never raised in any of Bigg's trials, while Townley's and Knatchbull's hung on the validity of the diagnosis and its implications for the *M'Naghten* rules. This may have been a function of time. Knatchbull and Townley were tried in the 1840s and 1860s, respectively. Bigg's encounters with the legal system began in the 1870s, and medico-legal interest in Bigg's case peaked in the 1880s. By then, moral insanity had become highly politicized, both within mental science and in the minds of courtroom observers. While most physicians agreed that non-delusional insanity existed, some, like Broadmoor's David Nicolson and Rockwood's Charles Clarke, groped for clinical terminology that was less freighted, and therefore less likely to invite controversy.

Charles Rosenberg writes that by the late-nineteenth century, moral insanity "no longer served a useful social purpose" and had become "obsolete, too indeterminate to serve any longer as a specific diagnostic category."[126] As moral insanity slowly fell out of favor among Anglo-American physicians, moral imbecility—connected to the rise of eugenic theories that centered "feeblemindedness"—and sexual psychopathy gained traction, ceding ground in turn to the figure of the modern "psychopath" in the mid-twentieth century. These conceptual descendants of moral insanity did not imply irresponsibility in the way that moral insanity seemed to in its Victorian heyday. Imbecility, instead, called for population management and the kind of social hygiene Clarke advocated in his later years. Psychopathy more often justified harsher punishment, not acquittal.[127]

Moral insanity's clinical imprecision did not empty it of meaning—quite the opposite. The diagnosis focused otherwise nebulous concerns about irresponsibility, prompting physicians, lawyers, and others to consider the many ways in which a subject of British law might be psychologically deficient even without exhibiting classical signs of mental disease. It articulated the connection between savagery and mental and moral degradation in Victorian evolutionary thought, and proposed that the psychic wounds of primitivism were analogous to brain disease—and should have similar legal consequences.

Most physicians and lawyers who believed in moral insanity thought that it was a severe illness afflicting a tiny minority of patients. Physicians who rejected the diagnosis doubted that it could be restricted to extreme cases. At a time when biological models of criminality were ascendant and when white Britons and colonized populations alike appeared increasingly vulnerable to savage impulses, moral insanity struck some critics as the beginning of the end of criminal responsibility. The lawyer Robert Lowe, to recall, described Knatchbull during his trial as "one of those persons for whom laws had not been made."[128] Moral insanity raised the possibility that there were, in fact, *no* persons for whom the common law had been made—no one to hold responsible, and no one to punish. What if savagery were not a rare mutation or a sickness but a core aspect of the human condition? And so, controversies about moral insanity spread around the British world, like knives secreted in the pockets of common-law jurisprudence.

CHAPTER 4

Murder and Metaphysics in Colonial Victoria

Alfred Deakin wrote many drafts of the speech he would give in court in May of 1892, but his argument never changed. He urged the jury to defy the "mobs of morbid & frenzied sensation seekers" who sought to corrupt Australian criminal justice with the "violent methods of lynch law." The evidence against the defendant was circumstantial. No one had seen the killing, witnesses' statements were contradictory, and the body of the victim, her nose smashed and her eyes rotted, was difficult to identify. Most of all, though, Deakin sought to persuade the jury that Frederick Bailey Deeming—bigamist, thief, fraudster, rumored epileptic, and killer of two of his wives and four of his children—was insane. The task would not be easy. Deeming was not the "wild beast" of legal myth. He spoke and dressed well. Instead, Deakin used the horror of Deeming's crimes to show the corruption of his mind. Deeming was more treacherous than Shakespeare's Iago or Edmund. He was "a monster so appalling" that one could not help but ask, "Is he human?"[1] On a scrap of paper, in notes he later crossed out, the lawyer described his client as one of many "persons dwelling in the borderland of crime & insanity."[2] Just as it was impossible to pinpoint the moment when day became night, Deakin explained, there was no clear boundary between sanity and insanity. Men like Deeming lived in the twilight, and no amount of judicial squinting could clearly distinguish them from the shadows.

Charles Rosenberg argues that for educated Americans in the late-nineteenth century, moral insanity and the problem of criminal responsibility were one and the same.[3] Moral insanity was also synonymous with criminal responsibility in the late-Victorian British Empire. Deeming's case, like the cases of Victor Townley, William Allnutt, and John Knatchbull, invited debate about the legitimacy of an unusual psychiatric diagnosis, and by extension about the fate of responsibility in an increasingly deterministic world. Tuke argued that moral insanity was a medical fact, which no alienist could deny in good faith. But Tuke was not a lawyer. His interest in legal questions was always subordinate to his commitment to mental science.

This chapter considers moral insanity through the legal work of one enterprising Melbourne lawyer, Marshall Lyle. Like Tuke, Lyle believed that moral insanity existed, and that alienists could detect it in their patients. But Lyle was not a physician. For him, moral insanity was the germ of a conceptual reorganization of criminal-law jurisprudence that should begin with the abandonment of *M'Naghten*. The criminal case files of the colony of Victoria, including Frederick Deeming's, are dotted with Lyle's letters, memos, and petitions. In the 1890s, these records show that Lyle became interested in the growing tension between how criminal law and mental science interpreted human behavior. Criminal anthropology, which posited that much criminality was biologically impelled, departed even further from the law's presumption that accused criminals were both sane and autonomous. Inspired by these scientific developments, Lyle embarked on a campaign against *M'Naghten*. He was determined to prove that the common law's approach to insanity was antiquated and, in capital cases, murderous.

To that end, Lyle identified potential test cases, in which he defended clients for free or for a pittance, and attempted to appeal those he lost in Australia to the Judicial Committee of the Privy Council in London. Although the committee's decisions did not bind either British courts or those of other colonial jurisdictions, its recommendations had moral and political authority that could, in time, shape imperial jurisprudence. Frederick Deeming's case offered Lyle the chance to challenge *M'Naghten* in a paradigmatic moral insanity case. Deeming was as bizarre, articulate, and dangerous a murderer as Tuke could have imagined. Even William Bigg, after all, never killed anyone. In court, Alfred Deakin told the jurors that insanity cases turned them into a "jury of metaphysicians."[4] Lyle hoped to exploit this opportunity. If he could persuade decision makers to accept the new, deterministic metaphysics that late-Victorian science propounded, then the process of reimagining the common law for the modern world could begin.

Lyle's story is also, to an extent, that of the imperial bar. By the late-nineteenth century, both New South Wales and Victoria, Australia's most important colonies, had proclaimed their transformations from convict backwaters into glittering centers of imperial innovation and ambition. "Marvelous Melbourne" was the jewel of Victoria, which by the end of the century was as populous and wealthy as California.[5] Their self-confident common-law system was an emblem of the success of the Australian colonies. Droves of British- and Irish trained lawyers, including Lyle, who was born in Ireland, traveled south in search of professional advancement and adventure. Their sons attended Australian universities that worked to match their British equivalents in rigor and sophistication. One legal historian writes that Australian judges and lawyers were "English to the core," and that their commitment to Anglo law—especially criminal law—only increased as the Australian colonies approached legislative independence.[6] Colonial Victoria overcame the "tyranny of distance" in part through its ostentatious fidelity to metropolitan criminal jurisprudence.[7]

The affinity of colonial lawyers for British legal culture did not, however, make them passive. In Victoria, Lyle joined an ambitious professional community eager to claim its place at the forefront of imperial legal thought and practice. Like many settler colonists, he believed that the "Better Britons" of the empire could inject global British civilization with the vigor and creativity lacking in a mother country that seemed increasingly sclerotic and conservative.[8] Lyle understood his work against *M'Naghten* as a contribution to common-law jurisprudence writ large—a purification of British legal principles, which perhaps a colonial innovator was best placed to undertake.

Lyle may have been an unusually zealous reformer. Lawyers and other officials who appeared alongside him in responsibility cases were far less outspoken. Deakin, for instance, made passionate speeches against Deeming's responsibility in court but did not push for clemency or an appeal through the available bureaucratic channels. Lyle's commitment to defining legal insanity went beyond the duties of a punctilious defense lawyer. Unsurprisingly, Lyle encountered significant resistance. Most lawyers and judges in Victoria and in England resisted entreaties to overthrow *M'Naghten*, whether they came from physicians or from their fellow jurists. Whatever they said in court in defense of their clients, few lawyers actually endorsed the systemic changes Lyle proposed. Without a robust concept of responsible subjecthood, some argued, British law and the empire built around it would be compromised. Instead of preserving British civilization, men like Lyle seemed poised to destroy it.

The cases that follow all involve Australians of European ancestry. Aboriginal Australians and migrants from outside Europe—from British India, the Middle East, and East Asia—appear later. This is because many Britons saw moral insanity as a peculiarly European, or at least white, affliction. It was a disease of civilization. Some even believed that insanity of all types was more common among whites. "Criminality, like insanity," wrote one British physician, "waits upon civilisation. Among primitive races insanity is rare; criminality, in the true sense, is also rare."[9] In colonial Victoria, Aboriginal Australians were not generally thought to have evolved beyond primitivism, and so their madness could not, by definition, take a form that involved degeneration from a more civilized state. Therefore, the moral insanity debate was almost exclusively about the nature of the European psyche, and the possibility that British law could not fairly or accurately assess the responsibility of even these "ideal" British subjects.

The 1892 trial of Frederick Bailey Deeming is among the greatest legal sensations in the history of Australia. His story has inspired true-crime writers since it first appeared in the Australian press.[10] Scandals like the one his case provoked invite participants and observers to test the limits of conventional categories and practices. In the colonies, hierarchies imported from Europe were less ossified, providing opportunities for redefinition, even fraud.[11] Deeming embodied the instabilities of status in several ways. He assumed many names and identities as he moved around the empire, which made him difficult to track. His false identities transgressed class boundaries, as he presented himself variously as a veteran, a prospector, and a gentleman. Once police had caught and identified him, his alleged insanity undermined efforts to develop a coherent explanation for his violence and to resolve his case. The trial and its aftermath ventured onto the precarious terrain of responsibility, made more unstable by the colonial context. Who was Deeming, and was he sane? What was the place of Australian judges, lawyers, and doctors in the imperial administrative order? In seeking to determine what the actual status of Deeming was—his true name, his life history, his class, his sanity, his guilt—officials also sought to clarify the status of law in the Australian colonies.

Deeming was born in Birkenhead, England, on 30 July 1854.[12] Until his arrest by police in March of 1892, it is difficult to say exactly where he went, or under which name he traveled. Deeming's police file contains one valiant attempt to produce a comprehensive timeline of his activities.[13] From what police could piece together, Deeming had worked as a plumber and gasfitter in Birkenhead until 1881. When he moved to Australia, he plied his trade in Sydney. Sometime in the early 1880s, he was joined by his English wife, Marie James, and first child. The couple soon had two more children. In 1886, he went into business independently, but a fire destroyed his premises. Under suspicion of insurance fraud, he fled to South Africa, leaving his family to follow. In 1888 or 1889, Deeming's wife and children returned to Birkenhead, and Frederick and Marie had a fourth child.[14] There were rumors that he masterminded a mining-property fraud in the Transvaal before escaping to Montevideo, where he was arrested and returned to England. Some said he escaped again, marrying a Scottish girl in Hull in 1890 while passing himself off as a retired Australian sheep farmer.

In 1891, Deeming's affairs come into sharper focus. In July, under the name Albert O. Williams, he rented a villa in Rainhill, Lancashire. In August, he killed his wife and children, and buried them in a pit under the hearth in their home. In September, he married Emily Mather and soon left with her for Melbourne, arriving in December. On 17 December, he bought cement from a local shop. Police would later discover Emily Mather's body under the hearth of the little house Deeming had rented on Andrew Street in Windsor, a suburb of Melbourne. Detectives believed that she had been killed on Christmas Eve.[15] In January of 1892, Deeming sailed from Sydney to Adelaide, introducing himself to passengers as Baron Swanston. Aboard the ship, he met a young woman named Kate Rounsevell and seduced her with jewelry and promises of marriage. He left in February for the Southern Cross Goldfields in Western Australia to make his fortune. Rounsevell was to join him once he had set up their marital home. On 4 March, however, a rank smell led Deeming's Windsor landlord and local police to his grisly secret.

Three members of the Melbourne police described the horror of slowly chipping the cement away from Emily Mather's corpse so that it could be transported to the city morgue. They recalled the stench, which clung to their skin and clothing so persistently that they had to burn their uniforms.[16] Mather had a cracked skull, and her throat had been cut. She had been buried in a nightdress, on her side with her knees tucked into her chest. Within thirty-six hours of the discovery of her body, Melbourne police had produced a twelve-page report on Deeming.[17] Sergeants Considine and Cawsey, two of Melbourne's fifteen detectives, worked on the case.[18] William Considine was a seasoned veteran, already in his twenty-first year on the force. When he retired, he was credited with capturing ten people who were later sentenced to death; Deeming's was among his greatest cases.[19]

Harry Cawsey, the junior partner, would remain with the police for nearly twenty years after the Deeming case, eventually rising to the rank of inspector. As an old man, he vividly remembered the day when the chief of the Criminal Investigation Branch called him into his office and said, "A woman's body has been found under a hearthstone in an empty house in Andrew Street, Windsor. Get on with it. I don't want to see you again until you bring in the man."[20] The detectives felt certain that the person who had rented the Andrew Street house as Drewin was the man they knew as Albert Williams, who had traveled to Melbourne on the *Kaiser Wilhelm II* from England that November. They made much of Drewin's purchase of cement from a local shop on 17 December, which they believed was bought "to conceal a premeditated crime."[21]

Frederick Deeming was a striver, fabulist, and dandy, with a penchant for ostentatious jewelry and a bushy ginger moustache. Samuel Bradley, a fellow passenger on the *Kaiser Wilhelm II*, remembered Deeming wearing "large quantities of jewellery quite exceeding good taste," including a large sapphire seal ring, diamond cufflinks and studs, and a watch with a heavy gold chain.[22] On the ship, Deeming claimed to have been a military engineer for nineteen years and boasted that he had been awarded the Victoria Cross for his service in various Egyptian campaigns. Deeming, reported Bradley, "though intelligent . . . is uneducated and tries to ape his superiors in conversation by the insertion of extraordinary aspirates where not required." Many witnesses also described Deeming's beloved pet canary, which he kept in an ornate brass birdcage with red stained-glass panels.[23] The press and the public delighted in the bathetic contrast between Deeming's buffoonish attempts at refinement and the violence of his crimes.

By mid-March of 1892, police had traced Deeming, known as Williams, to Rainhill. Melbourne police began writing to New Scotland Yard in London beginning on 5 March 1892. Sergeant Cawsey provided detailed descriptions of both Emily Mather and Deeming, including accounts of his military affectations and a catalogue of his gaudy jewelry. Mather was "26 to 28 years of age, about 5 feet high, slim build, dark clear complexion, large dark eyes, brown hair of very luxuriant growth, long thin nose, slightly roman, high cheek bones, upper front teeth all false, rather large ears especially the lobs [*sic*]."[24] Lancashire police quickly confirmed their identities. Mather's mother, Dove, told police that Williams had appeared in Rainhill in June 1891. He had claimed to be an inspector of stores in the Indian Army or the Bengal Cavalry, wounded many times in battle, and the wealthy son of a veteran of the Crimean

War. Dove Mather reported that her daughter had mailed letters from each port on her journey to Australia. A last letter, dated 28 December 1891, was in her new son-in-law's hand. It announced the newlyweds' plans to sail for Hong Kong in the New Year.[25]

Australian police took pains to keep the public away from Deeming. Once he was in custody in Perth he had to be smuggled back into Melbourne, past the determined mobs of newspapermen and readers desperate for a sign of the prisoner.[26] On 1 April 1892, while uniformed policemen stationed at Port Melbourne acted as decoys, a ship carrying Deeming quietly landed at St. Kilda, where plainclothes officers and a discreet waggonette waited to convey him to Melbourne Gaol.[27]

On 22 April 1892, Deeming appeared in court for the first time. He was arraigned at the Supreme Court of Melbourne before Henry Hodges, a Liverpool-born judge known for his temper and his tendency toward moderation in criminal sentencing. Hodges would also preside over Deeming's trial the subsequent week.[28] Deeming's defense team consisted of his solicitor, Marshall Lyle, and barristers Alfred Deakin and William Forlonge. The Crown prosecutor in the case was Robert Walsh, another Irish lawyer who had left Dublin for Victoria, where he made his fortune practicing mining law during the gold rush. Until 1859, all the barristers working in colonial Victoria had first passed the bar in Britain or Ireland.[29] Irish-trained lawyers, like Walsh and Lyle, dominated the profession. They had come seeking the social and economic advancement that could elude Celtic professionals in the United Kingdom, which one Irish émigré described as "over-stocked" with lawyers.[30] Deeming pled not guilty. The defense called for a postponement to gather more evidence from England and elsewhere to support an insanity defense, but Hodges denied the request.[31]

Unlike many of his colleagues, Alfred Deakin was born and educated in Australia, although his parents were British immigrants. He grew up in suburban Melbourne and studied law at the University of Melbourne. After an undistinguished early legal career, he drifted into journalism, where he excelled, which led toward prominence in colonial politics.[32] He was a liberal and a fervent advocate of Australian federation within a strong imperial framework. In 1891, Victoria suffered an economic bust so devastating that historians have described it as "Armageddon."[33] Deakin lost both his and his father's savings in late 1890 and was forced to resume his law practice. He was steadily recouping his losses in 1892. Although he took no fee for his work in the Deeming case, the trial boosted his notoriety. Deakin would later become attorney general and, in 1903, prime minister. William Percival Forlonge, the Australian-born

MR. MARSHALL LYLE, COUNSEL FOR THE DEFENCE.
[From a Photo. by Messrs. Tuttle & Co., Melbourne.]

Marshall Lyle. This photograph of Lyle was printed in the lavishly illustrated penny dreadful, *History of the Windsor and Rainhill Tragedies: Being a Full Account of the Career of Frederick Bailey Deeming, Alias Williams, Alias Swanston, Alias Lawson, Alias Ward, Alias Lord Dunn, Alias Dawson, Alias Duncan, Alias Drewin, &c., &c.*, 2nd ed. (Adelaide: Frearson's Printing House, 1892), p. 63. The author was anonymous. Credit: State Library of New South Wales, PAM 89/1170.

and -trained junior defense barrister in Deeming's case, was less influential, and information about his life and career is scarce.

In an eerie and possibly fanciful coincidence, an Australian newspaper reported that Frederick Deeming and Marshall Lyle had lived across from each other on Andrew Street in December 1891. One day, a brusque stranger had frightened Lyle's elderly housekeeper by asking to come in so that he could take in the view of his own rented villa, number 57. She had refused, and Lyle moved house shortly thereafter. The housekeeper later identified Deeming as the stranger. For Lyle, as for Deakin, representing Deeming was a chance to raise his public profile.[34] Unlike Deakin, for whom legal practice was a means to a financial end, Lyle loved the work and saw the Deeming case as a way to change the law as well as to build his practice. Judging from his letters and petitions, Lyle was an ambitious, theatrical, and passionate man, reluctant to yield to authority, quick to recruit the press to his causes. He considered himself a humanitarian and a friend of science, including criminal anthropology and studies of mental illness. In Deeming, he saw another opportunity to inveigh against what he had for some time seen as systematic flaws in jurisprudence and the administration of criminal justice.

As Lyle had anticipated, the Deeming case prompted a new, focused debate over responsibility and legal insanity. "There is no doubt," declared one

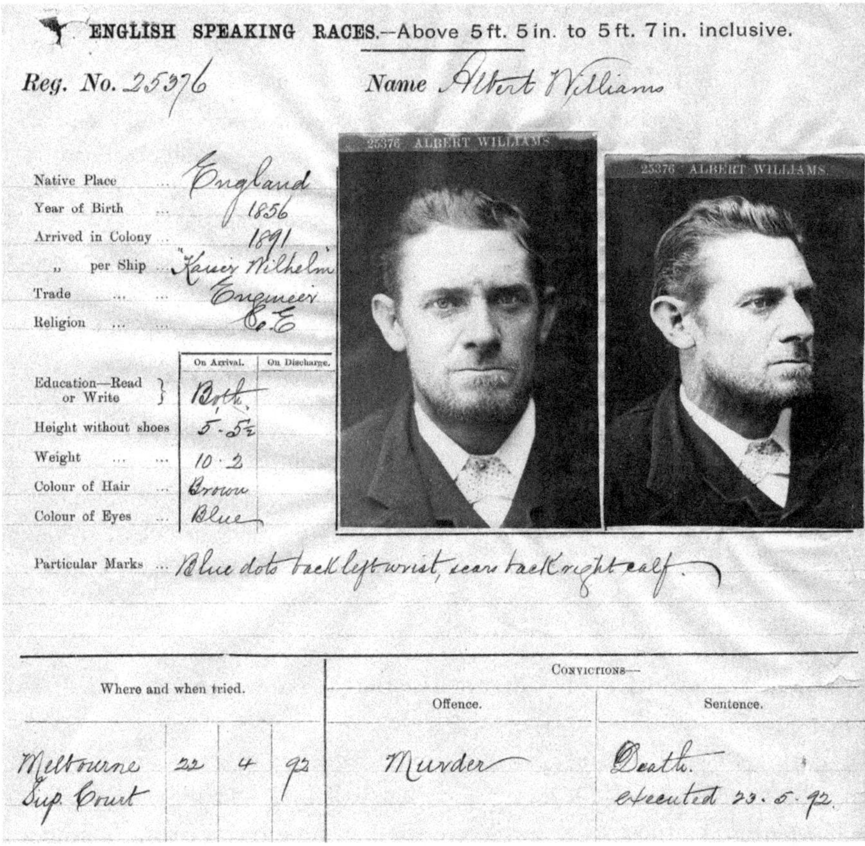

ENGLISH SPEAKING RACES.—Above 5 ft. 5 in. to 5 ft. 7 in. inclusive.

Reg. No. 25376 Name Albert Williams

25376 ALBERT WILLIAMS

25376 ALBERT WILLIAMS

Native Place ... England
Year of Birth ... 1856
Arrived in Colony ... 1891
" per Ship ... Kaiser Wilhelm
Trade ... ... Engineer
Religion ... ... C.E.

	On Arrival.	On Discharge.
Education—Read or Write	Both	
Height without shoes	5-5½	
Weight	10.2	
Colour of Hair ...	Brown	
Colour of Eyes ...	Blue	

Particular Marks ... Blue dots back left wrist, scars back right calf.

Where and when tried.				Convictions— Offence.	Sentence.
Melbourne Sup. Court	22	4	92	Murder	Death. executed 23.5.92.

Frederick Bailey Deeming. The photograph is from the "criminal history sheet" for Albert Williams/Frederick Bailey Deeming, a copy of which Marshall Lyle sent to Cesare Lombroso in 1898. Credit: Provincial Record Office of Victoria, VPRS 8369.

columnist for the *South Australian Register*, "that the whole subject of insanity and its relation to crime and punishment is in a state of uncertainty and suspense."[35] Lyle was prepared for the attention. He kept abreast of "the recent strides of medico-legal science and criminal anthropology," cultivated contact with leading figures in these fields, and believed elite science should supersede what he saw as outdated legal tradition and popular understandings of insanity and criminality.[36] For example, he corresponded in the 1890s with Cesare Lombroso, the Italian founder of the field of criminal anthropology (or positivist criminology), who argued that criminal tendencies were heritable, and who revived scientific and public interest in phrenology and other physiological accounts of criminality. Some years after Deeming's trial, Lyle compiled criminal files, including photographs and demographic information of offenders, to send to Lombroso in Italy.[37] One file included photographs of Deeming wearing a polka-dotted bow tie and a scrubby beard, his hair swept behind protruding ears. He pressed his lips together in a slight sneer, staring at the camera from beneath a furrowed, heavy brow.[38]

Lyle also wrote to Havelock Ellis, the English physician best known for his studies of human sexuality. Ellis, the son of an English sea captain, had his own Australian connection. He made a number of journeys to Australia in his youth and later spent four years in New South Wales working as a teacher and tutor. In 1879, he returned to England to pursue a career in medicine. He became interested in eugenics, formally supporting campaigns for voluntary euthanasia, abortion, and sexual reforms.[39] In 1890, he published *The Criminal*, a work of criminal anthropology. The book had gone through five editions by 1914. The third edition, published in 1903, included the same photograph of Deeming, wearing a spotted bow tie, that Lyle had sent to Lombroso.[40] In *The Criminal*, Ellis thanked Lyle for sending him seventeen photographs of criminals from New South Wales along with the portrait of Deeming, which Lyle considered the "most characteristic of that noted criminal."[41]

Many commentators described Deeming as either an "instinctive criminal" or insane. While the difference under the common law could be one of life and death—death for the criminal, life in an asylum for the madman—Ellis argued that differentiating between the two was absurd. He praised Lombroso for breaking down the wall between madness and criminality. Madmen and criminals, Ellis wrote, were "both recognised as belonging to the same great and terrible family of abnormal, degenerate, anti-social persons."[42] Philosophical attempts to assert a metaphysical basis for responsibility and free will had failed, in Ellis's view. People were welcome to act as though they were choosing agents and entitled to punish those who committed harmful acts, but free will was at best a useful fantasy. Ellis even suggested abandoning the term "responsibility" altogether and replacing it with "social reaction." By dispensing with responsibility and its emphasis on desert, society could better embrace the kind of social engineering that reformers like Ellis believed was the only solution to crime. Society should "react" to criminality prophylactically—in preventive treatment of those with criminal tendencies, for example—and punitively, though with a focus on rehabilitation.

Ellis and Lyle were of like mind. Both believed that British common law clung to a definition of responsibility that was scientifically unsound and socially destructive. Lyle had to argue that Deeming was insane if there was to be any chance of saving his life. His true aim, however, was not to enlarge the definition of legal insanity to encompass non-delusional subtypes but to chip away at metaphysical notions of responsibility so that a hereditarian, social-scientific model could take its place.

The cases that came before Deeming's and that formed its bedrock in Victorian law reveal just how important Deeming's case was for Lyle and other lawyers interested in the reform of criminal responsibility. The most important immediate precedent was the case of William Colston. At 5 A.M. on a March morning in 1891, William Colston, a carpenter and former sergeant in the British Army, drunkenly passed out on the road to Mr. Davis's orchard in the village of Narbethong, some fifty miles northeast of Melbourne. He awoke, still drunk, and made his way to the Davis house. He knew Mr. and Mrs. Davis well and was unsurprised when Mary Davis, never a paragon of modesty, answered the door in her nightdress. He was only slightly perplexed when she suddenly pulled him down onto her bed and shouted for her husband as, Colston said, "Davis and I had always laughed at it,—considering her eccentric."[43]

As Colston went on to explain in his confession, the situation escalated rapidly. Instead of laughing off the indiscreet scene, Colston alleged that Mr. Davis demanded £5 in exchange for his silence about the assault on his wife. Colston resentfully agreed to the blackmail, thinking that he could persuade Davis to change his mind while the men walked through the orchard to retrieve some of Colston's things. They argued, and Colston suddenly decided that "although he [Davis] had always laughed and seemed to understand it before—he must have been in the plot." "I collard [*sic*] the axe off his shoulder and hit him twice, and drew my brisk knife and cut his throat for he seemed to me then only as vermin."[44] Colston then returned to the house, struck Mary Davis with the axe, and ransacked the place to make it seem as though there had been a robbery.

Colston was soon caught, interrogated, and transferred to Melbourne Gaol, to be tried at the Supreme Court. Given his confession, his only chance of avoiding a capital sentence was to convince the jury that he had been insane at the time of the killings. Lyle acted as Colston's solicitor and led his insanity defense. In late April, the Victorian colonial government appointed six men to examine Colston—two for the Crown, including the resident physician of Melbourne Gaol, Dr. Andrew Shields, and four for the defense.[45] The doctors failed to agree, and the trial was postponed to allow more consultants to interview the prisoner. For three months, medical men regularly visited Colston. Exhibit I in his trial was a write-up of one physician's sanity test. In the test, four doctors watched Colston for signs of "paralysis," considered a symptom of "general paralysis of the insane" (probably tertiary syphilis), while Colston took dictation.[46] "Colston passed the ordeal in a most satisfactory manner," wrote Shields, "too satisfactory I fear rather for himself and his prospects, or for the theory of insanity."[47]

Dr. Edward Rosenblum, the senior medical officer of the Yarra Bend Asylum, found the writing test persuasive evidence of Colston's mental faculties. Conversations with Colston convinced Rosenblum that there was no reason to believe that he "did not understand the nature of his actions & knew that he was doing wrong."[48] Here, the alienist used the formulation of insanity set out in the *M'Naghten* rules. Colston may have been mentally ill by some medical definition, but many of his doctors felt that he was unlikely to meet the criteria for legal insanity. Another doctor, a regular visitor to Melbourne Gaol, summed up the issue: "There are dozens of men now about Melbourne with a number of the peculiarities Colston has."[49] The implication was clear: If Colston were insane, how many murderers could be said to be sane?

Colston was of such general interest to the Australian medical community that one of his interviewers, Dr. James Jamieson, presented the case to the Medical Society of Victoria.[50] In a September 1891 article, published in the *Australian Medical Journal*, Jamieson reflected on the difficulty of analyzing a defendant's sanity in a courtroom. Most of the medical men who evaluated Colston agreed about his symptoms: his impassive countenance, facial twitching, stilted speech, uneven pupils, and drooping right lip. But they differed in their interpretations. Physicians might reasonably attribute Colston's symptoms to incipient general paralysis of the insane, or perhaps to Bell's palsy, or to too many drunken nights spent outdoors, or nothing at all. If elite physicians could not agree, what hope did ordinary men have? The jurors in Colston's case would be asked to wade through a morass of complex and contradictory medical testimony. Jamieson did not think they were up to the challenge. The average juror, wrote Jamieson, "suddenly called from his shop or office," was unqualified to weigh in on such an "intricate question in nerve pathology." Moreover, British adversarial courtroom procedure encouraged lawyers to seek unequivocal statements from their witnesses and to discredit the opinions of opposing experts. "To investigate the question before the Court," lamented Jamieson, "as one of scientific interest or importance, is the last thing thought of."[51]

Australian physicians were at pains to show that they diagnosed prisoners with moral insanity at great personal and professional cost. At the November meeting of the Victorian branch of the British Medical Association, another of Colston's doctors, John William Yorke Fishbourne, presented on the case. He explained that he had defended Colston out of a sense of duty, not to advance his career. Rather, "to declare a man insane meant a storm of derision from the public and press, as well as a decided opposition from all Government officials," in addition to the "inconvenience and unpleasantness of attendance to give evidence in the court." On meeting Colston, Fishbourne immediately noticed his strange twitches and slurs—which he considered clear indications of brain disease. A second interview, attended by physicians including Henry Maudsley's nephew, Dr. Henry Carr Maudsley, confirmed the diagnosis of "moral perversion." Another physician, Dr. John Springthorpe, also concluded that Colston was mad. "If ever we have the misfortune to again attempt to serve a demented criminal," he advised his colleagues, physicians should force lawyers to ask, "What is the standard of right and wrong by which the law judges, and what amount of knowledge constitutes legal knowledge?"[52]

Colston was unrepentant and surprisingly calm as he contemplated his fate. He wrote Shields a letter to thank him for his kindness, in which he ruminated on why he, a steady former soldier and upright laborer, had resorted to extreme violence. Colston's theory was that he had taken too readily to military discipline. "I must have been bottling up my temper for the last eighteen years or so," he surmised. He took a philosophical view of his predicament: "Since Cain killed Abel and was allowed to live, marry, and rear a family, I suppose murders will occur in spite of the punishment in store."[53] Colston's apparent nonchalance and good humor struck some of his doctors and many in the press as an indication that he was either a lunatic or a "supreme egotist." That is, he was either profoundly insane or so cold-hearted that he was unperturbed by either murder or the prospect of his own demise.[54] Did his indifference to death make Colston sick or evil? Lyle and the expert witnesses for the defense came down firmly on the side of mental disease. A verdict of insanity in the case would pry open *M'Naghten*'s terms so that men like Colston could squeeze through.

Colston's trial began on 15 July 1891. His lead barrister was Dr. William L. Mullen, a physician and lawyer who specialized in legal cases that raised medical questions, and in the medical treatment and diagnosis of insanity. He would serve as the medical superintendent of three Australian asylums before he committed suicide by prussic acid poisoning, just over a year after losing his first wife and three weeks after marrying his second.[55] At trial, Mullen examined many medical men who testified that Colston had been insane at the time of the killings and was still insane and incapable of standing trial. The jury, however, was unconvinced. They found him sane at the time of trial, sane when he committed the crime, and guilty of willful murder.[56]

Lyle was angry. There was a rule at Melbourne Gaol that medical men could only interview prisoners in the presence of the jail's medical officer, Shields, which Lyle felt had undermined the defense.[57] His main objection, however, was that the judge—Justice Hickman Molesworth—had wrongly instructed the jury to apply the *M'Naghten* definition of insanity. The defense argued that this was the incorrect definition of "insane" under the terms of the Victorian Crimes Act of 1890.[58] The act referred to, and borrowed the language of, the metropolitan Criminal Lunatics Act (1800), which had created England's "pleasure men" in the wake of the Hadfield trial. The 1800 act did not include a definition of insanity, and neither did the Australian 1890 Act.

Lyle's legal strategy here is not completely transparent. It seems likely that when he referred to the Victorian Crimes Act, he meant to imply that Molesworth was wrong to read a *M'Naghten* insanity standard into the statute because it was based on a British law that predated *M'Naghten* by forty-three years. If so, then this approach was a long shot. The 1800 act left the definition of insanity ambiguous, but this was precisely the ambiguity that the House of Lords had sought to eliminate with the *M'Naghten* rules. By the end of the nineteenth century, Britain and its colonies had embraced the *M'Naghten* definition, if ambivalently. Thus, Molesworth's instructions to the jury on the legal definition of insanity were consistent with Victorian law and British precedent. Lyle's true argument was that the prevailing definition of legal insanity in the British common-law system was unjust. His objection to Molesworth's reading of the 1890 act was not really about the fine points of statutory interpretation. It was a direct challenge to the settled law of the British world.

Lyle saw Colston's case as a chance to attack *M'Naghten* in the highest court of the British Empire, the Judicial Committee of the Privy Council. The Judicial Committee, also known as the Board, was the imperial court of last resort. It emerged in its modern form in 1833, with the Judicial Committee Act. Its members included the judges of the English House of Lords, eminent judges from high courts and courts of appeal from Great Britain, India, and other colonies, and politically powerful laymen, such as the Lord

Chancellor, the vice chancellor, and all previous holders of these offices.[59] Petitions for appeal were sent direct from the colonies to the Queen, who then referred them to the Board for consideration. The judges read the documents forwarded from the colonial court or from the petitioner's lawyers, considered the evidence, and issued a recommendation to the monarch as to how the case should be decided. The Board issued these recommendations in open court.[60] The Lord Chancellor was the president of the council and was responsible for deciding which judges should sit in each case. At least four members of the committee had to hear a case for their recommendation to be valid.[61]

The Judicial Committee was a peculiar entity. Although routinely referred to as a court, its inclusion of lay members, its special relationship to the monarchy, and its immense jurisdiction all set it apart from the highest courts in the colonies, or in Britain. Henry Reeve, then the registrar of the Privy Council, described the Judicial Committee's jurisdiction in 1872 as "founded . . . essentially on the prerogative; it has existed since a very early period, and it is not strictly limited to the functions of a court of justice; it partakes of an administrative and executive character which it is extremely difficult to define."[62] Two English barristers wrote in 1901, "[The Judicial Committee's] authority is probably unique. Its jurisdiction is undoubtedly more extensive, whether measured by area, population, variety of nations, creeds, languages, laws or customs, than that hitherto enjoyed by any Court known to civilization."[63]

There was no guarantee that the Judicial Committee would agree to hear a case. Defendants in criminal cases, or their lawyers, had to apply for special leave to appeal; these cases were heard "as an act of grace" and as an exercise of the royal prerogative, not as a matter of right. Therefore, Marshall Lyle's first hurdle would be to persuade the Judicial Committee to grant him leave to appeal on Colston's behalf. To do this, he had to convince the committee that the case raised important matters of law that demanded review at the highest imperial level.[64] And so, as soon as the Melbourne Supreme Court announced Colston's conviction, Lyle began to sift through precedents in order to draft his petition. On 10 August 1891, however, Lyle discovered that the Victorian Executive Council, a government body presided over by the colony's governor, the Earl of Hopetoun, was preparing to discuss the Colston case. Hopetoun, a Scottish nobleman, had traveled to Melbourne to assume his governorship in 1889, at the age of 29. He was slight, gracious, and not especially clever. Despite his aristocratic air, his easy manner and love of horseback riding charmed the public. Hopetoun (like Deakin) supported

Australian federation, and eventually served as the first governor-general of the Commonwealth of Australia.[65]

Hopetoun preferred retail politics to hard policy, but he relished the routine tasks of government. Among the most important was his leadership of the Executive Council, which had the power to review capital convictions and exercise the prerogative of mercy. Lyle, caught off guard by the council's decision to move ahead in its review of Colston's sentence, wrote in haste to explain why the review should be delayed: "This case is one not alone of supreme importance to the individual concerned, but to the administration of justice. The rule creates a precedent as to all cases of insanity of a non-delusional character. It is the first time any such question has been ruled upon since McNaughten's case. It must affect the power of the medical profession to restrain the large and daily increasing number of non-delusional insane, whom medical science and asylum experience determine as the most dangerous to the community, but whom the so-called test in Colston's case decide [*sic*] are perfectly sane."[66]

On the same day, Lyle also wrote to the attorney general of Victoria, William Shiels, to ask him to stop the Executive Council from considering the case before his petition for leave to appeal to the Privy Council had been decided. In a memorandum to Lord Hopetoun a week later, Shiels claimed, not entirely correctly, that the *M'Naghten* rules of a half-century's vintage had been "universally acted upon in English Jurisprudence" since their promulgation. In his view, Colston had to hang.[67]

Shiels and the Executive Council had every reason to doubt that Lyle would succeed in bringing Colston's case before the Judicial Committee. Throughout its history, the committee had been largely unwilling to hear appeals in criminal cases. The court expressed its position in an 1863 case, *Falkland Islands Company v The Queen*: "The inconvenience of entertaining . . . [a]ppeals in cases of a strictly criminal nature is so great, the obstruction which it would offer to the administration of justice in the Colonies is so obvious, that it is very rarely that applications to this Board" should succeed.[68] The Judicial Committee had taken this approach to criminal appeals throughout the nineteenth century, which Lyle and Victorian officials well knew.[69]

Still, Lyle's cause was not entirely quixotic. Since the 1860s, the Privy Council had agreed to hear occasional criminal appeals, including some from the Australian colonies. In 1867, for example, Henry Louis Bertrand, a defendant from New South Wales, alleged that there had been serious procedural irregularities in his trial. For the first time, the Judicial Committee allowed a criminal appeal. In its decision in *Bertrand*, the judges reiterated their general reluctance to decide criminal matters, as these were likely to lead to "mischief and inconvenience."[70] Criminal appeals were not impossible, though. The court established a series of conditions under which leave might be granted. They would hear a case if it raised "questions of great and general importance" that were likely to affect future cases; if "the due and orderly administration of the law" were to be "interrupted, or diverted into a new course, which might create a precedent for the future"; and if there were "no other means of preventing these consequences."[71]

Lyle believed that Colston's case satisfied the *Bertrand* conditions. The idea, however, that a strict application of the dominant legal rule, *M'Naghten*, risked "diverting [the law] into a new course" was exceptionally difficult to argue. The petition relied on Lyle's ability to distinguish delusional from non-delusional insanity, and to show that finding a non-delusional lunatic sane under *M'Naghten* was a travesty of justice. Victoria's attorney general, Shiels, explicitly rejected the notion that the Colston case represented a diversion from established legal principles. In fact, he quoted directly from *Bertrand* in his letter encouraging the Executive Council to proceed with Colston's execution.[72]

Lyle rested much of his argument for Colston's leave to appeal on two other Australian criminal cases, *Supple* and *Levinger*. In 1870, Irish newspaperman Gerald Henry Supple chased two men through the streets of Melbourne, brandishing a gun. Witnesses described him as generally amiable and temperate but prone to fits of temper over imagined slights.[73] One friend testified that Supple had seemed to be "breaking down" in the weeks before the incident.[74] As he ran, he fatally shot a stranger with a bullet intended for a colleague of his at the Melbourne *Age*, whom he instead wounded in the arm. It came out at trial that Supple was paranoid, believing that his friends were slandering him. The jury returned an unusual verdict. They found the defendant guilty of murder but added, "We are unanimous in believing that the pistol was discharged accidentally."[75]

Supple's lawyers petitioned the Judicial Committee for leave to appeal, on the question of how the law should regard the accidental killing of a victim by a defendant who intended to murder someone else. Leave was granted. Supple's supporters in Victoria managed to secure a commutation, however, and the Privy Council appeal was ultimately dropped. Supple spent seven years in prison in Melbourne and was released upon the death of his intended victim. He then moved to New Zealand, where he died at the age of seventy-five.[76]

The second case, that of Hugo Levinger, also seemed to offer Lyle some leverage. Levinger, a Bavarian, was accused of killing an unnamed South Sea Islander aboard the *Young Australian* as it sailed near Polynesia. The crew were accused of slave trading.[77] Levinger was reported to have said, when the emaciated corpse of an Indigenous man had been thrown overboard, "here will be a loss of £5.10."[78] By the time of Levinger's trial, the rest of the *Young Australian*'s crew had already been convicted of murder.[79] The legal controversy in the case was procedural. The ship's owner was Irish, it sailed under the Union Jack, and it had departed from Sydney, bringing Levinger under British jurisdiction. Because he was a foreign national, though, a mixed jury composed of six "aliens" (foreigners) and six British subjects heard his case.[80] Levinger tried to peremptorily challenge one of the alien jurors but was denied.[81] He was convicted of manslaughter and sentenced to seven years' hard labor. In the wake of the trial, his lawyers successfully appealed to the Judicial Committee, which decided in Levinger's favor.[82]

Levinger raised a narrow, technical question about common-law rights and mixed juries. *Supple* might have incited much broader discussion about the relationship between criminal acts and intention, but once the appeal was withdrawn interest in the case faded. Neither appeal centered on the defendant's insanity or challenged a prevailing legal standard. Lyle's petition was bold but ultimately flimsy. The Executive Council in Melbourne, eager to settle Colston's fate and unconvinced by his lawyer's arguments, informed an irate Lyle that it would proceed on schedule.

Outraged, Lyle responded that he and his client, as British subjects, had a right to appeal directly to the Queen through her Privy Council. He accused the Supreme Court of Victoria and the Executive Council of overthrowing medical science, and of sinking to the "lowest level of Lynch law." Invoking American mob justice and the legacy of slavery was a common rhetorical tactic among nineteenth-century Britons, for whom the comparison served as a particularly pointed indictment.[83] In alleging that the execution of nondelusional but insane prisoners so debased British law—especially when there was a chance, however slight, of a successful appeal—Lyle made the strongest case he could in Colston's favor. He threatened to notify metropolitan authorities that Hopetoun was acting contrary to law, and begged the Executive Council to consider the constitutional import and "lamentable consequences" of its decision.[84] The members of the council were unmoved. The council met, considered Colston's case, and declined to commute the sentence. Colston was hanged on 24 August 1891 at ten o'clock in the morning, at

Melbourne Gaol. The newspapers reported that he went quietly, and that he praised the justice and mercy of the Victorian legal system until the end.[85]

After Colston's death, Lyle was determined not to lose again. Deeming was tried over four days in April and May 1892. Much of the testimony concerned his sanity. Medical men took the stand, some telling colorful tales of his childhood poverty, insane parents, and history of confinement to lunatic asylums. Others flatly denied that anything Deeming said could be trusted. Andrew Shields, the prison surgeon, was a skeptic. "It is my opinion," he said, "that the prisoner is not insane. I cannot believe anything he says on his own testimony." Although Shields did not believe it, he reported to the courtroom what Deeming had told him about his life. Deeming claimed, for instance, that he had no memories from before the age of eleven or twelve, and that he blacked out every year on his birthday. His dead mother haunted him, whispering evil things to him at night. He also said he had once pushed a woman off a pier for calling him Mad Fred.[86] Another medical witness for the prosecution, the superintendent of a lunatic asylum, told the court that Deeming was feigning insanity. Deeming might have lacked the responsibility of an "ordinary average man" and was likely an "instinctive criminal," but he possessed sufficient moral sense to know right from wrong.[87]

Dr. John Springthorpe, who had defended Colston in 1891, elected to do his part to challenge *M'Naghten* by testifying on Deeming's behalf.[88] Springthorpe had, by then, risen to the leadership of the Victorian branch of the British Medical Association. He emphasized Deeming's childhood history of want and cruelty, lingering on the malevolent ghost of his mother, who supposedly goaded him to kill and told him that he was "born to hang." Springthorpe read out a statement by Deeming in which he claimed that his second wife, Emily Mather, had secretly hired a man to kill his first wife, Marie James, so that they could be married. Deeming also claimed that Emily was still alive, having broken his heart and absconded. He did not know whose corpse had rotted beneath the stones at Andrew Street. Springthorpe believed that these were "distortions, exaggerations, delusions, hallucinations," but that Deeming's lies, and some suspicious scars on his scalp, suggested syphilis or epilepsy.[89]

John Fishbourne, who had also defended Colston, spoke for Deeming, too. Despite his twenty-year career in the treatment of the insane, Deeming unsettled him, and his testimony reflected this ambivalence and uncertainty. Fishbourne was "inclined to think" Deeming's delusions were real; he was

This cartoon, entitled "The Big Murder Inquest: In Court" (21 May 1892), depicts scenes from Frederick Bailey Deeming's inquest and trial. Harry Chaplin, a mid-twentieth-century collector of Victorian ephemera, glued it into a scrapbook devoted to the Deeming case. Credit: State Library of Victoria, MS 12158, F Box 2763/2.

"inclined to believe" that Deeming was sincere; he had "reason to think" Deeming's family history was true; it "might be possible" for an epileptic not to have known that murder was wrong. The defense's hedging did not persuade the jurors. They found Deeming guilty, and he was sentenced to death. In addition, the jurors considered three questions submitted to them by Justice Hodges: "(1) Is the prisoner now insane? Ans. No; (2) If it had been proved that his father and mother had been in a Lunatic Asylum and that he had been twice in a Lunatic Asylum, would you have been of opinion (a) That he is now insane? Ans. No; (b) That he was insane at the time the act charged against him was done? Ans. No."[90]

As soon as Hodges pronounced Deeming's sentence, Lyle began a campaign to stay the execution while he requested leave to appeal to the Privy Council. He argued that Deeming was insane, that the evidence against him was circumstantial, and that the press coverage had prejudiced the jury. After his defeat in the Colston affair, he also saw Deeming's case as a second chance to press his case against the *M'Naghten* definition of insanity. "You have doubtless read in the public press that the prisoner . . . is some unique moral monster," Lyle wrote to the Executive Council. This effort to cast Deeming as a rare aberrance was misguided. In reality, Deeming represented "a class which is rapidly increasing with the so called civilisation of our times. He is the typical criminal of the century . . . he stands knocking at the door of English conscience and thought."[91]

The criminal anthropologists and physicians who defended moral insanity and so-called moral monsters like Deeming were heralds, in Lyle's view, of a new age in which scientific, technocratic population management replaced the moralistic, individualized adjudication of traditional criminal justice. The connections Lyle had to Lombroso and other European social theorists likely informed his understanding of legal insanity as an epoch-defining problem. He was keen to convince the Executive Council that Deeming's case raised issues of not only imperial but also global importance, and that an international network of jurists and physicians would scrutinize the result.

To that end, he drew the council's attention to recent cases tried in Austria and the United States. Continental Europe had learned a hard lesson after the autopsy of executed serial killer Franz Schneider in Vienna that year, which supposedly showed that the man suffered from "brain dropsy."[92] A series of London *Times* articles described the Schneider case, which had riveted Western audiences. In 1891, Schneider, a muscular man with "high cheek bones, hollow cheeks, and a sandy beard and moustache," with an expression of "repulsive ferocity," and his wife, Rosalie, had lured a series of servant girls to secluded spots in the Vienna suburbs. Together, they killed the young women and stole their clothes and money. More than a thousand ticket holders had crammed themselves into the hall of the Vienna Courts of Justice to watch the couple's trial, held in late January 1892.[93] They followed the drama through opera glasses and smuggled wine and bread into the courtroom so as not to lose their seats during the lunch recess. Ultimately, the jury found both defendants guilty and sentenced them to death.[94] Rosalie Schneider's sentence was commuted to life imprisonment. Franz Schneider was hanged that spring with the help of three hangman's assistants who dangled from his legs and arms as he slowly suffocated.[95]

The trial notes that Alfred Deakin made show that he too considered the Schneider case a cautionary tale.[96] After the execution, as Lyle noted, newspapers reported that an autopsy of Franz Schneider's brain showed incontrovertible evidence of brain disease.[97] One Australian columnist believed that the autopsy proved that "the law had hanged one who, in all likelihood, was totally irresponsible for doing what is not a crime unless the agent is responsible. That is, the law had probably committed another murder." Deeming, the columnist warned, would likely be the law's next victim.[98]

The United States had been shamed in the same way in the famous Guiteau case, in which Lyle reminded the Executive Council that a post mortem had shown that the prisoner was a victim of "brain disorder."[99] In 1881, Charles Julius Guiteau shot President James Garfield, who died two months later. Rosenberg writes that the Guiteau affair became, in its time, "something of a milestone in the popularization of hereditarian explanations of insanity and criminality."[100] The publishers of an 1882 collection of documents, interviews, and commentary about the case raved, "This trial developes [*sic*] the insanity question as it has never before been opened."[101] His lawyers argued that Guiteau was morally insane and irresponsible. They lost, Guiteau was hanged, and the results of a brain autopsy showed no physical evidence of insanity.[102] Despite the vociferous disagreements among the medical experts who testified during the trial, however, most physicians believed, by the 1890s, that he had been obviously and chronically insane.[103]

By the time of Deeming's trial, several well-placed experts had come to see Guiteau's and Schneider's hangings as embarrassments to their governments. Lyle and Deakin urged the Melbourne Supreme Court to avoid similar disgrace. Deeming's case, in Lyle's view, was Australia's chance to show that it could rise above the mob, accept scientific reality, and change its approach to criminal responsibility. Hanging Deeming would prove, once again, that British civilization was built on the faulty premise that most people who committed violent crimes acted rationally and out of malice, rather than under biological compulsion. To ignore the scientific evidence that violence was often the product of inheritance or illness was deeply unfair; to execute the insane, criminal. Only doctrinal change could save Britain's reputation and preserve the dignity of its law. Better yet, the Australian colonies could use the case to demonstrate that they were more modern and humane than Europe or America, leading the common law rather than simply following it.[104]

Lyle described his client as suffering from "complete absence of the moral sense."[105] The interactions Deeming had with police, lawyers, and medical men reinforced the impression that he was eerily unfeeling. One morning after his arrest in Southern Cross, Western Australia, Deeming casually remarked to one of his police guards that a murderer must have a terribly troubled conscience. The constable replied, "Yes. It would be a cold-blooded man to commit a murder like that," to which Deeming responded, "But a man who has lived a good life up to the murder need not fear. He can only die once."[106] Lyle's claims that Deeming represented the new normal, the "criminal of the century," were meant to prompt his interlocutors to change their ways. But instead, the truth that Lyle claimed to preach entrenched official hostility to reform. After all, if the criminal of the future were to be as harsh and calculating as Deeming, then the law of the future would have to rise—or sink—to the challenge.

At trial, Deeming was sentenced to die on 23 May 1892. On 19 May, the Judicial Committee of the Privy Council convened at Whitehall before a large audience to hear the petition for special leave to appeal. Two London lawyers of Irish extraction, Gerald Geoghegan and Henry Hamilton Lawless, appeared on Deeming's behalf.[107] The lawyers complained of how little time they had had to prepare their case, and the limited evidence they had been able to access, mostly from press clippings and telegrams.[108] Deeming's funds were running low, and Lyle had scrambled to acquire a free copy of Justice Hodges's Notes of Evidence to cable to London the day before the hearing.[109]

The official petition that the London lawyers submitted contained none of Lyle's sweeping indictments of *M'Naghten*. Instead, Geoghegan and Lawless asked the Judicial Committee to delay the execution of Deeming until new evidence of his familial history of insanity, in the form of affidavits from his brother and sister-in-law, had arrived in Australia.[110] Perhaps the London lawyers dismissed Lyle's campaign against *M'Naghten* as unrealistic. The breakdown in communication among the solicitors might also have been determinative. In any event, the members of the Judicial Committee criticized the petition as poorly drafted and insubstantial. In their eyes, it was merely a complaint about the jury's conclusion that Deeming was sane. It was established Privy Council jurisprudence that the Judicial Committee would accept the factual determinations of lower courts.[111] Although the committee did have the power to order cases to be retried and to instruct courts to consider new evidence or to disregard faulty evidence, this was virtually unheard of in criminal cases. The petition failed.[112] Commenting on the decision, an Australian newspaper praised the committee for declining to interfere. The reporter held, with some pride, that Deeming's trial in Australia had been conducted "with as much care and regularity as those in the United Kingdom." Deeming was one of a class of "moral monstrosities"—criminal lunatics, but lunatic "in one sense of the word" only.[113] Whatever that sense of "lunatic" was, it made Deeming loathsome, but responsible and punishable under imperial law.

Deeming and his partisans must have known that their chances of securing a reprieve were slim. On 17 May, Lyle wrote to the governor to inform him that Deeming wished to donate his brain to science after his death.[114] Earlier that week, the Victorian branch of the British Medical Association had written to the attorney general to express its official interest in acquiring the brain.[115] Two days before the execution, the attorney general declined the request. The official justification for withholding the brain was that Deeming should be treated like any other executed criminal.[116] In truth, it is likely that the government was keen to put the Deeming matter to rest. Havelock Ellis, for one, was appalled at the Victorian authorities' refusal to turn over the brain. "The action of a government in such a sense," he wrote, "can only be regarded as due to a fear that its mistakes will be exposed."[117]

Deeming wrote his final will and testament a few days before the execution. He bequeathed most of his property, including his writings, to Lyle. He also left him "a drawing to enable him to secure money buried in Lamu, East Africa."[118] He gave valuable items, including a flask, rings, gold cufflinks, and a plot of land, to the governor of Melbourne Gaol and a number of warders.[119] The clergyman who had attended him in jail received a Bible, Deeming's brother in London, a watch; there was nothing for Kate Rounsefell but a copy of an earlier will (in which she had been left a percentage of his estate), "as a token of the lies she told in court."[120] Deeming was hanged at Melbourne Gaol, on schedule, at 10 A.M. on 23 May 1892. The *Argus* published a piece on the execution, dilating on Deeming's restless last night. Deeming made no grand statement before he died. Some observers heard him cry "no," while others claimed he said, "Lord receive my spirit," but most noticed only unintelligible gurgling. In an interview, the clergyman said that Deeming was "the most complex human problem [he] ever attempted to solve."[121]

Deeming was dead, but Marshall Lyle did not give up. The 1894 case of Martha Needle, a bold and profligate killer, gave Lyle yet another chance to argue for sweeping criminal-law reform. Needle was born in 1864, raised by her mother, Mary, and her stepfather, Daniel Foran, a laborer, in Port Adelaide. Her mother was a drunk, and Martha claimed that she had tried to slit her daughter's throat as a child.[122] Detectives could never prove the attempted murder, but they did discover that Foran had been convicted of indecently assaulting his stepdaughter.[123] Martha married Charles Needle when she was seventeen. The couple settled in the Melbourne suburb of Richmond and had three daughters, Mabel, Elsie, and May. Within six years, all three children and Charles were dead, struck by a mysterious illness that caused severe vomiting. Martha took up with a new man. He and his brother moved into her home in Richmond. Soon the brother was dead, another brother was ill, and Martha Needle had been arrested for murder.[124] She had dosed all her victims with "Rough-on-Rats," a commercially available rat poison.[125]

Justice Hodges heard Needle's case. She was under the supervision of Andrew Shields at Melbourne Gaol. Lyle, her solicitor, bombarded the governor, attorney general, and Crown solicitor with letters, memos, and petitions. In a letter to the governor, Lyle described Needle as belonging to the notorious "woman poisoner class," a group of thousands of women known to be insane but put to death anyway by cruel governments.[126] These arguments recalled those Lyle had made about Deeming's instinctive criminality. By the time of Needle's case, however, Lyle had broadened his program of legal reform to include the abolition of capital punishment. In 1894, he had become a special correspondent of the Howard Association for the Prevention of Crime, the British penal reform society dedicated to the modernization of criminal law and penal practices, and committed to abolishing the death penalty.[127] Founded in 1866, the association advocated for "the promotion of the best methods of the Treatment and Prevention of Crime and Pauperism." Lord Brougham, the legal reformer who had led the overhaul of the Judicial Committee decades earlier, headed its first list of patrons.[128] The members of the Howard Association were broadly sympathetic to criminal anthropology, and to the idea that

Martha Needle. Credit: Provincial Records Office of Victoria, VPRS 516, p. 2, vol. 11, p. 409.

criminality was at least partially hereditary and biological. They campaigned for more lenient, reformatory sentencing on the ground that criminals were dangerous, surely, but also sick and deserving of compassion.

Archival records suggest that Lyle had come to his general rejection of capital punishment through his deep discomfort with the insanity defense. The Howard Association, conversely, developed its jaundiced view of legal insanity through its members' interests in broad-based penal reform, including opposition to capital punishment. By the end of the century, the laws surrounding criminal insanity in the British world were in such disarray and disrepute that the association used them to sow more general doubt about the legitimacy of capital punishment. "If public opinion is not yet quite prepared to demand the Abolition of Capital punishment," the author of the association's 1896 Annual Report commented, "there can be no reasonable doubt that the Law of Murder, as relating to Homicidal Insanity, ought to be altered; for its present state is the occasion of scandals."[129] Late-nineteenth-century criminal anthropology—and its suggestion that criminals suffered from biological weaknesses that predisposed them to criminal behavior—cemented the bond between capital punishment and insanity. One former secretary of the Howard Association, William Tallack, described his thoughts as he walked along a hallway, thickly padded to prevent inmates from dashing their heads against the stone walls, in a ward for mentally disturbed prisoners at a London prison. "Supposing I had been born under such defective bodily conditions as these men," he wondered, "and had experienced their subsequent privations and temptations, should not I also have probably committed some act which had brought me, as a felon, instead of a visitor, to this place?"[130]

Lyle took up the Howard Association's position that all criminality, or at least most of it, was caused by a pernicious combination of hereditary weakness and an environment conducive to vice. He had learned from his failures in the Deeming and Colston cases. Convincing the authorities that Needle was insane would not necessarily save her. He even accepted that "there are greater reasons for punishing some of the insane, than the sane," although never for putting anyone to death.[131] And so, Lyle was careful to point out the practical, social benefits of a more scientific approach to criminal insanity, thereby shying away from the purely principled arguments he had made in *Deeming*.[132] In his many letters about Needle, he often mentioned the need for scientific and medical expertise to improve public safety. "We believe," he wrote to the Crown Law Department, "that there can be no successful warfare against crime and criminals, until the principle be recognised that the scientific examination of the dangerous members of society is the duty of the State."[133]

Martha Needle was found guilty of murder and sentenced to death.[134] The sentence was carried out, despite protests from Lyle and other supporters, on 23 October 1894. Her partner, whose brothers had been killed and sickened, was a frequent visitor during her time in jail. Needle went calmly, standing proudly on the trapdoor outside the condemned's cell. One reporter described her as "an inscrutable psychological problem" and a "callous, hardened criminal and a woman of the very worst type."[135] Lyle tried to use the *Colston*, *Deeming*, and *Needle* cases as instruments to advance what he considered to be a humane, scientific, modern approach to the criminal law. He was disappointed. In 1895, he reported to the Howard Association on Australia's continued affection for the death penalty. "The striking fact is," he wrote, "that murders have increased, notwithstanding that the scaffold has been so busy."[136] Lyle was a special correspondent of the association until 1898, after which it seems that his interests finally drifted away from criminal justice.[137]

The debate over *M'Naghten*, illustrated most starkly in contests over the existence of moral insanity, featured an apparent paradox: British civilization seemed to require both fidelity to the common law and the bold embrace of modern scientific truths. Increasingly, responsibility contests suggested that Britain could not do both. Under these circumstances, the *M'Naghten* rules seemed to offer the best—perhaps the only—compromise. Defendants whose mental abnormalities seemed clearly to undermine their ability to understand what the common law required of them could be spared, along with Britain's reputation as a civilized state. At the same time, the rules were narrow enough to preserve the presumption that the vast majority of the law's subjects were sane and subject to judgment, preserving in turn the legitimacy of British criminal law. If scientific determinism and legal liberalism were antinomies, then *M'Naghten*'s flaws could be understood as necessary concessions to the contradictory demands of civilization, rather than errors that could be corrected.

CHAPTER 5

Less Responsible Subjects

In late June 1872, in the town of Warrington, Cheshire, on the Mersey River, Joe Davenport came home late. His wife, Margaret, told him to look upstairs. On the bed were the bodies of his young daughters, Margaret Ann and Elizabeth Jane. Next to the bed, he saw the bucket of water in which his children had drowned. He called for help, and the police soon arrived and arrested Margaret. A newspaper reported that she said, in response to the news that she had been charged with murder, "They are both in Heaven, and I have tried to strangle myself, but I have failed. I have cut both my wrists thinking I should bleed to death; if you will let me sit by this fire, I shall be dead by morning."[1]

"Family troubles" had caused the "extreme mental depression" that deluded Margaret Davenport into thinking that "she had a perfect right to take the lives of her children," according to the governor of the prison where she awaited her trial.[2] A local policeman remembered her as melancholy and friendless, given to reading "religious books." Two years before the killings and shortly after she delivered her youngest child, Davenport had been discovered more than once wandering the streets at night naked or in just a night dress. Her father and grandfather were of "weak intellect," her aunt was in an asylum, and her cousin was also unwell. The policeman suspected that Davenport had been "very much neglected by those whose duty it was to make her home cheerful and happy."[3] When the Liverpool Assizes arrived in August, she was found insane upon arraignment. Soon thereafter, she was transferred to Broadmoor, to remain there at Her Majesty's pleasure.

When she killed her daughters and tried to take her own life, Margaret Davenport was newly pregnant. It is unclear whether she knew it. She gave birth to another daughter, Elizabeth Margaret, at Broadmoor in late February 1873.[4] William Orange and other asylum authorities did not trust Davenport with her child, and the two were housed in separate wards. Margaret's husband, Joe, pled poverty and would not take custody of his daughter. It seems likely that the baby became a ward of her mother's parish, although her fate is uncertain. In 1885, a Broadmoor official noted in a form that Davenport had given birth to five children, of whom four had surely died. In response to a question about the number then living, the official wrote: "One? Baby born here, where is it?"[5] Joe died in 1889. In 1890, "demented, incoherent, incapable of taking care of herself," Margaret was transferred to the Rainhill Asylum, near the village where Frederick Bailey Deeming would kill his wife and children in August of the subsequent year.[6]

Gender was an essential but often unmarked aspect of Victorian concepts of responsible personhood.[7] So, too, was race, with which gendered ideas of responsibility intersected. The middle-class men who made up most of the empire's official and professional castes saw even healthy, white, Protestant Englishwomen as to some extent mentally compromised. These women were considered, as Antoinette Burton writes, "the inferior sex in the superior race."[8] But when it came to matters of the mind, lines between sex and race could blur. Just as the concept of moral insanity drew on ideas about degeneration and racial hierarchy to explain the violence of the supposedly atavistic sufferer, women's violence also seemed to demand a civilizational explanation. Frequent comparisons among the mental capacities of white women, children, and nonwhite peoples could color accounts of female insanity and responsibility with a racial tinge. Like colonial populations and most children, women were not categorically irresponsible under British law. They were, however, a presumptively "less responsible" class, for whom many Victorians believed that legal accommodations ought to be made. The challenge for jurists and other officials was, as always, where to fix the boundary between mental weaknesses that obviated criminal responsibility, justifying mercy, and those that were of no legal consequence. Infanticide cases like Margaret Davenport's tested the limits of women's criminal responsibility and were intimately, if at times obliquely, connected to Victorian efforts to define responsible subjecthood in a diverse empire.

Infanticide, in which a mother killed her own young child, was the most common form of lethal female violence in nineteenth-century Britain. By 1875, more than 80 percent of insanity pleas entered by female defendants were made in response to indictments for assault and murder. Of these violent crimes committed by women, the victim was usually a child.[9] Broadmoor admissions records for the early 1880s, for example, conform roughly to this pattern. In 1880, forty-six men, including Thomas Maltby, were admitted to the hospital, as were sixteen women. Of the new female patients, eight had been charged with murder. Of those eight, six had killed young children. In 1881, of thirteen female patients admitted to Broadmoor, seven had assaulted their own children. In 1882, out of sixteen women, the figure was nine.[10] In the nineteenth century, a defendant accused of infanticide was charged with murder under Anglo law. A separate statutory offense of infanticide, carrying penalties analogous to those for manslaughter, would only be created in the 1922 Infanticide Act.

What could possess a mother to kill? In Margaret Davenport's case, observers identified neglect, heredity, and pregnancy as potential factors. We might also add grief, although legal and medical authorities made little of her losses: two of her children had died before the day on which Davenport killed her remaining daughters. No one expressed any doubt that she was insane, whatever the cause. In cases involving apparently motiveless or disturbing homicides, judges, jurors, and other officials often reached for creative interpretations of insanity. In the context of infanticide, arguments about the defendant's emotional state found traction in ways that would have been inconceivable in moral insanity cases. Judges could sympathize with a woman's despair or shame but were often quicker to condemn a man's rage.[11] When a mother accused of infanticide seemed incontrovertibly sane under *M'Naghten*, the promise of executive review meant that conviction was only the narrowest choke point in a stream of official inquiries into the state of her mind.

Puerperal insanity, also called puerperal fever or puerperal madness, was a medical diagnosis frequently applied to women who became mentally disturbed during pregnancy, childbirth, and the first few months postpartum. Physicians saw the female reproductive system as inherently unstable and changeable, and many believed that it interfered with a woman's rationality, self-control, and emotional equilibrium.[12] Puerperal insanity was the best known of the reproductive disorders. The diagnosis featured prominently in British works on mental disease beginning in the 1830s. James Cowles Prichard, the British ethnologist and alienist, wrote in 1837 that puerperal madness was "by no means infrequent."[13] French physician Étienne Esquirol agreed, attributing one-twelfth of the cases of female insanity treated at the Salpêtrière Hospital in Paris to pregnancy and lactation.[14]

Nineteenth-century mental science strongly associated puerperal insanity with female violence, especially infanticide. In his *Principles and Practice of Medical Jurisprudence*, Alfred Swaine Taylor described the usual course of the illness. "The woman is gay and joyous, laughing, singing, loquacious, inclined to talk obscenely, and careless of everything around. She imagines that her food is poisoned." After hours or days of giddy paranoia, the new mother succumbed to her violent impulses. Some women killed in a "sudden fit of delirium." But others, Taylor wrote, killed their children "with a full knowledge of the wickedness and illegality of the act; so that the legal test of responsibility of a knowledge of right and wrong cannot be applied in such cases."[15] In his view, these women could not satisfy the *M'Naghten* rules. A strict application of the test for legal insanity should have resulted in their conviction for murder.

And yet, Taylor noted that judges and juries regularly found even women who acted with "full knowledge of the wickedness and illegality of the act" legally insane, or else acquitted them outright. At times, this was because defense lawyers argued that puerperal insanity caused cognitive distortions so severe that sufferers could not understand the nature or quality of their actions or that they were wrong, bringing them within the *M'Naghten* criteria. Often, however, defense lawyers worked outside the formal limits of legal insanity, appealing to decision makers' broader sense of how, and why, women went mad. Defense lawyers might claim, for instance, that her puerperal insanity had made it impossible for a woman to resist violent impulses, or that deep despair or fear had overwhelmed her. They might describe their client's psychic pain as insanity as part of a legal strategy (to justify her acquittal on the ground of insanity) and a rhetorical device, but this veneer could be thin. Many infanticidal women were not considered "insane" even by the more elastic standards of mental science or the commonsense understandings of their friends and neighbors. The status of women as innately less responsible subjects who were prone to mental imbalance and emotional disregulation made the verdict that they were legally insane more acceptable, and more likely. An acquittal on the ground of insanity was a crude but effective proxy for the more generalized mental weakness attributed to all women, especially new mothers.

Victorian understandings of motherhood and maternal instinct could also sway jurors toward mercy on the basis that a woman's crime was, itself, her punishment. As Taylor put it, the suffering of a woman who killed her child, "fully aware of the nature of the act, and that it is contrary to the laws of God and man," was sufficient; the law should add no more.[16] Evidence that a woman had doted on her infant and prepared to care for it before the killing suggested that the crime was the result of a momentary perversion or a malfunction in a mother's delicate organism. This emphasis on an infanticidal woman's tragic love for her child was notably muted in cases against women who killed the children of strangers, employers, or clients. The lower-class women who operated the infamous late-Victorian "baby farms," where poor women left their babies in often dangerous group care settings, were particularly reviled.[17] The sympathy accorded to infanticidal women was thus conditional on their adherence to Victorian visions of feminine vulnerability, and on the pain the crime itself inflicted on them. Women whose violence seemed to be motivated not by despair, fear, or trauma but by cupidity or anger transgressed against both femininity and the law. They would be punished.

Female criminals appeared more frequently in the records of eighteenth-century English courts than in those of later centuries. Scholars have argued that this reflected the steady retreat of female deviance from the purview of the criminal courts. Women became less likely to be viewed as the authors of their own violent acts, for which they were subject to punishment and moral condemnation. Instead, a medicalized, biological model of female deviance presumed women's diminished responsibility, and justified their diversion to hospitals and reformatories rather than prisons.[18] Some commentators estimate that in the early-eighteenth century, women composed between 30 percent and 45 percent of those indicted at London's Old Bailey before falling to below 10 percent by 1895, a rate that has held steady ever since.[19] Even though women were a minority among convicted criminals, they represented a sizable proportion of killers: one scholar estimates that women made up 40 percent of all those tried for murder in England.[20] Near the end of the century, official statistical records began to break murders down by the age of the victim. Infanticide had come to be seen as an offense apart, with a distinct, and distinctly feminine, offender profile. Women were indicted for less than 25 percent of murders where the victim was over the age of one but made up nearly all of those tried for the murder of victims aged under a year.[21]

As women's criminal responsibility seemed to shrink, their imagined propensity to insanity—the clearest medical indication of irresponsibility—grew.

Elaine Showalter argues that insanity mutated, in popular consciousness, from a male disease into an aspect of the female condition between the eighteenth century and the end of the nineteenth.[22] Nineteenth-century English women were twice as likely as men to be acquitted on the ground of insanity, even when their crimes were the same.[23] By the 1850s, women outnumbered men in the English asylum population, although most inmates in Victorian criminal asylums were male.[24] Female killers were unlikely to be executed even if they were convicted. Between 1800 and 1899 in England and Wales, 172 women were executed, compared with 3,365 men. Female killers were far more likely to find themselves subject to indefinite detention in criminal asylums than condemned to death, especially after 1870.[25]

In the second half of the nineteenth century, Britons across the empire claimed to have detected an increase in the incidence of infanticide. In one 1851 letter to the editor of a London newspaper, the author decried the "horrible and too prevalent crime of infanticide," which had become "the stain of our country."[26] In 1857, the same paper ran an essay warning, "Infanticide . . . has become so stereotyped a fact in the annals of crime that our sensibilities have grown deadened by its frequency."[27] An 1862 article summarizing a physician's comments during an infanticide trial described the crime as "so common . . . that the police seemed to think no more of finding a dead child than they did of finding a dead cat or a dead dog."[28] Countless pieces in this vein expressed Victorians' fear that infanticide was, as Anne-Marie Kilday writes, "spreading like a contagion."[29] The press, with the cooperation of medical experts, fed a "moral panic" so widespread and profound that many came to see infanticide as "the greatest social evil of the Victorian era."[30]

Some blamed the apparent spike in infanticide on overcrowding in urban slums, poverty, women's employment, alcohol, Catholicism, and male violence, among other factors.[31] Modern, city life, in particular, seemed to loosen the communal bonds that supposedly discouraged infanticide, and its associated sexual impropriety, in smaller towns and villages. Anonymity facilitated vice and violence in London and other metropolises, where young men and women had only to "turn the next street corner to become a particle in an ocean of unknown human beings," in the words of one writer in 1863.[32]

Other commentators instead offered civilizational explanations. One strand blamed degeneration and an increase in "barbarism" among the British public. The process of degeneration had been accelerated, according to some, by the cultural and racial contamination inherent in imperial governance.[33] India had long been considered a hotbed of infanticide, especially against infant girls. East India Company officials were at times praised for their efforts to stamp out the practice among Indian communities accused of being "addicted to infanticide."[34] Others, in contrast, excoriated the Company for having "prop[ped] up heathenism" and ignored child killing to avoid conflict with colonial populations and to protect revenues.[35] After the 1857 Rebellion and the advent of Crown rule in India, some anticipated that direct governance of the subcontinent would lead to more interventionist anti-infanticide policies. But others predicted that closer ties to India would lead to the "Indianizing" of British society (what this entailed was generally opaque), worsening the epidemic of child killing in Britain itself.[36]

Another version of the civilizational argument held that the growth of infanticide was, in contrast, "the chief and most terrible" consequence of the civilizing process. One writer for the London *Era* wrote in 1857, "The crime of child murder may be said to be indigenous to a state of refinement and luxury."[37] The refinement he objected to most was the "vast and most injurious amount of false sentiment and unjustified compassion" that judges heaped upon women who did not deserve their "unhealthy pity." The bourgeois sentimentalism of judges and other officials was a symptom of modern decadence, which had led to impunity for those "heartless parents" who killed their children "with no more compunction than they would have served a dead cat."[38] Another *Era* article, published in 1863, took up the theme: "Smiles on the face and murder in the heart, and this is the state of society to which a high degree of civilisation and morbid philanthropy have reduced the people of England."[39]

The 1861 Offences Against the Person Act was the last major overhaul of British legislation governing child killing of the nineteenth century. The act criminalized the abandonment of children under the age of two, and also extended the scope of existing prohibitions against procuring abortions or miscarriages and against concealing the birth of a child.[40] Nineteenth-century women suspected of infanticide were often indicted on charges of concealment. The offense was easier to prove and carried a moderate two-year maximum sentence, often more palatable to judges and jurors than a murder conviction. In her analysis of trends in indictments and convictions for both infanticide and concealment, Kilday notes a sharp peak in the early 1860s, coinciding with the height of the panic. Given the secret nature of infanticide and related crimes and the fact that the registration of births was not mandatory before 1874, we cannot know whether this rise was due to more aggressive reporting, investigation, and prosecution of child killing, or whether it represented a genuine increase in the number of children killed in England and Wales.[41]

Victorian judges were accustomed to attributing female violence to the workings of powerful biological forces, at least in part. Therefore, late-nineteenth-century theories of racial and civilizational decline did not threaten fundamentally to alter women's existing status as less responsible subjects. White men as a class had more to fear from degeneration, which proposed that they, too, were potential victims of inherited mental unsoundness.[42] Controversies over the responsibility of male defendants in homicide cases tapped into this fear. Judges and jurors in the British world represented the ideal subject, both legally and politically. They were, by their own reckoning, educated, industrious, temperate, and independent. The more a defendant resembled this ideal, the easier it was for judges to imagine themselves in the prisoner's box. In assessing the sanity of men like themselves, judges confronted the precariousness of their own psychic equilibrium.[43]

Women were different. Already marked as psychologically and physically distinct from the men who judged them, their alleged insanity did not appear to redound on responsible subjecthood in general. To recall, responsibility cases were "typical exceptions": relatively infrequent but at the same time familiar, regular episodes in the course of criminal justice. Female defendants in such cases were, themselves, also "typical exceptions." Their violence placed them outside the bounds of female propriety, but the mental weakness and emotional febrility that seemed to provoke it were accepted aspects of normal womanhood. Therefore, when officials considered how to respond to homicidal women who killed without an appreciably rational motive, they made decisions more freely and with greater confidence. They believed that they could restrict the consequences of any "exceptional" verdicts to "exceptional" (female) defendants, thus preventing the erosion of responsibility that other cases, including moral insanity cases, seemed to portend.

To British jurists, women were therefore a special class, but they were not an entirely distinct one. Victorian medico-legal understandings of gender and sexual difference drew on the evolutionary theories that informed many popular accounts of race and civilizational hierarchy. Theorists regularly analogized female brains and those of "uncivilized" people, speculating that they were similarly underdeveloped and deficient. Insanity among women, both white and nonwhite, was a deviation from an already compromised norm. Accused mothers in infanticide cases were presumed to be less competent than the average male defendant before the question of their sanity was ever mooted. The core problem in such cases was to establish the degree of mental impairment of the accused and the appropriate legal consequences of her actions. While the idea that male sanity should be understood as a continuum, not a binary, was controversial in some circles, Victorian medical and legal accounts of the female psyche embraced the idea of female sanity as a spectrum. In the same way, and often in reference to the same biological and evolutionary processes, mainstream Victorian thought situated the nonwhite peoples of the British Empire along a civilizational continuum, with direct consequences for how colonial officials formulated their responsibility.

Victorian understandings of incompetence were a tangle of ambiguous, often internally contradictory ideas of the influence of gender, race, and age on human mental states. Consider, for example, the adage "ontogeny recapitulates phylogeny," closely associated with German scientist Ernst Haeckel, who formulated the principle in 1866. Individual organisms, Haeckel argued, developed by recapitulating the evolutionary stages previously undergone by their species.[44] In this view, a human fetus resembled humanity's ancient ancestors, while a mature adult assumed evolution's peak form. This understanding of evolution made primitivism and immaturity homologous. Primitive societies were underdeveloped—from a "civilized" perspective, literally juvenile—as were the psyches of supposedly primitive individuals. Indeed, writers and administrators described colonized peoples across the globe as perpetual children in need of imperial stewardship. The ubiquity of British references to the "Mother Country" fostering its "infant colonies" shows the power of the metaphor.[45]

Recapitulation offered a pithy explanation for what many believed ethnological and medical evidence revealed about the resemblances among women, children, and "savage" peoples.[46] In his account of human sex difference in his 1871 *Descent of Man*, Charles Darwin wrote that in women "the powers of intuition, of rapid perception, and perhaps of imitation, are more strongly marked than in man; but some, at least, of these faculties are characteristic of the lower races, and therefore of a past and lower state of civilisation."[47] Women physically resembled children, Darwin observed, and the formation of their skulls was "intermediate between the child and the man."[48] Victorian approaches to women's responsibility thus both echoed and rehearsed colonial authorities' configuration of the responsibility of Britain's racialized subject populations.

Women were childish, but not children, or at least not for long. Many nineteenth-century scientists noted that women reached puberty at a younger age than men did, a process that some claimed occurred even earlier among nonwhite women. One British physician, reflecting conventional wisdom, argued in 1893 that Indian girls reached sexual maturity at the age of only eleven.[49] The imagined precocious puberty of women and nonwhite peoples did not, however, imply the earlier onset of competent adulthood. In fact, many theorists imagined that precocity resulted in arrested development. Women's smaller stature, higher voices, and inability to grow a beard signaled their perpetual adolescence and their diminished access to the rationality and emotional moderation of adulthood.[50]

Interestingly, and in tension with recapitulation theory, colonial populations tended to be subject to both Victorian fantasies of immaturity and early, or even innate, senility. In 1872, J. Russell Reynolds, a London-based physician, defined "softening of the brain" as "a disease characterized during life by impairment of mind, sensibility, and motility, and after death by diminished consistence and degeneration of the cerebral substance." The condition was, he wrote, "essentially a manifestation of decay," brought about by advanced age.[51] This process of mental putrefaction accelerated in warm climates, where it was correlated with general physiological and moral decline.[52] Anthropologist Lawrence Cohen argues that in the nineteenth century colonial officials saw Indian minds as "naturally soft" and "in a sense congenitally senile."[53] Victorian racial understandings of aging and mental incompetence varied by colony and within colonial populations. For example, C. J. O'Donnell, the superintendent of the 1891 Bengal census, wrote that the "Negritic races" of India were remarkable for their "abundant fecundity" and their "singular short-livedness." Castes higher in the social and civilizational hierarchy displayed the opposite pattern. "As their position is higher in the social scale," he wrote, "they progress in length of years and decline in number of offspring."[54]

The consequences of these intertwined ideas about female and colonial incompetence for criminal responsibility were multifaceted. For some crimes, the deviation of women and racialized people from the white, male, responsible ideal mediated against responsibility. In infanticide cases, the presumption of female mental weakness could justify more lenient legal treatment, either in the form of acquittals on the ground of insanity or, more often, in lighter sentences or commutations. This was especially true in cases where women, mentally fragile at the baseline, were judged also to be mentally ill. Likewise, cultural-defense cases, as later chapters show, could induce legal authorities to accept natural or innate incompetence, rather than disease, as a mitigating factor in determining fault and calibrating punishment.

Neither common-law jurisprudence nor British political philosophy, however, countenanced a world where all women and all nonwhite men were categorically irresponsible and immune from the jurisdiction of criminal justice. Like adolescents, criminal defendants who deviated from the responsible ideal occupied a liminal space. They were less competent, certainly, but were they genuinely *in*competent? Although the analogy to adolescence sometimes broke down, as in the context of colonial senility, it is useful for understanding how women fared in criminal courts. Adolescents, eventually "juvenile delinquents," were subject to criminal prosecution and punishment, but their susceptibility to outside influence and their mental and moral underdevelopment urged mercy and promised the possibility of reform.[55] Similarly, as Victorian visions of gender calcified, women's physical and mental vulnerability came to justify lower sentences, fewer executions, less corporal punishment, and the diversion of "wayward" women from traditional prisons to reforming institutions and hospitals.[56] Women, like adolescents, were often, as one historian puts it, "more sinned against than sinning."[57]

Criminal anthropology adapted the biological insights of ethnology and Darwinian natural science for use in criminal justice. No book on female criminality was more influential than Cesare Lombroso's *La donna delinquente* (*The Criminal Woman*), first published in Italian in 1893 and translated into English in 1895. Although Lombroso had earlier published *L'uomo criminale* (*The Criminal Man*) in 1876 and it filtered into British understandings of biological criminality, his theories competed with those of other British and European thinkers such as Ellis, Galton, Spencer, and Krafft-Ebing. In fact, *Criminal Man* did not appear in English translation until 1911.[58] *The Criminal Woman*, in contrast, served as a core text on female criminality in the West until the 1970s.[59] In the book, which in the original Italian edition stretches to almost seven hundred pages, Lombroso used statistical analyses of the anatomy and appearance of large populations of both "normal" and "criminal" women to build a theory of female degeneration and instinctive criminality. He subdivided female criminals into a variety of types, including the murderer, the poisoner, the arsonist, the infanticidal woman, and the prostitute. Lombroso was perturbed by the female "born criminal"—a subcategory of especially violent, perverse women who lacked moral sentiments and displayed male sexual characteristics, especially a selfish and reckless eroticism. Women were like children, he wrote, "deficient in the moral sense; and . . . vengeful, jealous, and inclined to refined cruelty when they take revenge." Normally, these traits were counterbalanced by women's "piety, maternity, sexual coldness, physical weakness, and undeveloped intelligence." When these traditionally feminine qualities were absent or weak, Lombroso argued that women became virilized—masculine in appearance, intelligence, and propensity to violence.[60]

For Lombroso, even women who were not "born criminals" were immature and lacking in moral sense. Poverty, heartbreak, exhaustion, or other stresses could bring on episodes of madness, including some that culminated in child murder. In his view, infanticide was often a crime of passion, which women committed to avoid the stigma of illegitimate motherhood or under pressure by dishonorable men. It was a crime "caused by public opinion and prejudice" rather than the mother's moral perversity.[61] Infanticide was shocking but ultimately comprehensible, and often excusable. Infanticidal women were victims of biology and male cruelty, as the next case, that of Irish immigrant and domestic servant Mary Fitzgerald, illustrates.

Mary Fitzgerald left County Kerry, Ireland, for Victoria in 1885.[62] She moved to the countryside, where a series of farmers hired her to cook and clean. She rarely stayed with a family long, never for more than two years. While most of her employers described her as industrious and upright, they also thought she was "peculiar," "nervous," or of "weak intellect." Her briefest placement ended after only two weeks. Her employer, a small-town draper, criticized her incompetent cooking, including an attempt to roast corned beef, which he attributed to her "vacant manner" and "wandering in her mind."[63] Another man remembered driving Fitzgerald to the doctor when she claimed that she had accidentally swallowed a pin, only to discover it later in her room. Another said that she experienced severe "fits" during which she "appeared as if out of her mind and raving," sometimes as often as fourteen times a day. A local doctor diagnosed her with hysteria and dysmenorrhea, acute menstrual pain, for which he prescribed large doses of bromide, a popular sedative and anticonvulsant.[64] In the twentieth century, Western physicians would abandon bromides due to the high risk of patients' developing bromism, a syndrome that can cause psychosis, hallucinations, confusion, disinhibition, and other mental abnormalities, in addition to physical symptoms.[65] The drug may have had some role in what was to come.

In 1892, Fitzgerald had been working for a year in rural Craigieburn. Her employer, Margaret Patullo, was pleased with her work, including her "plain cooking." Fitzgerald, Patullo said, was "not at all stupid."[66] That May, however, Patullo accused her of concealing an illegitimate pregnancy. Fitzgerald burst into tears and admitted "it was all her fault." Patullo agreed to keep her on until she gave birth and to hire her back after the baby arrived.[67] In September, Fitzgerald collected her pay and left Craigieburn.

On a rainy night in early September, she knocked on an old friend's door in the nearby town of Benalla. Jane Sergeant had not heard from Fitzgerald in more than a year, but she quickly made up a pallet for her husband, Richard, in the shed. She and Mary, both heavily pregnant, squeezed into Jane's bed. Mary related that she had been abandoned by an abusive husband and claimed to be only six months along. Jane was skeptical, and indeed Mary gave birth to a healthy son just a week later. She bathed and nursed him tenderly, and accepted gifts of swaddling clothes and napkins from Jane and Richard. After three weeks, she asked Richard to drive her to town, announcing her plan to catch the next morning's early train to Beechworth, where she hoped to find a new situation. She was very quiet on the road. She carried two bundles, one her baby wrapped in calico, and the other, clothes and necessities.[68] On the morning of 30 September, Fitzgerald, wearing a dark dress and black hat adorned with flowers, boarded a train, carrying only one bundle. Late that night, she arrived at her former employer Margaret Patullo's house in Craigieburn. She told her that the baby had died.

Two days later, a teenaged boy was gathering wildflowers in a paddock in Benalla. He stumbled upon a small hole filled with nine inches of water. A baby, so perfect that the boy thought it might be a "wax doll," lay in the hole, its knees breaking the surface of the still pool.[69] When police came to collect the child's body, they found a woman's footprints in the mud and some pieces of white cloth strewn nearby. A local doctor who noticed that the baby had a small depression on his left temple remembered using forceps to deliver an infant boy at Jane and Richard Sergeant's home three weeks before.[70] Suspicion quickly settled on Mary Fitzgerald. Within a week, Margaret Patullo read newspaper reports on the baby's death and the search for his mother. Perhaps in a final act of kindness, Patullo allowed Fitzgerald, weeping, to leave her house before alerting the authorities. But Fitzgerald did not get far. Police arrested her on 18 October in the Melbourne city center. On the way to jail, the arresting officer said, "Well you know you have a child and I know where it is," to which Fitzgerald replied, "If you know where it is what do you want to ask me about it for[?]"[71]

Fitzgerald was tried for murder at the Benalla assizes on 15 November 1892 before Justice Joseph Henry Hood of the Supreme Court of Victoria. No experts in mental science participated in the trial. This alone was not determinative. As other cases described in this book show, medical understandings of insanity and responsibility could influence jurors and inspire judges even in the absence of expert medical testimony. Infanticide readily evoked widespread beliefs in the destabilizing effects of childbirth and nursing on women's minds.[72] In this case, however, a lack of evidence of insanity may have hurt Fitzgerald's fortunes. After deliberating for two hours, the jury found Fitzgerald guilty of murder. In a concession to her misery, they recommended that the Executive Council spare her life "on account of her feelings at the time the crime was committed."[73] The lawyer for Fitzgerald, Thomas Windsor, complained that he had been assigned her case only a week before the trial, and that several witnesses who could have testified to her "weak intellect" had not appeared in court. In letters he sent after her conviction, Windsor argued that she had been "so overwrought, perplexed and frensied [*sic*]" on the morning of the killing that she was "morally unaccountable" for her actions. She had made no effort to conceal her crime and had returned, Windsor believed, "by force of habit" to Patullo's house—proof of a "want of directing power in the mind."[74]

Perhaps Fitzgerald was indeed "not herself" when she drowned her child and returned, like a migrating bird, to her former employer's home. Alfred Swaine Taylor and other medico-legal experts often framed puerperal mania as a disorder of the will that produced a sudden, irresistible impulse to kill. Windsor's account of Mary's behavior draws on this characterization and a related one, which Joel Eigen describes as "unconsciousness" or a disruption in the "forensic assumption that the person is 'continuous.'" Witnesses' descriptions of Fitzgerald as "vacant," coupled with a "want of directing power in the mind," could represent the cruel semiconsciousness that Taylor described as sufficient punishment for infanticide. This form of "'overridden' consciousness," in Eigen's phrase, produced tender mothers fully aware of the violence they did to their children but powerless to stop it.[75] Hood, the judge, took a less psychiatric view of the case, but agreed that Fitzgerald deserved mercy. He wrote that she had been "feebly defended," and that she was "young ignorant and stupid and apparently deserted in her trouble by all."[76]

The Benalla branch of the Woman's Christian Temperance Union (WCTU) sent a petition to the Earl of Hopetoun, the governor of Victoria, requesting mercy in Fitzgerald's case. By the end of the nineteenth century, the WCTU, founded in the 1870s in the United States, had grown into a global network of Christian, evangelical, woman-led reform societies. Victorian chapters adopted a broad welfare agenda, campaigning for liquor control, better conditions for laborers, and female suffrage.[77] Like their counterparts in

Britain and America, Australian WCTU activists advocated "social purity"—a single, stringent standard of sexual morality applicable to both men and women—and tended to see infanticide, like abortion, as a product of male sexual aggression rather than female wickedness.[78]

Fitzgerald's plight attracted their attention. She was, they wrote, an "unfortunate prisoner" abandoned by her seducer, who had "put an end to a life in a fit of despair and when in a state of madness." WCTU chapters around the world were renowned for their massive petitioning campaigns.[79] True to form, the Benalla WCTU's petition garnered 733 signatures in only three days.[80] Victoria's Executive Council commuted Fitzgerald's death sentence to three years' hard labor. A Benalla newspaper congratulated the members of the WCTU on their success.[81]

Mary Fitzgerald fitted neatly into nineteenth-century understandings of the infanticidal woman. She was an unmarried domestic servant, far from friends, family, and homeland. Moreover, she was Irish. Scholars have noted the long-standing English vision of the Irish as pathologically infanticidal, the target of Jonathan Swift's famous satire, *A Modest Proposal* (1729). Swift proposed that the solution to poverty and overpopulation in Ireland was to kill and eat Irish babies. Swift's black joke skewered English callousness and Irish fecundity, echoing the popular theory that Irish Catholics' reproductive patterns drove the economic and moral degradation of the nation. The trope of Irish infanticide reemerged in late-Victorian imperial discourse alongside allegations that colonial populations—in Ireland, India, and elsewhere—had a malign influence on British civilization at home and abroad.[82]

Discourses of colonial inferiority, including an innate proclivity to infanticide, followed working-class Irish women like Mary Fitzgerald across the world. Large numbers of Irish immigrants traveled to colonial Australia in the nineteenth century, first as transported convicts, then as subsidized migrants dispatched to increase free-settler numbers, and later as fortune seekers drawn by the mid-century gold rushes. Most settled in the eastern colonies of Victoria and New South Wales. While fewer Irish immigrants struck out for the Australian colonies than for the United States or Britain in the nineteenth century, they made up a larger share of the total settler population. At the time of Australian federation in 1901, approximately a quarter of white Australians were Irish born or of Irish descent.[83] Some Irish migrants were middle-class professionals, including a substantial population of lawyers chasing economic opportunity and political influence, but most were single men and women from rural areas. Young, unmarried women formed the majority of late-nineteenth-century Irish emigrants, especially from the western counties, including Mary Fitzgerald's native Kerry.[84] Most migrants to Australia were Catholic and, like Fitzgerald, sought work and fellowship in farm communities and country towns.[85]

English suspicion of Irish Catholics dovetailed with pan-imperial concerns about apparently high rates of madness among the Irish, in Ireland as well as in the diaspora. The middle of the nineteenth century saw a rapid expansion of the public, or pauper, lunatic asylum system in Ireland, with the construction of twenty-two new institutions. These included the Central Criminal Lunatic Asylum at Dundrum in Dublin, opened in 1850 in the wake of the devastating Great Famine of 1845–1849. High mortality and emigration rates during and after the famine, as well as changes to the system of land inheritance, produced social and economic upheaval. The Irish Dangerous Lunatics Act of 1838 empowered justices of the peace to consign anyone suspected of mental unsoundness and criminal intention to detention in an asylum, with few procedural safeguards.[86] Admissions to Irish asylums soared.

In a widely read article published in 1894 in the *Journal of Mental Science*, Thomas Drapes, the superintendent of the district asylum at Enniscorthy, reflected on the apparent increase in insanity in Ireland. Drapes mooted many possible causes but settled on a civilizational narrative that emphasized colonial Ireland's inability to adapt to nineteenth-century conditions. He speculated that even the humble "plodding peasantry" of Ireland suffered from the "stress of modern life." As Irish farmers were outcompeted in an increasingly globalized market for agricultural goods, "great depression" set in. Ireland's backwardness was not only economic but also racial. The "quick-witted, passionate, versatile, and vivacious Celt," a "naturally emotional race," was prone to mental instability and emotional excess.[87]

The Irish peasants of the imperial diaspora had launched themselves into the volatile modernity to which Drapes and others believed they were constitutionally unsuited. The poverty and social dislocation many had fled continued in their new homes. Frederick Norton Manning, a prominent nineteenth-century Australian alienist, estimated that the asylum population of Victoria in 1887 was 25 percent Irish born, with Irish women representing 29 percent of female asylum inmates. According to the 1891 census, Victoria had the highest proportion of Irish-born immigrants in Australia—38 percent—and the highest rate of committals to psychiatric institutions.[88]

Some explicitly associated failed experiments in imperial migration with rising insanity rates in Ireland. From the mid-1870s to the mid-1890s, Irish emigration was highest from County Kerry, Mary Fitzgerald's birthplace. Daniel Hack Tuke, the English alienist, considered the poverty of the region, with its high eviction rates and small, unproductive farms, to be the primary cause of the disproportionate levels of both emigration and insanity there. He also guessed that one-time emigrants were returning home "mental wrecks" after unsuccessful ventures overseas, worsening domestic poverty and overburdening public asylums.[89] Ireland was a benighted colony, degraded further by its population's intercourse with the wider empire. Scholars dispute why, exactly, so many Irish immigrants found themselves in Australian asylums.[90] The clear association of Irish women with insanity, however, likely helped to convince the Executive Council to spare Mary Fitzgerald's life.

Windsor, Fitzgerald's lawyer, drew on medical and medico-legal discourses of the weakness of the female psyche, particularly of women's self-control, in the weeks after birth. He did not explicitly describe his client as "insane" but instead presented her violence as habitual, unconscious, and unthinking. Judge Hood, conversely, presented Fitzgerald as pathetic and desperate. She was not an automaton but a miserable young woman, badly mistreated by the man who had used and abandoned her. The fact that she had left her child to drown in a secluded but well-trafficked field revealed her low intelligence, not madness or a disordered will. For the petitioners of the WCTU, meanwhile, the crime Fitzgerald had committed was born of despair and madness. Male cruelty had upset her mind and broken her heart, leading directly to her baby's death.

This ambiguity among her advocates about the state of her mind reflected Victorian approaches to infanticide and women's culpability. Infanticide defenses in eighteenth- and nineteenth-century British trials relied heavily on the evocation of women's suffering and emotional distress. The agony of childbirth, for example, provided a ready explanation for women's violence, making infanticide intelligible and marking it as a distinctively female crime.[91] Dana Rabin writes that infanticide trials were opportunities for middle-class judges and jurors to display their "awareness of working-class pain and the acceptance of the subjectivity of the poor."[92] Pity for poor mothers and scorn for the men, whether rich or poor, who had exploited them revealed a refined social conscience. At a time when "sensibility"—the capacity for empathy and deep feeling, especially in response to suffering—was a mark of refinement, infanticide cases such as Fitzgerald's attracted exaggerated expressions of compassion and sentiment.

Of course, legal and medical officials' sympathy for infanticidal mothers did not expunge the horror of their violence. The deaths of infants and children at their mothers' hands continued to shock the Victorian conscience, and to devastate those left behind. Even if infanticidal patients recovered their sanity, as many did, the pain of their crimes endured. Broadmoor patient Sarah Allen's case, for example, captures the ambivalence infanticidal mothers encountered upon their release. Allen, the wife of a river-steamer captain, tried to drown her three young children in the Thames in 1855. One, her eleven-month-old son, survived. Doctors believed that "over lactation" had caused her to believe that "all of her children were in a serious diseased condition." She was found not guilty on the ground of insanity and delivered to Bethlem in 1856.[93] Later, she was among the first cohorts of criminal patients to be transferred from Bethlem to Broadmoor, in 1863.

For more than a decade, her carers described Allen as intermittently violent and mentally disordered. By the early 1870s, Broadmoor authorities had declared her sane and were ready to discharge her. Despite the entreaties of asylum staff, however, her husband, William B. Allen, would not accept Sarah into his custody, and refused to do anything else to facilitate her release.[94] One physician who interviewed him reported that William "should feel that his life was not safe from her" if she were to be released, and that she "spoke and looked when he last saw her exactly as she had done . . . on the day when she threw her three children into the water." Their only living son had a nervous disposition, and William feared that Sarah's release would "have a bad effect upon his mind."[95] Despite pressure from asylum authorities, William held firm. "It is miserable enough for me to know that she is confined," he wrote, "but my life would be unendurable if I knew that my son or myself might at any moment be another victim to her resentment."[96] Asylum staff kept up their campaign throughout the summer of 1872, even forwarding William letters from Sarah in which she begged for his support. By July, he was miserable. He grieved for his wife but could not help her. He tried, he wrote, "to be resigned under the heavy load which has destroyed the whole happiness and comfort of my life. But I have done my feeble utmost for my unfortunate wife, and I must humbly leave the issue to the maker of us all."[97] Ultimately, Sarah Allen was discharged into the care of her sister in late August 1872. Three days after she left Broadmoor, she sent Orange a note in which she reported, "I am quite well free from my old complaints I hope you will excuse this as I am going out shopping they want me to look very nice [*sic*]."[98] Medical and legal officials could declare patients responsible or irresponsible, sane or insane. Medico-legal experts could not, in many cases, dictate how the friends and relatives of prisoners and patients understood their violence, or their guilt.

Pity was powerful in infanticide cases, but misery alone could not formally justify an acquittal. As in instances where the *M'Naghten* criteria seemed to preclude lenience in court, jurors, lawyers, and judges often relied on executive authorities to weigh sentiment and circumstance in their review of a defendant's sentence. When the jury recommended mercy for Mary Fitzgerald "on account of her feelings," the question of whether emotion or insanity inspired her crime became irrelevant.[99] Sadness, too, had a script. Fitzgerald had no husband, but she was not as poor or friendless as many reports suggested. Margaret Patullo, her employer, agreed to keep her on despite her illegitimate pregnancy, exposing herself to the risk of social censure. Jane Sergeant, who would nearly die of blood loss during her own confinement shortly after Mary's, welcomed Mary into her home and cared for her through the end of her pregnancy and her son's first weeks. Many of her former employers sent their own petition to Hopetoun in which they described her as "an honest industrious girl of good character but of weak intellect" who was "not in her right mind" when she killed her child.[100] Perhaps Fitzgerald's identity—as a woman, as Irish, and as an unmarried, working-class migrant—obscured these kindnesses and contributed to the success of her request for a commutation. Her supporters were able to portray her as lonely and wretched, even as she had cradled her child in her friend's bed.

Violent women, especially infanticidal mothers, struck many Victorians as sick and sad, not hateful. There was greater diversity in the interpretation of male violence. Most white men, even men who were poor and marginal, were presumed to be masters of their fates. In cases where fathers killed their children, though, the presumption of male responsibility was unusually fragile. Filicidal fathers benefited from some of the same flexibility that judges and jurors showed in cases involving mothers. For example, Victorian concepts of masculinity and fatherhood could excuse paternal violence through reference to intense suffering, especially shame, and could also portray a child's death as sufficient, self-inflicted penance.

Case records from across the British Empire indicate that doctors and lawyers often assumed that men whose victims included only their children and, sometimes, their wives, were insane. This was not always true, as the convictions of Frederick Deeming and Lakshman Dagdu, who killed his two young daughters while he was feverish and with whose story this book began, show. Still, many male defendants persuaded jurors and officials to be merciful with stories of personal tragedy and terrible loss. If they were acquitted on the ground of insanity, fathers who killed their children faced shorter terms in mental hospitals and were more likely to be released than other men deemed criminally insane. In a study of Broadmoor, Jade Shepherd analyzed the cases of eighty-five "paternal child-murderers" committed to the asylum between 1868 and 1900. These men were more than three times more likely to be discharged from the asylum, after an average confinement of eleven years, than the average male patient. This relative leniency stemmed from the patients' status as bereaved fathers. While 71 percent of male Broadmoor patients who killed children not their own died in confinement, only 45 percent of men who killed their own children lost their freedom permanently.[101]

Like mothers, fathers who killed their children and pled insanity were expected to conform to a narrative of paternal despair. Defense lawyers and sympathetic witnesses described fathers as affectionate, sober, and kind, desperate to protect and provide for their families. Looming destitution, the death of a spouse, or the prospect of losing custody of the children led some fathers to the "terrible paradox" of killing a child in order to protect it.[102] In such cases, men killed in a daze, often waiting patiently for their arrest or presenting themselves, either dreamy and vacant or utterly distraught, at police stations. Men who killed in anger, in public, or for an ignoble motive—such as to conceal an adulterous affair—were more likely to be excluded from the class of violent fathers who could be labeled mad.

Physicians and laypeople described parental killers in psychiatric terms similar to those applied to the morally insane, whose sudden violence was a result of impaired self-control and emotional perversion. Love and suffering were the bright lines between these populations. Parents who killed out of love or because they experienced suffering—whether pursuant to childbirth, heartbreak, or financial ruin—were not threats to the public. Their violence was private, contained within the family. Their crime was its own punishment. The morally insane, motivated not by pain but by jealousy, rage, or even whimsy, were unpredictable and unrepentant. In both kinds of case, legal responsibility hinged not on the degree of the defendant's mental disorder but on its emotional quality.

Gender complicated responsibility in ways that were most visible in cases involving parental child killing. These cases underscore the capaciousness of irresponsibility, and its sensitivity to circumstance. While *M'Naghten* apparently held firm against its many critics, judges, jurors, physicians, and members of the public interpreted legal insanity broadly in individual cases. Many subjects of British law, at home and in the empire, fell short of the autonomous, liberal ideal while apparently satisfying the law's minimum threshold for criminal responsibility.[103] Gender, race, character, emotion, or even luck dictated how persons in this middle space, between manifest insanity and full mental capacity, would be judged. While female defendants in homicide cases were more likely to be found insane either at trial or after, some women—like the Australian poisoner Martha Needle—still died for their crimes. Likewise, masculinity did not necessarily imply responsibility or imperviousness to excesses of sentiment. The nature of the crime was also paramount, not just the identity of the accused. Familial violence did not seem to demand the intervention of the state with the same urgency that extra-familial killings did. In these cases of domestic homicide, public officials retreated from *M'Naghten*, and both mothers and fathers could argue that desperation diminished their responsibility.

Although *M'Naghten* defined insanity narrowly, women and men who killed their children were often held to different, more flexible standards and were treated with compassion by the institutions of British criminal justice on the basis of their mental anguish. Legal authorities reassured themselves that flexibility in such cases merely proved the rule—that in all but exceptional circumstances, responsibility ordered criminal justice in the British world. But could the expansive approach to irresponsibility practiced so openly in child-murder cases truly be contained? Even if British and imperial authorities declined to admit it, arguments about the mental weaknesses of white, British women chimed with arguments about the backwardness of Indigenous peoples, which sounded in unexpected ways in Britain and beyond.

CHAPTER 6

The Infanticidal Imperative

While searching for a lost goat, a man found a little girl's body floating in an abandoned well. The girl's mother, identified in colonial case records as Mussumat (roughly, "Mrs.") Neemia, and grandmother had reported her missing the previous afternoon.[1] The family, members of a humble agricultural caste, lived in a village in the Nerbudda valley in colonial India. Neemia shared a house with her husband, her three-year-old daughter and her month-old infant, her mother-in-law, her brother-in-law, and a niece.[2]

Neemia quickly confessed. She told village leaders and police that shortly before dawn she had been seized with the notion that she should throw her older child into the well because "it was written in her destiny" and "God put it in her head."[3] She confessed again the next night. Three days later, she retracted her confession, claiming that she had been bewildered by grief. Instead, she said the death was an accident. The well was on the road to the nearby *mowha* fields, where Neemia and her family spent long days picking flowers. It was unprotected by a barrier, making it potentially deadly to a child wandering at night.

At Neemia's trial for murder in December 1851 at the Court of Sessions for Saugor and Nerbudda Territories in the North-Western Provinces, the judge was skeptical. He did not believe that the child, who was sickly and usually crawled even though she could walk, had fallen into the well while searching for her mother. Instead, he initially suspected that "some illness, consequent on parturition," like puerperal fever, had led to the crime. But, since her relatives reported that Neemia had been in apparent good health, the judge changed course. He concluded that a "sudden impulse to criminality" had prompted her to commit the "unnatural act," "for some motive, of which the spring is quite hidden."[4] Her "infant in arms," whom she had brought into the courtroom, saved her from the scaffold. She was sentenced to spend the rest of her life in the Saugor jail.

Medical and legal theories about the ways that childbirth could compromise a woman's mental and emotional health traversed the British Empire. In India as elsewhere, judges and other legal authorities regularly treated infanticidal mothers with forbearance on the ground that they were not fully responsible for their crimes. And yet, as Neemia's sentence of life imprisonment suggests, lenience admitted to degrees. The only physician involved in Neemia's case was a colonial medical officer stationed in nearby Lullutpore, whom the judge rebuked for taking a "peculiar view of his obligations" and refusing to autopsy the victim's body.[5] According to the case report, the judge independently raised the possibility of puerperal insanity; it was, after all, a ready explanation for maternal violence. Finding little witness support for his theory, the judge instead substituted a sudden "impulse to criminality" that more closely resembled homicidal monomania or moral insanity, although he did not name either condition. As the previous chapter showed, a diagnosis of puerperal insanity could vitiate responsibility. A diagnosis of monomania or, especially, of moral insanity, in contrast, implied the sufferer was dangerous, and it could justify harsher punishment.

Where did this leave Neemia? Since her relatives claimed nothing was amiss before the killing and no medical witness took the stand to argue that her family had missed signs of illness visible only to experts, she had little chance of a successful insanity defense. The judge was content to report that Neemia's "sudden impulse" "ha[d] to be inferred" in the absence of a more satisfying explanation. Still, he urged mercy for Neemia. Her baby and, perhaps, the judge's lingering doubts about her sanity spared her execution or transportation.[6] But Neemia's punishment was severe in comparison with similar cases involving white defendants in Australia or England. There is no firm evidence, for instance, that Neemia was transferred to a hospital or that her long sentence was ultimately commuted. Women convicted of infanticide were disproportionately likely to receive mercy, and it is possible that Neemia was granted a pardon. Her case, however, predated the mass pardons that British Indian authorities would adopt after 1857, in celebration of Queen

Victoria's late-century jubilees. In the event that a woman was not pardoned, she would usually only be eligible for release after more than a decade of incarceration.[7]

Debates about the limits of sanity in the British world were also, implicitly and explicitly, about the nature of legal personhood and responsible subjecthood. Given this, psychiatric categories, including legal insanity, had racial and civilizational dimensions. In British cases involving white, Protestant defendants, the relationship between responsibility and civilization was usually assumed, rather than openly contested. However, cases where the accused seemed to break from the Anglo ideal—as in the previous chapter's case of Irish servant Mary Fitzgerald—drew medical and legal authorities to engage more directly with the understandings of racial or cultural fitness that underwrote Victorian concepts of personhood. Indian cases, like Neemia's, further expose how the politics of medical incapacity and those of racial inferiority met.

Some symptoms of mental disease were formally adopted as excusing conditions in nineteenth-century British and British imperial law, most visibly in the *M'Naghten* rules. The mental weakness that elite Victorians associated with non-European populations did not, however, provide a distinct defense to criminal responsibility. Controversies surrounding moral insanity suggest that many jurists, and some physicians, were eager to separate mental disease from civilizational deficiency. Otherwise, cultural practices labeled primitive or savage by colonial officials risked blending into forms of insanity that British jurists and medical officials held to be exculpatory. In fact, it seemed to some that crimes that manifested putative cultural ills ought to be punished more severely. This included infanticide, which colonial officials tended to regard as a congenital weakness of Indian culture. And yet, in the wider empire, both male and female infanticide was often held to be prima facie evidence of insanity, or at least of diminished responsibility. Cases involving infanticidal Indian women therefore tested the boundary between mental illness, which could excuse violence, and cultural pathology, which some thought required exemplary punishment.

Across the British world, women's violence against their children was simultaneously and contradictorily "unnatural" and overdetermined. Women as a class were vulnerable, gentle, and innately nurturing. And yet, their vulnerability made them ripe for corruption. Trauma, poverty, shame, and coercion, worsened by adherence to non-Christian faiths or superstitions, could easily produce mental illness or unleash primitive impulses. In the eyes of many colonial officials, Indian women shared white, British women's feminine weaknesses and were additionally subject to noxious cultural influences. Indian officials were faced with a quandary: Were Indian infanticidal mothers *less* responsible than their white, Protestant counterparts and therefore even more deserving of clemency? Or did Indian women's presumed barbarism make them *more* responsible (or at least more threatening) and therefore subject to greater punishment?

British efforts to describe the cultural and racial peculiarities of Indians, and to guide fellow officials in the investigation and prosecution of crime in India, led medical and legal experts to create a new field: Indian medical jurisprudence. Unlike in the settler colonies, colonial officials in India accepted that mass emigration from Britain and other parts of Europe to India was impossible, although many worked to anglicize Indian structures of power and prestige. Since demography would never remake India in England's image, the supposedly immutable difference of Indian society ultimately dictated colonial policy.

Neemia's case, including the judge's irritation with the lazy Lullutpore medical officer, provides a glimpse into the world of British Indian medico-legal officialdom. Indian medical and legal authorities were, for the most part, in the direct employ of the colonial government, as members of either the civil service or the military. This was true both before and after the 1857 Rebellion, after which the British Crown claimed sovereignty over the subcontinent, displacing the British East India Company. Indian medical jurisprudence became a cornerstone of the British administrative project in the second half of the nineteenth century. Many self-identified forensic experts were members of the Indian Civil Service, the powerful network of British administrators that, in 1879, had included the truculent bureaucrat Thomas Maltby. Specialists in medical jurisprudence, most of them current or former Civilians, wrote textbooks cataloguing the challenges of legal medicine in India, from detecting novel poisons to slowing the putrefaction of corpses in the tropical heat. Their forensic expertise circulated quickly through imperial networks, finding special traction in other British colonies with hot climates, such as Egypt.[8]

Infanticide was one of the core subjects of Indian medical jurisprudence. Norman Chevers, a founder of the field, wrote in 1856 that killing female children was "the chief and most characteristic crime of six-sevenths of the inhabitants of British India."[9] Although colonial officials occasionally diagnosed Indian mothers, and even fathers, with mental illnesses after they had killed their children, they most often described Indian maternal infanticide as deliberate, rather than psychotic. As in Neemia's case, experts in mental science were rarely called to testify. Instead, judges, at times with the encouragement of lawyers or other courtroom officials, or perhaps in response to a report by a medical officer, took it upon themselves to distinguish madness from malice, and personal tragedy from custom and conspiracy.

Indian medical jurisprudence, which infused British medico-legal knowledge with Anglo-Indian ethnology, reflected the colonial state's obsession with taxonomy. Cases involving Indian defendants more often stressed accurate classification than the ambiguity of responsibility. Colonial officials cared about whether a mother killed her child because she was insane, afraid, or ashamed, or whether her act was a calculating femicide. The abstract judicial or even metaphysical questions that responsibility cases raised in other contexts were secondary, however, to the more urgent project of collecting information deemed useful for controlling colonial populations.

Authorities in England and elsewhere sought access to women's private spaces, to women's bodies and secrets. In India, infanticide posed even greater epistemological challenges. Communities guarded their traditions against the colonial state and its officials, who navigated unfamiliar languages, cultures, and natural environments. Infanticide cases were, therefore, tests of colonial knowledge and of the proper functioning of the medical and legal branches of the British Indian state.

The nineteenth-century British Indian court system was complex, with separate criminal and civil systems whose names, jurisdictions, and procedures shifted over time. The three Presidencies of Bombay, Madras, and Bengal were subdivided into regions, districts, and subdistricts, which existed alongside semiautonomous princely states and other colonial administrative units. Prior to 1860, criminal and civil cases involving Indian parties were decided according to "Anglo-Muhammadan" law, which purported to fuse aspects of Islamic legal tradition with British principles. The Rebellion of 1857 led to territorial and administrative reforms that steadily reshaped the legal and jurisdictional landscape.[10] For our purposes, the most important aspect of the rich and complicated history of law in colonial India is the well-known division of the law into two spheres: the "personal" and the rest, including criminal law. The formal, institutionalized pluralism of Anglo-Indian law set it apart from law in other British colonies, where pluralism was ubiquitous but generally informal, covert, or strategically ignored. While Britain's Indian subjects were generally entitled to govern intimate relationships and private affairs using the "personal" laws of their confessions (hence "Hindu" and

"Muslim" law), albeit administered through the institutions and procedures of the colonial state, criminal law in India was substantially British in content if not always in form by the middle of the nineteenth century.[11] The Indian Penal Code (1860) codified swathes of common-law jurisprudence, much of it (although not all) a distillation of British criminal-law doctrines. Indian jurisprudence related to insanity and responsibility from the 1850s to the 1880s cleaved particularly close to common-law principles. Even under Anglo-Muhammadan criminal law in the first half of the century, approaches to homicide were highly anglicized. Therefore, it should not surprise us that debates about responsibility and sanity in Indian courts often echoed British and wider imperial developments and controversies.

Criminal justice in colonial India was not sui generis, but it was distinctive. Legal responses to infanticide displayed the characteristic dualism of Anglo-Indian law, which paired metropolitan norms with concessions to India's supposed exoticism. Britons explained Indian infanticide, particularly the killing of infant girls, or "female infanticide," as a cultural practice, which they incorrectly believed to be sanctioned by both Islam and Hinduism.[12] Colonial Britons distinguished sharply between female infanticide, in which the community or family shared the blame, and infanticide in which the child's gender was not a factor, where the mother herself was presumed to be at fault. Isidore Bernadotte Lyon, the author of a popular medical jurisprudence textbook, divided infanticide in India into these two forms. The systematic killing of infant girls was a crime "special to the East," while infanticide involving illegitimate children or within very poor families echoed patterns in Britain and elsewhere. Lyon did note, however, that while European women accused of infanticide were most often unmarried, the accused in Indian cases was "very frequently a Hindoo widow," who was traditionally expected to remain chaste after her husband's death.[13]

While female infanticide had been a concern of the East India Company from the late-eighteenth century, infanticide control was a priority for the mature colonial state of the later nineteenth.[14] Infanticide, both customary and stochastic, was difficult to detect. Infants are intensely vulnerable to deliberate violence, but also to the traumas of birth, disease, and neglect. The British state faced additional hurdles in India, where etiquette surrounding childbirth called for strict seclusion and privacy in the early days of a child's life. Lalita Panigrahi writes that Indian women in some regional communities avoided contact with outsiders, so that "the women of northern India were a sealed book to the stranger."[15] Policing and prosecuting infanticide in India required substantial institutional resources, including the political will to intervene in potentially explosive cultural and familial matters. The information-gathering apparatus of the modern colonial state made the intrusive monitoring, detection, and prosecution of infanticide possible.[16]

British administrators identified the Punjab and the neighboring North-Western Provinces, present-day Uttar Pradesh and surrounding regions, as unusually infanticide prone, and they targeted certain high-caste groups—especially the wealthy Rajputs—for special scrutiny. Britons tended to attribute female infanticide to the financial pressure of having to provide a daughter's dowry; to fears that a daughter might pollute a family's line through marriage to a lower-caste man; and to a general contempt for women and their subordination to men in Rajput tradition. This caste-based account persisted despite clear evidence from colonial investigations that female infanticide also occurred in lower-caste, Muslim, Sikh, and Buddhist communities. Scholars have seen this as a reflection of the place of infanticide in British Christian, especially missionary, discourse, where commentators associated the practice with elite Hinduism and presented conversion to Christianity as its only antidote.[17]

Neemia's case was published in 1853 in the *Decisions of the Nizamut Adawlut of the North Western Provinces*, the series of law reports that digested important cases heard at the Nizamat Adalat in Agra, then the highest criminal court in the North-Western Provinces. Local magistrates referred defendants accused of serious crimes to Sessions judges. If the defendant was convicted and sentenced either to death or to imprisonment for life, the Nizamat Adalat reviewed the case.[18]

The North-Western Provinces was an administrative region of the Bengal Presidency in northwest British India. First established in 1836 by the East India Company, the provinces merged with the conquered kingdom of Oudh in 1858. A year after his retirement from the Bengal Civil Service, folklorist William Crooke described the North-Western Provinces in poetic terms.[19] To the north of the province were "stupendous mountains covered in eternal snow," succeeded by a "dense jungle and abundant vegetation," "a line of malarious woodland and vast savannah of grass and reeds," and finally an alluvial plain whipped by seasonal winds hot as "the breath of a furnace." Crooke estimated the area of the provinces at 107,503 square miles, with a total population of nearly forty-eight million—roughly equal to that of the United Kingdom. One subdivision, Lucknow, had more inhabitants than Ireland, Scotland, Sweden, or Canada.[20]

Indian Civil Service (ICS) men like Crooke were eager to convey the sheer scale of India to the uninitiated in Britain's small, cramped islands. In part, this was a way to celebrate the achievements of the comparatively minuscule staff of the British Indian state. The ICS was an elite corps, created in 1858 after the end of Company rule. Recruits who could pass its rigorous entrance exams were offered professional advancement, adventure, and a chance at wealth—or, at least, a generous pension, fixed at a handsome £1,000 a year after twenty-five years' service. About a thousand Civilians claimed authority over more than three hundred million Indians. Tax collection, criminal justice, agricultural production, public health, infrastructure, and social welfare all fell under their remit. There was a clear chain of command, supported by a robust bureaucracy in which subordinates reported to their superiors, who issued instructions passed down from higher authorities. But, as was true in every colonial administrative system, metropolitan control was often more symbolic than real, with each tier of officials exercising considerable discretion and creativity in how it interpreted its instructions and mandate. Distance not only from London but also between colonial officials and offices in India empowered Civilians to act semiautonomously, with their instincts and personal libraries to guide them. Instructions could take weeks to travel from Britain to India, and longer still to wind through regional bureaucratic networks. Its size and diversity made India appear particularly unknowable to British interests. This encouraged the devolution of decision making to lower-level agents, whom distant officials relied on for information about local circumstances.[21]

Many ICS officials wrote books about the places where they were stationed, which the government sometimes published and distributed widely.[22] Some, such as William Crooke and Thomas Maltby, wrote manuals that fashioned their experiences into distinct fields of expertise. Even civilians who did not produce memoirs and guidebooks thought of themselves as experts, combining their knowledge of Indian ethnology, climate, geography, and economy with other professional identities, as magistrates, medical officers, revenue collectors, engineers, or surveyors, among others. They were proud of what they knew, and of their place at the interface of imperial politics and village life.

Colonial officials were caught between the empire's grand ideals and the exigencies of quotidian administration. Lawyers faced the problem of how to translate the abstract principles of common-law jurisprudence into sound decisions in particular cases. In this way, lawyering was a fractal of governance. Both processes relied on a class of professional men to bring ideals to earth. It was their task to make the inevitable compromises that real life demanded, while preserving the empire's motivating, justifying legal ideology.

Neemia's case hints at the improvised decision making of colonial officials, who spun theories about a defendant's responsibility with little oversight and few compunctions. Another case heard at the Agra Nizamat Adalat in 1853 also shows how medical, ethnological, and legal knowledge shaped colonial interpretations of infanticide. On a November evening in the town of Kurhul in the North-Western Provinces, two midwives examined a young woman named Mussumat Nisseea. She was bleeding heavily and lactating, which suggested that she had recently given birth. A civil surgeon inspected Nisseea's body, confirming the midwives' findings. He took Nisseea into custody. Earlier that night, the body of a newborn girl, umbilical cord still attached to her placenta, had been found dead in a pond near a butcher shop.

The next morning, Nisseea confessed. She told the police that her husband had left her two years before, and that she had begun an affair with a cousin. After her husband wrote to announce his plans to return, Nisseea's mother-in-law had brought her, heavily pregnant, to Kurhul. While her mother-in-law was out, Nisseea's daughter was born. She had strangled the baby and concealed the body in a basket covered with long grass until night fell, and then had stolen outside to throw it in the pond. Her mother-in-law noticed the blood on Nisseea's clothes but said nothing.

At trial before Henry Unwin, a British Sessions judge, Nisseea retracted her confession. She said that her child had been stillborn, two months premature, and she threw the body into the pond because no one had been home to bury it. Unwin was joined by three Indian counselors, known as "assessors": a high-caste Brahmin, a landholding *zamindar*, and a *vakil*, or "pleader," a kind of low-level lawyer. The first two men believed Nisseea's story. The third assessor, the pleader Mujlis Rae, voted to convict her of murder. Unwin concurred with Rae. There was no conclusive proof that the baby had been born alive, and the absence of marks of violence on the body and the intact umbilical cord introduced notes of uncertainty. Still, Unwin was confident Nisseea was guilty; she had every motive to kill her child and had confessed at least twice before trial. Disregarding the opinions of the two assessors who moved to acquit her, Unwin sentenced Nisseea to imprisonment for life with "labour suited to her sex."[23]

As required when courts of Session sentenced defendants to life imprisonment or death, the Nizamat Adalat in Agra reviewed the case. The judge,

Samuel Sneade Brown, also found Nisseea's confession damning, as were her "strong motives for destroying the fruit of her illicit intercourse with the expected arrival of her husband."[24] The judge added that when word had reached Nisseea that her child's body had been discovered, "smitten perhaps by remorse," she had cried out and admitted her guilt within earshot of her neighbors. He confirmed her sentence.[25]

Judge Brown was born in Bath, the son of a retired Civilian who had spent much of his career in Bengal. Brown achieved top marks at Haileybury, the East India Company's training college in England, winning the prize for Persian. He arrived in Calcutta in 1827, at the age of eighteen, and slowly ascended the administrative ranks.[26] In 1878, after Brown had retired, his nephew collected and published his youthful letters to his mother and sisters, which chronicled his first fourteen years in the service. He wrote about the boredom and loneliness of life in India, marked by paperwork and the death, from disease and misadventure, of his few friends. "I lament my youth," he wrote in 1836, "wasted in this melancholy country, and I look forward to my future years of service with a sickening feeling."[27]

Brown's jaundiced view of his Indian career, at least in these early years, extended to his understanding of British rule and Indian national character. A devout Christian whose maternal grandfather was a clergyman, he complained that the colonial government had devoted insufficient resources to the education of the Indian population. Unlike the "savages" of New Zealand, he argued that Indians' minds were neither blank nor open but beset by prejudice and intense superstition. Indian Muslims were "fiercely intolerant"; the superstitions of Hindus could "be traced in every action of their lives, in almost every word they utter." He likened Indians' Indigenous beliefs to "chains" riveted on their minds, holding their reason in an "iron grasp."[28]

Brown was skeptical, however, about the colonial government's ability to free Indian minds. British rule was, from the perspective of Indigenous people, "a pure despotism." "They enjoy, under our laws, many advantages which they never even dreamt of under their own tyrannical rulers; but if they have nothing to dread," Brown allowed, "they have at the same time nothing to look forward to. They feel themselves to be a conquered people."[29]

Brown heard Nisseea's case more than twenty years later, just months before his retirement. Power and a prestigious post at the court in Agra may have softened his cynicism about the possibilities of British rule. Still, he is unlikely to have abandoned his suspicions that religion and culture had pernicious effects on the minds of Britain's Indian subjects. For Britons, infanticide was a telltale sign of Indian "prejudice." Even though Nisseea's crime was not female infanticide in the strict sense, British officials saw infanticides committed by Indian defendants—including those in which the circumstances and even judges' theories invited analogies to domestic British models—through the lens of cultural pathology. Infanticide exposed the friability of British medico-legal taxonomy. While statutes and colonial political discourse at times distinguished clearly between allegedly customary female infanticide and other infanticides, the barrier between cultural or racial explanations for violence and medical or personal ones was porous.

A brief account of the specter of female infanticide elucidates the political and institutional context in which British Indian officials configured the responsibility of infanticide defendants. In an 1857 book on infanticide, John Cave-Brown, a British chaplain working in Bengal, wrote that during the Mynpooree famine of 1838, "mothers were known to consign their children alive to a watery grave, that they might be spared the agony of witnessing the death-struggles from hunger which they could not alleviate."[30] In the wake of the crisis, the resident magistrate, the same Henry Unwin who tried Nisseea's case fifteen years later, dispensed alms to the poor, slowly becoming familiar with the people of the local villages. As "his heart became more keenly alive to their necessities," Unwin was disturbed to realize that there seemed to be no girls among the village children.[31] He suspected that the villagers were practicing female infanticide.

Colonial administrators in the region had long been aware of infanticide but had prioritized efforts to suppress the more public practice of sati and the purported menace of thuggee (assaults by members of what were called "criminal tribes").[32] Unwin raised the alarm with his superiors, setting up a surveillance system in which police and magistrates reported on the birth and well-being of female infants and children. Similar surveillance and registration systems were soon exported to neighboring districts.[33] Unwin claimed great success for his efforts, although nineteenth-century reports and contemporary scholarship cast doubt on the new measures' effectiveness.[34] Census after census seemed to confirm Unwin's findings, suggesting that female infanticide was a systemic blight on northern India.[35] Isidore Bernadotte Lyon, the medical jurisprudence expert, quoted shocking statistics originally cited in Chevers's book suggesting that of thirty villages surveyed in Mynpooree, eleven had no girls at all; out of all thirty, there were only thirty-seven girls, compared with 329 boys.[36]

British concern about female infanticide, and infanticide in general, grew after the end of Company rule. Population data, though partial and unreliable, suggested that gender ratios remained unbalanced. Families continued to resist colonial efforts to monitor their private lives, which officials met with mounting paranoia. Colonial agents increasingly tied female infanticide to other social ills, including the kidnapping of girls for marriage, prostitution, and the growth of criminal tribes fueled by an increase in illegitimate births.[37] The patchwork of prohibition measures did not seem to be working. Moreover, medical uncertainty and strict standards of proof in murder cases made infanticide difficult to prosecute.

While many officials perceived female infanticide as uniquely harmful to morality and social stability, any infanticide case raised doubts about the smooth functioning of British justice. Even if they found a body, which was never guaranteed, medical officers struggled to prove that infants had been born alive and to establish a clear cause of death. Willful neglect resembled poverty, and medical experts could not reliably distinguish accidental injury from violence. Corroborating evidence, including eyewitness testimony, was often absent or, in officials' view, untrustworthy. Poisons could elude detection. Even if an infant had clearly been poisoned, proving the identity of the poisoner could foil prosecutors. The distance between many villages and police stations, and between police stations and medical officers, compounded these uncertainties. By the time a body made its way to a physician, it was often so decomposed that a postmortem was next to pointless.[38]

Any Indian mother who killed her child in the North-Western Provinces was likely to encounter officials, like Unwin, who had strong views on infanticide and the condition of Indigenous women. But Anglo judges and accused women were not the only parties in British Indian criminal trials. The colonial legal system in India relied heavily on Indian personnel and expertise. There were not enough white Britons to staff, or even to oversee, the massive legal-administrative institutions of the colonial state. So colonial officials depended on the knowledge and legal skill of locals but at the same time were anxious to circumscribe their influence.

This tension manifested itself in many ways, including through the "assessor" system, developed in India and later exported across much of British Africa. In 1843, the East India Company had adopted the system in many criminal trials. Lay participation in British Indian trials, however, remained uneven.[39] Under the assessor system, Sessions judges selected two or three Indian assistants who observed the trial, proposed lines of questioning, shared local knowledge and expertise, and delivered opinions on the verdict. Sorab P. N. Wadia, a Parsi lawyer, described the process. When a court of Session was convened, the judge selected assessors by lot from among the local Indian elite. The trial proceeded with all "its attendant pompousness," after which assessors conferred and delivered their verdict. Judges were not, however, bound by assessors' recommendations. If a judge disagreed with the assessors, he was entitled to pass his own sentence. Such trials were, in effect, "trial before and by a single individual," Wadia wrote, "a stranger to the language of the accused, a stranger to the caste customs, and much more, a total stranger to the prevalent native habits and opinion." Wadia denounced the assessor system as "farcical and unmaintainable," a waste of assessors' time that needed to be "ended or mended" as soon as possible, in favor of jury trials.[40] Assessors across the British Empire were "conveniently impotent," a superficial sop to Indigenous participation that involved no true colonial power sharing.[41]

Nisseea's trial before Unwin showcased the relative powers of British judges and Indian assessors. The case report is spare. Still, it offers some hints of differences of perspective among the men who judged her. Two assessors, named in the report as Rambux and Singh Thakoor, moved to acquit her. Rambux, described as a Brahmin, argued that a premature infant born in "such cold weather" would probably have died. Thakoor, a landholder, agreed, and noted that Nisseea's heavy postpartum bleeding meant that her daughter was "clearly a seven months' child."[42] Chevers summarized Nisseea's case (although he gave her name as Miseea) in his 1856 book. He seems to have regarded Thakoor's statement about excessive bleeding with derision, as he punctuated it ("since so much blood flowed!") with an incredulous exclamation mark.[43]

It is possible that Nisseea's bleeding was the result of a traumatic birth. A very premature infant would have stood little chance of survival. On the other hand, Rambux and Thakoor might have been doing what British jurors did routinely in infanticide cases: acquitting out of sympathy. Nisseea's husband had been away for two years. As a married woman, her primary source of financial and personal support was her husband's family. An illegitimate birth would have left Nisseea and her child vulnerable to violence or abandonment.[44] Her mother-in-law, who had brought her to Kurhul, might have helped her, or pressured her, to destroy her child in order to save her marriage. The assessors, sensitive to these familial dynamics, might have wished to spare Nisseea further pain. Wadia, for one, believed that jurors—and, presumably, assessors—were more likely to be merciful than a judge sitting alone. A juror was "free from that 'harshness of heart,' and strictness of judgment" that were "inseparable from the office of a judge," and could temper the letter of the law with mercy and attention to circumstance.[45]

If Rambux and Thakoor spoke for the heart, the third assessor, Mujlis Rae, may have spoken for the law. As a vakil, Rae was a professional litigator.[46] Vakils underwent notoriously difficult training, which in the early-twentieth century included six years' study and rigorous examinations in both English and at least one Indian language.[47] The recommendation by Rae to convict Nisseea might have demonstrated his commitment to the strict enforcement of the law, and the "harshness of heart" Wadia thought that legal training engendered.

The punishment Nisseea received was indeed harsh. She, like Neemia, was tried according to British legal principles that crossed imperial jurisdictions. Yet, neither had the benefit of trial by jury, where pity could move jurors, and judges, to treat infanticidal mothers mildly. If she had been an Englishwoman from a rural county who had been abandoned by her husband, seduced by her cousin, and pressured into killing her daughter by her mother-in-law to avoid shame and destitution, a jury might well have acquitted her. If she had been convicted at trial, neighbors, members of women's aid organizations, or the judge himself might have written to the government to request a lighter sentence or a pardon. As it was, those who judged Nisseea saw her crime not as a personal tragedy but as further proof of the cruelty and primitivism of Indian social life.

Poverty, lust, exhaustion, stupidity, despair, and mental disease could push parents anywhere to kill. Britons saw the systematic elimination of female infants, however, as a specifically "Indian" custom, unthinkable in any other place. Infanticide in India was thus both familiar and strange. Depending on how officials categorized a child's death, infanticide could fit within established imperial medico-legal paradigms or could call for radical legal innovation and investigative techniques developed specifically for use in India.

The Female Infanticide Act (1870) was one such innovation—the government's response to the creeping sense of crisis surrounding infanticide in India. James Fitzjames Stephen, who began his tenure as Law Member of the Viceroy's Council in 1869 and remained in office until 1872, fixed his considerable legislative energies on infanticide. Detractors urged caution. Rajputs made up a sizable proportion of the Indian Army and had a history of grievance against the colonial state. Subjecting them to intensified state control over personal and communal matters risked provoking another rebellion.[48] Despite the risks and in keeping with his ambitious program of statutory reform and codification, Stephen rejected noninterference: for him, British authorities could not ignore infanticide without betraying the civilizing mission that undergirded colonial rule.[49]

The act Stephen championed amplified penalties for child murder and created an elaborate surveillance and eradication program, applied to rural areas where British administrators believed the practice was most entrenched.[50] It was a massive enterprise. An evolving, public list of "guilty" villages and clans identified thousands of families who would be subject to long-term, invasive government monitoring. The act's flaws were clear from its inception, including the fundamental and widely acknowledged lack of reliable demographic statistics.[51] The law's results were mixed, at best. Governments took steps to prevent and punish infanticide across the British world. In India, infanticide control went much further, becoming an expensive and complicated state project. The civilizing mission thus turned on medico-legal and ethnographic knowledge.

Metropolitan British experts in medical jurisprudence, such as Henry Maudsley and Alfred Swaine Taylor, wrote works that circulated across the world even as their authors spent most of their lives in England. Other professionals, in contrast, made their livings and their names primarily in the colonies. A group of British doctors and lawyers, most attached to the East India Company's service and, later, to the ICS or to the Indian Medical Service, a branch of the Indian military, developed sophisticated bodies of legal and scientific scholarship. This literature was central to the Indian colonial administration, where divisions among the core institutions of the state—the judiciary, the military, the political executive—were highly fungible. Men with medical training could serve as surgeons, coroners, public health officials, or (really, *and*) holders of political or administrative offices over the course of their careers. Magistrates and judges often filled a variety of administrative posts, perhaps collecting revenue or overseeing land reform, before, after, or alongside their judicial functions. Because civil officials often served in remote outposts or far from other colonial administrators, they were expected to be generalists. A thriving Anglo-Indian press churned out handbooks, guidebooks, textbooks, and dictionaries to counsel officials and, in duller moments, to entertain and educate them. As the nineteenth century progressed, more of these works were written by experts who staffed India's burgeoning universities and colleges, many of whom had also spent time at elite schools, hospitals, and Inns of Court in England and Scotland.

British experts in India, including judges and medical officials, were familiar with European theorists and institutions. They were eager to claim their place alongside their metropolitan peers through their mastery of European and American literatures and techniques. They also emphasized the many challenges—as well as the pleasures—of life in the colonies, and the value of their hard-won expertise in all matters Indian. These men could find themselves torn between metropolitan forms and ideas and their self-presentation as dashing, innovative medical adventurers.

Norman Chevers, the author of the most famous work of Anglo-Indian medical jurisprudence, illustrates this ambivalence. He was born in Kent in 1818, the son of a Royal Navy surgeon who was a veteran of the Battle of Trafalgar. He completed his medical education at Glasgow at the age of twenty-one, after stints at the Royal Navy Hospital Haslar and Guy's Hospital in London. After nine years in London working mainly as a pathologist, he joined the East India Company medical service in Bengal Presidency, where he steadily climbed the ranks.[52] His *Manual of Medical Jurisprudence* was first published in 1856. Five hundred copies were printed at the expense of the government of India, with four hundred sent to judicial officers and one hundred placed at Chevers's disposal.[53] He intended the book as a supplement to Taylor's *Manual of Medical Jurisprudence,* which went through twelve British editions between 1844 and 1891 and twelve American editions between 1845 and 1897.[54] In his work, Chevers claimed that a separate, Indian medical jurisprudence was necessary. In India, he argued, crimes were committed "under circumstances entirely dissimilar to those which call for the like investigations in Europe," especially offenses involving "Unsoundness of Mind, Identity, Suicide, Torture, &c." He set the tone for the expanded 1870 second edition of the *Manual* with a frontispiece depicting an instrument supposedly "used in the murder of a child in a temple at Jessore."[55]

Chevers believed that Indian "national character" was the main determinant of criminality in India. "It would probably be impossible," he wrote, "to point to any races of men whose great crimes more distinctly emanate from and illustrate their national character, than is the case with those various classes of natives who inhabit the British possessions of India."[56] Only by developing a scientific understanding of the "'pathology' of crime in India," and an intimate knowledge of Indian culture, could British authorities secure order in the subcontinent.[57] Chevers's emphasis on order over uplift departs from the vision of humane governance advanced by some parties in the responsibility contests of the later nineteenth century. For him, the conscientious application of medical jurisprudence and the efficient and accurate prosecution of the guilty plotted the surest path to the consolidation of British rule in India.

The belief, widespread among colonial administrators, that Indians were compulsive liars complicated both medical diagnosis and efforts to determine

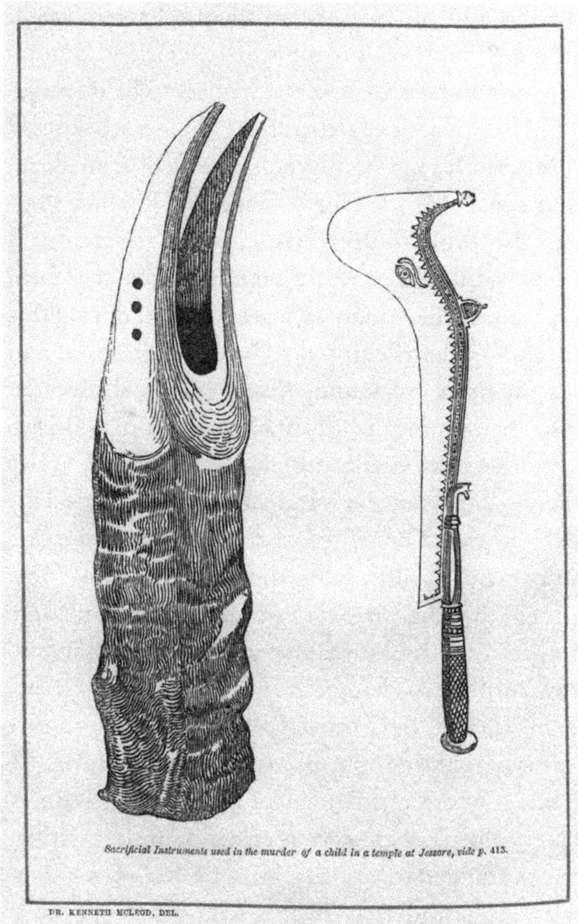

Chevers credited this drawing to Dr. Kenneth McLeod, who was working as a civil surgeon in Jessore in 1866 when he was called to investigate the alleged sacrifice of a five-year-old boy to the goddess Kali. It evokes the exotic, violent superstition that Chevers associated with Indian "national character." Credit: Medical Historical Library, Harvey Cushing/John Hay Whitney Medical Library, Yale University.

truth in court. The field of medical jurisprudence was intended to give colonial courts the tools to reconstruct events in criminal cases without the need for Indian testimony. Historian Elizabeth Kolsky describes the law of evidence, oath taking, and medical jurisprudence as "truth-technologies," conceived to combat the perceived epidemic of Indian perjury.[58] This obsession continued into the nineteenth century. "The great difficulty," wrote a medical jurisprudence expert in the 1890s, "with which all magisterial and judicial officers in India have to contend, is the false evidence which daily comes before them. It is, probably, no exaggeration to say that a case scarcely comes before a criminal court, in which there is not a certain amount of false evidence."[59]

Writing on the law of evidence in India in 1862, Calcutta lawyer Joseph Goodeve claimed that "Hindu law" allowed a witness to give false testimony in any case involving a Hindu, and in fact *required* the witness to lie if the accused were a Brahmin who might otherwise face death.[60] Goodeve belonged to a family of colonial administrators, many of whom traveled in medical, legal, and literary circles in Bengal. Henry Hurry Goodeve, Joseph's stepbrother, an army surgeon who also wrote futurist fiction, joined the faculty at the new Calcutta Medical College in the 1830s, a period of liberal reform across the British world.[61] The college, like many colleges founded during this period, offered Indian and British students culturally "British" education and professional training. At the same time, the abiding distrust colonial administrators had of Indians blunted their ambitions of ushering India into British modernity. Women were considered especially unreliable.[62] Modern white women could make excellent witnesses, but Indian women—especially women who observed purdah, and who benefited least from "intermingling with civilized life"—were prone to "absurdity, lying, and contradiction."[63]

British imperial ideology held that the condition of women was a measure of civilization. As a result, imperial political discourse used practices like sati, child marriage, and female infanticide to denigrate Indian culture.[64] Catherine Hall writes, "For the colonial state, the incapacity of Indian men to care properly for their women was a sign of their incapacity to rule themselves."[65] Predictably, then, Joseph Goodeve wrote approvingly of British Indian courts' policy of universally admitting women's testimony as evidence of the gentility and protection that British rule extended to women. His simultaneous indictment of women's credibility, though, undercut this liberal boast.[66]

Chevers's account also included equivocal treatments of credibility. References to lying often appeared alongside confident assertions that the science of medical jurisprudence could expose Indian dissembling. Chevers compared the medical jurist to the "hunter and the brutetamer" who "tracks out and lays bare the evidence of [the accused's] crime, almost with the certainty of an irresistible fate." In a footnote on the same page, Chevers quoted Menu (Manu): "As a hunter traces the lair of a wounded beast by drops of blood; thus let a King investigate the true point of justice by deliberate arguments."[67] Indian mendacity risked compromising British claims to be doing justice, but also entrenched British rule by excusing its failures and inefficiencies.[68] Bernard Cohn famously argued that "the conquest of India was a conquest of knowledge."[69] Experts in medical jurisprudence in British India intended to make the circumstances of, and motivations for, Indian crime intelligible, and therefore subject to control.

British hubris and insecurity together structured colonial rule, and medical jurisprudence was a microcosm of the colonial predicament.

Efforts to determine the sanity of Indian defendants taxed officials invested in the imperial myths of Indian difference and mendacity: how could responsibility or mental abnormality be determined among people Britons routinely construed as innately abnormal? The Indian Penal Code codified the language of *M'Naghten*. "A person who, at the time of doing [an act], by reason of unsoundness of mind, is incapable of knowing the nature of the act, or that he is doing what is either wrong or contrary to law" could not be convicted of an offense.[70] Chevers believed that the British physicians called to give opinions in homicide cases struggled to distinguish cultural pathology from mental illness, and to tell the difference between malingering and genuine distress. How could British medical experts divide "the ravings of Monomania" from Indians' sane but "ridiculous and unnatural" religiosity?[71]

Worse, ICS physicians with specialist training or experience in mental science were thin on the ground. While many surgeons encountered insanity in their clinical practice or as expert witnesses in legal cases, few were specialists. Chevers was concerned about Indian medical officers' lack of exposure to mental science. He described the trials a "young Civil Surgeon, upon whose fiat depends the life or death of a Native" might face in cases involving responsibility quandaries. Here, his interest was in improving the professional skill of colonial officers, rather than wading into the morass of philosophical and medical disputes about legal insanity. For Chevers, caution would serve. For instance, he urged medical officers to refrain from giving "dangerous and untenable" opinions, especially given the propensity of Indian accused to lie.[72]

As in other jurisdictions, responsibility cases in India broadcast the restraint and sophistication of British law, and the willingness of colonial authorities to bind themselves to their principles. The result was a complex medical ethics for physicians involved in Indian insanity cases. For instance, Chevers counseled medical men against curing prisoners of their madness before trial, and so reducing their chances of being found not guilty by reason of insanity.[73]

Over time, medical jurisprudence experts' concern about the inexperience of British medical men in India diminished. As the colonial medical establishment professionalized, practitioners developed closer ties with the metropolitan medical community. The East India Company medical corps had been seen for some time as a place for inferior physicians, and its asylums as incubators of corruption and amateurism. Pay and pension increases in the early-nineteenth century, however, helped to boost the Company's medical prestige. From 1822, medical staff had to have secured a diploma from one of the Royal Colleges of Surgeons in London, Dublin, or Edinburgh, or an equivalent formal qualification. The introduction of competitive exams in 1855 helped to promote imperial service in India as a viable option for career-minded physicians.[74] Chevers, for his part, eventually rose to the position of principal of the Calcutta Medical College, where he was also professor of medicine and, for some years before his retirement in 1876, president of the Faculty of Medicine and deputy surgeon general. He spent his last decade in London, where he inveighed against emerging understandings of germ theory and insisted that poisoned soil caused cholera.[75]

Isidore Bernadotte Lyon's *Text Book of Medical Jurisprudence of India, with Illustrative Cases* was first published in 1888 and epitomizes the more sophisticated and anglicized medico-legal culture of late-nineteenth-century India. It quickly became the premier Anglo-Indian medico-legal authority. The book went through four editions during Lyon's lifetime, with five more published posthumously.[76] Lyon was a member of the Bombay branch of the Indian Medical Service. He served as the Bombay government's official Chemical Analyser, the head of a network of laboratories and chief tester of samples for state institutions, including the courts.[77] Chemical examiners assumed increasingly prominent administrative and scientific roles beginning in the 1870s, with their average annual caseload in Bombay swelling from a few dozen cases in the 1860s to almost three thousand by the 1910s.[78] Lyon was also professor of chemistry and medical jurisprudence at Grant Medical College in Bombay. His publisher, Thacker and Spink, was one of the best-known Anglophone booksellers in India, with headquarters in London.[79]

In the preface to his *Medical Jurisprudence*, Lyon praised Chevers for his pioneering work. Unlike his predecessor, though, Lyon did not conceive of his book as an appendix to a metropolitan text but saw it as a complete, self-contained guide. Accordingly, Lyon surpassed Chevers's coverage, providing accounts of such topics as "Drowning, Hanging, Strangulation and Suffocation"; "Death from Heat, Cold, Electric discharge and Starvation"; "Wound and mechanical injuries" and—a reflection of his chemical expertise—nineteen chapters on poisons. He also included two chapters on insanity and devoted considerable attention to the new Indian statutes on evidence and procedure, the Indian Evidence Act of 1872 and the revised Code of Criminal Procedure (Act X of 1882). He was more concerned with the professional training of medical officers in their legal and medical responsibilities than with the exposition of "native character." His introduction signaled this shift in emphasis from Indian criminality to the ethics and responsibilities of medical officers in court. Lyon began his work with "Hints for Guidance in Giving Evidence," including, "Do not state as fact things which are merely matters of opinion," and, "Be careful to draw no stronger inference, and give no stronger opinion than the facts warrant you doing."[80]

This attention to Indian medical jurisprudence developed in tandem with the colonial administrative state, and against a backdrop of growing racist sentiment among whites in India.[81] An influx of white Europeans not employed by the colonial state disrupted the administration's attempts to apply and extend newly codified legal standards, including the Evidence Act (1872) and the Code of Criminal Procedure (1872). Unruly "non-official Europeans" resisted official efforts to design laws and legal processes that offered formal equality to Indians, even if discrimination on racial or cultural grounds remained ubiquitous.[82] The Code of Criminal Procedure attracted special criticism. Indians acquired the right to qualify as magistrates in India's country towns, or *mofussils*, in 1869. The 1872 code made white Britons subject to the jurisdiction of mofussil courts, ending a privilege entitling them to trial in the high courts at Presidency Towns for criminal offenses. They retained the right to be tried only by white British magistrates despite the logistical hassles and professional awkwardness this often produced.[83]

Simmering racial resentment boiled over when C. P. Ilbert, Law Member of the government of India, proposed legislation in 1883 that would withdraw whites' immunity to trial by Indian magistrates. The outrage of both official and nonofficial Britons in India, known to some as a "white mutiny," persuaded the government to back down. An anemic revised version of the Ilbert Bill proposed that white British subjects would be subject to trial by Indian judges, but with a right to demand a jury at least half composed of white Britons or Americans. White women were especially vocal in their objections to the Ilbert Bill. They argued that it would expose them to sexual predation, alleging that Indian magistrates belonged to a culture that did not value or protect women. Gendered discourses—particularly the notion that Bengali magistrates were "effeminate" and therefore unfit judges—concealed the true aim of the bill's critics: the preservation of white racial privilege. As liberals insisted on legal racial equality in India, Britons, both official and nonofficial, defended their supremacy through attacks on Indian attitudes toward women and the masculinity of Indian men.[84]

Sometimes, the increase in racial animus among Europeans in India produced obviously biased judgments in criminal cases, with medical jurisprudence supplying the "evidence" that allowed whites to escape punishment.[85] Many high-court judges, however, continued to think of themselves as the guardians of centuries of British legal wisdom, and as crucial checks on executive power.[86] As racial conflict became more pronounced in India, some of the texts most complicit in codifying colonial racism became more studied, neutral, and anglicized in tone and content. Crass claims to white racial superiority—as opposed to cultural sophistication—still met some resistance.

For example, throughout his discussion of insanity in India, Lyon did not mention "natives" or "Indians" (or "Europeans," for that matter). Although he, like Chevers and many other British colonial medical officials, entertained connections between Indian drug use and insanity, Lyon was skeptical. He observed, for instance, that the majority of cases of cannabis-induced insanity were in fact just cases of intoxication.[87] Elsewhere, he cited English works on the nature and prevalence of insanity without making any adjustments for Indian patients or colonial conditions.[88]

Amid racial controversies like the one surrounding the Ilbert Bill, asserting that Indians' brains were anatomically inferior might have struck authors of medical jurisprudence texts as inflammatory. Moreover, in late-nineteenth-century India, some prominent anticolonial activists were repurposing old theories of brain-based racial difference, including phrenology, to argue for Indian equality and against British colonial domination.[89] A cultural account of difference, based more on the mind than the brain, avoided controversy and bolstered British liberal attachment to a rhetoric of colonial improvement. Nineteenth-century British imperial ideology relied, after all, on the idea that British rule was both benevolent and civilizing. The open secret that colonized peoples could never grasp the brass ring of civilization and regain their liberty only intensified Britons' fealty to liberal institutions, especially when it came to matters of law.

In this respect, the 1885 prosecution of Lakshman Dagdu for the murders of his two young children—with which this book opens—provides an instructive contrast with the earlier cases of Neemia and Nisseea. Both women were tried before the heyday of Indian medical jurisprudence, before Crown rule, and before the sweeping codification projects of the later nineteenth century. While the judges in both women's cases very likely drew on knowledge they had acquired from British medical and legal textbooks and precedent, in addition to their experiences in the colonies, they did not cite these sources directly. Dagdu's case was different. The judges, Birdwood and Jardine, leaned heavily on medico-legal authorities and metropolitan cases, and expressed significant doubts about the wisdom of strict adherence to the *M'Naghten* standard of section 84 of the Penal Code. Partly, this reflected the heightened intensity of the responsibility debates in the 1880s, when theories of degeneration, criminal anthropology, and a more mature and assertive field of mental science chipped away at old certainties. Gender mattered, too. Neemia and Nisseea, as Indian women, were doubly removed from the common-law model of the responsible, white, male subject. Ascertaining their responsibility did not seem to engage the core doctrines of criminal jurisprudence. As a man, Dagdu was closer to the legal ideal. The question of his responsibility demanded fuller consideration and bit more deeply into the principles of British criminal justice. As Indian colonial law became increasingly anglicized and medical jurisprudence flourished, responsibility became more openly contentious.

Another late-nineteenth-century text, *Outlines of Medical Jurisprudence for Indian Criminal Courts* (1891), by James Dunning Baker Gribble, a retired member of the Madras Civil Service and a former judge, and Patrick Hehir, a surgeon in the Bengal Army, returns us to the question of medical jurisprudence as a means of perfecting colonial governance. Hehir began his medical training in the lowly Military Subordinate Medical Department before obtaining a commission in the Indian Medical Service.[90] The first edition of the book, which Gribble wrote alone, was well received both in India and in England, and it was adopted as a textbook by the Madras government and used as a source in various Civil Service examinations. The book went through multiple editions, reaching its sixth and final version in 1929. Gribble and Hehir cited Chevers, Taylor, Lyon, and the English physician Forbes Winslow, among other European and colonial authorities. Like Lyon, they emphasized the institutional and professional inadequacies of both British colonial and Indian medical and legal personnel, rather than innate differences between populations. Gribble and Hehir noted the lack of medico-legal knowledge among "police, vakeels and magistrates" and the poor quality of evidence gathered for trial. "An elementary knowledge of [medical jurisprudence] might possibly save many an innocent man from punishment," they wrote, "or obtain the conviction of the guilty."[91]

Gribble and Hehir could not resist allusions to mendacity, which remained the central problem Indian medical jurisprudence purported to solve. The native mind was, "generally speaking," they wrote, "unable to understand that the truth 'unadorned is adorned the most.'" And yet, diverging here from Chevers's mid-century account, Gribble and Hehir did not blame Indian mendacity entirely on poor character. They granted that false evidence was "as often given or concocted through fear as through enmity or evil motives." Indians had a legitimate fear of capital punishment, and police corruption, torture, and extortion could result in false confessions. Moreover, lying could be double-edged, resulting in the exoneration of the guilty and, worse, the conviction of the innocent.[92] While Indians, in Gribble and Hehir's view, still needed civilizing, the colonial administrative system, which included both British and Indian officials, was flawed. A thorough understanding of medical jurisprudence could improve colonial justice and help Britain to deliver the liberal order it had promised.[93]

Near the end of his career, Hehir published *The Medical Professions in India* (1923), where he complained about the "Indianization" of the Indian Medical Service.[94] The culprit, in his view, was Indians' affection for an inferior Indigenous medical tradition. Still, Hehir rejected both physical accounts of Indian inferiority and allegations that colonial administrators were prejudiced against Indian physicians. "A European who feels that he could not serve under an Indian for one reason or another," he wrote, "must be differently constituted from the majority of us."[95] The difference between Europeans and Indians, in his view, was one of culture and civilization, which were mutable, rather than biology and race, which were not. At a time when Indian difference was being imprinted on some parts of the body, it was being erased from others, including the brain.[96]

There was no clear line between the physical and the mental or, in modern terms, nature and nurture.[97] Still, language mattered. Variations in how medico-legal experts and other officials described the purported mental difference of Indigenous people, in India and elsewhere, reflected their politics, justifications of empire, relationships to history, and professional loyalties. Configurations of mental difference also had legal consequences. A woman suffering from puerperal insanity might survive her encounter with British criminal justice; a woman who bowed to cultural pressure to commit infanticide might not. As later chapters show, the legal consequences of "cultural" crime could be unpredictable in the British world.

Colonial administrators were preoccupied with what Ishita Pande calls "colonial numerology"—the effort to know and to organize colonial society by gathering massive amounts of quantitative data.[98] Statistical information about gender balance was the lynchpin of efforts to detect and suppress female infanticide. In contrast, though medical jurisprudence texts included quantitative data, they primarily offered summaries of medical and legal cases threaded together with aphorisms, anecdotes, and the wisdom of experience. This was the type of medico-legal knowledge that shaped Indian courts' approaches to insanity and infanticide, especially in cases in which violence could not easily be classified as customary. Understanding the subtle signs of insanity, or the hallmarks of a deliberate killing, was work that required intuition, intelligence, and a practiced hand. From Chevers to Gribble and Hehir, experts in medical jurisprudence tried to guide novice practitioners toward truth so that they could fulfill their duties to the empire and safeguard the integrity of British rule. Indian infanticide cases illustrate how medico-legal expertise helped the colonial state to know its subjects, to train its administrators, and to govern through law.

Despite limited personnel and incomplete information, the late-nineteenth-century colonial state claimed to deliver British justice to its Indian and British subjects alike. The full and fair consideration of a defendant's criminal responsibility was, many reasoned, one of Britain's legal gifts to India, and a symbol of imperial self-restraint. James Fitzjames Stephen remarked in 1868, "Nobody cares about criminal law except theorists and habitual criminals."[99] His flippancy elides the political and emotional valence of British criminal jurisprudence. British Indian judges and physicians closely followed wider imperial controversies about insanity and culpability, and asked themselves how these issues changed, or failed to change, on the subcontinent.

CHAPTER 7

The Savage Heart of Empire

Jimmy Governor and his friend Jacky Underwood burst into the Mawbey house in Breelong, in the Australian colony of New South Wales, one late July night in 1900.[1] Wielding axes and clubs, the intruders fell upon Sarah Mawbey, five of her children, her young niece, and Helen Kerz, a teacher who boarded with the family. Sarah's husband, John Thomas Mawbey, and older sons were staying at the family's former homestead nearby.[2] John came running, boots unlaced and screaming for help. He found his daughter Grace and the teacher, Helen, lying near a creek. He carried Grace, bloodied and moaning, to the house. He later found another daughter, Hilda, dead in the creek. Grace, Hilda, their brother Percival, and Helen died that night. Sarah Mawbey survived only long enough to name her attackers.[3]

The killings led to one of the longest, most theatrical manhunts in Australian history. Hundreds of police, trackers, and volunteers fanned out across the colony. They caught Jacky Underwood quickly, but Jimmy Governor and his brother, Joe, went on the lam for nearly four months. The brothers robbed and killed as they went, taunting police with notes and clues.[4] In October, ninety-nine days later, police caught Jimmy. They shot Joe dead four days later.[5]

In the second half of the nineteenth century, many alienists and lawyers across the British Empire argued that the legal definition of insanity set out in the *M'Naghten* rules was unjust, as we have seen. The rules did not encompass many of the often-subtle manias and disorders of moral sense that might afflict an accused murderer. Although *M'Naghten* endured, defendants convinced juries to find them not guilty by reason of insanity, or persuaded colonial governors to commute their capital sentences to terms of imprisonment. Judges, lawyers, doctors, and political authorities improvised more capacious ideas of insanity in the interstices of the legal system. Even as *M'Naghten* remained unchanged in principle, flexible approaches to criminal responsibility proliferated.

Indigenous defendants, including Aboriginal Australians like Jimmy Governor, could face racial barriers to a successful insanity plea. It was conventional wisdom among doctors and colonial officials operating in many imperial jurisdictions that racialized people were less susceptible to insanity than their European counterparts. Modern life, with its anxieties, anomie, and nervous shocks, could easily upset the sensitive white mind. Nonwhite colonial subjects, according to many Victorians, were insulated from these stresses by their dullness and rough organization.[6]

And yet, the protective effects of primitivism could be shattered. Historians of psychiatry in Africa and the United States have argued that white physicians in the late-nineteenth and early-twentieth centuries often believed that Africans and African Americans went mad because they were culturally, and perhaps biologically, underdeveloped and therefore could not adapt to civilized society.[7] Megan Vaughan, in her work on Nyasaland (now Malawi), writes that colonial officials theorized that Africans experienced a psychically damaging culture shock ("deculturation") when they entered European-style schools, cities, and factories.[8] In 1890, the alienist Frederick Morton Manning, who had earlier expounded on the susceptibility of Irish-born Australians to madness, delivered a paper at the Intercolonial Medical Congress of Australasia entitled "Insanity Among the Australian Aborigines." He argued that insanity had been rare among Aboriginal Australians before British conquest, but that they were sickening rapidly due to greater contact with "civilization."[9] Victorian racial theories could support or undermine arguments for an Indigenous person's insanity. Either way, Indigenous accused were trapped in a civilizational matrix in which their responsibility could not be understood except through reference to their purportedly primitive nature.

Sometimes, Indigenous people invoked their alleged lack of civilization and naivete to blunt the force of colonial criminal law. Especially in the context of crimes inter se or property offenses, colonial authorities could justify moderate punishment—often touted as proof that British rule was merciful and humanitarian—on the ground that Indigenous people struggled to abide by British legal rules. In such cases, a defendant's culture could operate as an analogue of insanity, constituting a kind of mental, and moral, handicap. Like white women, defendants whom colonial authorities understood as "uncivilized" were not categorically irresponsible but, rather, less responsible. Qualities that in middle-class, white men signaled insanity—impulsivity, aggression, violence, the inability to internalize the values enshrined in law—were the normal province of Britain's "uncivilized" subjects.

What were the legal consequences of these subjects' ineluctably diminished responsibility? Women who killed their children, as previous chapters showed, had access to arguments against their responsibility that exceeded the scope of *M'Naghten*. Although their punishments could remain quite severe, especially for Indigenous women in the colonies, they were unlikely to die on British gallows. Indigenous men and women accused of other crimes could also use their status as less responsible subjects to argue for greater latitude in the application of British criminal justice. As in infanticide cases, arguments against such defendants' responsibility might take the form of insanity pleas but could also be expressed through less formal appeals to emotion, liberal humanitarianism, or the need for legal pluralism in colonial contexts. Though there was no formal "cultural defense" under British criminal law, culture-based defenses were nevertheless common. This cultural dimension of responsibility ran just under the surface of every criminal case, including cases involving only white Britons who, for example, failed to live up to the standards of bourgeois respectability.

Previous chapters described how shifts in the scientific approach to insanity challenged the jurisprudential model of criminal responsibility. Moral insanity, in particular, seemed to suggest that those who committed violent and disturbing crimes were, almost by definition, the victims of mental pathologies that obviated responsibility. This chapter takes up that specific strand of Victorian thinking about cognitive ability and connects it to race, or culture, or civilization and the effects of race science on the jurisprudence of criminal responsibility. Criminal anthropology buttressed the idea that moral insanity was a legitimate mental disease by positing that criminality was the product of biological predispositions. Meanwhile, and in parallel, Victorian race science's emphasis on hierarchy and human evolution offered a tidy explanation for violence. Many advocates for the existence of moral insanity believed that the condition was atavistic—the recrudescence in a sufferer's brain of qualities from an earlier evolutionary stage. Responsibility cases involving defendants marked as "primitive" echoed moral insanity cases and asked officials to consider the implications of a world in which very few subjects of the common law were supposed to be civilized enough to follow it.

Jimmy Governor was a man trapped between two worlds. He was of mixed Aboriginal and European descent (he was often called a "half-caste" in the Australian press) who had married a white woman, Ethel Page, in 1898. Page was sixteen years old and five months pregnant when she and Governor married. Governor had grown up in an Aboriginal community at the fringes of Australian settler society. Like many Aboriginal men, he worked odd jobs for white farmers.[10] At the time of the killings, he and his brother Joe and his friend Jacky had been hired to fix the Mawbeys' fence. Jimmy had recently clashed with John Mawbey over his pay and rations.[11] At his trial for the murder of Helen Kerz, the teacher, Jimmy described the abuse his family suffered. Marriages between Europeans and Aboriginal Australians were especially taboo among white settlers.[12] On the evening of the Breelong killings, Governor explained, he had gone to the farmhouse to confront Sarah Mawbey. "Did you tell my missus that any white woman who married a blackfellow ought to be shot? . . . Did you ask her what sort of nature did I have—black or white?" Jimmy asked Sarah. She and Helen Kerz laughed at him "with a sneering laugh," and Kerz said, "Pooh, you black rubbish, you want shooting for marrying a white woman."[13] At that, Governor told the court, he started hitting the women and could not stop.

Aboriginal people of mixed parentage were trapped between the safe houses of legal insanity and what we might see as claims to cultural incapacity, or the cultural defense. Aboriginal people with European ancestry occupied a fraught position in the colonial Australian imagination. At the turn of the twentieth century, white Victorians predicted the inevitable decline and disappearance of Australia's Aboriginal peoples, which historian Russell McGregor has called the "doomed race theory."[14] What Patrick Wolfe describes as the "logic of elimination" that underpinned Australian settler colonialism became more complex, however, as it encountered people of Aboriginal and European heritage. In the late-nineteenth century, self-styled experts argued that biological Aboriginality could be "bred out" over three generations—a person with one-sixteenth Aboriginal ancestry or less was, in their view, "white." To engineer the gradual "whitening" of the Aboriginal population, government officials mandated the separation of people of mixed descent from the broader Aboriginal population. Expelled from reserves, those of mixed parentage often led difficult lives in makeshift settlements on the outskirts of rural towns. Their sons and daughters

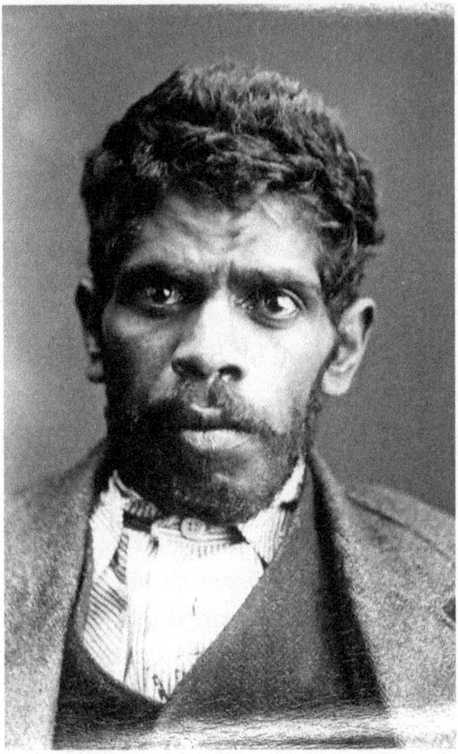

Jimmy Governor, 11 April 1900, Darlinghurst Gaol. Credit: NSW State Archives and Records, Gaol Inmates/ Prisoners Photos Index, 1870–1930, 3/6066, no. 8194.

were the first targets of the systematic removals of the "Stolen Generations," in which Aboriginal children were taken from their families and sent to youth institutions or, later, put up for adoption by white families.[15] Policies promoting interracial marriages encouraged people of mixed descent to become the spouses and, eventually, the parents of white Australians. One South Australian member of Parliament argued in 1910 that while "an aboriginal remained an unsophisticated child of nature all his life, a half-caste could easily be educated and civilized," before boasting about a girl of Euro-Aboriginal descent whom he had removed from her community and who "remained in his family until she was married to a white man—a respectable mechanic."[16]

The Australian colonies and, from 1901, the Australian Commonwealth pursued Aboriginal absorption with anxious determination. Interracial marriage, the strategy's core technology, threatened systems of social ordering premised on categorizing people by racial identity and indulging white preoccupations with racial purity.[17] To the surprise and dismay of many settlers, moreover, the Euro-Aboriginal population appeared to be increasing.[18] Rather than taking their assigned place at the bottom of white society, people of mixed descent often chose to live in Aboriginal communities, whether on official reserves or in informal camps. They built families with people of varying degrees of Aboriginal heritage, foiling official plans for their children's "whitening." Questions of class also complicated debates over biological absorption. Ethnologists, incipient eugenicists, and policy makers generally assumed that Euro-Aboriginal people would marry lower-class whites, leading some to fear the further degeneration of this troublesome segment of the settler population.[19]

In the late-nineteenth and early-twentieth centuries, officials and members of the general public became increasingly concerned about the preservation of white Australian racial stock in the face of what they saw as the twin menaces of immigration, especially from Asia, and the growth of the Euro-Aboriginal population. Newspaper headlines bemoaning the "Yellow Peril" of a "global Asiatic invasion" and the "Half-Caste Problem" proliferated.[20] The first independent Australian government, led by Edmund Barton, passed the Immigration Restriction Act (1901), which strictly favored white, European migrants over those from China, India, and the Pacific Islands. The increasingly intrusive and brutal Aboriginal assimilation policies of this era were, Wolfe argues, an "internal correlate" of the immigration-focused "White Australia Policy."[21]

Jimmy Governor's barrister was Francis Stewart Boyce, an ambitious young lawyer who would make his name in the case before going on to become a Supreme Court judge and politician.[22] He argued at trial that Sarah Mawbey and Helen Kerz had cruelly provoked Governor, and that the common-law partial defense of provocation should diminish his crime from murder to manslaughter.[23] Boyce built this defense on Governor's race. "Here was a man of no high feeling or high sentiment," he told the jury, "a rover under the roof of Heaven, a man who by his environment and nature had not learned to control himself as other men had. Could we, who had neglected, despised, and taunted the aboriginals, expect them to exercise the ordinary human control[?]"[24] Governor's lack of self-control was not his fault; settler society had not done enough to civilize him.

But Governor was also, Boyce argued, white and had married a white woman. Although marriages between white settlers and Aboriginal people were a central plank of Australian absorptionism, these relationships had a prescribed form. While marriages and sexual relationships, both coerced and consensual, between white men and nonwhite women were relatively common, especially on the frontier, relationships between white women and nonwhite men remained transgressive.[25] By marrying Ethel Page, Governor seemed to assert his right to participate in settler society—a claim the women of the Mawbey household took it upon themselves to reject. His heritage and his marriage made Governor, Boyce argued, "a man of sensitive nature—a better man than most blacks . . . and the taunts hurled at his wife were doubly felt by him." His rage at the insults against his wife betrayed his European sense of manly honor and chivalry. When Helen Kerz called him "black rubbish," Governor could forbear no longer—"the savage heart, tainted with the thirst of blood, burst through reason." In Boyce's estimation, Governor was doomed: a husband with the noble sentiments of a white man and the impulsivity and proclivity to violence of an Aboriginal person. The jurors were unmoved. They deliberated for only ten minutes before returning a guilty verdict.[26]

The timing of the case prompted commentators to connect Governor's fate with the fate of all Aboriginal people in the new Australian nation. On 1 January 1901, while the colonies celebrated their independence, Governor waited for death in a Sydney jail cell. One journalist complained that his hanging would spoil the festivities by reminding white Australians that their "civilization" rested on the violent subjugation of "savage" Aboriginal peoples. "Truly," he wrote, "[it is] an unfortunate period for the vindication, to the extreme degree of the laws of white civilisation! . . . [T]hose at all acquainted with the aboriginal races will recognise that they have not the same appreciation of barbaric acts as the superior and disciplined white races."[27] Queen Victoria died on 22 January 1901. Three days later, Jimmy Governor walked to the drop, pressing a cigarette between his lips.[28]

His fate might have been different if he had not been Aboriginal. A white man could have argued that the brutality of his crimes was evidence of madness. "If a white man were the author of such atrocities," wrote a journalist, "and without more motive, then he would be put down as a homicidal maniac."[29] The alternative—a defense based on Aboriginal custom or ignorance of British law—would also almost certainly have failed. Because Governor was not fully Aboriginal (in colonial eyes), Indigenous tradition could not sanction or explain his violence. That his victims were white settlers, including women and children, made mercy politically unpalatable. Boyce tried to plot a middle path, arguing that his whiteness made Governor proud, and his Aboriginality made him violent. Considering the plight of people of mixed parentage, one journalist observed, "his desires, if he possesses any, are perverted, and he is liable to fits of passion which transform him into a fiend. . . . [D]ivided as these are between a race that won't hold them as equals and another to whose depths they cannot sink, their case is hardly less sad."[30]

Indigenous defendants, including people of mixed heritage like Jimmy Governor, troubled colonial officials charged with applying the "laws of white civilization" to people whom Victorian racial thinking explicitly excluded from that civilization. At trial, Boyce argued that the "savage heart" of his client made it impossible for him to control himself in the face of racist abuse.[31] Boyce might easily have substituted the word "mind" for "heart." For the lawyer, Governor's indigeneity was akin to a mental disability, one that the common law ought to regard as similar to insanity. In an 1865 article, Robert Dunn, a British ethnologist, crudely articulated the imagined connection between race and cognitive ability when he argued for the similarity "between the narrow, low, and receding forehead in the skull of the poor idiot or degraded Bushman."[32] "So striking and so great, indeed," Dunn continued, "is the intellectual inferiority of the Bushman, the Australian, and the Negro to that of the Indo-European, that their claims even to our common humanity have been denied to them."[33] British judicial discourse constantly questioned the amenability of Indigenous people to common-law justice on the ground that they were impulsive, passionate, and dull. What was criminal law, premised as it was on self-control and understanding, to do?

Late-Victorian colonial officials attempted to square their belief in the mental weakness of Indigenous people with the mission to "civilize" them, including through the sound and judicious application of British law. Notwithstanding differences of culture, class, crime, and jurisdiction, Indigenous people forced to live under a British legal system seemed destined to commit crimes. In the opinion of some white Victorians, they were victims of a biological legacy that they could not deny and a legal order that they could not follow. In *The Pathology of Mind*, Maudsley put it vividly: "A precocious savage who had the ill fortune to develop a moral sense among savages would probably have no greater chance of survival than a tiger which developed a sudden horror of bloodshed." "[A]nd a low savage in a civilized society," he wrote, "must needs fare almost as badly as a carnivorous animal would fare in a land of herbivorous animals which it was forbidden to eat."[34]

British concerns that they had asked too much of their Indigenous subjects affected the operation of criminal justice in the colonies. For example, in a case tried in Australia's Northern Territory in 1900, Charles Dashwood, a white judge, argued that three Aboriginal men should be discouraged from pleading guilty to killing a pig with intent to steal it because he "did not favor natives being allowed to plead guilty unless it was clearly shown that they understood the nature of the charge." In the same court, on the same day, an Aboriginal man known as Long Peter was tried for the murder of another Aboriginal man, identified in colonial records as Jimmy. Jimmy died during a settling of scores between two Aboriginal communities following the accidental killing of an old woman, Long Peter's sister. Although the judge instructed the jurors that, technically, "no cognizance could be taken of individual or tribal customs as serving to excuse offenses against British law," he encouraged them to consider "the general facts as to the habits or customs prevailing among the natives" in determining the defendant's culpability. Ultimately, the jury convicted Long Peter of manslaughter and strongly recommended his pardon on the ground that his "act was the outcome of tribal custom."[35] He was released after three months.

Dashwood was no warrior for Aboriginal rights. In 1893, he had famously sentenced ten Aboriginal defendants to death within his first three days on the Northern Territory bench.[36] The widespread colonial belief that Indigenous people could not conform to foreign, "civilized" law could, however, lead in some cases to less punitive outcomes for Aboriginal defendants. Other colonial officials rejected Dashwood's approach and parried that the only way to bring civilization and justice to Britain's colonial subjects was to enforce British law without exception—even if applying the law in such cases involved, ironically, abandoning traditional understandings of mens rea and guilt.[37]

Concepts of race, culture, and civilization tended to overlap and blur in the Victorian era, and there were no meaningful or consistent boundaries between them in British legal policy or discourse. British officials slipped easily among religious ("Christian," "infidel"), civilizational ("primitive," "civilized"), and racial ("European," "African") categories as they thought and wrote about the differences between themselves and the people they ruled. The ideas of British social theorists such as Herbert Spencer, E. B. Tylor, and John Lubbock—especially their interest in the evolution of human societies from savagery to civilization—appeared in British courtrooms.[38] Colonial officials, however, including jurists, rarely quoted directly from these early anthropological texts. Largely, the distinctions among various social scientific schools of thought were lost in their translation into the everyday common sense of colonial administration. Mark Francis, writing about nineteenth-century Canada, describes the concept of civilization as a "reservoir filled with the thoughts of scholars and missionaries." When officials drew from this reservoir, they generally did so without much reflection, and if queried, "would have replied that they had no need of theories."[39]

This characterization of British officialdom holds across the British Empire. Jimmy Governor's lawyer, Boyce, for one, did not need to provide a scientific account of the history of civilization or human evolution to argue that Governor was innately prone to violence and deficient in self-control. By the turn of the twentieth century, white Australians assumed the psychological and physical difference of Aboriginal people. Boyce's task, in court, was to convince the jury that these differences went some way toward excusing Governor's violence—a much harder sell to settlers who could imagine their own farmhouses splattered with the blood of their wives and children.

Although lawyers, doctors, and officials might have drawn on the reservoir of civilizational thinking haphazardly, to borrow Francis's metaphor, it is important to step back and consider some of the thinkers whose theories filled it. In the second half of the nineteenth century, British alienists and social theorists became increasingly preoccupied with the connections between theories of racial decline and understandings of criminality. Their interest in how "savagery" might affect both crime and criminal responsibility was bolstered by the proliferation of writings about degeneration by Continental European authorities.

In an 1894 article published in the *Journal of the Anthropological Institute of Great Britain and Ireland,* Sir Thomas Smith Clouston reflected on the state of criminal anthropology in Britain.[40] Clouston, an aristocratic Scottish alienist and asylum superintendent, wrote extensively on mental disease. Like many educated Victorians, he was convinced of the importance of criminal anthropology. "I think the time is very near," he wrote, "when some knowledge of it will be required of all medical men, and especially of all lawyers and the higher officials of our prisons."[41] When the doctors, lawyers, and prison officials of Britain finally embraced criminal anthropology as their European counterparts had done, they would need to consider the evolutionary sources of criminality. In particular, Clouston explained, Britons would need to confront "the not fully evolved man who might do his work well enough in a primitive society, but who cannot accommodate himself to the conditions of a highly organised and largely artificial modern society."[42]

The two most influential Continental thinkers who promoted degeneration in the late-nineteenth century were Bénédict Auguste Morel, a French alienist and amateur ethnologist, and Cesare Lombroso, the early criminologist who collected photographs of criminals, including Frederick Deeming.[43]

The late-nineteenth-century understanding of degeneration was strongly associated with Morel, whose 1857 *Traité des dégénérescences physiques, intellectuelles et morales de l'espèce humaine et des causes qui produisent ces variétés maladives* (Treatise on the Physical, Intellectual, and Moral Degeneration of the Human Species and the Causes of These Morbid Variations) was popular among Britons worried about crime.[44] As Clouston put it, "the term 'degeneracy' is in the mouths of all writers on the subject since Morel's great work was written."[45] Morel was the superintendent of the Saint-Yon lunatic asylum in northern France when he first published his *Traité*. He was also a corresponding member of several medical societies, including the Royal Academy of Medicine in Turin, where Lombroso worked. Morel began the *Traité* by lamenting the recent growth in the number of epileptics, "idiots," and criminals in Europe and the United States.[46] As a young man, he had become convinced that the physical and moral histories of man could not be studied in isolation, and that ethnology and mind science were natural bedfellows.[47] He was particularly taken with Prichard's *Natural History of Man* (1843), in which Prichard argued for the single origin of humanity (monogenism) while meticulously cataloguing the physical and moral differences of various "tribes of the human family."[48] Morel, however, was much more pessimistic about the trajectory of human development than Prichard had been.

Morel took a comprehensive view of the causes and effects of degeneration. He believed that insanity, criminality, and the primitive state of non-European peoples foretold humanity's creeping decline to its primordial state. While criminality and insanity were not identical, Morel maintained that immorality, misery, and alcoholism were frequent causes of intellectual disturbance.[49] Degeneration was so variegated that it could be detected everywhere. No one was safe. This vision of human evolution in free fall dominated late-nineteenth-century social science.[50] Maudsley, unsurprisingly, admired Morel, whom he praised for his lucid account of "the brute brain within the man's."[51]

Lombroso based his explanation for crime on a belief in the innate violence and impulsivity of non-European peoples. In 1876, he was appointed to a professorship in legal medicine at the University of Turin. That year, he published his most famous work, *The Criminal Man*.[52] He initially speculated that criminality among whites was often the result of isolated instances of atavism among unlucky individuals. Scholars have noted, though, that Lombroso's understanding of primitivism became more sweeping over time, drawing closer to Morel's account of degeneration as a widespread, intergenerational blight by the 1880s. For Lombroso, criminals were throwbacks to a savage past, subject to the violent impulses of pre-civilized man. Criminality was inborn and biological, detectable in sloped brows, large jaws, and other features.[53] Lombroso argued that criminal Europeans shared many physical and mental traits with "primitive man"—proof that criminality was as ineluctable as evolution.[54] Nicole Rafter argues that one of Lombroso's earlier, still untranslated works, *L'uomo bianco e l'uomo di colore* (*The White Man and the Man of Color*) (1871), shows the centrality of race and primitivism in his account of criminality. Rafter describes how in *L'uomo bianco* Lombroso compared the skulls of Indigenous peoples to those of apes, arguing that Indigenous Americans and other racialized people were morally and physically similar to white criminals.[55] Lombroso was not alone in describing criminality as an aspect of savagery, nor was he the first to posit that non-European peoples were less civilized than Europeans. He also had many critics, especially among British intellectuals. Biological, determinist theories of criminality like his, however, made it more difficult for British jurists to ignore the implications of degeneration and stadial theory for criminal-law jurisprudence.

The late-Victorian obsession with civilizational and racial taxonomy in the empire reflected concerns about Britain's future.[56] Victorians saw their society as technologically advanced, commercially sophisticated, and territorially ambitious. The empire had expanded in the last decades of the century, as Britain pushed aggressively into Africa. Scientific advances, especially Darwinism, complemented an increasingly secular vision of the universe, dominated by the rational, self-disciplined individual. As Britain hurtled toward liberal modernity it was natural, to the educated middle class, that some categories of people—women, children, criminals, paupers, laborers, Irishmen, and the colonized masses—should be left behind. There were differences among an Irish farmer, an English thief, and an Indian lawyer, writes George Stocking in his history of British anthropology, but all were believed to lack the intelligence, foresight, and self-restraint of the truly civilized.[57]

Britain's rapid industrialization struck many Victorians as dangerous, and not only for those categories of white Britons deemed constitutionally incapable of meeting the expectations of an increasingly sophisticated and dynamic society. Commentators also worried that the pace of change could cause individual and social breakdown. Clouston, for example, wrote, "The continual process of too sudden adaptation to new environments and new conditions that is going on in our modern life constitutes . . . one of the great causational factors of criminality as I believe it does of certain forms of insanity."[58]

Moreover, many social theorists questioned whether middle-class British men had escaped their savage origins. Civilization was fragile. Herbert Spencer, for one, argued that humanity was still tethered to its primordial moorings.[59] Contemporary Europeans, with their humane societies, charities, and vegetarianism, had largely transcended their bloodthirsty past—but not completely. Europeans who adopted "primitive" customs in "primitive" places suffered from the "barbarizing of colonists"; American "Lynch law" proved that Europeans could easily succumb to savagery.[60] Even in England, Britons' "savage selfishness" was evident in their shameless gambling, their reckless commercial speculation, and their jostling at the doors of theaters.[61] British believers in degeneration saw threats to their civilization everywhere, including in London's prisons, poorhouses, taverns, and tenements.

"Savagery" was more than a threat to the United Kingdom, however. It was a fact of empire. Many millions of people whom some Britons considered "savage" lived under British rule in the colonies. Their skulls adorned the desks of well-to-do physicians and professors. "Savagery" was thus a domestic and an imperial question. When Victorian theorists described the conquest of primitive peoples by civilized ones as natural, they complicated the moral justification for the British imperial project. According to this view, Britons were pawns of nature, playing their assigned part in evolution. In his 1926 *Crime and Custom in Savage Society*, legal anthropologist Bronislaw Malinowski wrote, "The study of the rapidly diminishing savage races is one of those duties of civilization—now actively engaged in the destruction of primitive life—which so far has been lamentably neglected."[62] Which was too bad, continued Malinowski, because anthropology could "help the white man to govern, exploit, and 'improve' the native with less pernicious results to the latter."[63]

Malinowski, although writing in the twentieth century, identified the nexus of anthropology, problems of governance, and ideas of civilizational uplift that unsettled late-Victorian imperial law. British ethnology abetted imperial governance. A belief in the inherent difference of colonized peoples could, however, also cast doubt on the integrity of Britain's most important tool for the everyday governance of its empire: the law.

However enthusiastically it was sometimes pursued, the incorporation of Indigenous peoples into the British criminal justice system proceeded in fits and starts. It was not until the 1830s, for example, that the Australian colonies forcefully asserted their criminal jurisdiction over the Aboriginal population.[64] In other colonies, the process took much longer. In 2001, John Comaroff coined the term "lawfare" to describe the efforts of the colonial state to conquer and control Indigenous people through law. In the same essay, he cautioned against taking British declarations of legal supremacy at face value. In fact, colonialism was "often an underdetermined, chaotic business, less a matter of the sure hand of oppression . . . than of the disarticulated, semi-coherent, inefficient strivings for modes of rule that might work in unfamiliar, intermittently hostile places a long way from home."[65] British imperial law in the nineteenth century bears out this core tension between aspirations to control Indigenous populations and the limits of the colonial apparatus of governance. These limits were primarily physical and financial—a paucity of resources and personnel—but could also be ideological. Even after authorities declared the preeminence of imperial jurisdiction over crime, they continued to question whether non-Europeans were appropriate subjects of British law.

To most late-Victorian Britons, the inferiority of colonized people was an axiom of imperial government. Although white, specifically white-British, supremacy was a useful justification for colonial rule, it made questions of criminal responsibility more complex. This complexity did not sabotage imperialism. Scholars have argued persuasively that the "rule of colonial difference" and the colonial liberalism that it underpinned did not undo the empire.[66] Although greed and violence often overcame their scruples, the lieutenants of empire remained sensitive to fault lines in the ideology of British rule, however. Sometimes, British officials interrogated the justice of expecting Indigenous people to think and act like Britons while simultaneously declaring that it was impossible for them to do so.[67] Defense lawyers and witnesses who introduced ethnographic evidence to argue that their clients were not responsible subjects hoped to exploit the apparent mismatch between Anglo legal principles and the mental and moral capacity of Indigenous defendants.

An Australian case involving an Indian defendant, Fatta Chand, shows colonial racial thinking at work. The jurists and commentators in Chand's case never mentioned Chevers's *Manual of Medical Jurisprudence for Bengal and the North-West Provinces* or any other ethnological or medico-legal treatise explicitly. They did not need to. Ideas developed by men like Chevers resonated around the empire. Whenever non-Europeans entered a British courtroom, whether as defendants or witnesses, they encountered a mire of popular ethnographic and social scientific knowledge. This knowledge could sometimes diminish their culpability for their criminal acts—but it also diminished their status as responsible subjects.

Fatta Chand arrived in Melbourne on the steamship *Nerbudda* on 25 January 1890. The economic boom of the 1870s and 1880s in Victoria had brought new waves of Indians, Afghans, and Syrians to the colony.[68] Like many new immigrants from Asia and the Middle East, Chand worked as a hawker selling small goods—aprons, scarves, jewelry—door to door. Hawkers peddled their wares in tony suburbs, on crowded city streets, and on Aboriginal reservations. They flowed through Melbourne society, seeping through the barriers that divided the respectable from the penurious. Hawkers needed a government license, which they could acquire only by demonstrating basic English proficiency in Hawker's License Courts.[69] Many who could not obtain a hawker's license worked illegally, living on the margins of a marginal trade.

A young Indian man named Juggoo Mull had accompanied Fatta Chand on his journey across the sea.[70] Mull was slight, sporting a beard and a moustache.[71] He received a hawker's license and lived with some twenty others in a house owned by Azamoo Khan, an Afghan wholesaler and overseer.[72] On the morning of 27 November 1890, a butcher in the town of Healesville noticed a pile of brush at the bottom of an embankment. He made his way down and shifted the branches, which lay across a patch of freshly disturbed earth. He dug away the dirt and uncovered a man's torso, with its arms missing. He dug deeper and saw a face.[73] It was Juggoo Mull.

Police arrested Chand.[74] He and Mull had worked together, hawking and taking odd jobs at the Aboriginal Station at Corranderk and on the road between the station and Azamoo Khan's house in Melbourne. Sergeants Considine and Cawsey, the detectives who would lead the manhunt for Frederick Deeming two years later, headed the investigation. Many witnesses described seeing Mull and Chand together a few days before Mull disappeared. Considine and Cawsey could not discover much about their suspect, but they believed that he had fallen into debt and had killed his friend to rob him.[75] Chand vehemently denied the charges.

Chand's anonymity and ethnicity complicated his path through the colonial justice system. Hawking without a license, he had avoided busy roads, urban centers, and strangers. Chand told prison surgeon Andrew Shields, who examined him at Melbourne Gaol, that he could not provide an alibi because he had deliberately avoided attracting attention.[76] Police investigations included the compilation of the personal histories (the "antecedents") of those arrested. These narratives were often detailed portraits that structured how lawyers, officials, and the public understood the crime and the suspect's motives. The report by Considine and Cawsey on Chand was short. They declared their ignorance of his life, "owing to the short time he has resided in the colony, his nationality and the nomadic life he has been leading."[77] His carefully cultivated anonymity hurt Chand. White experts filled in the gaps in his biography with generalizations about Indian character plucked from popular ethnology. Victorian authorities knew little about him, but they believed they knew enough. He was a canvas onto which officials could project images of how Indians behaved—how they killed, what they wore, what they believed—without the inconvenience of first having to erase the traces of a life.

Chand was tried at the Supreme Court in Melbourne. Gilbert Smith, a journalist and self-proclaimed "Oriental interpreter," took the stand for the defense. Smith claimed to have known Mull and Chand for some time. He told the court that Chand could not speak English well, "although he might be able to say 'You buy' and things of that sort." Chand was the last man to see Mull alive. The judge, Hickman Molesworth, explained in his instructions to the jury that the evidence against Chand was "purely of a circumstantial character." Eleven jurors voted to convict Chand of murder. One man, however, insisted that the evidence against Chand was too flimsy to justify a guilty verdict. After ten hours of deliberation and despite Molesworth's cajoling, the jury could not agree, and a new trial was ordered.[78] Chand was tried again three weeks later, before a different judge. In his closing address, Chand's lawyer, William Forlonge, who also appeared in the Deeming trial, argued that the case was one of mistaken identity. Forlonge, as Australian lawyers often did, impugned the reliability of nonwhite witnesses. He disputed the evidence given by the Aboriginal inhabitants of Coranderk on the ground that "the aboriginals might easily be mistaken in recognizing Fatta Chand." He invoked the canard of Indian mendacity and declared that "he did not hesitate to charge the Hindoo witnesses with perjury."[79]

The evidence in this new trial was the same, but the judge's instructions to the jury were not. According to one journalist, the judge accepted that the evidence against Chand was circumstantial but added, "If juries refused to act on circumstantial evidence then half the criminals would be allowed to go free."[80] After deliberating for three hours, the jurors returned a guilty verdict. They did not recommend mercy.

There were problems with the trial. Smith, Chand's interpreter, wrote to the governor, the Earl of Hopetoun, objecting to how Chand's Indian identity had been discussed in court. The Crown prosecutor had argued that only an Indian could have killed Mull, because Hindu murderers regularly dismembered their victims. Smith contended that there was no such "invariable practice." Moreover, if he were forced to identify one, it would be poisoning. Smith disputed the testimony of Aboriginal and white witnesses placing Chand with Mull on the day of the murder, as he claimed that Indians were notoriously difficult to tell apart. He argued that a Muslim amulet found at the crime scene would never have been kept by either Mull or Chand, as Hindus. Finally, Smith described Chand as "a stranger in a strange land," "a poor unfortunate Hindu, destitute and pleading for a fair trial." "Here is an Indian hawker," Smith wrote, "sneaking through a district, . . . unable to speak English, fearful of arrest for having no license, locked up in gaol without money, defended by the Crown as a pauper, called upon to prove where he was the week the murder was committed!! Could he have done so?"[81]

On 14 April 1891, the members of the Executive Council considered the case. They interviewed the judge. They looked at some of the exhibits and read Smith's letter. After a "prolonged discussion," the council directed that Chand's death sentence be carried out in two weeks' time.[82] In the run-up to his execution, the public's fascination with Chand grew. It was customary for a spiritual adviser to minister to condemned prisoners, but no Hindu religious official could be found in Victoria. Eventually, authorities mustered a "Brahmin" from a "nearby colony," but Chand "repelled" him. A Protestant clergyman who claimed to have visited his village in India attended him in his last days.[83] The prisoner was inconsolable and refused food. The press hazarded, ghoulishly, that Chand was scheming to "[cheat] Jones, the hangman, of his £5 hanging fee" by starving himself to death. "Eternal misery" supposedly awaited Hindus who ate food prepared by Christians or were executed by them.[84] One newspaper reported that Chand "broke down" when the noose was placed around his neck, protesting his innocence in his native tongue.[85] Another reporter interviewed a "well-known Hindoo interpreter" who thought little of Chand's declarations of innocence because, purportedly, Hindus believed that confession only worsened a prisoner's suffering. Chand made one dying request: "Tell [my father] I'm dead, but do not tell him that I was hanged. Say I died of cholera, and that my body was burned."[86]

Colonial authorities, including his partisans, could not interview his family, could not prove where Chand had been on the day Juggoo Mull was killed, and could not have visited Chand's village in Punjab. Despite these real limitations, much of their ignorance about him was willful or feigned. Chand's English might have been poor, but Gilbert Smith, a second court interpreter, and the minister who visited Chand in prison all spoke his language. None of them shared anything personal about him with the authorities. Only Smith tried to intervene with the Executive Council on his behalf, and he largely ignored Chand's biography in favor of arguing in generalities about Indians. Chand was in police custody for months, but still authorities loudly claimed almost total ignorance about him as an individual, while often boasting of their familiarity with the culture of Indians, or "Hindoos," as a people. Colonial authorities—and Chand's own lawyers—undervalued the testimony of the most direct witnesses in the case, including Chand's supplier, Khan, the Aboriginal Australians who recognized Chand from his visits to Coranderk, and the men who shared his house. They were not white settlers, and so could not be trusted. Chand did have connections in Victoria, but in the minds of the Australian police, jurors, and jurists in his case, these connections were not enough to tie an Indian man to Melbourne. His voice rarely pierces the reams of newspaper articles and letters about him. But Chand *was* speaking—to the minister, to the prison doctor, to interpreters, to coworkers, and even to the men who gathered to watch him die.

Cultural defenses did not always fail. The case of the Rani Swarnamoyee of the Bengali *zamindari*, or estate, of Cossimbazar, about 125 miles north of Calcutta, shows the power of culture in imperial courts. Swarnamoyee won her case before the Judicial Committee of the Privy Council in one of only a handful of criminal appeals heard by the committee in the nineteenth century. The story behind the case came to light in the 1960s, when Somendra Chandra Nandy, a descendent of Swarnamoyee, discovered a cache of documents in boxes and trunks in his ancestral home, ultimately publishing a family history.[87] His *History of the Cossimbazar Raj* (1986) begins with Krishnanath, Swarnamoyee's husband.

In 1844, the year of his death, Krishnanath was the heir of Cossimbazar. His father had died, leaving his son under the watchful eye of the Bengal Court of Wards and under the thumb of his mother and grandmother. Although he was an avid horseman, Krishnanath was thin, pale, and sickly. As a teenager, he married Swarnamoyee, then only eleven years old. He soon sued his mother and grandmother over their alleged financial mismanagement of his estate, keeping physicians in his retinue to guard against retaliatory poisoning. When he reached eighteen, the age of majority under British law, Krishnanath's money troubles were abating. He and Swarnamoyee lived in a grand house in the countryside, and Krishnanath acquired a large collection of Arabian horses and English hunting hounds. He patronized the arts and pursued interests in horticulture, physics, astronomy, mining, and shipping.

In 1841, the Indian government officially awarded him the title of Raja Bahadur, and in 1842, Swarnamoyee gave birth to a daughter.[88]

There were dark rumors in Cossimbazar that Krishnanath had threatened to flog Swanamoyee for failing to produce a son, and that he had tried to kill his infant daughter by leaving her on the floor of an empty room. In the summer of 1844, Krishnanath, then twenty-two, was drinking heavily, and Swarnamoyee was pregnant with their second child. The management of the zamindari was in disarray, and tax revenue was falling. In September of 1844, a box of jewels went missing. Krishnanath's servant Keshab Sarkar accused another servant against whom he bore a grudge, whom guards then beat and tortured. When the local magistrate heard about the servant's treatment, he issued orders for Krishnanath's arrest. Krishnanath fled to Calcutta, knowing he would be pursued. In late October, the servant died of his injuries. On hearing the news, Krishnanath fatally shot himself through the eye with a double-barreled shotgun.[89]

When her husband died, Swarnamoyee assumed the stewardship of the Cossimbazar Raj. She studied languages and the zamindar system, traveling across the land in a palanquin, announced by drums and flanked by elephants, swordsmen, and carts full of money and provisions.[90] Legal difficulties plagued the estate, however. In June 1845, Swarnamoyee gave birth to a second daughter. With no male heir, her place in Cossimbazar was in doubt. Krishnanath had hastily drafted a series of new wills in the days before his suicide, in which he purported to leave almost all of his property to his servant Keshab Sarkar.[91] Swarnamoyee and her supporters drafted a memorial to the Queen in which they argued that her husband had not been in his right mind when he wrote the final will.[92] The case went to court in India, where the will was ruled invalid and Swarnamoyee retained control of the estate. Krishnanath's relatives were unsatisfied, however, and colluded with East India Company officials to pursue the matter further.

In July 1863, one of many lawsuits challenging the inheritance was appealed to the Judicial Committee of the Privy Council in London. The central issue was the legality of suicide in India. Under the British law of *felo de se*, suicide was a crime, and a suicide's personal property was forfeited to the Crown. The appellants in the case, the government of Bengal, argued that Anglo criminal law applied to both Indians and Europeans in Calcutta when the rajah had committed suicide in 1844. They asserted that India was a "barbarous country," and that the British had brought their laws with them as conquerors.[93] Therefore, much of Krishnanath's estate was rightfully government property.

This argument rested on an interpretation of *Calvin's Case*. The case, decided by the English Court of King's Bench in 1608, was the most famous articulation of the nature of subjecthood and jurisdiction in common-law jurisprudence.[94] Robert Calvin was a child from Edinburgh who inherited property in England shortly after the union of Scotland and England in 1603.[95] The court held that all those governed by the King of England at the time of their birth were British subjects, including Calvin. Edward Coke's decision in *Calvin's Case* cast subjecthood as a moral relationship fixed in natural law. This formulation lived on long after Calvin was dead and buried. William Blackstone, in his eighteenth-century *Commentaries,* wrote that subjecthood was a "natural allegiance" that was "intrinsic, and primitive."[96] The bond between subject and sovereign was portable, difficult to transfer, and survived even treason.[97]

The relationship between political subjecthood and legal subjecthood in the British Empire was ambiguous. In *Calvin's Case,* Coke wrote that if a Christian king conquered a Christian territory, then the laws of that territory were presumed to remain in force unless explicitly altered by the conqueror. If a Christian king defeated an infidel kingdom, however, "there ipso facto the laws of the infidel are abrogated, for that they be not only against Christianity, but against the law of God and of nature."[98] Daniel Hulsebosch argues that the case has often been misinterpreted to mean that Britons overseas always brought the common law with them. Hulsebosch contends that Coke's judgment was in fact far narrower: status as a British subject only entitled a person to the protections of the common law inside Britain. Those living in British dominions overseas were subject to various laws depending on their legal traditions and the circumstances and degree of their colonization by the Crown.[99]

The appellants in Swarnamoyee's case aimed to convince the Judicial Committee that India was an infidel country that had been conquered by the Crown, and thus was subject to the common law. Lord Kingsdown, who delivered the Judicial Committee's decision, was not persuaded. Kingsdown praised Lord Stowell's well-known decision in the *Indian Chief* (1800) case, in which he considered the jurisdiction of British law over an American official living at the British factory at Calcutta. Stowell explained that in the Western world, alien merchants and native peoples mixed easily. "But in the East," he continued, "from the oldest times, an immiscible character has been kept up; foreigners . . . continue strangers and sojourners, as all their fathers were."[100] Stowell found that the American official had become, to some extent, legally

British while under British protection in Calcutta. *Indian Chief*, however, was remembered primarily for Stowell's account of British India as fundamentally heterogeneous. British law superseded Mughal or other strands of Indian law in British factories and ports but not beyond. Britons had not, and probably would not, integrate into wider Indian society; British and Indian life, and law, were incompatible.

Kingsdown followed Stowell's lead. He described Mughal India as a "very populous and highly civilized country, under the government of a powerful Mahomedan ruler"—hardly an empty or barbarous wasteland. The judges found that British law was not applicable to Indian Hindus or Muslims at the time of the first British settlement, and that only express alteration of Indian law by the Crown could have brought Indians under its jurisdiction. In addition, even when British civil and criminal law was explicitly applied to India, as the judges agreed it had been in Calcutta by the Charter of 1726, British law did not extend to non-Christians if this produced "intolerable injustice and cruelty."[101] The Indian Penal Code of 1860 did not classify suicide as a punishable offense, although it did criminalize abetting suicide and suicide attempts.[102]

The British Indian government's efforts to assert the criminality of suicide in 1844 struck the members of the Judicial Committee as insensitive. There were many British laws that they felt were unsuitable for Indians. For instance, to punish Indians for polygamy under British bigamy laws would have been "monstrous." The British prohibition against the "heinous offence" of having carnal knowledge of young girls was, in the judges' view, inappropriate in a place where girls were often married at or under the age of ten.[103] Turning at last to suicide, Kingsdown argued that self-murder was a crime primarily against the King, who lost a subject, and against the Christian commandments. Part of the common-law punishment for suicide was the victim's exclusion from burial in consecrated ground. This was no punishment at all for non-Christians, which the committee took as evidence that the European law of felo de se was not applicable to Indians. In non-Christian countries suicide "deriv[ed] its moral character altogether from the circumstances" and could be either meritorious or immoral.[104] The appellants' appeal against Swarnamoyee was dismissed.

The Judicial Committee may have rejected the notion that India was "barbarous," but its judges never suggested that British rule in India was illegitimate. The committee heard Swarnamoyee's case in London in 1864, when Victorian civilizational and ethnological thinking dominated imperial ideology. Kingsdown's contempt for bigamy, child marriage, and suicide was clear. The judges did not doubt the superiority of British law, or of Britons who were supposed to be enlightened enough to be judged under it. Hindu and Muslim Indians' deficient moral sense forced a deviation from British legal principles. Indians would experience metropolitan suicide law as cruel, not just. In the eyes of the Judicial Committee, the victory of Swarnamoyee in the case proved her people's inability to participate fully in British civilization.

Aboriginal Australians and Indians occupied very different places in the Victorian racial cosmology. There was little agreement about where various cultures should be placed along the civilizational scale, although settled, militarized, and monotheistic peoples tended to rate higher than nomadic peoples with less transparent (to Europeans) traditions of belief and governance.[105] Aboriginal Australians were almost always classed among the least civilized peoples, while Indians usually fared better. Class also inflected the civilizational classification of individuals and groups within populations; an Indian noble was more likely to be described as "civilized" than was a humble peddler.[106] Charles Darwin, not known for ethnographic overstatement, wrote in *The Descent of Man* (1871) that he considered Aboriginal Australians to be only a short evolutionary "break" away from the gorilla.[107] Criminal cases involving Aboriginal Australian defendants therefore particularly tested Britons' faith in the universal applicability and justice of British law.

Aboriginal Australians' relationship to British colonial governments was often in question in the nineteenth century.[108] Damen Ward argues that many Australian colonial officials were zealously exceptionalist; that is, they believed that British law was culturally specific, and that it was unfair to expect Indigenous peoples to meet the standards of the most civilized legal system in the world.[109] Ward analyzes an 1837 essay, "Exceptional Laws in Favour of the Natives of New Zealand," in which the author argues that laws can only govern parties of roughly equal power, "but where one of the parties is immeasurably inferior to the other, the only consequence . . . will be to destroy the weaker under a show of justice."[110] In the same year, the authors of the report of the British Parliamentary Select Committee on Aboriginal Tribes wrote that to require Indigenous people to observe British laws would be "absurd, and to punish their non-observance of them by severe penalties is palpably unjust."[111] The report expressed the Evangelical, reformist committee's belief that imperial violence and cupidity had tainted the civilization that British rule promised.[112]

The passionate paternalism that animated the Select Committee waned with the nineteenth century. Lisa Ford argues that from the 1830s white settlers in the colonies grew increasingly intolerant of Indigenous exemptions from common-law authority.[113] Sir George Grey, for example, who served terms as governor of South Australia, New Zealand, and the Cape Colony, saw the exceptionalists' humanitarianism as misguided. He thought that uncivilized laws, not biological destiny, kept Indigenous people primitive. Aboriginal Australians were, he wrote, "as apt and intelligent as any other race of men," but their laws were so debased that "it would appear . . . impossible that any nation subject to them could ever emerge from a savage state."[114] Although efforts to use British law to govern Aboriginal Australians increased in the mid-nineteenth century, officials still made many formal and informal exceptions to common-law jurisdiction. Australian legal historians have noted that white authorities were reluctant to prosecute Aboriginal people for crimes committed inter se even into the twentieth century.[115] Partly, this reluctance stemmed from logistical difficulties. Few white Australians spoke Indigenous languages. Investigating crime in Aboriginal communities could strain police resources. Racist tropes about the untrustworthiness of Aboriginal witnesses further discouraged authorities from spending time and money gathering what they assumed was faulty evidence.[116] Cases in which colonial authorities hesitated to investigate, prosecute, or punish Aboriginal Australians should not, though, be seen only as artifacts of official neglect or resource scarcity. Officials' apparent derogations from criminal justice policies can also reveal uncertainty about the applicability of common-law standards to Aboriginal people, including thresholds of criminal responsibility.

In one 1858 case, two Aboriginal men, known to colonial authorities as Old Man Billy and Young Man Billy, were accused of hitting another Aboriginal man, identified as Johnny, over the head and then drowning him in a river. Old Man Billy and his nephew Young Man Billy were charged with murder, and their case was tried at Ballarat, about seventy miles west of Melbourne.[117] The principal witness in the case was an Aboriginal woman known as Kitty, who testified that she had seen "the Billys" strike Johnny with a rock. The judge and jury found her account persuasive but made much of the fact that she was "unsworn" and so, in their eyes, unreliable. The jury found both men guilty of murder but strongly urged mercy. In a letter to the Executive Council of Victoria, the judge supported the recommendation "on the ground of their ignorance of our customs. And the peculiar nature of their own."[118] Both men's sentences were commuted from death to seven years' hard labor.[119]

Although the sentence was not death, it was severe. Old Man Billy died in April 1859, after he and Young Man Billy had been at work breaking stones in a prison stockade for months. The cause of death was officially recorded as dropsy. He was forty.[120]

In 1860, an Aboriginal man known as Peter but who called himself Mun-gett was accused of raping a seven-year-old white girl in a small town in the Pentland Hills, about forty miles outside Melbourne.[121] Like Jimmy Governor, it seems possible, based on newspaper reports, that Mun-gett was of mixed European and Aboriginal heritage. He and everyone around him, however, considered Mun-gett Aboriginal, both culturally and racially.[122] His case was tried at the Supreme Court in Melbourne. One of his barristers entered a special plea before the trial. The lawyer argued that his client belonged to a sovereign Aboriginal tribe, and that he "did never become subject to, or submit himself, or otherwise acknowledge allegiance to, our said Lady the Queen."[123] Mun-gett demanded the right to be tried by a tribal court with customary jurisdiction over serious crimes. Newspapers reported that this was the first case in Victoria in which an Aboriginal person refused to plead on the ground that he was not a British subject.[124] After some debate, the lawyer agreed to reserve the question of Mun-gett's status as a British subject to be heard before the full court, in the event of a conviction.[125]

William Thomas testified in Mun-gett's defense. At the time, Thomas worked as the Guardian of Aborigines, an office created in the late 1830s in which colonial governments across the empire engaged "Guardians" or "Protectors" to supervise Aboriginal communities and, in theory, protect them from violence and exploitation.[126] Thomas did little to further Mun-gett's cause. He told the jury that for Aboriginal Australians, "the more civilized the worse," and that Peter had lately begun living among settlers.[127] Here, Thomas expressed the colonial belief in the danger of "civilization" for native people, which also shaped accounts of Jimmy Governor's responsibility forty years later. Thomas argued that Mun-gett's contact with European society had unbalanced his mind, unleashing violent impulses. Under cross-examination, Thomas declared, Aboriginal Australians "know right from wrong. [Mun-gett] is punishable for Rape. It is a crime. They have laws for almost every offence. He would be punished for Rape by the father. It would be a blow to the head." Only under reexamination by the defense did Thomas add, "They [Aboriginal people] never put them to death for Rape."[128] Mun-gett was found guilty and sentenced to death. The Supreme Court, sitting in full, convened some months later to consider the special plea. "The Court did not call on the Solicitor-General for any reply," the Melbourne *Argus* reported, "but held that the Queen's writ runs throughout this colony, and that British law is binding on all peoples within it; and that the conviction was good."[129] Mun-gett's sentence was later reviewed by the Executive Council and commuted to fifteen years' hard labour.[130]

R v Peter set the precedent in Victoria for the subjection of Aboriginal Australians to British criminal law. Some months later, defense counsel in a manslaughter case involving an Aboriginal couple attempted to distinguish *Peter*, in which the defendant was Aboriginal but the victim was white, from cases where both parties were Aboriginal. In *R v Jemmy*, the full Supreme Court heard the special plea that the colonial courts should allow Aboriginal people to be tried by their customary courts for crimes inter se. Lawyers for the defense compared Aboriginal Australians to Indigenous Americans, to the Irish, and even to Normans after the Conquest. In response, the court affirmed *Peter* and the supremacy of imperial jurisdiction. Chief Justice Stawell added, however, "It is not intended to decide that in no case might there be a concession to a subject race of immunity from the laws of the conquerors living among them."[131]

Some, including Australian Supreme Court judges, have taken *Peter* and *Jemmy* as proof that criminal law applied equally to Europeans and Aboriginal people in the second half of the nineteenth century.[132] Against this view, I propose that both *Peter* and *Jemmy* should instead be seen as evidence that jurisdiction over non-Europeans was not a settled matter for imperial jurists. In *Peter*, the Supreme Court entertained the argument by Mun-gett that he was not a subject of the Queen, and the Executive Council commuted his sentence. In *Jemmy*, the chief justice explicitly circumscribed the court's decision, leaving open the possibility of legal concessions to conquered peoples in future cases. Although no nineteenth-century cases successfully challenged the principle of imperial legal supremacy, in practice colonial courts regularly considered and often made accommodations for Indigenous defendants.

These political, jurisdictional questions might seem at some remove from criminal responsibility, which was a matter internal to criminal-law jurisprudence applicable only to defendants who had already been declared subject to British jurisdiction. Even after British courts declared their supremacy, however, debates about who was a full subject of British law continued. All responsibility cases engaged jurisdictional issues, at least to a degree. Insanity cases, for instance, asked legal decision makers to determine whether courts should cede their authority to hospitals and medical personnel. In cultural-defense cases, questions of political jurisdiction shaded into jurisprudential, even moral, ones, as officials contemplated the legal implications of the empire's insistence on colonial difference. Political subjecthood brought the empire's denizens into British courts, but determinations of legal subjecthood—conceived in terms of mental capacity—dictated what happened there.

In principle, responsible subjecthood—and the attendant authority of criminal courts to punish a defendant for transgressions—required only a basic level of cognitive capacity and understanding.[133] Irresponsibility, as we have seen, was difficult to prove. In practice, though, the case records of the empire show that officials often applied a robust understanding of responsible subjecthood, one which allowed defendants to claim that their responsibility was diminished or extinguished on many grounds, from culture and gender to pain and illness. In cases where Indigenous defendants pled cultural incapacity, officials had to consider how the law should serve an imperial civilizing mission that was ever, inevitably, incomplete. Sir George Grey might have been certain that "the only way to prevent great crimes on the part of the natives, and massacres of these poor creatures as the punishment of such crimes, [was] to check and punish their excesses in their infancy." But not all shared his belief that Indigenous peoples would, or could, distinguish the common law's lessons from its violence.[134]

CHAPTER 8

Cannibalism and Culpability

Charles-Borromée Rouleau was a stipendiary magistrate in Canada's North-West Territories, which stretched from the barren islands of the Arctic Circle to the northern border of the United States, and from present-day Alaska to the eastern shores of Hudson Bay. On 25 September 1885, Rouleau tried three Cree men for murder in a courtroom in Battleford, a small town on the banks of the North Saskatchewan River in the Canadian prairies. The defendants, Charles Ducharme, Wawasehowein (Dressy Man), and Wahsahgamass (Bright Eyes), were unlikely killers. Ducharme was eighty-five, still tall, with a laborer's build.[1] He was born at the turn of the century in Pembina, the site of the oldest European settlement in the Dakotas. At the time, the settlement had recently acquired its first fur-trading post. Twenty-three years later, surveyors noticed that Pembina was not in Canada at all; it was two miles below the forty-ninth parallel.[2] Wawasehowein was a married man of sixty-five and slight, with dark grey eyes. Wahsahgamass was only eighteen.[3]

The men were accused of killing an old woman named Riskeyak, known in English as She Wins. Witnesses described how Riskeyak was carried to the site of her execution wrapped in an animal skin. She knelt on the hide, surrounded by dozens of onlookers, both Cree and Euro-Canadian. Ducharme struck her on the side of the head with a green poplar stick. She fell to the ground. Wahsahgamass raised his pistol and shot. The powder scorched her bloodied hair. Wawasehowein then approached and buried his ax in her neck.[4] A jury of six white settlers deliberated for twenty minutes before convicting the two older men of murder, a capital offense. Wahsahgamass, perhaps because of his youth, was sentenced to twenty years' imprisonment for manslaughter.[5] Three days later, Rouleau forwarded his papers from the case to Ottawa, the colonial capital. He included a note in which he disagreed with the jury's decision to convict Ducharme and Wawasehowein of murder. "Taking into consideration their degree of civilization," he wrote, "the impression under which they were, that they could and were in duty bound to do away with their victim, I think that in law the degree of malice was not sufficient to justify the Jury to bring a verdict of murder."[6] Rouleau argued that Ducharme and Wawasehowein felt "duty bound" to execute Riskeyak because her frail form concealed a dark and dangerous nature: she was a *wendigo*, a cannibal creature that stalked human prey in the boreal forests of the western plains.[7]

Like many members of the imperial judiciary, Rouleau did not believe that Indigenous defendants should, or even could, be held to the standards of behavior and cognition required by British criminal law.[8] In his view, Ducharme, Wawasehowein, and Wahsahgamass did not have the guilty minds of murderers; their actions were misguided but not criminal.

This chapter uses a group of cases tried in 1885 in the North-West Territories to show the connection between insanity and culture in imperial jurisprudence, and the importance of amateur ethnology in trials involving Indigenous defendants. Controversies over the culpability of Indigenous accused related directly to colonial efforts to pacify Indigenous nations, including debates about the role of colonial courts in disciplining and educating Indigenous people.[9]

I begin and end with the 1885 wendigo case and the legal debates it inspired among colonial officials as they considered the defendants' honest belief in phenomena that they, as jurists and administrators, swore were not real. I also describe the case of Kakisikutchin (Swift Runner), a rumored wendigo and convicted murderer whose crimes colonial officials would long remember. These cases connect to the trial of Louis Riel, a French-speaking Catholic man of Métis (mixed European and First Nations) heritage. In 1885, Riel led the most significant military challenge by Indigenous forces against the colonial Canadian state. Ducharme, Wawasehowein, and Wahsahgamass's story is entangled with Riel's. It contrasts sharply with the case of another Indigenous man, Louison Mongrain, who escaped execution because white settlers considered him noble and "civilized" rather than noble and strange.

In the 1850s, the buffalo herds began to dwindle. First Nations, including the Ojibwa, Saulteaux, Assiniboine, and Cree, competed for scarce natural resources with the Métis and with white settlers who steadily flooded the western plains. To survive, many Cree turned to agriculture and, reluctantly, to the colonial reservation system.[10] In 1867, the British North America Act united the province of Canada (modern-day Quebec and Ontario), Nova Scotia, and New Brunswick, creating the Dominion of Canada. The new polity moved quickly to consolidate its power. The Hudson's Bay Company (HBC) had long administered Rupert's Land and the North-West Territory, the land between Ontario and the British Columbia border beyond the Rocky Mountains. The HBC operated a network of trading posts in the region, dealing in furs and other goods. In 1870, the Company purported to sell the territories it had claimed to the Canadian government. Indigenous and Métis communities resisted these incursions against their sovereignty in the Red River Rebellion. Louis Riel, a charismatic Métis politician and self-proclaimed prophet, led the movement, which induced the Canadian government to negotiate individual land claims and to create the new province of Manitoba. Still, Canadian Prime Minister Sir John A. Macdonald dreamed of enticing commercial investors and white settlers to the prairies. He described Indigenous people as "quite loyal" but determined to resist colonial interference. "They would have preferred their present wild and semi-barbarous life," huffed Macdonald in 1870, "to the restraints of civilization that will be forced upon them by the Canadian Government and the new settlers."[11]

Over the next several years, North-West Cree leaders, especially Mistahimaskwa (Big Bear) of the Fort Pitt region in the district of Saskatchewan, negotiated with the Canadian government for administrative autonomy and access to the buffalo herds.[12] Paranoia and mistrust reigned. In an 1883 report, Assistant Indian Commissioner Hayter Reed warned that the Fort Pitt Cree intended "to test the powers of the authorities once more." The solution to this inchoate threat, Reed thought, was intrusive policing: "It is by meeting the Indians at every step and often by anticipating their intentions that one can be successful and not wait until their plans are formed, for then nothing can stop them."[13] The government adopted increasingly punitive policies to force Indigenous people to conform to colonial fantasies of "civilization," often withholding rations from impoverished and restive people.[14]

In 1885, long-standing grievances erupted. Mistahimaskwa and his allies argued that armed insurrection against the Canadians would never succeed. In-

Charles-Borromée Rouleau, August 1872, photographed in Ottawa by William James Topley. Credit: Topley Studio/ Library and Archives Canada, MIKAN no. 3451111.

stead, the Cree resisted the government by refusing to follow orders, holding traditional gatherings, cooperating across communities, and moving their camps without permission. The colonial authorities responded with violence, false promises, and strategic starvation.[15] The Métis, led by Louis Riel, declared war.[16]

Charles-Borromée Rouleau, the judge in the Ducharme case, was a French Catholic lawyer, originally from Lower Canada (Québec). Appointed to his post in 1883, he had moved his household, including his wife and two children, from Ottawa to Battleford in the dead of winter. The town of Battleford became the territorial capital of the North-West Territories in 1876. Its homes and government buildings were overshadowed by the hulking Fort Battleford, a North-West Mounted Police (NWMP) garrison perched on the high ground between the Battle and North Saskatchewan rivers.[17] Battleford was surrounded by Cree reserves. The 1885 North-West census estimated that the district of Saskatchewan, where Battleford was located, then contained 6,260 "Indian" inhabitants, 2,594 Métis, and only 1,892 whites out of a total population of 10,746.[18] As discontent grew among the Indigenous peoples of the North-West, so did the police presence in the region. The NWMP complement at

Battleford, the most heavily manned station in the Territories, had 103 men in 1884 and 197 by the end of 1885. Police numbers in the whole of the North-West swelled rapidly during the Resistance. Six hundred and eight recruits joined the NWMP in 1885, nearly doubling its forces in the space of a year, to 1,039 men.[19]

Life as a stipendiary magistrate in the North-West was lonely and hard. Until 1885, there were never more than three stipendiary magistrates in the whole territory; in 1885, a fourth was added to assist with the legal business churned up by the Resistance.[20] Magistrates rode such enormous circuits, often by sleigh, that it was not unusual for trials to be delayed for half a year while judges made their way to far-flung communities.[21] Rouleau spent the first months of his time in Battleford complaining about his moving allowance.[22] Rural Saskatchewan was very different from the more cosmopolitan cities of Ottawa, Montreal, and Québec where he had begun his legal career. In a letter to the minister of justice in Ottawa, he described some of the difficulties of his new post. Most people spoke Cree, and Rouleau, who spoke only English and French, could not "make them understand anything pertaining to the administration of justice."[23] Indigenous people seeking legal advice came to his house every day that court was not in session, and Rouleau had to scour the neighborhood for interpreters.[24]

Shortly after hearing the Ducharme case, Rouleau wrote to the minister of justice. He forwarded his notes of evidence in the case and expressed his displeasure with Ducharme and Wawasehowein's capital sentences. He hung his argument on the fact that the defendants lacked "actual malice"—a malevolent motive—which he contended should reduce their culpability.[25] The minister, John Sparrow David Thompson, rejected Rouleau's recommendation. "The condemned men fully intended to take the life of their victim," wrote Thompson, "and . . . they took her life without any lawful excuse or justification. This in law amounts to murder. The design to do such an act is malice. A felonious act done wilfully is done, in the eye of the law, maliciously."[26]

This objection was technical. Rouleau had erred, according to Thompson, by telling the jury that Ducharme and Wawasehowein needed to have experienced "actual malice" in order to be guilty of murder.[27] Malice, sometimes called "malice aforethought," is interchangeable with "intention" in criminal law. "Actual malice," on the other hand, moves away from this legal definition toward a more colloquial one, in which malice resumes its usual connotation of wickedness. In 1894, Oliver Wendell Holmes Jr. described actual malice as "a malevolent motive for action, without reference to any hope of a remoter benefit to oneself to be accomplished by the intended harm to another."[28] According to Rouleau, the accused in the Ducharme case believed that they were executing a dangerous creature. They might have killed with the law's malice but not with the "actual" malice or maliciousness that Rouleau thought necessary to justify their deaths. Thompson's view was in line with criminal-law doctrine. Rouleau, however, was in the North-West trying the Cree, living among them, and struggling to understand them. His empathy for the accused—and perhaps his belief in the irreconcilability of the British imperial and Cree belief systems—drove him to depart from the mainstream understanding of criminal responsibility in order to work, at trial and after, to save them.

While Rouleau had only two years' experience in the North-West, Thompson had none. Thompson was a former attorney general of Nova Scotia who would become an architect of the Canadian Criminal Code of 1892. He would also serve as prime minister of Canada from 1892 until he died of a heart attack over lunch at Windsor Castle in 1894.[29] Thompson, an east-coast lawyer, had been appointed to the Ministry of Justice only days before Rouleau's letter arrived. He initially had little patience for what he viewed as superstition. To him, the strangeness of Cree culture and the resistance to British norms that it represented called for the harsh and didactic imposition of imperial criminal law, not leniency. "If the Indians in that Territory are to be made amenable to the law at all," he wrote, "it seemed to him [Thompson] that a case of very cruel and deliberate murder of an inoffensive old woman was a crime calling for exemplary punishment."[30]

Thompson believed that Indigenous people had to be assimilated, forcibly if necessary, into colonial society. For many Canadian officials, the civilizing mission acquired a new urgency in the wake of the Resistance. At a meeting of the North-West Council, the Territories' governing body of which Rouleau, as stipendiary magistrate, was a member, Edgar Dewdney, the lieutenant governor, addressed the assembled. "The fond hope which Canada had so long entertained of being able to manage the large number of Indians resident in these Territories, without a resort to arms, has unfortunately during the present year, been dispelled," he said.[31] The supposed wendigo Riskeyak was not a direct casualty of the Resistance. And yet, her death seemed to offer the Canadian government an opportunity to flex its authority and continue its efforts to transform its rebellious Indigenous subjects into loyal ones.

Thompson made little of the mentions of cannibalism in the documents Rouleau sent him. Rouleau's notes of evidence were cursory and summarized the testimony of only two witnesses.[32] François Dufresne, a Métis man, said that he had seen Riskeyak hobble into camp two days before her death. On the day of the killing, she had crouched in her tent, apparently ill. Dufresne learned that Riskeyak was a cannibal. Soon, he watched her die.[33] Paskwy Ak, a Cree witness, corroborated Dufresne's account, adding, "I heard the old woman say it would be better for them to take her away from the camp and kill her, because if they did not, that she would destroy the women and children."[34] Although Thompson quoted this last snippet of evidence in his account of the role of "superstition" in the case, he did not linger on its meaning or consider it legally important.

If the minister had known more about wendigos, allusions to cannibalism might have given him pause. The wendigo has a long history. Anishinaabe scholar and storyteller Basil Johnston describes it as a kind of malevolent manitou, or spirit.[35] The wendigo was a giant predator that concealed itself in blizzards and in the dense, boreal forests of the subarctic. Its hunger for human flesh could never be sated; even as it feasted, it starved. It was, Johnston writes, a loathsome creature, "gaunt to the point of emaciation, its desiccated skin pulled tautly over its bones. . . . What lips it had were tattered and bloody from its constant chewing with jagged teeth."[36] The wendigo was a parasite, slowly transforming its host into a monster.[37] Johnston's contemporary account of the wendigo captures historical reports of the wendigo in the Ducharme case and others like it.[38] Today, some Indigenous scholars have understood the creature as a metaphor for greed and selfishness; as a legal category describing those who violate taboos; or as an expression of mental illness.[39]

Outside Indigenous communities, the wendigo has been described as a "celebrated" and "perennial staple" of Algonkian mythology, and also as the defining symptom of a culture-specific psychiatric disorder.[40] Beginning in the 1920s, wendigos became objects of social-scientific fascination, evidence of the purported exoticism and primitivism of First Nations peoples. In the 1970s, some scholars argued that the wendigo was a symbolic expression of a community's horror when a member indulged in cannibalism.[41] Others countered that the wendigo was a postcolonial construct, born out of Western racism and fear of Indigenous people, who only, if ever, resorted to cannibalism in cases of extreme privation and social disorder.[42] Some explained the wendigo as a label applied to social outcasts and weak members of Indigenous communities in order to justify their execution.[43] In the late-twentieth century, scholarship on wendigos focused on so-called wendigo "psychosis," in which a sufferer became convinced that he or she had become, or would become, a wendigo. While some have argued that no one has ever really suffered from the disorder, others believe some patients genuinely imagined that they were supernatural beasts with an aching desire for human flesh.[44]

Historians, for their part, have noticed a concentration of wendigo cases in the colonial archive during the late-nineteenth century, followed by a near-total disappearance in the first half of the twentieth century.[45] The 1885 Resistance was the last major military encounter between Canada's Indigenous peoples and the imperial state. The consolidation of colonial authority that followed, the waves of settlers, the entrenchment of the reservation system, and the elaboration of the Western judicial system eroded the cosmology in which the wendigo hunted. In the last decades of the nineteenth century, though, wendigos were not faint memories or children's tales. For both Europeans and Indigenous peoples, cannibalism was frighteningly real.

In 1879, Kakisikutchin, a Cree man, stood trial at Fort Saskatchewan in northern Alberta. He was charged with murdering his wife, Charlotte, at Open Hills Creek near the Athabasca trail. The judge was Hugh Richardson. Richardson was born in London in 1826, immigrating to Canada at the age of six. He was called to the bar in Toronto in 1847.[46] He would try Louis Riel and his allies at Regina six years later. The jury in Kakisikutchin's trial included three English-speaking Métis and four white men who were "up on the Cree language."[47] Kakisikutchin had an interpreter but no defense counsel.[48] He and Charlotte had been married for several years and had six children, including an infant daughter.[49] Charlotte's father, Kis-Sie-Ko-Way, testified that he last saw the family on the banks of a lake about a day's walk from the nearest Hudson's Bay trading post. They parted ways shortly after the snow began to fall. In the winter, Cree communities often split into small, mobile groups who could seek scarce game over a larger territory.[50] No one was surprised when Kakisikutchin's family disappeared into the woods.

When Kis-Sie-Ko-Way next met his son-in-law in the spring, Kakisikutchin said "he was the only one left. That his wife was brave she had shot herself that two of his children had died and he had buried their bodies as well as he could, and that the rest of his family had then left him."[51] Another witness recounted Kakisikutchin's story. Charlotte, sick, had left some of her children in the woods to die and later shot herself through the breast out of guilt—or maybe so that her husband would abandon her and save their last

Kakisikutchin (Swift Runner), 1879–1880, Fort Saskatchewan. Credit: George M. Dawson/ Library and Archives Canada, PA-051141.

surviving child, a little boy.[52] Kakisikutchin tried to carry his son to safety but weakened as he starved. Eventually, he left the boy and returned alone. But Kis-Sie-Ko-Way could not help but notice that Kakisikutchin "did not look very poor or thin, or as if he had been starving."[53]

In June, Kakisikutchin and three policemen set out to find the bodies of his wife and children in the forest. The officers would not let their prisoner go free until they had verified his story. Kakisikutchin plotted a circuitous path, explaining that snow and leaves had hidden the graves or that bears had eaten the corpses.[54] After much cajoling, he led the police to his son's grave. The fifteen-year-old boy's body was emaciated but intact. The next day, Kakisikutchin reluctantly brought his escort to the grave of his wife and two youngest children. Skulls, bones, hair, and clothing were strewn around a series of campsites. The policemen found entrails in the campfires.[55]

"The skulls and bones had all been boiled," said one medical man during Kakisikutchin's trial, "and the long ones appeared so broken that the marrow could be extracted."[56] The defendant asked no questions and called no witnesses. Near the end, a policeman read out a confession by Kakisikutchin. He admitted to killing and eating one of his sons before the eldest died of starvation and to having threatened to do the same to Charlotte if she objected. He eventually did kill her.[57] The family was never more than a day's walk from food and rescue. When asked if he wanted to say anything to the jury, Kakisikutchin replied, "No. I did it."[58] The jury found him guilty. The sentence was death.

In a letter to the Justice Department, Hugh Richardson marveled at the enormity of Kakisikutchin's crime. He described Kakisikutchin as unusually intelligent—"rather above ordinary Indians"—and apparently sane.[59] On 27 October, the Governor-General-in-Council reviewed the case and set the execution for 20 December.[60] Sixty First Nations and Métis people trudged through thick snow into the prison yard to watch the hanging. A sheriff reported that there was talk of "deeds of cruelty that were to accompany the execution," but Indigenous onlookers left the hanging satisfied with its humaneness.[61] The case also attracted official attention. Justice Minister Alexander Campbell wrote to the prime minister, Macdonald, to speculate about Kakisikutchin's motives.[62] Judicial executions were always likely to draw crowds. This time, there was an additional reason why the people of Fort Saskatchewan were so interested in Kakisikutchin. He was rumored to be a wendigo.

Kakisikutchin's is perhaps the most famous modern wendigo case. And yet, Kakisikutchin's legal file includes none of the explicit discussion of wendigos that marked that of Ducharme, Wawasehowein, and Wahsahgamass. There is no evidence that authorities debated commuting Kakisikutchin's sentence. While colonial officials often described Riskeyak as "crazy" and "insane," Richardson rejected the idea that Kakisikutchin was mad. The brutality of the crime and his confession likely contributed to a summary decision and a swift execution. Still, such stunning violence was hard to forget. In 1885, as Richardson presided in trials of Indigenous defendants, he might well have reflected on the extraordinary events at Fort Saskatchewan. Charles Rouleau, though new to the North-West, took a basic understanding of wendigos as a given. Thompson, the justice minister who had never sat in a prairie courtroom, did not know that allegations of cannibalism among the Cree were not figments of a "primitive" imagination: the wendigo was a nightmare recently made flesh, and there were court records to prove it.

The wendigo raises complicated questions for outsiders about what to believe. This was true for nineteenth-century colonial authorities, and it is true for most scholars today. When the Ducharme case was tried, colonial authorities assumed that the supernatural wendigo did not exist, but that human cannibals like Kakisikutchin did. However, the reality of the wendigo was not the focus of the legal or moral debate about what to do with Riskeyak's executioners. Rather, what Ducharme, Wawasehowein, and Wahsahgamass *believed* about the wendigo drove their culpability.

Cree legal scholar Hadley Friedland has lamented the preoccupation of historians with wendigo executions, and with sensational tales of monsters and cannibals.[63] She writes that this emphasis on the supernatural aspects of the wendigo and on establishing the "'honestly held' *belief* in the *wetiko*" detracts from the legitimacy of the legal processes involved in identifying, quarantining, and, if necessary, executing those accused of posing threats to their communities as wendigos. Some of the legal forms developed to manage wendigos, Friedland argues, might be useful within Indigenous communities today, regardless of the "reality" of wendigos themselves.[64] Rather than interrogating either the nature of wendigos in the historical record or what people in the past believed about them, she urges scholars to focus on what wendigo cases can tell us about Cree legal tradition.

Friedland's position is persuasive, especially from a policy perspective. Instead, historians might prioritize not the "genuineness" of Cree belief in the wendigo but how colonial officials formulated, tested, and responded to the idea of this belief. The controversy in the Ducharme case inhered in how colonial authorities tried to determine, and to judge, what the defendants thought they were doing when they executed Riskeyak. Rouleau, like many white missionaries, officials, and traders in the North-West, believed in the belief in wendigos.

To situate Riskeyak's execution within nineteenth-century Cree law, it is important to consider what the band Mistahimaskwa led thought about her condition in the spring of 1885. Ducharme, Wawasehowein, and Wahsahgamass left no personal correspondence explaining why they killed her. The colonial archive also cannot tell us much about Cree spiritual and legal tradition. Contemporary Indigenous scholarship offers some guidance. John Borrows, a scholar of Indigenous law in Canada, has argued that nineteenth-century wendigo cases allow us to grasp a valuable and humane strand of Anishinaabe tradition, in which people acted collectively to evaluate, support, and, in extreme cases, remove individuals who threatened the safety of the community.[65]

Who was Riskeyak, and how did she understand what happened to her? She appears only in traces in the archive. Paskwy Ak, a Cree witness, said that Riskeyak's daughter reported that her mother had begun refusing food. The Reverend Charles Quinney, a white captive, described a meeting with Riskeyak during which he learned that she had not slept for seventeen nights.[66] All agreed that she was elderly and weak, although the case records do not reveal her precise age or the symptoms of her illness. Riskeyak spent her last days confined to her tent while an anxious crowd lingered outside. She was not alone. Family members visited her often, as did many of the white and Métis prisoners of war who had been taken captive by Cree forces. François Dufresne, the Métis man who worked as an HBC interpreter, testified that the Cree urged him and other prisoners to check on Riskeyak. "On the day she was killed," recounted Mooswar, another Cree witness, "I heard her say that if she were not killed before sundown she would kill all the children & eat them."[67]

Riskeyak ailed for weeks. Frequent visits suggest her community watched for signs of improvement and possibly attempted a cure. Her condition and her confinement were not sudden or secret, and her kin, including her daughter, seem to have agreed about the nature of her affliction. Documents also suggest that Riskeyak believed that she was becoming a wendigo. Many witnesses averred that she begged for death before her execution, as she feared that her transformation was nearly complete. The Cree tried, according to one white Canadian lawyer, to persuade their white captives to kill Riskeyak for them. When they refused, Ducharme, Wawasehowein, and Wahsahgamass offered to do the perilous work.[68] Before striking her, Ducharme reportedly declared, "My friends you asked everybody to kill that woman and nobody would do it. After I strike her, don't say I struck the old woman and laugh at me."[69]

That Riskeyak welcomed her death is only an inference. The witnesses in the Ducharme case may have had their own reasons for portraying her as a willing victim, and some details cut against this theory. For example, Dufresne testified that the Cree compelled a white prisoner to bind Riskeyak's legs before her execution.[70] This use of restraints troubles the notion that Riskeyak wanted to die. Or, the bindings might have been a wise precaution, lest the wendigo inside Riskeyak attack as her death approached. It is also possible that the community decided to end the frail old woman's life because she was a drain on scarce resources, or because her execution by the Cree before the captured settlers declared Cree sovereignty. One letter hints at an ulterior motive for Riskeyak's killing. Quinney, the captive clergyman, believed that she "had prophesied the success of the troops over the Indians and hence the feeling of the camp was against her," although he later abandoned this theory.[71] While there are other interpretations of the archival evidence, I think that Riskeyak's killing was not capricious or cruel but a legal response to the threat she posed. Ducharme, Wawasehowein, and Wahsahgamass were executioners, not murderers. Still, we cannot know that Riskeyak wanted to die.

Officials and other white settlers in the North-West acted as intermediaries between Indigenous people and authorities in Ottawa. They were self-appointed cultural interpreters, translating the wendigo into the language of criminal responsibility. Whether or not the Cree believed in wendigos, at least some white Canadians, including traders, missionaries, lawyers, and judges like Rouleau, thought that they did. According to Rouleau, the fear Ducharme, Wawasehowein, and Wahsahgamass had of wendigos meant that their motives were good, even honorable. Rouleau and men like him could demonstrate their value by educating the colonial government about Canada's new subjects in the west. The Ducharme case was an opportunity for North-West legal authorities to show that they and the law they practiced had integrity, doctrinal sophistication, and compassion. This was especially important considering the fates of other Indigenous prisoners taken during the Resistance, including its leader, Louis Riel.

A bowl of blood connected the Ducharme case to Riel's. The Métis occupied a cultural and political space in the settler imagination between French Catholics, their coreligionists, and their First Nations cousins. At Riel's trial, held in July 1885, white lawyers on both sides struggled to make sense of Métis identity. The defense argued that Indigenous and European patrimonies were at war within Riel, as they had been within the colony. They claimed that this made him mentally unstable. Early in the trial, the defense called Thomas Mackay, a settler and pro-government military volunteer.[72] Mackay described his visit to Riel's headquarters, a shack next to a church. As they negotiated, Riel yelled, "You don't know what we are after—it is blood! blood! We want blood! It is a war of extermination! Everybody that is against us is to be driven out of the country."[73] The defense seized upon Mackay's mention of blood:

> Q. What was on the table when you went into the council chamber?
> A. Some tin dishes and some spoons, some fried bacon and some bannocks.

Louis Riel studio portrait, c. 1875. Credit: Unknown/Library and Archives Canada, e011156891.

Q. Any blood on the dishes?
A. No. I did not see any.
Q. Will you swear that there was not? Will you swear that some of them were not eating cooked blood at the time?
A. Not that I saw.[74]

Mackay would not admit that he had seen Riel eating blood, but the rhetorical effect of the questions might have satisfied the lawyers.[75] Eating blood out of a bowl, as opposed to in a sausage or a pie, might have seemed odd to white members of the jury, but not shocking. Evocations of blood eating might, however, also have struck a deeper, more sinister chord among settlers who remembered Kakisikutchin.

Riel and the 1885 Resistance loom over every account of the extension of colonial authority in the Canadian west. Riel was a hero, a traitor, and a politician. He was also a defendant in a criminal trial in a British colonial court. This aspect of his life best elucidates judicial negotiations about culture and responsibility in the late-nineteenth century. During his trial and after, his defense counsel drew on his medical history to argue that Riel was insane and irresponsible, and that he should therefore be acquitted of treason and confined to a hospital. Prosecutors, conversely, tried to explain Riel's religious fervor and military leadership as normal expressions of a sane, if exotic, Métis sensibility. In their view, his Euro-Indigenous ancestry, like Jimmy Governor's, made Riel more volatile but also more sophisticated—sufficiently "civilized" to be obviously guilty. Riel's prosecutors' arguments departed dramatically from those that officials crafted to explain Riskeyak's killing, where the First Nations status of the defendants became powerful evidence of their incapacity and lack of civilized understanding. In both cases, despite their different outcomes, ethnological arguments about the mental state of the accused were essential to how officials articulated their responsibility and justified the government's responses to their crimes.

After the Red River Rebellion of 1870, Riel spent time in the United States before returning to Montreal, where he had attended seminary school as a boy.[76] In the mid-1870s, his sanity began to fray. He was admitted to a lunatic asylum in Longue Pointe, Québec, in 1874. In 1876, he was transferred to the Beauport asylum near Montreal under the name Louis David Riel, where he remained for eighteen months.[77] Doctors diagnosed Riel with monomania, megalomania, and melancholia.[78] He spun grandiose religious theories and declared himself a prophet. He composed many poems and songs during his confinement, including the stanza below:

> I am Kept as a poor insane
> In the Lunatic Asylum.
> But the world's judgment is vain.
> Man without god, is without brain.
> And fit for the Cage of Barnum.[79]

Riel also kept up a lively correspondence. In one letter to Elzéar-Alexandre Taschereau, archbishop of Québec, he followed his signature with a string of titles: "Prophête, Pontife infaillible, Prêtre Roi [selon] la charité du Sacré Coeur de Jésus Christ."[80]

After his release from Beauport in 1878, Riel returned to the United States. There, he reportedly spent time in an asylum in Washington Territory before moving to Montana, marrying, and settling into life as a schoolteacher.[81] In 1884, a delegation of Métis traveled to Montana to ask him to lead them in a war against the Canadian government.[82] Riel knew that returning to Canada might cost him his life. Shortly before his death, he reminisced, "I told them that to me it was a question of life or death; that in doing so I must contend with a rope about my neck; but my reply was, if my brothers require it I am ready to lay down my life for my brothers."[83] After a year of preaching, planning, and fighting, Riel convinced many Métis, First Nations, and even some white settlers to join his cause. They began seizing property and arms in Saskatchewan in the spring of 1885. During the Resistance, Riel's top lieutenants passed a resolution declaring that he was indeed a prophet.[84] After an early victory at Duck Lake in late March, Riel and his troops were quickly overrun. Outnumbered and outgunned by Canadian military forces, he surrendered in mid-May after the disastrous battle at Batoche. Newspapers across Canada celebrated his forces' defeat as a defining moment in the history of British North America.[85]

Riel doubted that he could have a fair trial in the North-West Territories. In a letter to his lawyers, written from jail, he pleaded to be tried before the Canadian Supreme Court. He wrote, "I humbly ask not to be treated as a murderer or shackled before the jury has decided; and I have confidence that it will find me not guilty. I am an American citizen. As such, I beg the Canadian government to accord me a 'fair play' trial."[86]

His protests had no effect, and Riel was charged with treason, a capital crime.[87] The Canadian government saved its harshest justice, its most fearsome lawyers, and the bulk of its money for Riel. Colonial authorities were reluctant to exacerbate Indigenous resentment by executing dozens of prisoners of war. In exchange for their guilty pleas, Crown prosecutors agreed to charge Riel's collaborators with felony-treason, a statutory offense for which they would serve a sentence of between three and ten years in prison, or even less in the likely event of a mass pardon once passions cooled.[88] For Riel, though, execution was almost inevitable. George Burbidge, deputy minister of justice and one of Riel's prosecutors, summed up the government's position: "Riel has so great an influence over the Half-breeds and Indians that the North-West would never be safe with him at large, and as long as he is in the Penitentiary or an Asylum there is a danger of his being set at large. If he escapes the gallows the Indians and Halfbreeds will really think that if he is not a prophet he is at least Divinely succored."[89] The authors of the *Canada Law Journal* gleefully predicted that he would be convicted "of the highest crime known to the law, taken as he has been red handed." But, they allowed, "due form and ceremony" should prevail, and the authorities must resist their urge to proceed with "unseemly haste."[90]

Louis Riel addressing the jury during his trial for treason in 1885 in Regina, Saskatchewan. Credit: O. B. Buell/Library and Archives Canada/1966-094, C-001879, e010933908.

Riel was tried before a jury of six settlers in Regina. The judge was Stipendiary Magistrate Hugh Richardson, who had presided in Kakisikutchin's trial years before. Richardson had been recently promoted to Regina from his post in Battleford, where Rouleau replaced him.[91] In 1885, the judge was fifty-nine, extravagantly bearded, and a retired lieutenant colonel in the Volunteer Militia. Richardson had heard three previous capital cases, all involving Indigenous defendants: Kakisikutchin's in 1879 and, as one journalist put it, "that of the Stevenson brothers, the Regina Halfbreeds, who were hanged for the murder of an unoffending man."[92] When Riel's defense counsel pressed for details about their client's alleged blood eating, they might have had Richardson in mind. He had surely not forgotten Kakisikutchin or the talk of cannibalism that circulated in Indigenous communities. Regina jurors, too, probably knew about wendigos. Hayter Reed, then Indian Affairs commissioner, described Riskeyak in an 1888 letter as a "crazy cannibal woman."[93] Riel was not openly accused in court of cannibalism or of being a wendigo. His lawyers might, nonetheless, have been invoking the settler belief that Indigenous people who ate blood and claimed to be wendigos were mad.

The prosecutors in Riel's case were daunting. Christopher Robinson, a barrister and trusted ally of Prime Minister John A. Macdonald, was senior counsel. Robinson was joined by Britton Bath Osler, a criminal lawyer from Toronto and a member of the influential Osler family; George Wheelock Burbidge, the deputy minister of justice; David Lynch Scott, the mayor of Regina and an organizer of Regina's home guard during the Resistance; and Thomas Chase-Casgrain, a Quebec lawyer who would later be burned in effigy for his role in Riel's prosecution.[94] The defense lawyers were a more motley bunch. They included French-Canadian criminal lawyer François-Xavier Lemieux and three other competent but little-known lawyers from central Canada, Charles Fitzpatrick, J. N. Greenshields, and T. C. Johnstone.[95] Riel had little money. In a note from the Regina jail, he wrote, "My family [is] very poor and abandoned in Saskatchewan," and asked his lawyers for news of them.[96] Riel relied on donations to fund his defense. Many supporters were from Québec, where he had spent many years. The province had a rancorous relationship with the Anglo-Saxon, Protestant, Conservative Macdonald government.[97]

His lawyers never contested the role Riel played in the Resistance. Instead, they impugned his sanity, hoping to trade the gallows for life in an asylum. This was risky, as most people, whether they thought he was a savior or a scourge, believed that Riel was sane. The liberal Toronto *Globe* printed excerpts from his diary, seized at Batoche, in serialized form, inviting the public to judge Riel's mental state for themselves. A reporter warned readers that the diary would "give no aid or comfort to those who build their hopes of the writer's release on the insanity plea. Very much the reverse. If all who are mentally astray only so far as these jottings indicate that Riel is, were shut up in our asylums, we should have to increase capacity of those establishments very considerably."[98]

In addition to their allusions to blood eating, his lawyers argued that his political vision for the North-West Territories—which Riel planned to divide into seven equal parts, each a homeland for a religious or ethnic group—was that of a madman.[99] The defense aggressively cross-examined witnesses who mentioned the "sevenths" plan.[100] One witness testified that Riel had schemed to give land to Poles and Hungarians, "and soon."[101] Prosecutors, on the other hand, portrayed Riel as the calm, rational commander of a traitorous army.[102] Witnesses described him as intelligent and calculating, and several recalled their humane treatment while prisoners of his forces.[103] His sevenths plan was unusual, but many of the groups to whom Riel wanted to allocate land—Métis, First Nations, white settlers, Irish Americans, even Poles—were either resident communities of the North-West or potential Catholic allies.

Lawyers both for Riel and against him pitched their battle about his sanity on his religiosity. His defense counsel expounded on his religious ecstasies, especially his claims that he was a prophet. They encouraged speculation that Riel intended to declare himself pope.[104] In response, the prosecution resorted to cultural arguments about the role of religion in the lives of the Métis. At times, they presented Riel as a fraudster who claimed divinity to foment Indigenous rebellion. They argued that his education and his years abroad had washed away his presumed Métis naivete, making him dangerous. Settler witnesses dilated on the fervent Catholicism of the Métis, whom they described as superstitious, gullible, and easily manipulated. One man said, "The Half-breeds are a people who need religion. Religion has a great influence on their mind. . . . If the prisoner had not made himself appear as a prophet, he would never have succeeded in bringing the Half-breeds with him."[105] Another witness described the Métis as "very religious" and attributed Riel's influence among them to the fact that "he was so religious and appeared so devout."[106]

Even if his religious beliefs were genuine, prosecution lawyers argued, this did not make Riel insane; grandiosity was typical among Indigenous Catholics. Father Alexis André testified, for the defense, that Riel was sensible when discussing literature and science but that "upon politics and religion he was no longer the same man; it would seem as if there were two men in him, he lost all control of himself on those questions." Riel was "completely a fool, in discussing these questions; it was like showing a red flag to a bull."[107] The prosecution countered that the Métis, like non-Europeans across the globe, were prone to zealotry. They pressured defense witnesses to concede that Riel's claims to divinity were not madness but cultural and racial peculiarity. One witness, Dr. François Roy, the superintendent of the Beauport asylum, diagnosed Riel with megalomania. Many sufferers, Roy explained in court, declared themselves prophets or kings. In an aggressive cross-examination, Osler impugned Roy's professionalism and refused the superintendent's requests to speak in French. Then, Osler turned to the question of prophets. He asked Roy if he had ever heard of Joseph Smith and Brigham Young, and if these founders of Mormonism were insane. Roy waffled. Osler asked if he would call "Brigham Young's ideas of prophetic inspirations inconsistent with knowledge of what is right and wrong." Roy, deflated, said he would need to study any patient for a few months before deciding.[108]

Riel's defense caricatured his faith and politics, insisting that his religiosity was neither cultural nor personal but insane. The defense needed Riel to seem "white" enough that the jury would interpret his eccentricities as insanity. The prosecution, conversely, portrayed him as typically Métis, and relied on tropes about Indigenous religious sentiment to explain his behavior. Prosecution lawyers also argued, in the alternative, that Riel was too intelligent and cosmopolitan to be anything but a criminal.

The defense called Dr. Daniel Clark of the Asylum for the Insane in Toronto as a witness.[109] Clark had been an expert witness in lunacy cases many times during his ten years as superintendent. He knew that *M'Naghten* was not about medicine. "I could convince any lawyer," he said, "if they will come to [the] Toronto Asylum, in half an hour, that dozens in that institution know right and wrong . . . and yet are undoubtedly insane. The distinction between right and wrong . . . is one of these metaphysical subtilities [*sic*] that practical men in asylums know to be false."[110] Clark believed that Riel was insane but left the question of his responsibility to the lawyers. Under cross-examination, the physician agreed that Riel could be both delusional and culpable. He testified that Riel "was not an ignorant man. He was not like an Indian who never read a newspaper, and knew nothing of the country around him. He had travelled, he had been in Ottawa, he had been in the United States, and he knew all about the power of Britain and the Dominion."[111] The jury might have been persuaded that Riel was a fraud, a Métis fanatic, or even a lunatic. But they did not think he was irresponsible. The insanity defense failed, and Riel was sentenced to hang on 16 November 1885.

Riel's lawyers appealed his case to the High Court of Manitoba without success. They then petitioned the Judicial Committee of the Privy Council for leave to appeal. In London, a newspaper reported, "the greatest lawyers of the realm [had] been summoned to attend the hearing, or rather consideration of the case."[112] The members of the committee declined. They reiterated in their judgment that it was the "usual rule . . . not to grant leave to appeal in criminal cases, except where some clear departure from the requirements of justice is alleged to have taken place."[113] Among other objections, Riel's lawyers challenged Richardson's jurisdiction and complained that there had never been a coroner's inquest or indictment.[114] The Judicial Committee dismissed these concerns. Departures from British metropolitan procedure were permissible in the colonies in the interest of "peace, order, and good government." "Forms of procedure unknown to the English common law," the judges noted, had already been widely established and acted on in India, and "to throw the least doubt upon the validity of . . . those words would be of widely mischievous consequence."[115] They also rejected any notion that Riel was not responsible for his acts due to "mental infirmity."[116]

With no Privy Council appeal forthcoming, mercy was Riel's only prospect. British authorities in London disagreed about whether to commute the sentence. Henry Herbert, the fourth Earl of Carnarvon who was then Lord Lieutenant of Ireland, wrote to the British prime minister, Lord Salisbury, to encourage him to push Ottawa toward clemency.[117] Everyone acquainted with Canadian politics, wrote Carnarvon, "can tell how delicate & serious such a case is and what *very* grave consequences it may have if a wrong decision is come to."[118] British officials warned that Riel's execution would inflame tensions between Québec and English Canada. Carnarvon reiterated the point in a letter to the colonial secretary, "[Sir John A. Macdonald] may be strong enough to hang Riel—who richly deserves it—but *I know* that it will be an act that . . . must add a fresh element of irritation to an already dangerous heap of combustibles."[119]

Many in the British government took the opposite view. They argued that Macdonald could not commute Riel's sentence without losing face, and that London would damage relations with the settler colonies if it demanded clemency. Carnarvon's cousin, Robert Herbert, long-serving permanent undersecretary of the Colonial Office, put it bluntly: "I do not think it would be possible, without running the risk of seriously embarrassing Sir John Macdonald, to move in any way at present in the Riel matter. . . . Sir John appears to have decided that he cannot condone this second act of rebellion."[120] In a letter to the Colonial Office, Lord Lansdowne, the governor-general of Canada, supported the Canadian government's decision to hang Riel. Lansdowne argued that Riel's death was necessary to justify executing the Indigenous men who had killed settlers during the conflict. Riel, in his view, had waged war on Canada, and his death would dissuade Indigenous forces from trying again. Lansdowne also praised the jury in Riel's case for refusing to equate what he saw as Indigenous mental weakness with legal insanity. "The admission, either by the courts or by the Executive," he wrote, "that in a country circumstanced in regard to its settlement as [is] the North-west Territories any person with a . . . mind subject to occasional illusions or accesses of religious or political fanaticism might break the law" with impunity would have "far reaching and disastrous consequences."[121]

Riel's lawyers' final option was to petition for a delay of the execution, so that a medical commission could be assembled to assess Riel's mental state. The Canadian government requested a report from Dr. Augustus Jukes, the physician monitoring Riel in the Regina jail. Jukes judged Riel sane. Riel also thought he was sane and was furious at his lawyers. "He has assured me over & over again," wrote Jukes, "that though life was sweet, even though the penalty was death, he would never consent to purchase immunity at the sacrifice of his mental integrity."[122] Ten days after the government received Jukes's report, Riel was hanged.

These episodes in Louis Riel's life show how insanity and culture were intertwined in responsibility decisions made by British colonial courts. Metropolitan authorities perceived the risk that ethnology could effectively become mental science. Cultural pathology might, very easily, become enshrined in common-law jurisprudence as mental pathology. The Canadian government needed a guilty verdict against Riel to vindicate its authority, to placate settlers, and to justify its treatment of other Indigenous defendants. Still, many white Canadians firmly believed—and even testified—that Riel was either insane or in the grip of a primitive religiosity that made responsibility impossible.

Louis Riel was the only person associated with the 1885 Resistance who was sentenced to death in Regina. The other capital cases against Indigenous defendants were tried before Rouleau, in Battleford. These included the cases of the men accused of killing settlers at a small settlement called Frog Lake, the site of an agency for the Department of Indian Affairs, as well as a trading post and a Roman Catholic mission.[123] Shortly after Riel and his forces declared war, many Cree joined the campaign. Energized by the rebels' early victories, some members of Ducharme, Wawasehowein, and Wahsahgamass's band attacked Frog Lake on 2 April 1885. The violence was deadly but brief. "The whole time of the massacre," a witness would later recall, "did not last more than the time to smoke a pipe."[124] Of the twelve settlers at Frog Lake, nine died. On 3 April, Francis Dickens, the dissolute son of author Charles Dickens and an inspector in the NWMP, wrote frantically to the authorities in Battleford, listing casualties and begging for rescue.[125] "We expect to be attacked at any minute," he wrote. "Please send reinforcements *as soon as possible.*"[126]

Ten days later, after a brief siege, Cree forces led by Mistahimaskwa seized the government station at Fort Pitt, about thirty-five miles southeast of Frog Lake. The fort consisted of six buildings nestled in a grassy plain near the Saskatchewan River. Four were occupied by HBC traders and their families, and two housed a detachment of twenty-four NWMP officers.[127] Negotiations between the residents of Fort Pitt and Mistahimaskwa's men floundered, and one NWMP constable, David Lattimer Cowan, was killed. The twenty-three surviving mounted policemen escaped upriver in a rickety scow, which the HBC traders had hastily constructed in the fort's central square days before.[128]

The twenty-eight civilians who remained behind, both white and Métis, became prisoners of the Cree.[129] They were well treated during the six weeks that most remained with the band. The prisoners circulated fairly freely within the encampment, becoming familiar and even friendly with their captors.[130] It was in the camp, in wartime, surrounded by captured HBC agents, that Ducharme, Wawasehowein, and Wahsahgamass executed Riskeyak. She died on or around 16 April 1885, only days after the capture of Fort Pitt.[131] The intimacy between the Cree and the Fort Pitt and Frog Lake prisoners precipitated by the war ensured that Riskeyak's execution did not go unnoticed by the colonial state. Within hours of their arrival, the white and Métis outsiders learned of the sick old woman crouched in a tent. Within days, many witnessed her death. Months later, when Ducharme, Wawasehowein, and Wahsahgamass stood trial for murder, they would testify about what they had seen.

On 6 November 1885, the day after Thompson submitted his initial report on the Ducharme case, the Governor-General-in-Council ruled that the law should take its course: Ducharme and Wawasehowein would be hanged on 27 November.[132] They were not the only ones. Eleven people died near Fort Pitt in April 1885: nine at Frog Lake, one NWMP officer at Fort Pitt, and Riskeyak. In the aftermath of the Resistance, twelve Indigenous men, including many from Mistahimaskwa's band, were tried for their murder.[133] Except for Wahsahgamass, whose charge was reduced to manslaughter, all were convicted. Rouleau was the judge in every case. In the spring of 1885, Indigenous forces had briefly taken Battleford. Rouleau had watched his house burn down from across the banks of the North Saskatchewan River.[134] He especially mourned the loss of his impressive library, which included British, American, and Canadian treatises, law reports, and statute books that he had brought with him to the North-West.[135] His legal judgments consistently emphasized jurisprudence over precedent, and he had a long-standing interest in judicial reform. He was also, according to one biography, "known to dislike Aboriginals."[136]

Rouleau, who in October was still waiting for his house to be rebuilt, heartily recommended the speedy execution of the Indigenous defendants convicted of killing white settlers.[137] Manachoos (Bad Arrow) and Kittimakegin (Miserable Man) were convicted, Rouleau crowed in a letter to Thompson, on the basis of evidence "so direct and conclusive that there can be no doubt as to their guilt." Another prisoner "richly deserve[d] . . . the sentence pronounced on him."[138] Rouleau decried the killings of white settlers as shocking and savage. In contrast, Riskeyak's death inspired curiosity. Because all the parties in the Ducharme case were Cree, white settlers, even in the wake of the Resistance, could interpret Riskeyak's death as a question of "superstition" and Cree tradition, rather than an act of war.[139]

Judgment of the Indigenous accused would be swift and cheap. "Firmness and severity on the part of the Government," wrote Osler, one of Riel's prosecutors, was essential.[140] Locating witnesses in remote settlements, taking statements, paying interpreters, and transporting lawyers and witnesses to courts in Regina and Battleford was slow and expensive, however. To economize, government authorities allowed most of Riel's allies to plead guilty to treason-felony in exchange for noncapital sentences. But killing was different. Indigenous defendants accused of homicide, particularly against settlers, would be given no quarter. "We thought of getting them to plead guilty and discharge[d] on recognisance," wrote Osler, "but . . . concluded that it is necessary to prosecute vigorously."

The post-Resistance trials were didactic dramas, performed to terrify and educate the colony's Indigenous subjects. At one trial, according to Osler, a lawyer "made a very eloquent speech in their [the defendants'] favour, but it had no effect as the sentences had been fixed before the court opened." The trials were lessons in colonial justice and administrative thrift. Battleford was closer to Frog Lake and Fort Pitt than Regina; the murder trials would happen there.[141] W. Prescott Sharp, the government prosecutor in the Battleford homicide cases, received strict instructions to avoid "any unnecessary expense."[142] Most Indigenous defendants in these cases called no witnesses, offered no affirmative defense, or pled guilty.[143]

Thompson, the minister of justice, did not immediately distinguish the Ducharme case from the stack of homicide files crowding his desk after the Resistance. Rouleau, though, thought it was different. He was moved not by the death of Riskeyak but by the plight of her killers. In his instructions to the jury in their case, Rouleau observed, "The parties were not civilized, and may perhaps have thought it was in self-defence; in that case it would be manslaughter."[144]

Sharp, the prosecutor, was equally perturbed. On 10 November, he wrote to Thompson to tell him more about wendigos. He had been dismayed to learn that the Governor-General-in-Council refused to commute the defendants' capital sentences. Sharp would later confess to the deputy minister of justice, Augustus Power, that he did not trust Rouleau to explain the wendigo to Ottawa authorities. "Doubts stole into my mind," he wrote, "as to whether the Magistrate took sufficiently full notes in the case & whether his report was clear." Sharp told Thompson that the Cree believed that the old woman was a "crazy person desirous of eating human flesh." Wendigos were nearly impossible to kill and possessed powers of resurrection. The whole band had agreed that Riskeyak had to die. Sharp was "informed by intelligent half breeds that the presence of such a person would strike terror into the hearts of whole camps of Indians." If this alone had not piqued Thompson's interest, Sharp's final observation surely did: "Wawasehowein clubbed Const. Cowan & knocked his brains out after Louison Mongrain killed him. He also cut his heart out."[145]

Louison Mongrain, a Cree man, was accused of the murder of Constable Cowan of the NWMP during the capture of Fort Pitt, on 15 April 1885.[146] Mongrain belonged to a band who lived on the Onion Lake reserve. He and others from Onion Lake joined Mistahimaskwa's encampment after the attack on Frog Lake, days before the seizure of Fort Pitt. Mongrain had brought George G. Mann, a government farm instructor, and Mann's family, with him when he left Onion Lake—a fact that would ultimately change his fate.[147] Rouleau was the judge in his trial, and Sharp the prosecutor. Although Mongrain was tried alone for Cowan's killing, the official complaint also named Wawasehowein as his accomplice.[148] The trial was set for 25 September 1885; the same day, and in the same courtroom, Ducharme, Wawasehowein, and Wahsahgamass stood trial.[149] Sharp, possibly because Wawasehowein had already been convicted of murdering Riskeyak earlier that day, entered a plea of *nolle prosequi*, declining to prosecute Wawasehowein for Cowan's murder.[150]

An NWMP constable was the first witness at Mongrain's trial. He told the court that he and Cowan, along with another man, stumbled across Mistahimaskwa's band on their return from a scouting mission.[151] The constable claimed the shooting was unprovoked, but this was a lie. In statements made after the trial, William Bleasdell Cameron, the sole male survivor of Frog Lake and a prisoner of Mistahimaskwa's band, told a different story.[152] Cameron and the constable had paraded directly before the group of Cree warriors who were demanding the surrender of the Fort, deliberately antagonizing them.[153] Negotiations shattered.[154] The constable was wounded in the ensuing firefight; Cowan, shot, fell from his horse.[155] One witness said that he saw two Cree men feel Cowan's body to see if he was still breathing. Then a man in a white blanket walked up to Cowan and fired two shots at close range.[156] Kasowakayo, a Cree man, said that he overheard Mongrain boasting that after Cowan fell, "he was lying on his back and [he] put his hands up saying don't brother and I fired two shots at him."[157] Other Cree witnesses testified that they had also overheard Mongrain's confession, shared around a campfire shortly after the incident.[158] The defense called only one witness, Mesinachassayo, who swore that he had seen Mongrain near Cowan, but that Mongrain fired no shots and had made no confession.[159] The jury found Mongrain guilty of murder and sentenced him to hang with the other convicted rebels on 27 November.

Unlike the other Cree men who shuffled through Charles Rouleau's courtroom in late September, Louison Mongrain had settler allies. A month after his conviction, Amelia McLean, HBC trader William James McLean's seventeen-year-old daughter, wrote to the government to beg for Mongrain's life. Amelia was the eldest of McLean's nine children. She had grown up in the North-West Territories at a series of trading posts and military forts, and she and her family had forged strong bonds among the Cree.[160] She was a gifted linguist who would later work as an Indigenous-language translator and amateur ethnographer.[161] Her letter explained that she had been told "that if I wrote down about that *good* Indian that is to be hanged on the 37th [*sic*] of Nov. and explain all about him, he will be saved." Amelia described Mongrain as a hero who had saved the McLean family and that of Farm Instructor Mann during the Frog Lake attack. Mongrain protected them and even "gave the Manns the last pot of flour he had." "He always said," wrote the girl, "he was a friend of the Whiteman's."[162] She was sure that Mongrain, whom she always called Louison, was innocent. She accused the prosecution's Indigenous witnesses of trying to frame him for murder as revenge for his kindness toward settlers.[163] Amelia spoke fluent Cree and offered her services in any way that "might help the best friend we had among the Indians."[164]

On receipt of the letter, authorities began an urgent search for the McLeans.[165] There was only a month left until Mongrain's execution. The family had left Saskatchewan for Fort Alexander in Manitoba, more than seventy-five miles across Lake Winnipeg from Stony Mountain Penitentiary, where Mongrain and the other condemned men were held.[166] S. L. Bedson, the prison superintendent, set out himself for Fort Alexander to find Amelia, since no one else would brave the ice-clogged lake until the spring thaw.[167] Finally, on 31 October, Bedson took depositions from Amelia and her father and sent the statements to Ottawa.[168] Amelia swore that Mongrain had saved her family's life. He had given them his horse, his food, his protection, and even a gun.[169] William McLean corroborated his daughter's account. Then his testimony turned to Wawasehowein. McLean said that Wawasehowein had told him that "Cowan was not dead when he was shot but that he [Wawasehowein] finished him with a club, he showed me the club which was bespattered with brains and blood, and boasted of the deed."[170] On 5 November 1885, the minister of justice recommended a commutation for Mongrain in light of the "courage and humanity" he showed toward the settler prisoners.[171] While Mongrain's sentence was being reviewed, Sharp's letter to the Ministry of Justice accusing Wawasehowein of cutting out Cowan's heart was being carried from Battleford to Ottawa.

The mercy dispensed by officials in Wawasehowein and Mongrain's cases shows the colonial judiciary's bifurcated vision of Canada's Indigenous people. Thompson praised Mongrain for his "humanity" twice in the recommendation for his commutation. Perhaps Thompson would have been equally struck by a white man's "humanity." It is also possible, however, that Mongrain's extraordinary kindness toward settlers, and the way they took up his cause, allowed Thompson to see him not as a victim of superstition or a casualty of evolution but a man. Amelia McLean's letter saved Mongrain's life by persuading colonial authorities that Mongrain was like them. Sharp's letters, meanwhile, saved Ducharme and Wawasehowein by convincing Thompson of the opposite.[172]

After reviewing Sharp's correspondence about the wendigo, the minister of justice wrote to the executive to request a stay of Ducharme and Wawasehowein's executions. Thompson explained that he had not initially understood the Cree fear of wendigos, such that the "killing of such a person appear[s] a commendable act." He blamed Rouleau for the oversight. "These features," he wrote, "were not developed in the evidence or explained by the magistrate who seems to have taken for granted that they would be known in the Department of Justice."[173] While he waited for the Governor-General-in-Council's response, Thompson tried to learn all he could about cannibals. In a longer report, Sharp divulged more about the case. Riskeyak's refusal of food was, in the Cree view, a classic symptom of wendigo affliction, as the creatures could eat nothing but human meat. There were rumors that even William McLean had feared that Riskeyak would eat his children.[174] Sharp also shared his own trial notes with Thompson, including the testimony of two additional Cree witnesses. Both reported that Riskeyak believed she was a wendigo.[175] Rouleau confirmed the intensity of wendigo panic. "There was no doubt," he wrote in response to Thompson's questions, "that the woman killed was crazy and threatened on several occasions to kill women and children, that [she] herself asked the favor of being killed, in order to avoid such a calamity."[176] He sent this last letter on 27 November, the day that eight Indigenous men convicted in Rouleau's court were hanged en masse in Battleford. Ducharme and Wawasehowein were not there. On 9 December 1885, following Thompson's revised recommendation for mercy, the Governor-General-in-Council commuted their sentences to life imprisonment.[177]

Mongrain, Ducharme, and Wahsahgamass were transported to Stony Mountain Penitentiary in the fall of 1885. Wawasehowein was sent to the jail in Regina. With Mongrain's sentence commuted, Thompson faced the unpleasant prospect of having no one to hang for the murder of an NWMP constable. Sharp had declined to prosecute Wawasehowein for Cowan's murder in September; the Cree man had not been acquitted. And so, colonial authorities instructed the prosecutor to gather evidence for a new trial. In May 1886, Sharp left Canada for Europe and transferred the case, still pending, to another lawyer, who had been junior counsel for the prosecution in Louis Riel's trial.[178] Six months later, a year after he had first been slated to die, Wawasehowein was still in Regina, waiting.[179] The day finally came on 11 March 1887. The judge in the case was Hugh Richardson, who had tried Riel and most of his allies in Regina in 1885. The prosecution struggled to locate witnesses, some of whom had died or moved away. In the end, the principal witnesses were François Dufresne, the Métis man who had testified against Wawasehowein in the Ducharme case, and his wife.[180] The evidence was patchy and unpersuasive, and the political imperative to convict Riel's sympathizers had faded in the years since the Resistance. Wawasehowein was found not guilty and sent to Stony Mountain to serve his sentence for the killing of Riskeyak.[181]

Two years after Ducharme, Mongrain, and Wahsahgamass arrived at Stony Mountain, and a few months after Wawasehowein joined them there, petitions began to arrive at the Ministry of Justice asking for their pardon and release. One group of Indigenous petitioners from Onion Lake wrote, "As the old woman was dangerous and wanted to kill some children, to eat, it was considered advisable to kill her, and it always has been the custom to kill them, with us: we did not consider we were doing wrong in doing so." They added that the prisoners had been urged to kill the "witch" by the whole camp, including the head HBC trader at Fort Pitt, William McLean.[182] A missionary joined their plea, adding that the Cree men had killed Riskeyak in legitimate self-defense and had never committed murder in their hearts.[183] Much of the testimony at the 1885 trial and the correspondence that followed mentioned McLean's alleged terror of the wendigo. If a white man, it was implied, could succumb to a "superstitious" belief in cannibals, then how could the Cree resist it? One Catholic priest, writing to request clemency for Wahsahgamass, expressed this sentiment clearly. "There is no doubt," he wrote, that McLean "counseled and urged the savages to rid themselves of that Wittiko woman, at all costs. If a magistrate [who is] supposed to be the interpreter of the law, counseled and urged a murder, what can we say of a poor child of 16, who shoots a corpse?"[184]

In 1887, the government was not yet ready to release its Indigenous prisoners. The Indian commissioner of the North-West Territories reflected, "The time for their release [was] not yet ripe." Better to wait, he judged, until mercy could serve a political purpose. After all, he wrote, "an opportunity may offer, when the exercise of clemency might be made to serve some important end, in connection with our relations with these Indians."[185] In 1889, the Canadian government at last pardoned Indigenous prisoners convicted of crimes related to the Resistance. The Crown had always intended to release them.[186]

Four years after Riel's execution, the Canadian state had proved it was fearsome, and wished to show it could be mild. And yet, as prisoners began to stream home to Saskatchewan from Stony Mountain, Mongrain, Wawasehowein, Ducharme, and Wahsahgamass were left behind. They alone were in prison for murder or, in Wahsahgamass's case, for manslaughter; the other prisoners had been charged with property offenses and treason-felony. They began to despair. The prison surgeon wrote to Bedson, the superintendent, to warn him that the Indigenous prisoners were sick and dying. "Since the release of the last three Indians with whom they were largely associated," the doctor noted, "they appear to have become downhearted and entirely discouraged at the prospect of their ever leaving here alive."[187] He urged Bedson to press for release, as they would not survive much longer in prison. On 3 August, Charles Ducharme, who at ninety was the oldest Indigenous prisoner by twenty years, died of "debility."[188] It was too late for him, but the others were luckier. Wawasehowein and Mongrain were released just over a month later. Wahsahgamass left Stony Mountain the following June.[189]

The Ducharme case had no obvious afterlife in the annals of Canadian or British imperial law. It was not reported and is almost never mentioned in histories of the Plains or of the Resistance. Other wendigo execution cases, however, continued to make their way into colonial courtrooms. One, *R v Machekequonabe* (1897), is the only wendigo case ever recorded in law reports.

In 1896, Machekequonabe, an Ojibwa man, was tried at Rat Portage in Western Ontario for killing his foster father, whom he had mistaken for a wendigo.[190] At trial, Machekequonabe's lawyer argued that the belief in wendigos was "a form of insanity to which the whole tribe is subject." The judge disagreed; it was "not insanity at all, but superstitious belief."[191] This dispute was, in many ways, about the legal consequences of primitivism. In such cases, there was little difference between the false beliefs of delusional insanity and the allegedly false beliefs of Indigenous cosmology. Both insanity and superstition, from the perspective of colonial officials, were the offspring of less capable minds. *M'Naghten* and legal insanity offered a path to freedom, or at least hospitalization, for those whose accounts of their mental disturbances found favor with judges and jurors. Cultural defenses that relied on imputations of culture-based incapacity, too, could shield defendants from the full force of colonial law, although more obliquely.

Machekequonabe was convicted of manslaughter in the lower court. The Ontario Divisional Court reviewed the case in 1897. The defense contended that Machekequonabe never intended to harm a human being, and that his mistake was reasonable by the standards of his people.[192] The judges disagreed, upholding the trial court's verdict in a two-sentence judgment.[193] *Machekequonabe* has become one of the best-known "Native law" cases in the common-law tradition.[194] The case has been interpreted as authority, both in Canada and elsewhere in the British world, for the principle that Indigenous peoples were bound by colonial law regardless of their religious and cultural beliefs.[195] Sidney Harring sees the case as evidence that "the very real and intricate cultural world of the Ojibwe found no recognition in Ontario courts."[196] And yet, *Machekequonabe* did not settle the question of whether, and to what degree, common-law courts should treat culture as exculpatory. As Harring notes, many whites were dismayed by the court's unwillingness to acknowledge Machekequonabe's fear that a wendigo stalked him in the night.[197] In the end, he received a six-month sentence, spending considerably less time in confinement than he might have if acquitted on the ground of insanity.

How should one understand Machekequonabe's manslaughter conviction, or Wahsahgamass's? What does the fact that Ducharme, Wawasehowein, and Mongrain avoided judicial execution say about law in the British Empire? Although Riel and most of the Frog Lake killers died, most of those who had participated in the Resistance lived. In the colonies as in England, mercy was a political tool that showed the strength of British criminal law, not its vulnerability.[198] But there is more to the 1885 trials than state terror. Although executive pardons, shorter sentences, and less punitive charges could serve the colonial state by dampening criticism and bolstering its humanitarian image, they were also signs of uncertainty and self-reflection in colonial governance, however attenuated or fleeting. British assertions of political or territorial sovereignty did not resolve the question of how to incorporate supposedly uncivilized colonial populations into a civilized legal order. Judges could force Indigenous people to submit to the law through violence, but violence alone could not build a lawful empire.

The Ducharme case and others like it show that imperial officials worried about their capacity to judge the minds and hearts of nonwhite defendants, especially Indigenous defendants who adhered to the laws of their people. The common-law preoccupation with intention made Rouleau, Thompson, and Sharp into amateur ethnographers, tasked with weighing the legal and moral consequences of an unevenly civilized empire. In the weeks after the Resistance, when judicial and administrative resources were taxed and settlers urged vengeance, they still contemplated the wendigo.

Conclusion

TWO PASSAGES TO INDIA

> Sail forth—steer for the deep waters only,
> Reckless O soul, exploring, I with thee, and thou with me,
> For we are bound where mariner has not yet dared to go,
> And we will risk the ship, ourselves and all.
>
> Walt Whitman, "A Passage to India" (1871)

E. M. Forster's *A Passage to India* (1924) culminates in a trial. Adela Quested, a young English woman, accuses Dr. Aziz, a Muslim man, of rape, an assault she claims Aziz committed in the Marabar Caves, a fictional place in British India. At Aziz's trial before an Indian magistrate, Adela is beset by doubt. When she rises to testify, she experiences a "new and unknown sensation" in which she does not "think what had happened or even remember in the ordinary way of memory" but relives the day of the attack, relating every detail to the rapt crowd.[1] Adela's vision does not show Aziz entering the cave behind her, and she withdraws the charges. The British spectators are furious. One tries to stop the proceedings on "medical grounds." Another speculates that a "nervous breakdown" caused Adela's outburst.[2] In the chaos, Adela wanders, dazed, from the courtroom into the street.

In Walt Whitman's "A Passage to India" (1871), canals and telegraph wires collapse the distance between East and West. The lands of the "vast terraqueous globe" hold "a festival garland, as brides and bridegrooms hand in hand," and the human soul, emboldened, embarks on a spiritual voyage to a metaphorical India in search of God. Whitman embraces the journey with "daring joy," for, he asks, "are they not all the seas of God?" Forster borrowed Whitman's title, but not his faith. *A Passage to India* is a modernist fable where nothing is certain and everything is disorienting.[3] Is Adela's vision accurate, or is it caused by a transient insanity, brought on by the stress of the trial? Forster will not say. For him, the empire is not a happy marriage; physical proximity cannot bridge the space between Britons and Indians. "Fear is everywhere," reflects Cyril Fielding, Dr. Aziz's friend, "the British Raj rests on it."[4] The trope of Indian mendacity appears often, casting doubt both on Aziz's protestations of his innocence and on the justice of colonial trials. The superintendent of police, opening the prosecution against Aziz, speaks the impolite truth when he grumbles, "Everyone knows the man's guilty, and I am obliged to say so in public before he goes to the Andamans [penal colony]."[5] Forster's characters at times distinguish between a "mystery" and a "muddle"—while mysteries can be cracked, muddles are messes without an underlying structure or secret logic.[6] At various points in the book, they describe India, colonialism, life, and racial conflict as "muddles."[7] The modernism of the twentieth century, with its emphasis on instability, subjectivity, and fracture, superseded the liberal faith in the pursuit of truth—about defendants' mental states as about human nature—that had animated the post-Enlightenment age. Responsibility controversies reflected the pain of that transition, from a world in which intelligence and industry could yield certainty to another, in which they could not.

In the late-nineteenth century, this book argues, developments in medicine and natural science collided with imperial ambitions to consolidate, regularize, and anglicize criminal law in the British world. At the time, British law seemed to demand a coherent approach to determining the responsibility of defendants in criminal cases, and the exemption of the insane from capital punishment. Mental science promised tools for dividing the sane from the insane, even as changing medical definitions of insanity made this exercise increasingly difficult. Ethnology and evolutionary theories, which shaped medical understandings of mental and moral acuity, helped to explain both insanity and criminality as functions of a natural hierarchy of civilizations. These scientific accounts presented much criminal behavior, especially violence, as unwitting or unchosen. Whether they were mad or simply uncivilized or under-civilized, many defendants in homicide cases argued that they were unfit for judgment under British law—political subjects, surely, but not responsible ones.

For British officials at home and in the colonies, these claims to irresponsibility could be defeated, but they could not be dismissed. Legal officials were loath to expel their medical colleagues, partners in imperial administration as in class and sensibility, from the criminal justice system. Nor could they disavow the civilizational, evolutionary, and racial theories that seemed to justify

British imperial ventures, including the imposition of Anglo common-law institutions on colonial populations. And so, faced with persistent, public challenges in responsibility cases, the physicians, lawyers, and administrators of the empire scrambled to articulate a legal order that could simultaneously protect fault-based liability for criminal acts and acknowledge the many ways in which defendants could fall short of responsible subjecthood.

The responsibility debates of the late-nineteenth century were symptoms of liberalism in crisis. British officials had the stomach to argue fine metaphysical points in responsibility cases at least in part because they thought the exercise was worthwhile. The mind was a mystery that could, with skill and persistence, be resolved. This optimism carried over into the imperial project. Responsibility cases exposed the tension between the liberal universal ideal, epitomized in the common law, and the civilizational chauvinism that underwrote the empire. Officials mostly believed that this apparent contradiction could be managed and its worst abuses tempered (for instance, through the commutation of capital sentences) until, with the ultimate success of the civilizing mission, it naturally disappeared. Doubt crept in, of course. Some feared that Britain could not civilize its colonies while its own civilization, battered by degeneration, was at risk. Others rejected the individualized adjustments to *M'Naghten* or to other aspects of responsibility that officials made in tough cases, demanding a formal, systemic change to legal approaches to fault and punishment. For them, technocratic, bureaucratic, scientific means of deterring crime and managing criminals were the way forward; the professionals and administrators of the empire were ready to serve.

In the early-twentieth century, scientific and medical objections to the *M'Naghten* orthodoxy continued, but judges became increasingly confident in their ability to make case-by-case exceptions without compromising the integrity of the criminal law. Judicial pragmatism dulled the scientific critique of criminal responsibility.[8] Still, the wounds the responsibility contests of the nineteenth century inflicted on common-law idealism remained. It was no longer possible for judges to defend the legal definition of insanity as a coherent, self-evident standard, supported by medical knowledge, logic, or common sense. Instead, the common-law doctrine of responsibility was stripped bare—revealed as expedient and maybe necessary, but misshapen, uneven, arbitrary. Responsibility came to seem like more of a muddle than a mystery. Nineteenth-century criminal-insanity cases distilled philosophical concerns about personhood, justice, and empire into one simple question: Guilty or not guilty? Despite thousands of verdicts, there was no answer.

The gap between the common-law concept of responsibility and the ways lawyers and judges applied it to individuals in court had been filled with intuition and assumptions about the fundamental intelligibility of other minds for so long that it had gone unnoticed. By the late-nineteenth century, the gap had become a gulf. Late-Victorian Britons' old certainties had given way. And yet, the ties of common-law jurisprudence would hold, at least for a few more decades. In a speech in 1921, Scottish lawyer Richard Burton Haldane, after a long stint as Lord Chancellor and a member of the Judicial Committee of the Privy Council, told a gathering of his peers, "The human mind is much the same all the world over. The differences are much less than the identities, and that has been our experience in the judicial committee."[9] For Haldane, human minds around the world were "much the same"—not identical, admittedly, but close enough to allow common lawyers to do their work.

Queen Victoria died in January 1901. Although it is rare for centuries, reigns, and historical eras to change in tandem, the advent of the twentieth century marked a shift, though not a complete break, in the history of imperial law. The South African War (1899–1902) rang in the new century on a bitter note. Although British imperial forces ultimately defeated the upstart Boer republics, they did so at obscene human cost. Images of women and children, especially white Boers, confined to concentration camps indicted the empire on an international stage, appalling Britons inclined to overlook similar violence against Indigenous populations. Britain was publicly stripped of its claims to colonial benevolence, perhaps even to civilization.[10] In Australia and Canada, increasingly independent Dominion governments drifted away from nineteenth-century understandings of formally color-blind, liberal "British justice," adopting overtly discriminatory immigration laws anchored in fears of white racial decline.[11] These were paired with domestic campaigns to eliminate Indigenous populations through systematic "whitening," both cultural and biological.[12]

Scholars caution that eugenic ideas, widely popularized in the first decades of the new century, were not novel, nor were they identical with modern concepts of race or racism.[13] Still, the idea that societies could be perfected only through breeding rather than under the benign sway of civilizing institutions, including a morally sound and internally coherent legal tradition, shifted focus away from metaphysical debates. Britain and its colonies suddenly seemed to have abandoned the civilizing mission in favor of a more brutal politics of military domination and racial purification. The civilizing mission had been brutally violent, but its advocates were confident that it was just. As the posture of civilization dropped away, the ugly, unvarnished, and undisguised truth of empire, which had always been visible to the colonized, was suddenly and unavoidably in many imperial and colonial officials' sights. The professionals who had husbanded the civilizing mission of the common law, the lawyers, doctors, and judges born into the optimistic liberalism of the early and middle decades of the nineteenth century, were older now, and tired. The responsibility controversies had exposed the apparent irreconcilability of traditional jurisprudential accounts of the autonomous individual and the deterministic, often pessimistic perspective of the new sciences. Human nature started to seem like a cosmic enigma, best offered up to God or perhaps an unfeeling universe—in any case, not a question to which judges, alienists, or lawyers could provide a satisfying response.

From 1843 to the present, *M'Naghten* has continued to define the contours of legal insanity in almost all common-law jurisdictions. Psychiatrists can now observe a living brain at the cellular level using machines Henry Maudsley imagined would reveal, once and for all, the physical causes of insanity. "The time will come," he wrote in *Responsibility and Mental Disease*, "when by the invention of improved instruments of research the insensible movements of molecules will be as open to observation as are the molar movements of the heavens, and when those that come after us will not fail to discover the physical causes of derangements."[14] Despite the passing of the British Empire and scientists' ability to observe the "insensible movements of molecules," *M'Naghten* lives on. The Law Commission of the United Kingdom, a statutory body with a mandate to review English law, recommended sweeping reform of insanity law in a 2013 report, because "both the test for unfitness to plead and the insanity defence are founded on nineteenth century legal concepts which have not kept pace with developments in medicine, psychiatry and psychology."[15] The recommendations were not implemented.

Part of the reason for *M'Naghten*'s persistence is the concern, voiced so often by Victorian officials and professionals, that a more capacious definition of insanity would allow violent individuals to escape the most severe punishment, undermining the deterrent force of the law and endangering the public. As knowledge about the brain deepens in the twenty-first century, so does a renewed anxiety that cognitive science will prevent the criminal justice system from punishing the most serious offenders.[16] As activists, physicians, and patients work to destigmatize mental illness, however, a general dissatisfaction with the persistence of nineteenth-century definitions of insanity grows.[17] This tension between condemnation and compassion, between impulses to punish and to treat, has endured alongside *M'Naghten.* Nineteenth-century debates about the meaning of criminal responsibility in a diverse and scientifically sophisticated world share so much with present-day debates that century-old cases, treatises, and newspaper articles often seem arrestingly contemporary.[18]

Now as in the nineteenth century, there is no distinct cultural defense under the common law. And yet, as they did over a century ago, cultural considerations play an overlooked but critical role in how judges, jurors, and political officials imagine and apply criminal-responsibility standards. Today, scholars of Anglo-American law debate the merits of formally enacting such a defense; many contend that it already exists covertly, and has for centuries.[19] Many have argued that the "reasonable man" of common-law tradition must reflect defendants' diverse identities and experiences.[20] British imperial authorities shared this ambivalence about both cultural defenses and the law's supposedly universal norms.

"Although universality of application is often used as one of the basic elements in any definition of law," writes legal anthropologist Sally Falk Moore, "universality is often a myth."[21] The *M'Naghten* rules did not, in practice, represent the only legally meaningful understanding of insanity. Culture did, in fact, operate as both an inculpating and a mitigating factor in criminal cases. In responsibility contests, officials bargained in the shadow of the law, as when they shunted the criminally insane directly to asylums to avoid scandal or the appearance of cruelty. Judges and jurors, in turn, bargained in the shadow of the prerogative of mercy, calculating that they could uphold rigid responsibility standards because the sting of a guilty verdict would be dulled by a respite after trial.

"Now it is a fact, abundantly exemplified in human history," observed Maudsley, "that a practice often lasts for a long time after the theory which inspired it has lost its hold on the belief of mankind."[22] Maudsley was referring to the *M'Naghten* definition of insanity, but he might just as easily have been describing the myth of liberal imperialism. In the end, Britain and its colonies clung to *M'Naghten* and to a narrative of a united and universal criminal law despite their growing suspicion that it was, at best, a noble lie. The story of responsibility in the empire is one of doubt and accommodation, conflict and negotiation, as the professionals who administered criminal law in the British world confronted the possibility that their justice system was, like their empire, unjust.

Abbreviations

ADB:	*Australian Dictionary of Biography*
ANL:	Australian National Library
AO:	Archives of Ontario
BAnQ-M:	Bibliothèque et Archives nationales du Québec, Montréal
BH:	Bethlem Hospital Archives
BL:	British Library
BRO:	Berkshire Records Office
CBC:	Criminal Casebooks of BH
CRIM:	Central Criminal Court Papers of TNA
CUL:	Cambridge University Library, Department of Manuscripts and University Archives
DCB:	*Dictionary of Canadian Biography*
HO:	Home Office Papers of TNA
IOR:	India Office Records of BL
LAC:	Library and Archives Canada
LHR:	*Law and History Review*
MH:	Ministry of Health Papers of TNA
OBP:	*Old Bailey Proceedings Online*
ODNB:	*Oxford Dictionary of National Biography*
PRO:	Domestic Records of TNA
PROV:	Provincial Record Office of Victoria
SAB-R:	Saskatchewan Archives Board, Regina

SAB-S:	Saskatchewan Archives Board, Saskatoon
SLV:	State Library of Victoria
TNA:	The National Archives, United Kingdom, Kew
VPRS:	Inward Correspondence Files, Provincial Record Office of Victoria (especially VPRS 264, Capital Case Files, and VPRS 1100, Capital Sentence Files)

Notes

INTRODUCTION

1. James Mackenzie Maclean, *Guide to Bombay: Historical, Statistical, and Descriptive* (Bombay, 1889), 406.
2. *Queen Empress vs Lakshman Dagdu*, in *The Indian Law Reports: Bombay Series* (Bombay, 1886), 512–19.
3. Secretary of State for India in Council, *The India List and India Office List for 1898* (London: Harrison and Sons, 1898), 367.
4. *Queen Empress vs Lakshman Dagdu* (1886), 515.
5. *Queen Empress vs Lakshman Dagdu* (1886), 512–19.
6. George H. Savage, *Insanity and Allied Neuroses: Practical and Clinical* (London: Cassell, 1884), 462.
7. In this book, I primarily use "British" to describe institutions and people with origins in Great Britain, wherever they were situated in the empire. I reserve "English" for those with specific ties to England itself. By "British" law, I mean case law, statutes, and jurisprudence originally developed mainly in England and Wales (as distinct, especially, from Scots law), wherever it was ultimately applied. Nineteenth-century officials, for their part, often referred to "British" rule and "British" justice but also to the precepts of "English" law. Some scholars have adopted "Anglo" law to circumvent this potential confusion, which I also use on occasion. On Scots law, see: Lindsay Farmer, *Criminal Law, Tradition and Legal Order: Crime and the Genius of Scots Law, 1747 to the Present* (Cambridge: Cambridge University Press, 2005).
8. Hannah Weiss Muller, *Subjects and Sovereign: Bonds of Belonging in the Eighteenth-Century British Empire* (Oxford: Oxford University Press, 2017), 14–15.

9. P. J. Cain and A. G. Hopkins, *British Imperialism, 1688–2000*, 2nd ed. (Harlow, UK: Longman, 2002); C. A. Bayly, *Empire and Information: Intelligence Gathering and Social Communication in India, 1780–1870* (Cambridge: Cambridge University Press, 1996); James Belich, *Replenishing the Earth: The Settler Revolution and the Rise of the Anglo-World, 1783–1939* (Oxford: Oxford University Press, 2009).
10. William Blackstone, *Commentaries on the Laws of England*, book 4, ch. 2, 11th ed. (London: A. Strahan and W. Woodfall, 1791).
11. Henry Campbell Black, *A Dictionary of Law* (Clark, NJ: Lawbook Exchange, 1891), 31; Elizabeth Papp Kamali, *Felony and the Guilty Mind in Medieval England* (Cambridge: Cambridge University Press, 2019).
12. Oliver Wendell Holmes, Jr. *The Common Law* (Clark, NJ: Lawbook Exchange, 1881), 3.
13. On the shift in emphasis from character to choice-based models of responsibility, see: Nicola Lacey, *Women, Crime, and Character: From Moll Flanders to Tess of the D'Urbervilles* (Oxford: Oxford University Press, 2008), 20–23.
14. James Fitzjames Stephen, *A General View of the Criminal Law of England* (London: Macmillan, 1863), 75–76.
15. On clues and conjecture in law, medicine, and history, see: Carlo Ginzburg, "Morelli, Freud and Sherlock Holmes: Clues and Scientific Method," *History Workshop Journal* 9 (1980): 5–36.
16. In this book, I refer to experts in mental science as either alienists or physicians. I use the anachronistic modifier "psychiatric" when referring to medical knowledge about the mind and the brain primarily for concision, in preference to "mental scientific" or similar terms. On terminology, see: Andrew Scull, "The Social History of Psychiatry in the Victorian Era," in *Madhouses, Mad-Doctors, and Madmen: The Social History of Psychiatry in the Victorian Era* (Philadelphia: University of Pennsylvania Press, 1981), 6.
17. Joel Peter Eigen, *Mad-Doctors in the Dock: Defending the Diagnosis, 1760–1913* (Baltimore: Johns Hopkins University Press, 2016).
18. James Fitzjames Stephen, *A History of the Criminal Law of England*, vol. 1 (London: Macmillan, 1883), 183.
19. Selected works on the history of responsibility include: Thomas Andrew Green, *Freedom and Criminal Responsibility in American Legal Thought* (Cambridge: Cambridge University Press, 2014); Susanna L. Blumenthal, *Law and the Modern Mind: Consciousness and Responsibility in American Legal Culture* (Cambridge, MA: Harvard University Press, 2016); Kamali, *Felony and the Guilty Mind in Medieval England*; Nicola Lacey, *In Search of Criminal Responsibility: Ideas, Interests, and Institutions* (Oxford: Oxford University Press, 2016); Eigen, *Mad-Doctors in the Dock*; Kimberley White, *Negotiating Responsibility: Law, Murder, and States of Mind* (Vancouver: UBC Press, 2007); Roger Smith, *Trial by Medicine: Insanity and Responsibility in Victorian Trials* (Edinburgh: Edinburgh University Press, 1981); Charles E. Rosenberg, *The Trial of the Assassin Guiteau: Psychiatry and the Law in the Gilded Age* (Chicago: University of Chicago Press, 1968); Nigel Walker, *Crime and Insanity in England: The Historical Perspective* (Edinburgh: Edinburgh University Press, 1968).
20. George W. Stocking, *Victorian Anthropology* (New York: Free Press, 1987), xi.

21. "Birdwood, Herbert Mills (1837–1907), Judge in India," *ODNB*; Rugby School, *Rugby School Register: 1874–1887* (Rugby, 1891), 44.
22. Daniel J. Hulsebosch, "The Ancient Constitution and the Expanding Empire: Sir Edward Coke's British Jurisprudence," *LHR* 21, no. 3 (2003): 439–82.
23. John Leonard Forde, *The Story of the Bar of Victoria* (Melbourne: Whitcombe and Tombs, 1913), 10; "Obituary," *Blue Mountain Echo*, 9 March 1923: 3.
24. HC Deb 11 February 1932 vol 261 cc1136–62.
25. P. A. Howell, *The Judicial Committee of the Privy Council, 1833–1876: Its Origins, Structure, and Development* (Cambridge: Cambridge University Press, 1979); D. B. Swinfen, *Imperial Appeal: The Debate on the Appeal to the Privy Council, 1833–1986* (Manchester, UK: Manchester University Press, 1987).
26. HC Deb 29 June 1900 vol 85 c85.
27. Lisa Ford, *Settler Sovereignty: Jurisdiction and Indigenous People in America and Australia, 1788–1836* (Cambridge, MA: Harvard University Press, 2010).
28. Radhika Singha, *A Despotism of Law: Crime and Justice in Early Colonial India* (Oxford: Oxford University Press, 1998).
29. J. F. Stephen to Mary Stephen, 18 February 1870, MS Add. 7349/7b, CUL.
30. Stephen, *A History of the Criminal Law of England* (1883), 1:183.
31. Ruth Harris, *Murders and Madness: Medicine, Law, and Society in the Fin de Siècle* (Oxford: Clarendon Press, 1989), 4.
32. Rosenberg, *Trial of the Assassin Guiteau.*
33. Blumenthal, *Law and the Modern Mind.*
34. Harris, *Murders and Madness.*
35. Lindsay Farmer, *Criminal Law, Tradition and Legal Order*, 173.
36. See: Issa Kohler-Hausmann, *Misdemeanorland: Criminal Courts and Social Control in an Age of Broken Windows Policing* (Princeton: Princeton University Press, 2018), 120.
37. HL Deb 16 April 1875 vol 223 cc1065–77.
38. Tal Golan writes that contests between legal and scientific authorities verged on "chaos." See: *Laws of Men and Laws of Nature: The History of Scientific Expert Testimony in England and America* (Cambridge, MA: Harvard University Press, 2004), 97.
39. Martin J. Wiener, *Reconstructing the Criminal: Culture, Law, and Policy in England, 1830–1914* (Cambridge: Cambridge University Press, 1990), 92–93.
40. Wiener, *Reconstructing the Criminal*, 97.
41. See: Lacey, *Women, Crime, and Character*; Mariana Valverde, *Diseases of the Will: Alcohol and the Dilemmas of Freedom* (Cambridge: Cambridge University Press, 1998).
42. Wiener, *Reconstructing the Criminal*, 109.
43. Penelope Edmonds and Hamish Maxwell-Stewart, "'The Whip Is a Very Contagious Kind of Thing': Flogging and Humanitarian Reform in Penal Australia," *Journal of Colonialism and Colonial History* 17, no. 1 (2016).
44. Singha, *A Despotism of Law*, xv.
45. Singha, *A Despotism of Law*, 233.
46. Wiener, *Reconstructing the Criminal*, 100.
47. *The Law of Capital Punishment: The Debate on the Motion for the Second Reading of the Bill for the Abolition of Capital Punishment. June 22, 1881* (London, 1881), 8.

48. Emphasis original here and in all subsequent direct quotations.
49. Howard Association, "Summarised Information on Capital Punishment," in *Law of Capital Punishment*.
50. On executions as political theatre in the colonies, see: Stacey Hynd, "Killing the Condemned: The Practice and Process of Capital Punishment in British Africa, 1900–1950s," *Journal of African History* 49, no. 3 (2008): 403–18.
51. See: John Darwin, *The Empire Project: The Rise and Fall of the British World-System, 1830–1970* (Cambridge: Cambridge University Press, 2009); C. A. Bayly, *The Birth of the Modern World, 1780–1914: Global Connections and Comparisons* (Malden, MA: Blackwell, 2004); C. A. Bayly, *Imperial Meridian: The British Empire and the World, 1780–1830* (London: Longman, 1989); Belich, *Replenishing the Earth*; P. J. Cain and A. G. Hopkins, *British Imperialism, 1688–2000* (New York: Longman, 2002); Ronald Robinson and John Gallagher with Alice Denny, *Africa and the Victorians: The Official Mind of Imperialism*, 2nd ed. (London: Macmillan, 1981).
52. Robinson, Gallagher, and Denny, *Africa and the Victorians*.
53. Ford, *Settler Sovereignty*.
54. Patrick Colquhoun, *A Treatise on the Police of the Metropolis*, 2nd ed. (London, 1796), xi.
55. Kirsten McKenzie, *Scandal in the Colonies: Sydney and Cape Town, 1820–1850* (Melbourne: Melbourne University Press, 2004); Paul Knepper, "Dreams and Nightmares: Drug Trafficking and the History of International Crime," in *The Oxford Handbook of the History of Crime and Criminal Justice*, ed. Anja Johansen and Paul Knepper (Oxford: Oxford University Press, 2016), 209.
56. Daniel Pick, *Faces of Degeneration: A European Disorder, c. 1848–1918* (Cambridge: Cambridge University Press, 1993).
57. Lindsay Farmer, *Making the Modern Criminal Law: Criminalization and Civil Order* (Oxford: Oxford University Press, 2016), 50.
58. See: Deana Heath, *Purifying Empire: Obscenity and the Politics of Moral Regulation in Britain, India and Australia* (Cambridge: Cambridge University Press, 2010).
59. Robinson, Gallagher, and Denny, *Africa and the Victorians*, 9.
60. Lauren Benton and Lisa Ford, *Rage for Order* (Cambridge, MA: Harvard University Press, 2016), 2.
61. See: Miles Ogborn, *Global Lives: Britain and the World, 1550–1800* (Cambridge: Cambridge University Press, 2008); Emma Rothschild, *The Inner Life of Empires: An Eighteenth-Century History* (Princeton: Princeton University Press, 2011); Linda Colley, *Captives: Britain, Empire and the World, 1600–1850* (New York: Anchor Books, 2004); Linda Colley, *The Ordeal of Elizabeth Marsh: A Woman in World History* (New York: Pantheon Books, 2007); David Lambert and Alan Lester, eds., *Colonial Lives across the British Empire: Imperial Careering in the Long Nineteenth Century* (Cambridge: Cambridge University Press, 2006); John McLaren, *Dewigged, Bothered, and Bewildered: British Colonial Judges on Trial, 1800–1900* (Toronto: University of Toronto Press, 2011); Zoë Laidlaw, *Colonial Connections, 1815–45: Patronage, the Information Revolution and Colonial Government* (Manchester, UK: Manchester University Press, 2005); Maya Jasanoff, *Liberty's Exiles: American Loyalists in the Revolutionary World*

(New York: Alfred A. Knopf, 2011); Diana S. Kim, *Empires of Vice: The Rise of Opium Prohibition across Southeast Asia* (Princeton: Princeton University Press, 2020).

62. See Antoinette Burton and Isabel Hofmeyr, *Ten Books That Shaped the British Empire: Creating an Imperial Commons* (Duke University Press, 2015); Bhavani Raman, *Document Raj: Writing and Scribes in Early Colonial South India* (Chicago: University of Chicago Press, 2012); Miles Ogborn, *Indian Ink: Script and Print in the Making of the English East India Company* (Chicago: University of Chicago Press, 2007); C. A. Bayly, *Empire and Information: Intelligence Gathering and Social Communication in India, 1780–1870* (Cambridge: Cambridge University Press, 1996); Asheesh Kapur Siddique, "Mobilizing the 'State Papers' of Empire: John Bruce, Early Modernity, and the Bureaucratic Archives of Britain," *Journal of Early Modern History* 22, no. 5 (2018): 392–410; Catherine Hall, *Civilising Subjects: Colony and Metropole in the English Imagination, 1830–1867* (Chicago: University of Chicago Press, 2002); Leslie Howsam, *Cheap Bibles: Nineteenth-Century Publishing and the British and Foreign Bible Society* (Cambridge: Cambridge University Press, 2002); Richard Harry Drayton, *Nature's Government: Science, Imperial Britain, and the "Improvement" of the World* (New Haven: Yale University Press, 2000).

63. Robinson, Gallagher, and Denny, *Africa and the Victorians*, xi.

64. Robinson, Gallagher, and Denny, *Africa and the Victorians*, xxi.

65. On the shared philosophical sensibilities of American doctors and lawyers, see: Susanna L. Blumenthal, "The Mind of a Moral Agent: Scottish Common Sense and the Problem of Responsibility in Nineteenth-Century American Law," *LHR* 26, no. 1 (2008): 99–159.

66. A. W. B. Simpson, *Legal Theory and Legal History: Essays on the Common Law* (London: Hambledon Press, 1987), 378.

67. A. W. B. Simpson, *Leading Cases in the Common Law* (Oxford: Clarendon Press, 1995), 12.

68. Mitra Sharafi, *Law and Identity in Colonial South Asia: Parsi Legal Culture, 1772–1947* (Cambridge: Cambridge University Press, 2014), 10.

69. See: Natalie Zemon Davis, *Fiction in the Archives: Pardon Tales and Their Tellers in Sixteenth-Century France* (Stanford: Stanford University Press, 1987), 4.

70. Michel Foucault, *Discipline and Punish: The Birth of the Prison*, trans. Alan Sheridan (New York: Vintage Books, 1977), 191–92.

71. On the subversive potential of the case history, however, see: Erik Linstrum, "The Case History in the Colonies," *History of the Human Sciences* 33, nos. 3–4 (2020): 85–94.

72. John Forrester, "If P, Then What? Thinking in Cases," *History of the Human Sciences* 9, no. 3 (1996): 1–25.

73. Forrester, "If P, Then What?" 10.

74. *John McLeod v The Attorney General New South Wales* [1891] UKPC 31 (23 July 1891).

75. See: E. P. Thompson, *Customs in Common* (New York: New Press, 1991); and A. W. B. Simpson, *Cannibalism and the Common Law: The Story of the Tragic Last Voyage of the Mignonette and the Strange Legal Proceedings to Which It Gave Rise* (Chicago: University of Chicago Press, 1984).

CHAPTER 1. GUILT AND THE GALLOWS

1. Shaw's Petition to the Queen, 2 March 1898, HO 144/22922.
2. Douglas Hay, "Property, Authority and the Criminal Law," in *Albion's Fatal Tree: Crime and Society in Eighteenth-Century England*, 2nd ed. (London: Verso, 2011), 17–64.
3. See Carolyn Strange, *Qualities of Mercy: Justice, Punishment, and Discretion* (Vancouver: UBC Press, 1996); Hynd, "Killing the Condemned."
4. Rob Turrell, "'It's a Mystery': The Royal Prerogative of Mercy in England, Canada and South Africa," *Crime, histoire et sociétés/Crime, History and Societies* 4, no. 1 (2000): 85–94.
5. Daniel Hack Tuke, "Historical Sketch of the Insane," in *A Dictionary of Psychological Medicine*, ed. Daniel Hack Tuke (London, 1892), 1.
6. *R v Shaw*, Judge's Notes of Evidence, 18 November 1897, HO 144/22922.
7. "The Murder of a Boy Near Sulgrave, Revolting Details," *Northampton Herald*, 20 November 1897, HO 144/22922.
8. Joseph Foster, *Men-at-the-Bar: A Biographical Hand-List of the Members of the Various Inns of Court* (London, 1885), 81; Henry Robert Addison et al., *Who's Who* (London, 1899), 475.
9. "The Murder of a Boy Near Sulgrave."
10. Alfred Swaine Taylor, *The Principles and Practice of Medical Jurisprudence* (London, 1873), 574.
11. Cogan's Report, 31 August 1897, HO 144/22922.
12. Judge's Notes of Evidence, HO 144/22922; Arthur Foss and Kerith Lloyd Kinsey Trick, *St. Andrew's Hospital, Northampton: The First 150 Years (1838–1988)* (Cambridge: Granta, 1989), 184.
13. "The Murder of a Boy Near Sulgrave."
14. Coroner's Depositions and Northampton Constabulary Memorandum, 21 July 1897, HO 144/22922.
15. G. Jason Phillips to M. White Ridley, 13 November 1897, HO 144/22922.
16. "The Murder of a Boy Near Sulgrave."
17. February 1843, trial of Daniel M'Naughten (t18430227–874), *OBP.*
18. February 1843, trial of Daniel M'Naughten (t18430227–874), *OBP.*
19. February 1843, Daniel M'Naughten, *OBP*.
20. Schedule A Form, D/H14/D2/2/1/75/46, Daniel MacNaughten Case File, BRO.
21. HL Deb 13 March 1843 vol 67 cc714–44.
22. M'Naghten's case [1843] UKHL J16 (19 June 1843).
23. Joel Peter Eigen, *Witnessing Insanity: Madness and Mad-Doctors in the English Court* (New Haven: Yale University Press, 1995), 77.
24. Daniel Hack Tuke, "Historical Sketch of the Insane," in *A Dictionary of Psychological Medicine*, ed. Tuke, 25.
25. John Charles Bucknill, *Unsoundness of Mind in Relation to Criminal Acts* (London, 1854), 119.
26. Mark Stevens, *Broadmoor Revealed: Victorian Crime and the Lunatic Asylum* (Barnsley, South Yorkshire: Pen and Sword Social History, 2013), 6.
27. Smith, *Trial by Medicine*, 23.

28. Bethlem case notes, 21 March 1854, D/H14/D2/2/1/75/46, Daniel MacNaughten Case File, BRO.
29. Broadmoor case notes, 28 March and 3 May 1865, D/H14/D2/2/1/75/46, Daniel MacNaughten Case File, BRO.
30. Henry Maudsley, *Responsibility in Mental Disease* (London, 1874), 178.
31. "The Sulgrave Murder," *Northampton Mercury*, 19 November 1897.
32. Wills's Notes of Evidence, Shaw Case, HO 144/22922, 19.
33. Carolyn Strange, "Patriarchy Modified: The Criminal Prosecution of Rape in York County, Ontario, 1880–1930," in *Essays in the History of Canadian Law: Crime and Criminal Justice in Canadian History*, ed. Susan Lewthwaite, Tina Loo, and Jim Phillips, vol. 5 (Toronto: University of Toronto Press, 1994), 207–51.
34. Harry Oosterhuis, *Stepchildren of Nature: Krafft-Ebing, Psychiatry, and the Making of Sexual Identity* (Chicago: University of Chicago Press, 2000), 40.
35. *The Ludgate* (London, 1894), 45.
36. Leslie Stephen, *The Life of Sir James Fitzjames Stephen* (London, 1895), 141.
37. J. F. Stephen to J. S. Mill, 9 April 1864, MSS Add. 7349/11.
38. Sir James Fitzjames Stephen, *A General View of the Criminal Law of England* (London, 1863).
39. J. S. Mill to J. F. Stephen, 12 April 1864, MSS Add. 7349/11.
40. K. J. M. Smith, *James Fitzjames Stephen: Portrait of a Victorian Rationalist* (Cambridge: Cambridge University Press, 1988), 126.
41. Smith, *James Fitzjames Stephen*, 126–37.
42. Thomas R. Metcalf, *Imperial Connections: India in the Indian Ocean Arena, 1860–1920* (Berkeley: University of California Press, 2008); Eric Stokes, *The English Utilitarians and India* (Oxford: Clarendon Press, 1959).
43. Sir William Wilson Hunter, *A Life of the Earl of Mayo, Fourth Viceroy of India* (London, 1875), 168.
44. "Stephen, Sir James Fitzjames, first baronet (1829–1894)," *ODNB*.
45. Stephen, *History of the Criminal Law of England*, 1:94–95.
46. Stephen J. Morse, "Thoroughly Modern: Sir James Fitzjames Stephen on Criminal Responsibility," *Ohio State Journal of Criminal Law* 5, no. 2 (2008): 509.
47. Stephen, *History of the Criminal Law of England*, 1:96.
48. See: Richard A. Posner, "The Romance of Force: James Fitzjames Stephen on Criminal Law," *Ohio State Journal of Criminal Law* 10, no. 1 (2012): 263–75.
49. Stephen, *History of the Criminal Law of England* (1883), 1:186. On the ways in which the mid-twentieth-century Hart-Devlin debate reprised disagreements between Stephen and Mill on public morality and harm in criminal law, see: Paul J. McCutcheon, "Morality and the Criminal Law: Reflections on Hart-Devlin," *Criminal Law Quarterly* 47, no. 1 (2002): 15–38. On the connection between Devlin's position and postwar multiculturalism, which one can also see in Stephen and Wills's nineteenth-century approach to insanity and culpability, see: Gregory Bligh, "Birth of Multiculturalism and Hart-Devlin Debate: The Crisis of the Standard of the Ordinary Englishman in Post-War British Common Law Studies," *Droit et société* 98 (2018): 159–78.

50. Wills to Ridley, 18 November 1897, HO 144/22922.
51. Judge's Notes of Evidence, HO 144/22922; Foss and Trick, *St. Andrew's Hospital, Northampton*, 184.
52. Étienne Jean Georget, *De la folie: Considérations sur cette maladie* (Paris, 1820), 110. Translation mine.
53. Étienne Esquirol, *Mental Maladies: A Treatise on Insanity*, trans. E. K. Hunt (Philadelphia, 1845), 320.
54. See: Joel Peter Eigen, "Lesion of the Will: Medical Resolve and Criminal Responsibility in Victorian Insanity Trials," *Law and Society Review* 33, no. 2 (1999): 425–60; Mariana Valverde, *Diseases of the Will*.
55. Eigen, *Witnessing Insanity*, 74.
56. Charles Chrétien Henri Marc, *De la folie, considérée dans ses rapports avec les questions médico-judiciaries* (Paris, 1840).
57. February 1843, Daniel M'Naughten, *OBP*.
58. Marc, *De la folie*, 229.
59. Marc, *De la folie*, 225.
60. William Orange, "Criminal Responsibility in Relation to Insanity," in *A Dictionary of Psychological Medicine*, ed. Tuke, 308.
61. Orange, "Criminal Responsibility," 318, 320.
62. Paul Garnier and Henri Colin, "Homicidal Monomania," in *A Dictionary of Psychological Medicine*, ed. Tuke, 593.
63. Maudsley, *Responsibility in Mental Disease*, 71.
64. Mary Elizabeth Braddon, *Lady Audley's Secret* (London, 1862), 85–86.
65. Arthur Conan Doyle and David Stuart Davies, *The Best of Sherlock Holmes* (London: Collector's Library, 2009), 393.
66. Wills to Ridley, 18 November 1897, HO 144/22922.
67. George Miller to Wills, 19 November 1897, HO 144/22922.
68. An Act for the Safe Custody of Insane Persons Charged with Offences, 39 & 40 Geo. III, c. 94. On Hadfield, see: Richard Moran, "The Origin of Insanity as a Special Verdict: The Trial for Treason of James Hadfield (1800)," *Law and Society Review* 19, no. 3 (1985): 487–519.
69. Stevens, *Broadmoor Revealed*, 8. Walker, *Crime and Insanity in England*, 81.
70. Sir Alexander Wood Renton, *The Law of and Practice in Lunacy* (London, 1897), 795.
71. The Trial of Criminal Lunatics Act (1883), 46 & 47 Vict, c. 38.
72. Eigen, *Witnessing Insanity*, 80–81.
73. The Trial of Criminal Lunatics Act (1883), 46 & 47 Vict, c. 38, s. 1.
74. Wills to Ridley, 19 November 1897, HO 144/22922.
75. Shaw's Petition to the Queen, 24 November 1897, HO 144/22922.
76. Judge's Notes of Evidence, 18 November 1897, HO 144/22922.
77. See: Havelock Ellis, *The Criminal*, 3rd ed. (London, 1903), 144.
78. Brayn and Nicolson Report on Shaw, 26 November 1897, HO 144/22922.
79. Richard von Krafft-Ebing, *Psychopathia Sexualis*, trans. Charles Gilbert Chaddock (Philadelphia, 1894), 379.
80. Brayn and Nicolson Report on Shaw, 26 November 1897, HO 144/22922.

81. Wills to Ridley, 29 November 1897, HO 144/22922.
82. Annual Report (1905), Broadmoor, HO 144/22922.
83. Notice of Death, 14 February 1947, HO 144/22922.
84. Wills to the Home Office, 3 December 1897, HO 144/22922.
85. March 1878, trial of Henry John Dodwell (t18780311–365), *OBP*.
86. Trial of Henry John Dodwell, *OBP*.
87. Schedule A form, D/H14/D2/2/1/936A, Rev. Henry John Dodwell Case File, BRO.
88. Henry Hawkins to Orange, 4 April 1878, D/H14/D2/2/1/936A.
89. Forbes Winslow's Report, Spring 1878, D/H14/D2/2/1/936A.
90. Alfred Swaine Taylor, *A Manual of Medical Jurisprudence*, 8th ed. (Philadelphia, 1880), 808.
91. Forbes Winslow, "The Case of the Rev. Mr. Dodwell," Correspondence, *British Medical Journal* (1878), 2, 271.
92. Winn's Report, 22 March 1878, D/H14/D2/2/1/936A.
93. "The Case of the Rev. Mr. Dodwell," *Journal of Psychological Medicine and Mental Pathology* 4 (1878): 321–25.
94. Orange and Gover's Report, 10 July 1878, D/H14/D2/2/1/936A.
95. Michel Foucault, "About the Concept of the 'Dangerous Individual' in 19th-Century Legal Psychiatry," trans. Alain Baudot and Jane Couchman, *International Journal of Law and Psychiatry* 1, no. 1 (1978): 9.
96. Thomas Bewley, *Madness to Mental Illness: A History of the Royal College of Psychiatrists* (Trowbridge, Wiltshire: Cromwell Press, 2008), 2–17.
97. Nicolson, William Orange's obituary, HO 144/158/A41007, 7.
98. Ralph Partridge, *Broadmoor: A History of Criminal Lunacy and Its Problems* (London: Chatto and Windus, 1953), 69.
99. Partridge, *Broadmoor*, 69–72.
100. Nicolson, William Orange's Obituary, HO 144/158/A41007, 1–3.
101. Nicolson, William Orange's Obituary, HO 144/158/A41007, 4.
102. H. Charlton Bastian to the Home Office, 20 April 1886, HO 144/158/A41007.
103. E. Leigh Pemberton to Sir Warwick Morshead, 24 March 1886, D/H14/A1/2/5/5 (1884–1897), 110.
104. Nicolson, William Orange's Obituary, HO 144/158/A41007, 4.
105. Dodwell to James Bray, Esq., 20 May 1878, D/H14/D2/2/1/936A.
106. Nicolson's Obituary, *Lancet* 220 (1932): 100.
107. Stevens, *Broadmoor Revealed*, 16.
108. Dodwell to J. Bray, Esq., 18 June 1878, D/H14/D2/2/1/936A.
109. Home Office to Broadmoor Board of Supervision, 22 November 1884, D/H14/A1/2/5/5 (1884–1897), 39.
110. Home Office to Broadmoor Board of Supervision, 5 November 1889, D/H14/A1/2/5/5 (1884–1897), 266.
111. Nicolson's Obituary, *Lancet* 220 (1932): 100–101.
112. Assheton Cross, HC Deb 25 February 1879 vol 243 cc1748–9.
113. "Maudsley, Henry (1835–1918)," *ODNB*.
114. "Conolly, John (1794–1866)," *ODNB*.

115. Maudsley and Blandford's Report, 17 September 1878, D/H14/D2/2/1/936A.
116. Maudsley, *Responsibility in Mental Disease*, 40.
117. Maudsley, *Responsibility in Mental Disease*, 44.
118. Mark Stevens, "Henry Dodwell" (2009), http://www.berkshirerecordoffice.org.uk/albums/broadmoor/henry-dodwell.
119. Henry Maudsley, *Body and Will: Being an Essay Concerning Will in Its Metaphysical, Psychological, and Pathological Aspects* (London, 1883), preface.
120. Maudsley, *Responsibility in Mental Disease*, 129.
121. Stephen, *History of the Criminal Law of England* (1883), 1:479.

CHAPTER 2. A CRIMINAL LUNATIC IN SEARCH OF A TRIAL

1. Reconstructed from witness statements, drawn from IOR/L/PJ/6/13, File 688.
2. Testimony of Bandi Paidi Gadu, IOR/L/PJ/6/13, File 688, 9.
3. Testimony of Atti Appaya, IOR/L/PJ/6/13, File 688, 13.
4. Louis Mallet to the Home Office, 15 May 1880, IOR/L/PJ/6/13, File 688.
5. Maltby's Petition to the Queen, IOR/L/PJ/6/130, File 1409.
6. *In re Maltby* [1881] 7 QB 18, 20.
7. Peter King, *Crime, Justice, and Discretion in England, 1740–1820* (Oxford: Oxford University Press, 2003), 1–2.
8. The Trial of Criminal Lunatics Act (1883), s. 1, 46 & 47 Vict, c. 38.
9. William Orange, "Presidential Address, Annual Meeting of the Medico-Psychological Association, 27 July 1883," *Journal of Mental Science* 29, no. 127 (1883): 330–31.
10. Walker, *Crime and Insanity in England*, 86.
11. Smith, *Trial by Medicine*, 21.
12. Norris to Ridley, 23 November 1899, HO 144/529/A36056.
13. Civil Service of India, *Times* (London, England), 8 August 1867, 10.
14. Thomas James Maltby, *A Practical Handbook of the Uriya or O'di'ya Language* (Calcutta, 1874).
15. Maltby, *Practical Handbook*, x–xii.
16. Maltby, *Practical Handbook*, vii.
17. *The New Annual Army List, Militia List, and Yeomanry Cavalry List* (London, 1881), 487.
18. Testimony of Major Butler, IOR/L/PJ/6/13, File 688, 2–3.
19. Testimony of Major Butler, IOR/L/PJ/6/13, File 688, 3.
20. Statement at the Madras Asylum, 1880, IOR/L/PJ/6/13, File 688, 34.
21. Testimony of William Elseworthy, IOR/L/PJ/6/13, File 688, 6.
22. Testimony of Alister Macnab, IOR/L/PJ/6/13, File 688, 7.
23. Testimony of Bandi Paidi Gadu, IOR/L/PJ/6/13, File 688, 10.
24. Maltby, Statement at the Madras Asylum, 1880, IOR/L/PJ/6/13, File 688, 34.
25. Maltby, Statement at the Madras Asylum, 1880, IOR/L/PJ/6/13, File 688, 35.
26. Maltby to R. Davidson, 19 April 1880, HO 144/60/93521.
27. Seymour D. Thompson, "Homicide in Self-Defence," *American Law Review* 14, no. 8 (1880): 560.

28. James Fitzjames Stephen, *A History of the Criminal Law of England*, vol. 3 (Cambridge: Cambridge University Press, 2014), 12–13.
29. Maltby (unlike his father) does not appear on the English "Law List," or on any other register of lawyers in London, the English countryside, or Madras. It is likely that his Civil Service training was his only formal education. I thank Edel Clarke at the Law Society, London, for her assistance in confirming Maltby's absence from the relevant lists.
30. Maltby's Petition to the Queen, IOR/L/PJ/6/130, File 1409.
31. Testimony of Kunuku Appayya, IOR/L/PJ/6/13, File 688, 16; and Summary of Witness Statements, IOR/L/PJ/6/13, File 688, 24–25.
32. Testimony of Buttana Tattigadu, IOR/L/PJ/6/13, File 688, 16.
33. Testimony of Aumanchi Suryanarayana, IOR/L/PJ/6/13, File 688, 1.
34. Testimony of J. Sunder Siva Row Pantulu, IOR/L/PJ/6/13, File 688, 19–20.
35. Testimony of J. Sunder Siva Row Pantulu, IOR/L/PJ/6/13, File 688, 20.
36. O. B. Irvine to the Chief Secretary to Government, 27 December 1879, IOR/L/PJ/6/193, File 108.
37. O. B. Irvine to the Chief Secretary to Government, 27 December 1879, IOR/L/PJ/6/193, File 108.
38. Indian Code of Criminal Procedure Being Act X of 1872 (London, 1872), s. 423.
39. O. B. Irvine to the Chief Secretary to Government, 3 January 1880, IOR/L/PJ/6/193, File 108.
40. Surgeon-Major J. Smith to the District Magistrate, Vizagapatam, 3 January 1880, IOR/L/PJ/6/193, File 108.
41. Norman Chevers, *A Manual of Medical Jurisprudence for Bengal and the North-Western Provinces* (Calcutta, 1856), 556.
42. *In re Maltby* [1881] 7 QB 18, 24.
43. See: David Arnold, *The Tropics and the Traveling Gaze: India, Landscape, and Science, 1800–1856* (Seattle: University of Washington Press, 2011).
44. Johannes Fabian, *Out of Our Minds: Reason and Madness in the Exploration of Central Africa* (Berkeley: University of California Press, 2000), 3.
45. Waltraud Ernst, *Mad Tales from the Raj: Colonial Psychiatry in South Asia, 1800–58* (London: Anthem, 2010), 59.
46. Maltby, Statement at the Madras Asylum, 1880, IOR/L/PJ/6/13, File 688, 34.
47. Arthur Henry Leapingwell to Government, 13 March 1880, IOR/L/PJ/6/13, File 688, 34.
48. Report of the Official Visitors of the Madras Lunatic Asylum, 23 February 1880, IOR/L/PJ/6/13, File 688, 32.
49. Maltby to Secretary of State for India, 19 April 1880, HO 144/60/93521, TNA.
50. Maltby, "How to Make a Government Lunatic," February 1880, IOR/L/PJ/6/13, File 688, 33.
51. Judicial Department Minute, 13 July 1880, IOR/L/PJ/6/18, File 996.
52. Orange and Nicolson's Report, 13 July 1880, IOR/L/PJ/6/18, File 996.
53. Home Office Directions to Louis Mallet, 2 May 1880, HO 144/60/93521; India Office to T. J. Maltby Sr., 20 May 1880, IOR/L/PJ/6/13, Files 711–12.
54. Public and Judicial Department Minute, 2 September 1880, IOR/L/PJ/6/23, File 1356.

55. Bewley, *Madness to Mental Illness*, 7.
56. Report of the Commissioners in Lunacy, 6 November 1880, IOR/L/PJ/6/26, File 1605.
57. Public and Judicial Department Minute, 2 September 1880, IOR/L/PJ/6/23, File 1356.
58. Public and Judicial Department Minute, 10 August 1880, IOR/L/PJ/6/18, File 996.
59. Public and Judicial Department Minute, 2 September 1880, IOR/L/PJ/6/23, File 1356.
60. Irvine to the Chief Secretary to Government, 29 January 1880, IOR/L/PJ/6/13, File 688, 1.
61. An Act to Authorize the Removal from India of Insane Persons Charged with Offences, and to Give Better Effect to Inquisitions of Lunacy Taken in India (1851), 14 & 15 Victoria, Cap. 81, *The Statutes of the United Kingdom of Great Britain and Ireland, 14 & 15 Victoria* (London, 1851), 463.
62. Public and Judicial Department Minute, 18 November 1880, IOR/L/PJ/6/26, File 1612.
63. *In re Maltby* [1881] 7 QB 18.
64. *In re Maltby* [1881] 7 QB 18, 22.
65. *In re Maltby* [1881] 7 QB 18, 24.
66. Maltby's Petition to the Queen, 1884, IOR/L/PJ/6/130, File 1409.
67. Maltby's Petition to the Queen, 1884, IOR/L/PJ/6/130, File 1409.
68. Henry Stilwell to the Home Office, 24 May 1881, HO 144/60/93521.
69. Notes in Response to Henry Stilwell's of 18 May 1881, HO 144/60/93521.
70. Notes in Response to Henry Stilwell's of 18 May 1881, HO 144/60/93521.
71. Commissioners in Lunacy to Home Office, 7 June 1881, HO 144/60/93521.
72. An Act to Consolidate and Amend the Laws for the Provision and Regulation of Lunatic Asylums for Counties and Boroughs, and for the Maintenance and Care of Pauper Lunatics, in England (1853), 16 & 17 Vict., c. 97, s. 88.
73. An Act to Make Better Provision for the Custody and Care of Criminal Lunatics (1860), 23 & 24 Vict., c. 75, s. 11.
74. Notes on the Letter from the Commissioners in Lunacy to Home Office on 7 June 1881, HO 144/60/93521.
75. Notes on the Letter from the Commissioners in Lunacy to Home Office on 7 June 1881, HO 144/60/93521.
76. C. E. H. Vincent to Home Office, 9 June 1881, HO 144/60/93521; Reginald Lucas, "Vincent, Sir (Charles Edward) Howard (1849–1908)," *ODNB*.
77. Notes on the Letter from the Commissioners in Lunacy to the Home Office on 7 June 1881, HO 144/60/93521.
78. Stilwell to Home Office, 5 July 1881, HO 144/60/93521; Notes on Stilwell's Letter of 5 July 1881, 7 July 1881, HO 144/60/93521.
79. Maltby's Petition to the Queen, 1884, IOR/L/PJ/6/130, File 1409.
80. Maltby's Petition to the Queen, 1884, IOR/L/PJ/6/130, File 1409.
81. Judicial Department Minute, August 1881, IOR/L/PJ/6/46, File 1111.
82. Maltby to Louis Mallet, August 1882, IOR/L/PJ/6/79, File 1357.

83. Donovan Williams, "Mallet, Sir Louis (1823–1890)," *ODNB*.
84. Newton Jennings, 13 January 1880, IOR/L/PJ/6/13, File 688, 27; Testimony of J. W. S. Butler, IOR/L/PJ/6/13, File 688, 3.
85. Maltby's Case History, 11 March 1880, IOR/L/PJ/6/13, File 688, 38.
86. *Times* [London], Wednesday, 27 March 1878.
87. Brayne's Report, 13 November 1897, IOR/L/PJ/6/463, File 2338.
88. Maltby's Petition to the Madras High Court, 16 October 1883, IOR/L/PJ/6/193, File 108.
89. Proceedings of the High Court of Judicature at Madras, 3 December 1883, No. 3780, IOR/L/PJ/6/193, File 108.
90. Maltby to Sir Philip Hutchins, 10 December 1897, IOR/L/PJ/6/467, File 2528.
91. Judicial Department Minute, 11 December 1884, IOR/L/PJ/6/142, File 2485.
92. Maltby to the India Office, 11 December 1884, IOR/L/PJ/6/142, File 2485.
93. Metropolitan Police Report, 27 October 1884, HO 144/60/93521.
94. G. Lushington's Notes on Buckingham's Telegram, 25 October 1884, HO 144/60/93521.
95. Metropolitan Police Report, 27 October 1884, HO 144/60/93521.
96. An Act to Make Further Provision Respecting the Removal of Prisoners and Criminal Lunatics from Her Majesty's Possessions out of the United Kingdom (1884), 47 & 48 Vict., Cap. 31.
97. HL Deb 20 May 1884 vol 288 cc815–16.
98. Colonial Prisoners Removal Act (1884), 47 & 48 Vict., c. 31, s. 9(2).
99. Criminal Lunatics Act (1884), 47 & 48 Vict., c. 64, s. 11(1).
100. Stilwell to India Office, 27 February 1885, IOR/L/PJ/6/148, File 385.
101. Stilwell to W. V. Harcourt, 25 February 1885, HO 144/60/93521.
102. Nicolson to India Office, 13 September 1886, IOR/L/PJ/6/183, File 1375.
103. Maltby's Petition to the Madras High Court, 18 May 1886, IOR/L/PJ/6/193, File 108.
104. Proceedings of the High Court of Judicature at Madras, 3 December 1883, No. 3780, IOR/L/PJ/6/193, File 108.
105. Proceedings of the High Court of Judicature at Madras, 11 November 1886, No. 3059, IOR/L/PJ/6/193, File 108.
106. Public Department Minute, 17 January 1887, IOR/L/PJ/6/193, File 108.
107. Orange to Home Office, 28 September 1885, HO 144/60/93521.
108. Notes on Maltby's Letter to Randolph Churchill, 28 September 1885, HO 144/60/93521.
109. Testimony of Mrs. H. Butler, IOR/L/PJ/6/13, File 688, 3.
110. Nicolson's Report, 3 February 1887, IOR/L/PJ/6/195, File 276.
111. Maltby to Accountant General, 25 June 1889, IOR/L/PJ/6/205, File 1110.
112. Maltby to Philip Hutchins, 10 December 1897, IOR/L/PJ/6/467, File 2528.
113. Brayn to Philip Hutchins, 22 December 1897, IOR/L/PJ/6/467, File 2528.
114. Maltby to Philip Hutchins, 23 February 1898, IOR/L/PJ/6/473, File 403.
115. Deaths Registered in July, August, and September, 1921, Easthampsted, Berkshire, 46.
116. Maltby Case Records, HO 144/60/93521; Thomas Maltby Case File, D/H14/D2/2/1 /1240, BRO. Maltby's Broadmoor file will not be open to researchers until 2022.
117. *In re Maltby* [1881] 7 QB 18.
118. Ernst, *Mad Tales from the Raj*, 29.

CHAPTER 3. LOVERS, MONSTERS, AND THE PROBLEM OF EVIL

1. *Medical Times and Gazette*, vol. 9 (London, 1854), 525.
2. Daniel Hack Tuke, *Prichard and Symonds in Especial Relation to Mental Science: With Chapters on Moral Insanity* (London, 1891), 102.
3. C. K. Clarke, "The Case of William B.—Moral Imbecility," *American Journal of Insanity* 43, no. 1 (1886): 86.
4. Tuke, *Prichard and Symonds*, 103–4.
5. On the confusion about Bigg's pardon, see: John Creighton to W. G. Metcalf, 23 October 1884, RG 10-291, B280641, AO.
6. Tuke, *Prichard and Symonds*, 104.
7. William Bigg Casebook Entry, Kingston Asylum, RG 10-292, AO, 226.
8. Clarke, "The Case of William B.—Moral Imbecility," 102.
9. Medical Superintendent's Journal, 25 August 1884, RG 10-295, AO, 304.
10. See: Nicole Rafter, "The Unrepentant Horse-Slasher: Moral Insanity and the Origins of Criminological Thought," *Criminology* 42, no. 4 (2004): 979–1008.
11. H. Sass and S. Herpertz, "Personality Disorders: Clinical Section," in *A History of Clinical Psychology: The Origin and History of Psychiatric Disorders*, ed. German E. Berrios and Roy Porter (London: Athlone, 1995), 635.
12. Waltraud Ernst, "Personality Disorders: Social Section," in *A History of Clinical Psychology: The Origin and History of Psychiatric Disorders*, ed. German E. Berrios and Roy Porter (London: Athlone, 1995), 646.
13. See: Markus Dirk Dubber, "The Right to Be Punished: Autonomy and Its Demise in Modern Penal Thought," *LHR* 16, no. 1 (1998): 113–46.
14. James Cowles Prichard, "Insanity," in *The Cyclopaedia of Practical Medicine*, ed. John Forbes, vol. 2 (London, 1833), 12.
15. *The Phrenological Journal, and Magazine of Moral Science, for the Year 1844* (1844): 169. See also: James Poskett, *Materials of the Mind: Phrenology, Race, and the Global History of Science, 1815–1920* (Chicago: University of Chicago Press, 2019).
16. James Cowles Prichard, *On the Different Forms of Insanity in Relation to Jurisprudence* (London, 1842), 19.
17. Prichard, *On the Different Forms of Insanity*, 30–37.
18. James Cowles Prichard, "Observations on the Connection of Insanity with Diseases in the Organs of Physical Life," in *Phrenological Journal, and Magazine of Moral Science, for the Year 1844* (1844): 169.
19. James Cowles Prichard, "Soundness and Unsoundness of Mind," in *The Cyclopaedia of Practical Medicine*, ed. John Forbes, vol. 4 (London, 1835), 53.
20. See: Thomas Mayo, *Medical Testimony and Evidence in Cases of Lunacy* (London, 1854), 64.
21. Mayo, 80.
22. "Knatchbull, John (1792–1844)," *ADB*. See also: Jan Wilson, "'An Irresistible Impulse of Mind': Crime and the Legal Defense of Moral Insanity in Nineteenth Century Australia," *Australian Journal of Law and Society* 11 (1995): 145.
23. "Supreme Court—Criminal Side," *Sydney Morning Herald*, 25 January 1844, 2.

24. "Lowe, Robert (1811–1892)," *ADB*.
25. "Supreme Court—Criminal Side," *Sydney Morning Herald*, 25 January 1844, 2.
26. L.E.G.E., "The Punishment of Death," *Zoist: A Journal of Cerebral Physiology and Mesmerism, and Their Applications to Human Welfare* 2, no. 7 (October 1844): 315. L.E.G.E. was likely the pseudonym of William Collins Engledue, a phrenologist and practitioner of mesmerism who cofounded the *Zoist* with John Elliotson in 1843. On the identity of L.E.G.E., see: "Illustrative Notices," *Reasoner: A Weekly Journal, Utilitarian, Republican, and Communist* 7 (1849): 237.
27. "A Memoir of J. Knatchbull," *Cornwall Chronicle*, 17 February 1844, 4.
28. John Knatchbull, "Life of John Knatchbull," in Colin Roderick, *John Knatchbull: From Quarterdeck to Gallows* (Sydney: Angus and Robertson, 1963), 125.
29. L.E.G.E., "The Punishment of Death," 295–316. On the *Zoist*, see: Alison Winter, *Mesmerized: Powers of Mind in Victorian Britain* (Chicago: University of Chicago Press, 1998), 154–55.
30. *Sydney Morning Herald*, 11 March 1845, 2.
31. "The Punishment of Death," 312–13.
32. "Execution of Knatchbull," *Morning Chronicle* (Sydney), 14 February 1844, 2.
33. Roderick, *John Knatchbull: From Quarterdeck to Gallows*, 241.
34. "Lowe, Robert (1811–1892)," *ADB*.
35. December 1847, trial of William Newton Allnutt (t18471213–290), *OBP*.
36. Allyson Nancy May, *The Bar and the Old Bailey, 1750–1850* (Chapel Hill: University of North Carolina Press, 2003), 225.
37. Forbes Winslow, *The Plea of Insanity in Criminal Cases* (London, 1843), 37.
38. December 1847, trial of William Newton Allnutt (t18471213–290), *OBP*.
39. Australian Joint Copying Project. Microfilm Roll 92, Class and Piece Number HO 11/17, Page Number 151 (78).
40. William Ballantine, *Some Experiences of a Barrister's Life* (New York, 1882), 210.
41. Wiener, *Reconstructing the Criminal*, 26.
42. Mayo, *Medical Testimony and Evidence in Cases of Lunacy*, 58.
43. George Victor Townley Casebook Entries, CBC/5, BH.
44. "The Trial of George Victor Townley, for Wilful Murder," *Derby Mercury*, 16 December 1863.
45. Bessie to Townley, letter read at trial, "The Trial of George Victor Townley, for Wilful Murder," *Derby Mercury*, 16 December 1863.
46. "The Rev. F. R. Bryans and the Late Miss Goodwin," *Dundee Courier and Argus*, 4 January 1864.
47. "The Trial of George Victor Townley, for Wilful Murder," *Derby Mercury*, 16 December 1863.
48. Townley's counsel did not attempt a provocation defense. The result could only have been a finding of manslaughter, not a "not guilty" verdict. On provocation, see: A. J. Ashworth, "The Doctrine of Provocation," *Cambridge Law Journal* 35, no. 2 (November 1976): 292–320.
49. "The Trial of George Victor Townley, for Wilful Murder," *Derby Mercury*, 16 December 1863.

50. "The Trial of George Victor Townley, for Wilful Murder," *Derby Mercury*, 16 December 1863.
51. J. F. Stephen to Mary Stephen, 3 December 1863, MS add. 7349/7a, CUL.
52. J. F. Stephen to Mary Stephen, 13 December 1863, MS add. 7349/7a, CUL.
53. J. F. Stephen to Mary Stephen, 11 December 1863, MS add. 7349/7a, CUL.
54. J. F. Stephen to Mary Stephen, 9 December 1863, MS add. 7349/7a, CUL.
55. J. F. Stephen to Mary Stephen, 13 December 1863, MS add. 7349/7a, CUL.
56. "The Mad Doctors Again," *Liverpool Mercury*, 15 December 1863.
57. "Murder Most Foul," *Western Times* (Exeter), 18 December 1863, 5.
58. "Intercession for George Victor Townley," *Daily Post* (Liverpool), 18 December 1863, 5; "The Wigwell Hall Murder," *Newcastle Guardian, and Tyne Mercury*, 19 December 1863, 2.
59. J. F. Stephen to Mary Stephen, 13 December 1863, MS add. 7349/7a, CUL.
60. Declaration of Charles James Townley, 17 December 1863, MH 51/60.
61. "The Execution of Townley," *Derbyshire Times and Chesterfield Herald*, 26 December 1863, 3.
62. Harwood to Waddington, 21 January 1864, MH 51/60; Certificate of Insanity for G. V. Townley, 29 December 1863, MH 51/60.
63. Examination of George Victor Townley before the Commissioners in Lunacy, Derby Gaol, 27 December 1863, MH 51/60.
64. "Respite of George Victor Townley," *Newcastle Courant*, 1 January 1864.
65. J. F. Stephen to Mary Stephen, 1 January 1864, MS add. 7349/7a, CUL.
66. J. F. Stephen to Mary Stephen, 3 January 1864, MS add. 7349/7a, CUL.
67. Derby Magistrates to Sir George Grey, 5 January 1864, MH 51/60.
68. "'Killing No Murder!' or the Strange Efforts to Save Townley," *Huddersfield Chronicle and West Yorkshire Advertiser*, 9 January 1864, 8.
69. "The Case of Townley," *Liverpool Mercury*, 16 January 1864; "The Townley Case—The Official Correspondence," *Manchester Times*, 16 January 1864.
70. "The Respite of the Murderer Townley," *Derby Mercury*, 20 January 1864.
71. Medical Report on Townley's Sanity, 28 January 1864, MH 51/60.
72. George Victor Townley Casebook Entries, CBC/5.
73. Waddington to Evans & Mundy, 1 February 1864, MH 51/60.
74. "The Suicide of George Victor Townley," *Journal of Mental Science* 11 (1866): 66–68.
75. "The Suicide of George Victor Townley," *Journal of Mental Science*, 11 (1866): 66, 77, 79, 82.
76. "Moral Insanity," *Journal of Mental Science* 11 (1866): 133–36.
77. "George Victor Townley," *Lancet* 1 (1865): 212.
78. Joel Peter Eigen, "Lesion of the Will: Medical Resolve and Criminal Responsibility in Victorian Insanity Trials," *Law and Society Review* 33, no. 2 (1999): 430.
79. Tuke, *Prichard and Symonds*, 58.
80. Tuke, *Prichard and Symonds*, 110.
81. Eigen, "Lesion of the Will," 428.
82. Tuke, *Prichard and Symonds*, iv.
83. Medical Superintendent's Journal, Kingston Asylum, 4 July 1881, RG 10-295, AO, 77.

84. Metcalf to Low, 10 March 1885, RG 10-291, B280641, AO.
85. Medical Superintendent's Journal, Kingston Asylum, 4 July 1881, RG 10-295, AO, 78.
86. Medical Superintendent's Journal, Kingston Asylum, 15 August 1885, RG 10-295, AO, 364.
87. Medical Superintendent's Journal, Kingston Asylum, 19 August 1885, RG 10-295, AO, 366.
88. Kenneth C. Dewar, *Charles Clarke, Pen and Ink Warrior* (Montreal: McGill-Queen's University Press, 2004).
89. Ian Dowbiggin, "Clarke, Charles Kirk," *DCB.*
90. C. K. Clarke, "The Care of the Insane in Canada," in *The American Journal of Insanity*, vol. 50 (Utica: Utica State Hospital Press, 1893), 381–85.
91. Clarke, "The Care of the Insane in Canada," 385.
92. Photograph of William Bigg, William Bigg Casebook Notes, Kingston Asylum, RG 10-292, AO.
93. William Bigg Casebook Notes, Kingston Asylum, RG 10-292, AO, 480–81.
94. C. K. Clarke to J. M. Wallace, 4 May 1886, RG 10-285: B111416, AO.
95. William Bigg Casebook Notes, Kingston Asylum, RG 10-292, AO, 200.
96. William Bigg Casebook Notes, Kingston Asylum, RG 10-292, AO, 225; Clarke, "The Case of William B.—Moral Imbecility," 97.
97. C. K. Clarke and J. Webster, "The Case of Wm. B.—Moral Imbecility," *Bulletin of the Ontario Hospitals for the Insane* 7, no. 4 (July 1914): 208–9.
98. Bigg's Family History, RG 10-285: B111416, AO.
99. C. K. Clarke to J. M. Wallace, 12 May 1886, RG 10-285: B111416, AO.
100. Cultural and biological evolutionism—which, respectively, attributed savagery to either cultural primitivism, potentially remediable through education, or biological primitivism, which was innate and intractable in individuals—had become largely indistinguishable by the end of the nineteenth century. See: Peter J. Bowler, "From 'Savage' to 'Primitive': Victorian Evolutionism and the Interpretation of Marginalized Peoples," *Antiquity* 66, no. 252 (1992): 721–29.
101. Edward Burnett Tylor, *Primitive Culture: Researches into the Development of Mythology, Philosophy, Religion, Art, and Custom* (London, 1871), 38.
102. Nancy Stepan, *The Idea of Race in Science: Great Britain, 1800–1960* (Hamden, CT: Archon Books, 1982), 49.
103. Roger Smith, *Inhibition: History and Meaning in the Sciences of Mind and Brain* (Berkeley: University of California Press, 1992), 174.
104. Henry Maudsley, *The Pathology of Mind: A Study of Its Distempers, Deformities, and Disorders* (London, 1895), 29.
105. Maudsley, *Responsibility in Mental Disease*, 173.
106. Maudsley, *Responsibility in Mental Disease*, 219.
107. Tuke, *Prichard and Symonds*, 110.
108. Tylor, *Primitive Culture*, 38.
109. Stephen, *A History of the Criminal Law of England* (1883), 1:184–85.
110. Blumenthal, "The Mind of a Moral Agent."

111. Nicole Rafter, *The Criminal Brain: Understanding Biological Theories of Crime* (New York: NYU Press, 2008), 38.
112. Green, *Freedom and Criminal Responsibility in American Legal Thought*, 15.
113. Valverde, *Diseases of the Will*, 45.
114. Matthew Stanley, *Huxley's Church and Maxwell's Demon: From Theistic Science to Naturalistic Science* (Chicago: University of Chicago Press, 2015).
115. W. S. Lilly, "Materialism and Morality," *Fortnightly Review* 40 (1 November 1886): 584–86.
116. T. H. Huxley, "Science and Morals" (1886), in Thomas H. Huxley, *Evolution and Ethics* (New York: D. Appleton, 1899).
117. Stephen, *A History of the Criminal Law of England* (1883), 1:160.
118. Maudsley, *Body and Will*, 8.
119. Clinical Casebook of the Hospital for the Insane, Hamilton, RG 10-285: B111416, AO.
120. Clarke, "The Case of William B.—Moral Imbecility," 102.
121. Clarke and Webster, "The Case of Wm. B.—Moral Imbecility."
122. Clarke and Webster, "The Case of Wm. B.," 227–31.
123. Ian Dowbiggin, "Clarke, Charles Kirk," *DCB*.
124. C. K. Clarke, "The Fourth Maudsley Lecture," *Public Health Journal* 14, no. 12 (1923): 538–41.
125. Stepan, *The Idea of Race in Science*, 117–18.
126. Rosenberg, *Trial of the Assassin Guiteau*, 252–53.
127. David W. Jones, *Disordered Personalities and Crime: An Analysis of the History of Moral Insanity* (London: Routledge, 2015).
128. "Supreme Court—Criminal Side," *Sydney Morning Herald*, 25 January 184, 2.

CHAPTER 4. MURDER AND METAPHYSICS IN COLONIAL VICTORIA

1. Alfred Deakin, Draft Address, MS 1540/6/19–28, ANL.
2. Alfred Deakin, Draft Address, MS 1540/6/184, ANL.
3. Rosenberg, *Trial of the Assassin Guiteau*, 254.
4. Alfred Deakin, Draft Address, MS 1540/6/19–28, ANL.
5. Belich, *Replenishing the Earth*; Asa Briggs, *Victorian Cities* (Berkeley: University of California Press, 1993), 278.
6. Bruce Kercher, *An Unruly Child: A History of Law in Australia* (St. Leonards, NSW: Allen and Unwin, 1995), 93–94.
7. See: Geoffrey Blainey, *The Tyranny of Distance: How Distance Shaped Australia's History*, 2nd ed. (Melbourne: Macmillan, 1982).
8. See: James Belich, *Paradise Reforged: A History of the New Zealanders from the 1880s to the Year 2000* (Honolulu: University of Hawai'i Press, 2001), 76.
9. Ellis, *The Criminal*, 370.
10. See: *Biography of Frederick Bayley Deeming: A Romance of Crime* (Melbourne, 1892); *Complete History of the Windsor Tragedy* (Melbourne, 1892); *The Criminal of the Century: A Complete History of the Career of Frederick Bayley Deeming, Alias Albert*

Williams, Alias Baron Swanston, &c., &c. (Sydney, 1892); *The History of a Series of Great Crimes on Two Continents* (Adelaide, 1892); *The Life of Deeming: The Murderer of Women and Children* (Melbourne, 1892); *Windsor and Rainhill Murders* (Melbourne, 1892). Also: John Steven O'Sullivan, *A Most Unique Ruffian: The Trial of F. B. Deeming, Melbourne 1892* (Melbourne: Cheshire, 1968); Rachael Weaver, *The Criminal of the Century* (Melbourne: Arcadia, 2006).

11. McKenzie, *Scandal in the Colonies*, 8.
12. "Deeming Insures His Life in Queensland," *Queenslander* (Brisbane), 9 April 1892, 709.
13. "Precis of Career of Frederick Bailey Deeming alias A. O. Williams the Windsor Murderer," VPRS 937/P0000/511, PROV.
14. Report of Sergeants Considine and Cawsey, "Re Antedecents of Convict Albert Williams under sentence of Death for Murder," 5 May 1892, VPRS 1100/P0000/1: Albert Williams, Capital Sentences Files, PROV.
15. Report of W. N. Considine, VPRS 937/P0000/511, PROV.
16. Report of Sergeant O'Loughlin, 6 May 1892, VPRS 937/P0000/511; Report of Constable Webster, 6 May 1892, VPRS 937/P0000/511; Report of Constable Kinniburgh, 12 May 1892, VPRS 937/P0000/511.
17. Considine and Cawsey's Report, 5 March 1892, VPRS 937/P0000/511.
18. "The Man Who Tracked Deeming," *Bombala Times* (New South Wales), 7 July 1933, 2.
19. "Resignation of Sergeant Detective Considine," *Argus* (Melbourne), 1 February 1893, 7.
20. "The Man Who Tracked Deeming."
21. Considine and Cawsey's Report, 5 March 1892, VPRS 937/P0000/511.
22. Samuel Bradley to Sydney Police Department, 8 March 1892, VPRS 937/P0000/511.
23. See Considine and Cawsey's Report, 5 March 1892, VPRS 937/P0000/511; Samuel Bradley to the Sydney Police Department, 8 March 1892, VPRS 937/P0000/511.
24. Victoria Police, Criminal Investigation Branch, to New Scotland Yard, 7 March 1892, VPRS 937/P0000/511.
25. Superintendent of the Lancashire Constabulary on 12 March 1892 to the Assistant Commissioner of Police, Criminal Investigation Department, New Scotland Yard [Copy], VPRS 937/P0000/511.
26. Telegrams from Perth for the Chief Commissioner of Police, Victoria, 21 and 23 March 1892, VPRS 937/P0000/511.
27. "The Trial," *Launceston Examiner*, 25 April 1893, 3.
28. "Hodges, Sir Henry Edward (1844–1919)," *ADB*.
29. Forde, *The Story of the Bar of Victoria*, 225–35.
30. Forde, *The Story of the Bar of Victoria*, 30.
31. "The Windsor Tragedy," *Inquirer and Commercial News* (Perth), 23 April 1892, 5.
32. "Deakin, Alfred (1856–1919)," *ADB*.
33. Belich, *Replenishing the Earth*, 209.
34. "A Lecture by Marshall Lyle," *Freeman's Journal* (Sydney), 18 June 1892, 18.
35. "The Defence of Insanity," *South Australian Register* (Adelaide), 2 April 1892, 6.

36. Lyle to Executive Council, 14 August 1891, VPRS/264/P0000/18, William Colston Capital Case File.
37. General Correspondence, 16 April 1898, Correspondence, Photos and History Sheets of Certain Male Criminals (1862–1902), VPRS 8369.
38. Deeming's History Sheet, Correspondence, Photos and History Sheets of Certain Male Criminals (1862–1902), VPRS 8369.
39. "Ellis, (Henry) Havelock (1859–1939)," *ODNB*; "Ellis, Henry Havelock (1859–1939)," *ADB*.
40. Ellis, *The Criminal*, 365.
41. Ellis, *The Criminal*, 381.
42. Ellis, *The Criminal*, 367.
43. Confession of William Colston, 31 March 1891, VPRS/264/P0000/18.
44. Confession of William Colston, 31 March 1891, VPRS/264/P0000/18.
45. "The Narbethong Murders," *Bendigo Advertiser* (Victoria), 22 April 1891, 2.
46. Exhibit I, Writing from Dictation by William Colston, 10 July 1891, VPRS/264/P0000/18. Judge's Notes, VPRS/264/P0000/18. "The Narbethong Murders," *Maitland Mercury and Hunter River General Advertiser* (New South Wales), 22 April 1891, 6.
47. Exhibit I, Writing from Dictation by William Colston, 10 July 1891, VPRS/264/P0000/18.
48. Statement of Edward Rosenblum, VPRS 30/P0000/841, William Colston Criminal Trial Brief.
49. Statement of Dr. Youl, VPRS 30/P0000/841, William Colston Criminal Trial Brief.
50. James Jamieson, "The Medical Aspects of the Colston Case," *Australian Medical Journal* 13 (15 September 1891): 433–44.
51. Jamieson, "The Medical Aspects of the Colston Case," 434–39.
52. John William Yorke Fishbourne, "Notes on the Colston Case," *Australian Medical Journal* 13 (15 December 1891): 586–604.
53. Colston to Andrew Shields, 13 May 1891, VPRS 30/P0000/841, William Colston Criminal Trial Brief.
54. "The Narbethong Murders," *Maitland Mercury*, 6.
55. "A Lunatic Asylum Tragedy," *Advertiser* (Adelaide), 21 August 1912, 8.
56. Judge's Notes, VPRS/264/P0000/18.
57. "The Narbethong Murders," *Maitland Mercury*, 6.
58. Statement of Hickman Molesworth on the Crimes Act, 21 July 1891, VPRS/264/P0000/18; An Act to Consolidate the Law Relating to Crimes and Criminal Offenders (Crimes Act) (1890), Act 54 Vict. No. 1079, s. 458.
59. An Act for the Better Administration of Justice in His Majesty's Privy Council (Judicial Committee Act, 1833), 3 & 4 William IV, Cap. 41 s. 1.
60. 3 & 4 William IV, Cap. 41, s. 3.
61. 3 & 4 William IV, Cap. 41, s. 5.
62. *Report from the Select Committee of the House of Lords on Appellate Jurisdiction* (London, 1872), 18.
63. Frank Safford and George Wheeler, *The Practice of the Privy Council in Judicial Matters* (London, 1901), xiii.

64. Safford and Wheeler, *The Practice of the Privy Council*, 732.
65. "Hopetoun, Seventh Earl of (1860–1908)," *ADB*.
66. Lyle to Executive Council, 10 August 1891, VPRS/264/P0000/18.
67. Shiels to Hopetoun, 18 August 1891, VPRS/264/P0000/18.
68. *Falkland Islands Company v The Queen* [1864] UKPC 10.
69. See: *Dillet v Graham* [1886] UKPC 18.
70. *Attorney General New South Wales v Henry Louis Bertrand* [1867] LR 1 PC 520.
71. *Attorney General New South Wales v Henry Louis Bertrand* (1867).
72. Shiels to Hopetoun, 18 August 1891, VPRS/264/P0000/18.
73. Judge's Notes, VPRS 264/P0000/6, Gerald H. Supple Capital Case File.
74. Testimony of Myles Garrett Byrne, Judge's Notes, VPRS 264/P0000/6.
75. Judge's Notes, VPRS 264/P0000/6.
76. "Death of Mr. G. H. Supple," *Freeman's Journal* (Sydney), 8 October 1898, 20.
77. Testimony of Henry Heath, Judge's Notes, VPRS 1095/P0000/14, Hugo Levinger: Accused of Murder, 1870; "The Alleged Murder on the High Seas," *Mercury* (Hobart), 25 June 1869, 4.
78. Testimony of Henry Heath, Judge's Notes, VPRS 1095/P0000/14, Hugo Levinger: Accused of Murder, 1870.
79. Memorandum for the Governor from Justice Williams, 1869, VPRS 1095/P0000/14, Hugo Levinger: Accused of Murder, 1870.
80. See: Marianne Constable, *The Law of the Other: The Mixed Jury and Changing Conceptions of Citizenship, Law and Knowledge* (Chicago: University of Chicago Press, 1994).
81. "Alleged Murder on the High Seas. Trial of Hugo Levinger," *Mercury* (Hobart), 22 June 1869, 3.
82. *Hugo Levinger v The Queen* [1870] UKPC 46.
83. Lyle to Executive Council, 14 August 1891, VPRS/264/P0000/18. See also: Binyamin Blum, "The Hounds of Empire: Forensic Dog Tracking in Britain and Its Colonies, 1888–1953," *LHR* 35, no. 3 (2017): 621–65.
84. Lyle to Executive Council, 14 August 1891, VPRS/264/P0000/18.
85. "On the Gallows," *Barrier Miner* (Broken Hill, NSW), 24 August 1891, 3.
86. Testimony of Andrew Shields, Judge's Notes, *R v Deeming*, VPRS 264/P0000/21.
87. Testimony of Thomas Dick, Judge's Notes, *R v Deeming*, VPRS 264/P0000/21.
88. Fishbourne, "Notes on the Colston Case," *Australian Medical Journal* 13 (15 December 1891): 599.
89. Testimony of John Springthorpe, Judge's Notes, *R v Deeming*, VPRS 264/P0000/21.
90. Judge's Notes, *R v Deeming*, p. 25, VPRS 264/P0000/21.
91. Lyle to Executive Council, 7 May 1892, VPRS 264/P0000/21.
92. "The Murderer Schneider," *Advertiser* (Adelaide), 21 March 1892, 5.
93. "An Austrian Murder Trial," *Times* (London), 26–28 January 1892.
94. "The Schneider Murder Trial," *South Australian Chronicle* (Adelaide), 19 March 1892, 19; "An Austrian Murder Trial," *Times* (London), 26 January 1892.
95. "The Schneider Execution," *Advertiser* (Adelaide), 19 March 1892, 7.
96. Alfred Deakin, Draft Address, MS 1540/6/185–188, ANL.

97. "A Murderer's Brain," *Geelong Advertiser* (Victoria), 22 March 1892, 3.
98. "Stray Notes," *Barrier Miner* (Broken Hill, NSW), 23 May 1892, 2.
99. Lyle to Executive Council, 7 May 1892, VPRS 264/P0000/21, 14.
100. Rosenberg, *Trial of the Assassin Guiteau*, 244.
101. Henry Gillespie Hayes and Annie J. Dunn Guiteau Dunmire, *A Complete History of the Trial of Guiteau, Assassin of President Garfield* (Philadelphia, 1882), vi.
102. "The Guiteau Autopsy," *Boston Medical and Surgical Journal* 107 (June–December 1882): 67.
103. Rosenberg, *Trial of the Assassin Guiteau*, 243.
104. Lyle to Executive Council, 7 May 1892, VPRS 264/P0000/21, 14.
105. Lyle to Executive Council, 7 May 1892, VPRS 264/P0000/21, 7.
106. Testimony of Evan Williams, Judge's Notes, *R v Deeming*, VPRS 264/P0000/21, 25.
107. "Deeming's Petition to the Privy Council: The Application Refused," *Manchester Guardian*, 20 May 1892, 8; "Career of Marshall Halt," *Observer* (Adelaide), 2 November 1929, 15.
108. "Deeming's Petition to the Privy Council: The Application Refused," *Manchester Guardian*, 20 May 1892, 8.
109. Lyle to Attorney General, 18 May 1892, VPRS 264/P0000/21.
110. "The Windsor Murder," *Daily News* (Perth), 17 May 1892, 3.
111. Safford and Wheeler, *The Practice of the Privy Council in Judicial Matters*, 732.
112. "Judgment of the Lords of the Judicial Committee of the Privy Council on the Petition for Special Leave to Appeal of Frederick Deeming, from the Colony of Victoria," 19 May 1892, VPRS 264/P0000/21.
113. "The Privy Council and the Deeming Appeal," *Wagga Wagga Advertiser* (New South Wales), 28 June 1892, 4.
114. Lyle to Governor, 17 May 1892, VPRS 264/P0000/21.
115. Augustus Kenny to Crown Law Office, 12 May 1892, VPRS 264/P0000/21.
116. "The Windsor Murderer," *Bendigo Advertiser* (Victoria), 28 June 1892, 3.
117. Ellis, *The Criminal*, 405.
118. The Last Will and Testament of Frederick Bailey Deeming, VPRS 7591/P2 Wills, unit 205, 51/087.
119. Deeming to J. Shegog, 21 May 1892, MS 12158, SLV.
120. The Last Will and Testament of Frederick Bailey Deeming, VPRS 7591/P2 Wills, unit 205, 51/087.
121. "The Windsor and Rainhill Murders," *Argus* (Melbourne), 24 May 1892, 5.
122. Memo of A. Shields, 12 September 1894, VPRS 264/P0001/02, Martha Needle Capital Case File.
123. Report of Detective Constable Priest, South Australian Police, 17 September 1894, VPRS 264/P0001/02.
124. Report of Sergeant A. E. Whitney and Constable R. Fryer of the Melbourne Police, 28 September 1894, VPRS 264/P0001/02.
125. Testimony of George Miller, Judge's Notes, *R v Needle*, 24 September 1894, VPRS 264/P0001/02.
126. Lyle to Governor, 5 October 1894, VPRS 264/P0001/02.

127. Howard Association, *Annual Report*, October 1894, 20.
128. William Tallack, *Howard Letters and Memories* (London, 1905), 144–45.
129. Howard Association, *Annual Report*, October 1896, 17; see also: Leon Radzinowicz and Roger Grahame Hood, *A History of English Criminal Law and Its Administration from 1750*, vol. 5, *The Emergence of Penal Policy* (London: Stevens, 1986), 681.
130. Tallack, *Howard Letters and Memories*, 258–59.
131. Lyle to Governor, 5 October 1894, VPRS 264/P0001/02.
132. See: Thomas A. Green, "Freedom and Criminal Responsibility in the Age of Pound: An Essay on Criminal Justice," *Michigan Law Review* 93 (1995): 1915–2053.
133. Lyle to Crown Law Department, 9 October 1894, VPRS 264/P0001/02.
134. Judge's Notes, *R v Needle*, 24 September 1894, VPRS 264/P0001/02.
135. "Execution of Martha Needle," *Clarence and Richmond Examiner* (Grafton, NSW), 23 October 1894, 5.
136. Howard Association, *Annual Report*, October 1895, 18.
137. Howard Association, *Annual Report*, October 1899.

CHAPTER 5. LESS RESPONSIBLE SUBJECTS

1. "Double Murder and Attempted Suicide at Warrington," *Glasgow Herald*, Saturday, 29 June 1872.
2. Schedule A Form, Margaret Davenport Case File, D/H14/D2/2/2/212, BRO.
3. Report of James Hunt, Chief Constable of Warrington Borough Police, 4 November 1872, Margaret Davenport Case File, D/H14/D2/2/2/212, BRO.
4. Orange to the Guardians of Warrington Union, 22 May 1873, Margaret Davenport Case File, D/H14/D2/2/2/212, BRO.
5. Criminal Lunatics Act 1884 patient information form for 1885, Margaret Davenport Case File, D/H14/D2/2/2/212, BRO.
6. Form transferring Margaret Davenport to Rainhill Asylum, 10 February 1890, Margaret Davenport Case File, D/H14/D2/2/2/212, BRO.
7. See: Rachel Ann Malane, *Sex in Mind: The Gendered Brain in Nineteenth-Century Literature and Mental Sciences* (New York: Peter Lang, 2005), 203.
8. Antoinette M. Burton, *Burdens of History: British Feminists, Indian Women, and Imperial Culture, 1865–1915* (Chapel Hill: University of North Carolina Press, 1994), 35.
9. Joel Peter Eigen, *Unconscious Crime: Mental Absence and Criminal Responsibility in Victorian London* (Baltimore: Johns Hopkins University Press, 2003), 71.
10. Rough book of admission, transfer, discharge and death, and crimes, 1880–83, D/H14/D1/6/1, BRO.
11. See: Carolyn Strange, "Masculinities, Intimate Femicide and the Death Penalty in Australia, 1890–1920," *British Journal of Criminology* 43, no. 2 (2003): 310–39; Krista J. Kesselring, "No Greater Provocation? Adultery and the Mitigation of Murder in English Law," *LHR* 34, no. 1 (2016): 199–225.
12. Elaine Showalter, *The Female Malady: Women, Madness, and English Culture, 1830–1980* (London: Penguin, 1987), 55.

13. James Cowles Prichard, *A Treatise on Insanity and Other Disorders Affecting the Mind* (Philadelphia, 1837), 222.
14. Esquirol, *Mental Maladies*, 126.
15. Alfred Swaine Taylor, *The Principles and Practice of Medical Jurisprudence* (London, 1865), 1122.
16. Taylor, *Principles and Practice*, 1122.
17. Ruth Ellen Homrighaus, "Wolves in Women's Clothing: Baby-Farming and the British Medical Journal, 1860–1872," *Journal of Family History* 26, no. 3 (1 July 2001): 350–72.
18. See: Lacey, *Women, Crime, and Character*.
19. Malcolm M. Feeley and Deborah L. Little, "The Vanishing Female: The Decline of Women in the Criminal Process, 1687–1912," *Law and Society Review* 25, no. 4 (1991): 720.
20. Lucia Zedner, "Women, Crime, and Penal Responses: A Historical Account," *Crime and Justice* 14 (1991): 319.
21. Zedner, "Women, Crime, and Penal Responses," 319.
22. Showalter, *The Female Malady*, 8.
23. See: Hillary Marland, "Disappointment and Desolation: Women, Doctors and Interpretations of Puerperal Insanity in the Nineteenth Century," *History of Psychiatry* 14, no. 3 (2003): 303–20; Carroll Smith-Rosenberg, "The Hysterical Woman: Sex Roles and Role Conflict in 19th-Century America," *Social Research* 39, no. 4 (1972): 652–78; Carroll Smith-Rosenberg and Charles Rosenberg, "The Female Animal: Medical and Biological Views of Woman and Her Role in Nineteenth-Century America," *Journal of American History* 60, no. 2 (1973): 332–56; Alison Bashford, *Purity and Pollution: Gender, Embodiment, and Victorian Medicine* (Basingstoke: Macmillan, 2000); Anne-Marie Kilday, *A History of Infanticide in Britain, c. 1600 to the Present* (Basingstoke: Palgrave Macmillan, 2013); Mark Jackson, *Infanticide: Historical Perspectives on Child Murder and Concealment, 1550–2000* (London: Ashgate, 2002); Josephine McDonagh, *Child Murder and British Culture, 1720–1900* (Cambridge: Cambridge University Press, 2003).
24. Showalter, *The Female Malady*, 52.
25. Lisa Appignanesi, *Trials of Passion: Crimes in the Name of Love and Madness* (London: Virago, 2014), 114–15.
26. "Increase of Infanticide," *Era*, 2 November 1851. *British Library Newspapers*.
27. "Infanticide and Its Reproach," *Era*, 17 May 1857. *British Library Newspapers*.
28. "Infanticide in the Metropolis," *Daily News*, 10 September 1862. *British Library Newspapers*.
29. Kilday, *A History of Infanticide*, 112.
30. Kilday, *A History of Infanticide*, 120.
31. See, for example: "The Alarming Increase of Infanticide," *Morning Chronicle*, 18 January 1861. *British Library Newspapers*.
32. "The Prevalence of Infanticide: How Is the Crime to Be Dealt With?" *Huddersfield Chronicle*, 15 August 1863, 4. *British Library Newspapers*.
33. Paul Knepper, "Dreams and Nightmares: Drug Trafficking and the History of International Crime," in *The Oxford Handbook of the History of Crime and Criminal*

Justice, ed. Anja Johansen and Paul Knepper (Oxford: Oxford University Press, 2016), 209.

34. "Female Infanticide in India," *Daily News*, 29 December 1859. *British Library Newspapers.*
35. "Female Infanticide in India," *Morning Post*, 11 September 1858, 6. *British Library Newspapers.*
36. McDonagh, *Child Murder and British Culture, 1720–1900*, 137.
37. "Infanticide and Its Reproach," *Era*, 17 May 1857. *British Library Newspapers.*
38. "Infanticide and Its Reproach," *Era*, 17 May 1857. *British Library Newspapers.*
39. "Infanticide and the Proposals to Cure It," *Era*, 29 March 1863. *British Library Newspapers.*
40. Kilday, *A History of Infanticide*, 118.
41. Kilday, *A History of Infanticide*, 122.
42. See: Robyn Martin, "A Feminist View of the Reasonable Man: An Alternative Approach to Liability in Negligence for Personal Injury," *Anglo-American Law Review* 23 (1994): 334; Cynthia Lee, *Murder and the Reasonable Man: Passion and Fear in the Criminal Courtroom* (New York: NYU Press, 2007).
43. Blumenthal, *Law and the Modern Mind.*
44. On Haeckel and Darwin, see: Robert J. Richards, *The Tragic Sense of Life: Ernst Haeckel and the Struggle over Evolutionary Thought* (Chicago: University of Chicago Press, 2008), 113–70.
45. Frederick Young, *On the Political Relations of Mother Countries and Colonies* (London, 1883), 18.
46. Cynthia Eagle Russett, *Sexual Science* (Cambridge, MA: Harvard University Press, 2009), 50–51.
47. Charles Darwin, *The Descent of Man: And Selection in Relation to Sex*, vol. 2 (London, 1871), 326–27.
48. Darwin, *Descent of Man*, 2:317.
49. Andrew Davidson, *Hygiene and Diseases of Warm Climates* (Edinburgh: Young J. Pentland, 1893), 16.
50. Russett, *Sexual Science*, 74–75.
51. John Russell Reynolds, *A System of Medicine: Local Diseases*, vol. 2 (Philadelphia: J. B. Lippincott, 1872), 446.
52. On putrefaction in eighteenth-century imperial medicine, see: Suman Seth, *Difference and Disease: Medicine, Race, and the Eighteenth-Century British Empire* (Cambridge: Cambridge University Press, 2018), 113.
53. Lawrence Cohen, *No Aging in India: Alzheimer's, the Bad Family, and Other Modern Things* (Berkeley: University of California Press, 2000), 20–22.
54. *Census of India for 1891* (Calcutta, 1893), 171–73.
55. Margaret May, "Innocence and Experience: The Evolution of the Concept of Juvenile Delinquency in the Mid-Nineteenth Century," *Victorian Studies* 17, no. 1 (1973): 7–29; Wiener, *Reconstructing the Criminal*, 131.
56. Wiener, *Reconstructing the Criminal*, 129–30.
57. May, "Innocence and Experience," 22.

58. Cesare Lombroso, *Criminal Woman, the Prostitute, and the Normal Woman*, trans. Nicole Hahn Rafter and Mary Gibson (Durham, NC: Duke University Press, 2004), 4.
59. On the persistence of Lombroso and classic criminological models of women's criminality into the twentieth century, see: Carol Smart, *Women, Crime and Criminology: A Feminist Critique* (Abingdon: Routledge, 2013), 27.
60. Lombroso, *Criminal Woman*, 183.
61. Lombroso, *Criminal Woman*, 203–4.
62. Police Report on Mary Fitzgerald, 21 November 1892, VPRS/264/P0000/20, Mary Fitzgerald Capital Case File.
63. Report of Victoria Police, Yarrawanga Station, 25 November 1892, VPRS/264/P0000/20.
64. Report of Victoria Police, Yarrawanga Station, 25 November 1892, VPRS/264/P0000/20.
65. M. W. P. Carney, "Five Cases of Bromism," *Lancet* 298, no. 7723 (1971): 523–24.
66. Judge's Notes of Evidence, *R v Fitzgerald*, 15 November 1892, VPRS/264/P0000/20.
67. Police Report on Antecedents of Mary Fitzgerald, 21 November 1892, VPRS/264/P0000/20.
68. Judge's Notes, *R v Fitzgerald*, 15 November 1892, VPRS/264/P0000/20.
69. Testimony of Hugh McDiermed, Judge's Notes, 15 November 1892, VPRS/264/P0000/20.
70. Testimony of Edward John McAdel, Judge's Notes, 15 November 1892, VPRS/264/P0000/20.
71. Testimony of Constable Charles James Wardley, Judge's Notes, 15 November 1892, VPRS/264/P0000/20.
72. Eigen, *Unconscious Crime*, 72.
73. Judge's Notes, *R v Fitzgerald*, 15 November 1892, VPRS/264/P0000/20.
74. T. O. Windsor to Law Society, 18 November 1892, VPRS/264/P0000/20.
75. Eigen, *Unconscious Crime*, 74–76.
76. J. H. Hood to Executive Council, 25 November 1892, VPRS/264/P0000/20.
77. Anthea Hyslop, "Temperance, Christianity and Feminism: The Woman's Christian Temperance Union of Victoria, 1887–97," *Historical Studies* 17, no. 66 (1976): 29–33.
78. Elizabeth Pleck, "Feminist Responses to 'Crimes against Women,' 1868–1896," *Signs: Journal of Women in Culture and Society* 8, no. 3 (Spring 1983): 455.
79. Hyslop, "Temperance, Christianity and Feminism," 43.
80. WTCU Benalla to Hopetoun, 26 November 1892, VPRS/264/P0000/20.
81. "Child Murder," *North Eastern Ensign* (Victoria), 29 November 1892, 3.
82. McDonagh, *Child Murder and British Culture*, 185.
83. Elizabeth Malcolm, "Searching for the Irish and Irish Studies in Australia," *Estudios Irlandeses* 14 (March 2019): 207.
84. Oonagh Walsh, "Gender and Insanity in Nineteenth-Century Ireland," in *Sex and Seclusion, Class and Custody: Perspectives on Gender and Class in the History of British and Irish Psychiatry*, ed. Jonathan Andrews and Anne Digby (Amsterdam: Rodopi, 2004), 72.

85. Malcolm, "Searching for the Irish and Irish Studies in Australia," 208.
86. Walsh, "Gender and Insanity in Nineteenth-Century Ireland," 69–79.
87. Thomas Drapes, "On the Alleged Increase of Insanity in Ireland," *Journal of Mental Science* 40 (October 1894): 531–33.
88. Elizabeth Malcolm, "Irish Immigrants in a Colonial Asylum during the Australian Gold Rushes, 1848–1869," in *Asylums, Mental Health Care and the Irish: 1800–2010*, ed. Pauline M. Prior (Newbridge: Irish Academic Press, 2017).
89. Daniel Hack Tuke, "Increase of Insanity in Ireland," *Journal of Mental Science* 40 (October 1894): 551.
90. See: Mark Finnane, "Asylums, Families and the State," in *History Workshop Journal* 20 (1985): 134–48; Patrick James O'Farrell, *The Irish in Australia* (Kensington, NSW: NSWU Press, 1987), 36.
91. Daniel J. R. Grey, "'The Agony of Despair': Pain and the Cultural Script of Infanticide in England and Wales, 1860–1960," in *Pain and Emotion in Modern History*, ed. Rob Boddice (Basingstoke: Palgrave Macmillan, 2014), 210.
92. Dana Y. Rabin, *Identity, Crime and Legal Responsibility in Eighteenth-Century England* (Basingstoke: Palgrave Macmillan, 2004), 109.
93. Schedule A Form, Sarah Allen Case File, D/H14/D2/2/2/2, BRO.
94. W. B. Allen to Orange, 24 May 1872, Sarah Allen Case File, D/H14/D2/2/2/2, BRO.
95. Dr. Cassidy's notes on interview with W. B. Allen, 14 June 1872, Sarah Allen Case File, D/H14/D2/2/2/2, BRO.
96. W. B. Allen to Orange, 15 June 1872, Sarah Allen Case File, D/H14/D2/2/2/2, BRO.
97. W. B. Allen to Orange, 13 July 1872, Sarah Allen Case File, D/H14/D2/2/2/2, BRO.
98. Sarah Allen to Orange, 30 August 1872, Sarah Allen Case File, D/H14/D2/2/2/2, BRO.
99. Judge's Notes, *R v Fitzgerald*, 15 November 1892, VPRS/264/P0000/20.
100. Employers' Petition to Hopetoun, VPRS/264/P0000/20.
101. Jade Shepherd, "'One of the Best Fathers until He Went out of His Mind': Paternal Child-Murder, 1864–1900," *Journal of Victorian Culture* 18, no. 1 (2013): 12–18.
102. Shepherd, "One of the Best Fathers," 5.
103. See: Susanna L. Blumenthal, "The Default Legal Person," *UCLA Law Review* 54, no. 1 (2006): 1135–1265.

CHAPTER 6. THE INFANTICIDAL IMPERATIVE

1. "Mussumat" is an honorific used for North Indian women, which appeared frequently in law reports and other official documents during this period. See: Stephen Legg, "Empirical and Analytical Subaltern Space? Ashrams, Brothels and Trafficking in Colonial Delhi," *Cultural Studies* 30, no. 5 (2016): 811.
2. W. Chichele Plowden, *Census of the N. W. Provinces, 1865*, vol. 1 (Allahabad, 1867), 109.
3. *Government v Mussumat Neemia* (1852), in *Decisions of the Nizamut Adawlut, North-Western Provinces, for 1852*, vol. 2 (Agra, 1853), 17.
4. *Government v Mussumat Neemia*, 18–19.
5. *Government v Mussumat Neemia*, 17.

6. *Government v Mussumat Neemia,* 19.
7. See: Alastair McClure, "Sovereignty, Law, and the Politics of Forgiveness in Colonial India, 1858–1903," *Comparative Studies of South Asia, Africa and the Middle East* 38, no. 3 (2018): 385–401.
8. Heather Wolffram, "Forensic Knowledge and Forensic Networks in Britain's Empire: The Case of Sydney Smith," in *Global Forensic Cultures: Making Fact and Justice in the Modern Era,* ed. Ian Burney and Christopher Hamlin (Baltimore: Johns Hopkins University Press, 2019), 305–24.
9. Norman Chevers, *A Manual of Medical Jurisprudence for Bengal and the North-Western Provinces* (Calcutta, 1856), 515.
10. Singha, *A Despotism of Law,* 80–120.
11. See: Jörg Fisch, *Cheap Lives and Dear Limbs: The British Transformation of the Bengal Criminal Law, 1769–1817* (Wiesbaden: F. Steiner, 1983), 1–7.
12. Daniel J. R. Grey, "Gender, Religion, and Infanticide in Colonial India, 1870–1906," *Victorian Review* 37, no. 2 (2011): 107. See also: Daniel J. R. Grey, "'It Is Impossible to Judge the Extent to Which the Crime Is Prevalent': Infanticide and the Law in India, 1870–1926," *Women's History Review* (ahead-of-print, 2020), 1–19.
13. Isidore Bernadotte Lyon, *A Textbook of Medical Jurisprudence for India* (Calcutta, 1889), 351.
14. Padma Anagol, "The Emergence of the Female Criminal in India: Infanticide and Survival under the Raj," *History Workshop Journal* 53 (2002): 76.
15. Lalita Panigrahi, *British Social Policy and Female Infanticide in India* (New Delhi: Munshiram Manoharlal, 1972), 15.
16. Anagol, "The Emergence of the Female Criminal in India," 77.
17. Grey, "Gender, Religion, and Infanticide in Colonial India, 1870–1906," 111–13.
18. Dharma Bhanu, *The Province of Agra: Its History and Administration* (New Delhi: Concept, 1979), 162.
19. See: Sadhana Naithani, *In Quest of Indian Folktales: Pandit Ram Gharib Chaube and William Crooke* (Bloomington: Indiana University Press, 2006).
20. William Crooke, *The North-Western Provinces of India: Their History, Ethnology, and Administration* (London, 1897), 4–7.
21. Clive Dewey, *Anglo-Indian Attitudes: Mind of the Indian Civil Service* (London: Hambledon, 1993), 3–5.
22. Maltby, *Practical Handbook*; Thomas James Maltby, *The Ganjam District Manual,* ed. G. D. Leman (Madras, 1882).
23. *Government v Mussumat Nisseea* (1853), in *Decisions of the Nizamut Adawlut, North-Western Provinces, for 1853* (Agra, 1854), 123–25.
24. *East-India Register and Army List* (London, 1855), 291.
25. *Government v Mussumat Nisseea,* 125.
26. Samuel Sneade Brown, *Home Letters: Written from India between the Years 1828 and 1841* (London, 1878), iii–iv.
27. Brown, *Home Letters,* 148, 157.
28. Brown, *Home Letters,* 113–14.
29. Brown, *Home Letters,* 113.

30. John Cave-Browne, *Indian Infanticide: Its Origin, Progress, and Suppression* (London, 1857), 75–76.
31. Cave-Browne, *Indian Infanticide*, 77–78.
32. Panigrahi, *British Social Policy*, 19.
33. Cave-Browne, *Indian Infanticide*, 80.
34. Panigrahi, *British Social Policy*, 113.
35. Panigrahi, *British Social Policy*, 22–23.
36. Lyon, *A Textbook of Medical Jurisprudence for India*, 352.
37. Panigrahi, *British Social Policy*, 133–37.
38. Panigrahi, *British Social Policy*, 92.
39. Sharafi, *Law and Identity in Colonial South Asia: Parsi Legal Culture, 1772–1947*, 193–198.
40. Sorab P. N. Wadia, *The Institution of Trial by Jury in India* (Bombay, 1897), 46, 80–3. On the jury in India, see also: Kalyani Ramnath, "The Colonial Difference between Law and Fact: Notes on the Criminal Jury in India," *Indian Economic and Social History Review* 50, no. 3 (2013): 341–63.
41. Sharafi, *Law and Identity in Colonial South Asia*, 198.
42. *Government v Mussumat Nisseea*, 124.
43. Chevers, *Manual of Medical Jurisprudence*, 524.
44. Anagol, "The Emergence of the Female Criminal in India," 86–87.
45. Wadia, *The Institution of Trial by Jury in India*, 85.
46. J. Duncan M. Derrett, "The Administration of Hindu Law by the British," *Comparative Studies in Society and History* 4, no. 1 (1961): 23.
47. Sharafi, *Law and Identity in Colonial South Asia*, 110–11.
48. Panigrahi, *British Social Policy*, 145.
49. Panigrahi, *British Social Policy*, 147.
50. Grey, "Gender, Religion, and Infanticide in Colonial India, 1870–1906," 110–11.
51. Panigrahi, *British Social Policy*, 156.
52. "Norman Chevers," *Plarr's Lives of the Fellows*, Royal College of Surgeons of England (19 April 2011), https://livesonline.rcseng.ac.uk/.
53. Robert P. Brittain, *Bibliography of Medico-Legal Works in English* (London: Sweet and Maxwell, 1962), 33.
54. Brittain, *Bibliography*, 184–86.
55. Norman Chevers, *A Manual of Medical Jurisprudence for India: Including the Outlines of a History of Crime Against the Person in India* (Calcutta: Thacker, Spink, 1870), inside cover.
56. Chevers, *Manual*, 5.
57. Chevers, *Manual*, 12–13.
58. Elizabeth Kolsky, *Colonial Justice in British India* (Cambridge: Cambridge University Press, 2010), 117. See also: Bernard Cohn, *Colonialism and Its Forms of Knowledge: The British in India* (Princeton: Princeton University Press, 1996), 69. On police efforts to deploy "truth machine" technologies in postcolonial Indian criminal justice, see: Jinee Lokaneeta, *The Truth Machines: Policing, Violence, and Scientific Interrogations in India* (Ann Arbor: University of Michigan Press, 2020).

59. James Dunning Baker Gribble and Patrick Hehir, *Outlines of Medical Jurisprudence for Indian Criminal Courts*, 2nd ed. (Madras, 1891), 11.
60. Joseph Goodeve, *The Law of Evidence as Administered in England and Applied to India* (Calcutta, 1862), 115.
61. Mary Ellis Gibson, ed., *Science Fiction in Colonial India, 1835–1905: Five Stories of Speculation, Resistance and Rebellion* (London: Anthem Press, 2019), 77–78.
62. See: Wendie Ellen Schneider, *Engines of Truth: Producing Veracity in the Victorian Courtroom* (New Haven: Yale University Press, 2016), 206–8.
63. Goodeve, *Law of Evidence*, 85–86.
64. On sati, see: Lata Mani, *Contentious Traditions: The Debate on Sati in Colonial India* (Berkeley: University of California Press, 1998).
65. Catherine Hall, "Of Gender and Empire: Reflections on the Nineteenth Century," in *Gender and Empire*, ed. Philippa Levine (Oxford: Oxford University Press, 2004), 55.
66. Goodeve, *Law of Evidence*, 88.
67. Chevers, *Manual*, 4.
68. Wendie Ellen Schneider, "Enfeebling the Arm of Justice: Perjury and Prevarication in British India," in *Modern Histories of Crime and Punishment*, ed. Markus Dirk Dubber and Lindsay Farmer (Stanford: Stanford University Press, 2007), 301.
69. Cohn, *Colonialism and Its Forms of Knowledge*, 17.
70. Indian Penal Code (1860), s. 84.
71. Chevers, *Manual*, 568.
72. Chevers, *Manual*, 533–34.
73. Chevers, *Manual*, 561.
74. Waltraud Ernst, *Mad Tales from the Raj: Colonial Psychiatry in South Asia, 1800–58* (London: Anthem, 2010), 73.
75. "Norman Chevers," *Plarr's Lives of the Fellows*.
76. Brittain, *Bibliography*, 112–13.
77. Lyon, *A Textbook of Medical Jurisprudence for India*. On the office of the Chemical Analyser or Chemical Examiner, see: Mitra Sharafi, "The Imperial Serologist and Punitive Self-Harm: Bloodstains and Legal Pluralism in British India," in *Global Forensic Cultures: Making Fact and Justice in the Modern Era*, ed. Ian Burney and Christopher Hamlin (Baltimore: Johns Hopkins University Press, 2019), 64–65.
78. David Arnold, *Toxic Histories: Poison and Pollution in Modern India* (Cambridge: Cambridge University Press, 2016), 112.
79. John Barnes et al., "A Place in the World," in *The Cambridge History of the Book in Britain*, ed. David McKitterick (Cambridge: Cambridge University Press, 2009), 631.
80. Lyon, *Medical Jurisprudence for India*, 12–13.
81. Martin J. Wiener, *An Empire on Trial: Race, Murder, and Justice under British Rule, 1870–1935* (Cambridge: Cambridge University Press, 2009), 132.
82. Elizabeth Kolsky, "Codification and the Rule of Colonial Difference: Criminal Procedure in British India," *LHR* 23, no. 3 (2005): 635.
83. Mrinalini Sinha, *Colonial Masculinity: The "Manly Englishman" and the "Effeminate Bengali" in the Late Nineteenth Century* (Manchester: Manchester University Press, 1995), 36.

84. Sinha, *Colonial Masculinity,* 34–40; Kolsky, "Codification and the Rule of Colonial Difference," 680.
85. Kolsky, *Colonial Justice in British India,* 136; Jordanna Bailkin, "The Boot and the Spleen: When Was Murder Possible in British India?" *Comparative Studies in Society and History* 48, no. 2 (2006): 462–93.
86. Wiener, *Empire on Trial,* 150.
87. Lyon, *Medical Jurisprudence for India,* 262.
88. Lyon, *Medical Jurisprudence for India,* 396.
89. James Poskett, *Materials of the Mind: Phrenology, Race, and the Global History of Science, 1815–1920* (Chicago: University of Chicago Press, 2019), 261. Erick Linstrum makes a similar point about twentieth-century psychology and psychometric testing in: *Ruling Minds: Psychology in the British Empire* (Cambridge, MA: Harvard University Press, 2016).
90. Dirom Grey Crawford, *A History of the Indian Medical Service, 1600–1913* (London: W. Thacker, 1914), 111–12.
91. Gribble and Hehir, *Outlines of Medical Jurisprudence,* 1.
92. See: Sharafi, "The Imperial Serologist and Punitive Self-Harm," 70.
93. Gribble and Hehir, *Outlines of Medical Jurisprudence,* 11–16.
94. Patrick Hehir, *The Medical Profession in India* (London, 1923), 1.
95. Hehir, *Medical Profession,* 51.
96. The spleen, for instance, became a site where racial difference was located in British India. See: Bailkin, "The Boot and the Spleen."
97. See: Gyan Prakash, *Another Reason: Science and the Imagination of Modern India* (Princeton: Princeton University Press, 1999), 145.
98. Ishita Pande, "Coming of Age: Law, Sex and Childhood in Late Colonial India," *Gender and History* 24, no. 1 (2012): 215.
99. 22 December 1868, Grant Duff Papers, quoted in George Feaver, *From Status to Contract: A Biography of Sir Henry Maine, 1822–1888* (London: Longmans, 1969), 101.

CHAPTER 7. THE SAVAGE HEART OF EMPIRE

1. "Fearful Outrage by Blacks," *Argus* (Melbourne), 23 July 1900, 5.
2. A nulla-nulla or waddy is a cudgel used by Aboriginal Australians in hunting and combat.
3. "The Breelong Murders," *Nepean Times* (Penrith, NSW), 28 July 1900, 3.
4. Katherine Biber, "Besieged at Home: Jimmy Governor's Rampage," *Public Space* 2 (2008): 3–4.
5. "The Breelong Murders," *National Advocate* (Bathurst, NSW), 26 July 1900, 2.
6. See: Maudsley, *Pathology of Mind,* 29.
7. On race, colonialism, and psychiatry, see among others: Martin Summers, *Madness in the City of Magnificent Intentions: A History of Race and Mental Illness in the Nation's Capital* (Oxford: Oxford University Press, 2019), 78; Megan Vaughan, *Curing Their Ills: Colonial Power and African Illness* (Stanford: Stanford University Press, 1991); Jock McCulloch, *Colonial Psychiatry and "the African Mind"* (Cambridge: Cambridge

University Press, 1995); Jonathan Sadowsky, *Imperial Bedlam: Institutions of Madness in Colonial Southwest Nigeria* (Berkeley: University of California Press, 1999); Sloan Mahone and Megan Vaughan, *Psychiatry and Empire* (Basingstoke: Palgrave Macmillan, 2007); Richard C. Keller, *Colonial Madness: Psychiatry in French North Africa* (Chicago: University of Chicago Press, 2007); Erik Linstrum, *Ruling Minds: Psychology in the British Empire* (Cambridge: Harvard University Press, 2016); Claire E. Edington, *Beyond the Asylum: Mental Illness in French Colonial Vietnam* (Ithaca, NY: Cornell University Press, 2019).

8. Vaughan, *Curing Their Ills*, 107–9.
9. Summary of "Insanity among the Australian Aborigines," 15 February 1890, *British Medical Journal* 1 (London, 1890): 375.
10. Katherine Ellinghaus, *Taking Assimilation to Heart: Marriages of White Women and Indigenous Men in the United States and Australia, 1887–1937* (Lincoln: University of Nebraska Press, 2006), 153–56.
11. "Breelong Murderers," *Brisbane Courier*, 28 July 1900, 9.
12. Ellinghaus, *Taking Assimilation to Heart*, 149.
13. "The Breelong Murders," *Warwick Examiner and Times* (Queensland), 28 November 1900, 3.
14. Russell McGregor, *Imagined Destinies: Aboriginal Australians and the Doomed Race Theory, 1880–1939* (Melbourne: Melbourne University Press, 2012).
15. Patrick Wolfe, "Land, Labor, and Difference: Elementary Structures of Race," *American Historical Review* 106, no. 3 (2001): 867–73.
16. "The Half-Caste Problem," *Advertiser* (Adelaide), 14 October 1910, 8.
17. Katherine Ellinghaus, "Absorbing the 'Aboriginal Problem': Controlling Interracial Marriage in Australia in the Late 19th and Early 20th Centuries," *Aboriginal History* 27 (2003): 186.
18. McGregor, *Imagined Destinies*, 142.
19. Stocking, *Victorian Anthropology*, 229–30; McGregor, *Imagined Destinies*, 174.
20. "Yellow Peril," *Telegraph* (Brisbane), 26 September 1903, 8.
21. Wolfe, "Land, Labor, and Difference," 873; Ellinghaus, "Absorbing the 'Aboriginal Problem,'" 185.
22. "Boyce, Francis Stewart (1872–1940)," *ADB*.
23. Kesselring, "No Greater Provocation?"
24. "The Breelong Tragedy," *Sydney Morning Herald*, 24 November 1900, 11.
25. Biber, "Besieged at Home," 33.
26. "The Breelong Tragedy," *Sydney Morning Herald*, 24 November 1900, 11.
27. "Jimmy Governor," *Narromine News and Trangie Advocate* (New South Wales), 4 December 1900, 3.
28. "Jimmy Governor Executed," *Richmond River Herald and Northern Districts Advertiser* (New South Wales), 25 January 1901, 2.
29. "Jimmy Governor," *Narromine News and Trangie Advocate* (New South Wales), 14 December 1900, 3.
30. "Victims of Vice," *Sunday Times* (Perth), 5 July 1903, 10.
31. "The Breelong Tragedy," *Sydney Morning Herald*, 24 November 1900, 11.

32. Robert Dunn, "Some Observations on the Psychological Differences Which Exist among the Typical Races of Man," *Transactions of the Ethnological Society of London* 3 (1865): 12.
33. Dunn, "Some Observations," 19. See "Dunn, Robert (1799–1877)," *ODNB.*
34. Maudsley, *Pathology of Mind,* 29.
35. "Circuit Court, Monday, September 24, 1900," *Northern Territory and Gazette* (Darwin), 18 September 1900, 3.
36. Thalia Anthony, *Indigenous People, Crime and Punishment* (New York: Routledge, 2013), 40.
37. See: Damen Ward, "A Means and Measure of Civilisation: Colonial Authorities and Indigenous Law in Australasia," *History Compass* 1, no. 1 (1 January 2003): 1–24.
38. See: Herbert Spencer, *Social Statics: Or, The Conditions Essential to Human Happiness* (New York, 1873); John Lubbock, *The Origin of Civilisation and the Primitive Condition of Man* (London, 1870).
39. Mark Francis, "The 'Civilizing' of Indigenous People in Nineteenth-Century Canada," *Journal of World History* 9, no. 1 (1998): 73.
40. T. S. Clouston, "The Developmental Aspects of Criminal Anthropology," *Journal of the Anthropological Institute of Great Britain and Ireland* 23 (1894): 215–25.
41. Clouston, "Developmental Aspects," 217.
42. Clouston, "Developmental Aspects," 225.
43. On understandings of degeneration advanced by Morel, Lombroso, and Maudsley and their national contexts, see: Pick, *Faces of Degeneration.*
44. Rafter, *The Criminal Brain,* 99; Bénédict Auguste Morel, *Traité des dégénérescences physiques, intellectuelles et morales de l'espèce humaine et des causes qui produisent ces variétés maladives* (Paris, 1857).
45. Clouston, "Developmental Aspects," 221.
46. Morel, *Traité des dégénérescences,* viii.
47. Morel, *Traité des dégénérescences,* xiv.
48. James Cowles Prichard, *The Natural History of Man* (London,1843).
49. Morel, *Traité des dégénérescences,* 377.
50. Valverde, *Diseases of the Will,* 51.
51. Maudsley, *The Pathology of Mind,* 116.
52. Rafter, *The Criminal Brain,* 65.
53. Cesare Lombroso, *Criminal Man,* ed. Mary Gibson and Nicole Hahn Rafter (Durham, NC: Duke University Press, 2006), 195. On atavism and degeneration in Lombroso's thought, see: Pick, *Faces of Degeneration,* 120.
54. Lombroso, *Criminal Man,* 222.
55. Lombroso, *Criminal Man,* 72–73.
56. Francis, "The 'Civilizing' of Indigenous People in Nineteenth-Century Canada," 55.
57. Stocking, *Victorian Anthropology,* 229.
58. Clouston, "Developmental Aspects," 221.
59. Spencer, *Social Statics,* 449.
60. Spencer, *Social Statics,* 450.
61. Spencer, *Social Statics,* 221–22.

62. Bronislaw Malinowski, *Crime and Custom in Savage Society* (London, 1926), xi.
63. Malinowski, *Crime and Custom,* xi.
64. Ford, *Settler Sovereignty.*
65. John L. Comaroff, "Colonialism, Culture, and the Law: A Foreword," *Law and Social Inquiry* 26 (2001): 306–11.
66. Partha Chatterjee, *The Nation and Its Fragments: Colonial and Postcolonial Histories* (Princeton: Princeton University Press, 1993).
67. See: Homi K. Bhabha, *The Location of Culture* (Routledge, 2012).
68. Belich, *Replenishing the Earth,* 359.
69. Nadia Rhook, "Listen to Nodes of Empire: Speech and Whiteness in Victorian Hawker's License Courts," *Journal of Colonialism and Colonial History* 15, no. 2 (2014).
70. "The Alleged Murder by a Hindoo," *Argus* (Melbourne), 2 March 1891, 10.
71. Testimony of Azamoo Khan, Judge's Notes, 23 March 1891, *R v Fatta Chand,* VPRS/1100/P0000/1.
72. "The Alleged Murder by a Hindoo," 9.
73. Testimony of Robert Allan, Judge's Notes, 23 March 1891, *R v Fatta Chand,* VPRS/1100/P0000/1.
74. Occasionally records list "Fatta" as "Patta," but almost all of the documents identify the defendant as Fatta Chand.
75. Report of Considine and Cawsey, Judge's Notes, 23 March 1891, *R v Fatta Chand,* VPRS/1100/P0000/1.
76. Memo from Andrew Shields, 30 March 1891, VPRS/1100/P0000/1.
77. Report on the Antecedents of Fatta Chand, 25 March 1891, VPRS/1100/P0000/1.
78. "The Alleged Murder by a Hindoo," 10.
79. "The Murder of an Indian Hawker," *Argus* (Melbourne), 25 March 1891, 9.
80. "The Hindoo Murder," *Riverine Herald* (Victoria), 25 March 1891, 2.
81. Gilbert Smith to Governor, 13 March 1891, VPRS 264/P0001/1.
82. Executive Council, Minute 22, 14 April 1891, VPRS 1080/P0000/28.
83. "On the Gallows," *Barrier Miner* (Broken Hill, NSW), 28 April 1891, 4; Captain Evans to A. P. Akehurst, 1 June 1891, VPRS 264/P0001/1.
84. "On the Gallows," 4.
85. "Execution of Fatta Chand," *Bowral Free Press and Berrima District Intelligencer* (New South Wales), 29 April 1891, 2.
86. "On the Gallows," 4.
87. Michael E. Scorgie and Somendra Chandra Nandy, "Emerging Evidence of Early Indian Accounting," *Abacus* 28, no. 1 (1992): 88–97.
88. Somendra Chandra Nandy, *History of the Cossimbazar Raj in the Nineteenth Century* (Calcutta: Dev-All, 1986), 200–229.
89. Nandy, *Cossimbazar Raj,* 272–81.
90. Nandy, *Cossimbazar Raj,* 468.
91. Nandy, *Cossimbazar Raj,* 293–306.
92. Nandy, *Cossimbazar Raj,* 428.
93. *Advocate-General of Bengal v Ranee Surnomoyee* [1864] UKPC 14 (22 July 1864), 3.

94. *Calvin's Case* [1608] 7 Coke Report 14 a, 77 ER.
95. Polly J. Price, "Natural Law and Birthright Citizenship in Calvin's Case (1608)," *Yale Journal of Law and Humanities* 9 (1997): 81.
96. William Blackstone, *Commentaries on the Laws of England*, book 1, ch. 10, 358.
97. *Calvin's Case*, 393.
98. *Calvin's Case*, 398.
99. Hulsebosch, "The Ancient Constitution."
100. *The Indian Chief* [1800] 3 Robinson's Reports 29.
101. *Advocate-General of Bengal v Ranee Surnomoyee* [1864], 3–5.
102. Indian Penal Code (1860), ss. 306 and 309.
103. *Advocate-General of Bengal v Ranee Surnomoyee* [1864], 5. The Age of Consent Act (1891) would raise the age of consent for all girls in India from ten to twelve.
104. *Advocate-General of Bengal v Ranee Surnomoyee* [1864], 6.
105. James Belich, *The New Zealand Wars and the Victorian Interpretation of Racial Conflict* (Auckland: Auckland University Press, 1986).
106. Bowler, "From 'Savage' to 'Primitive,'" 727.
107. Charles Darwin, *The Descent of Man and Selection in Relation to Sex*, 2nd ed. (New York, 1896), 156.
108. See: Ann Hunter, "Boundaries of Colonial Criminal Law in Relation to Inter-Aboriginal Conflict (Inter Se Offences) in Western Australia in the 1830s–1840s," *Australian Journal of Legal History* 8, no. 2 (2004), 215–36.
109. Ward, "A Means and Measure of Civilisation," 8.
110. Edward Jerningham Wakefield and John Ward, *The British Colonization of New Zealand* (London, 1837), 400.
111. *Report of the Parliamentary Select Committee on Aboriginal Tribes (British Settlements)* (London, 1837), 127.
112. On the Select Committee, see: Elizabeth Elbourne, "The Sin of the Settler: The 1835–36 Select Committee on Aborigines and Debates over Virtue and Conquest in the Early Nineteenth-Century British White Settler Empire," *Journal of Colonialism and Colonial History* 4, no. 3 (2003).
113. Ford, *Settler Sovereignty*, 3.
114. George Grey, "A Report upon the Best Means of Promoting the Civilization of the Aboriginal Inhabitants of Australia," in *Further Information Respecting the Aborigines*, by the Aborigines' Committee of the Meeting for Sufferings (London, 1842), 25.
115. Mark Finnane, "'Payback,' Customary Law and Criminal Law in Colonised Australia," *International Journal of the Sociology of Law* 29 (2001): 303.
116. Finnane, "'Payback,'" 304.
117. Judge's Notes of Evidence, 25 October 1858, *R v Old Man Billy and Young Man Billy*, VPRS 264/P0000/1.
118. Williams to Executive Council, 26 October 1858, VPRS 264/P0000/1.
119. "Melbourne News," *Bendigo Advertiser* (Victoria), 2 November 1858, 2.
120. "Inquest on A Murderer," *Argus* (Melbourne), 4 June 1859, 5.
121. Judge's Notes, 5 July 1860, *R v Peter (An Aboriginal)*, VPRS 264/P0000/2.
122. "Law Report," *Argus* (Melbourne), 29 June 1860, 6.

123. "Criminal Sessions," *Argus* (Melbourne), 16 February 1860, 3.
124. "Victoria," *South Australian Register* (Adelaide), 21 February 1860, 3.
125. "Criminal Sessions," *Argus* (Melbourne), 21 February 1860, 7.
126. Kenneth D. Nworah, "The Aborigines' Protection Society, 1889–1909: A Pressure Group in Colonial Policy," *Canadian Journal of African Studies* 5 (1971), 80.
127. Testimony of William Thomas, Judge's Notes, 5 July 1860, *R v Peter (An Aboriginal),* VPRS 264/P0000/2.
128. Testimony of William Thomas, Judge's Notes, 5 July 1860, *R v Peter (An Aboriginal),* VPRS 264/P0000/2.
129. "Law Report," *Argus* (Melbourne), 29 June 1860, 6.
130. "Colonial News," *Maitland Mercury and Hunter River General Advertiser* (New South Wales), 24 July 1860, 4.
131. "Law Report," *Argus* (Melbourne), 7 September 1860, 6.
132. Martin Kriewaldt, "The Application of the Criminal Law to the Aborigines of the Northern Territory of Australia," *University of Western Australia Law Review* 1 (1961–62): 20.
133. Blumenthal, "The Default Legal Person."
134. Grey, "A Report upon the Best Means of Promoting the Civilization of the Aboriginal Inhabitants of Australia," 27–28.

CHAPTER 8. CANNIBALISM AND CULPABILITY

1. Stony Mountain Penitentiary Admissions Book, 1885, LAC RG 13, T-11095.
2. Ruth Swan and Edward A. Jerome, "The History of the Pembina Métis Cemetery: Inter-Ethnic Perspectives on a Sacred Site," *Plains Anthropologist* 44, no. 170 (1 November 1999): 82.
3. Stony Mountain Penitentiary Admissions Book, 1885, LAC RG 13, T-11095.
4. Testimony of Francis Dufresne, LAC RG 13, vol. 1423, File 207A, Ducharme Capital Case File.
5. Rouleau's Notes of Evidence, Forwarded to the Minister of Justice on 28 September 1885, LAC RG 13, vol. 1423, File 207A.
6. Charles B. Rouleau to Minister of Justice, 28 September 1885, LAC RG 13, vol. 1423, File 207A.
7. There are several alternative forms and spellings of wendigo used among First Nations peoples. Common variants include *witiko, witigo, windigo, wintigo,* and *wittikow.* Variations on the Cree form, *wihtikow*, spelled *witigo*, are generally used in the Charles Ducharme and Wawasehowein capital case file. I have adopted the most common English form—wendigo—here. See Robert A. Brightman, "The Windigo in the Material World," *Ethnohistory* 35, no. 4 (1 October 1988): 337–79.
8. Terminology can be complicated when describing Indigenous Canadian communities. In general, both Métis and groups sometimes known as "Indian" can be accurately described as Indigenous. "First Nations" is often preferred today in Canada, although First Nations does not, usually, include the Métis. Here, I have referred to both the Métis and the Cree as Indigenous and Aboriginal but have restricted "First Nations" to the Cree and Ojibwa nations. See Edward J. Hedican, *Applied*

Anthropology in Canada: Understanding Aboriginal Issues (Toronto: University of Toronto Press, 2008), 5–8.

9. On capital punishment and Indigenous defendants in Canada, see: Jacqueline Briggs, "Exemplary Punishment: TRL MacInnes, the Department of Indian Affairs, and Indigenous Executions, 1936–52," *Canadian Historical Review* 100, no. 3 (2019): 398–438.
10. John L. Tobias, "Canada's Subjugation of the Plains Cree, 1879–1885," *Canadian Historical Review* 64, no. 4 (1983): 526.
11. MacDonald to Carnarvon, 14 April 1870, Add MS 60803, Carnarvon Papers.
12. Tobias, "Canada's Subjugation of the Plains Cree, 1879–1885," 521.
13. Hayter Reed to the Indian Commissioner, 28 December 1883, LAC RG 10, vol. 3668, File 10644.
14. Fort Pitt Historical Society, *Fort Pitt History Unfolding: History of the Hudson Bay Post and the School Districts of White Eagle, Harlan, Frenchman Butte, Rock Bottom, Onion Lake, Fort Pitt* (Fort Pitt, SK: Fort Pitt Historical Society, 1985), 37.
15. Tobias, "Canada's Subjugation of the Plains Cree, 1879–1885," 536.
16. The Métis people described in this chapter were, like Louis Riel, French-speaking and Catholic. There were, however, Métis groups in the nineteenth century of Scottish and English heritage, many of whom were Protestant Christians and spoke English. Hedican, *Applied Anthropology in Canada*, 7–8.
17. Walter Hildebrandt, *Views from Fort Battleford: Constructed Visions of an Anglo-Canadian West* (Regina, SK: Canadian Plains Research Centre, 2008), 19–20.
18. "Census of Part of the North-West Territories of Canada, August, 1885," *Journal of the Statistical Society of London* 49, no. 2 (1886): 476.
19. Annual Report of the Commissioner of the North-West Mounted Police Force, Dominion of Canada Sessional Papers, vol. 6 (1886), 13.
20. W. F. Bowker, "Stipendiary Magistrates and the Supreme Court of the North-West Territories, 1876–1907," *Alberta Law Review* 26 (1988): 270.
21. Bowker, "Stipendiary Magistrates," 267–68.
22. Letters between Charles Rouleau and the Ministry of Justice, November 1883–February 1884, LAC RG 13-A-2, vol. 58, File 1594.
23. Rouleau to Alexander Campbell, 4 December 1884, LAC RG 13-A-2, vol. 61, File 1315.
24. Rouleau to Campbell, 4 December 1884, LAC RG 13-A-2, vol. 61, File 1315.
25. Rouleau to Minister of Justice, 28 September 1885, LAC RG 13, vol. 1423, File 207A.
26. Thompson's Report, 5 November 1885, LAC RG 13, vol. 1423, File 207A.
27. Thompson's Report, 5 November 1885, LAC RG 13, vol. 1423, File 207A.
28. Oliver Wendell Holmes Jr., "Privilege, Malice, and Intent," *Harvard Law Review* 8, no. 1 (25 April 1894): 2.
29. "Thompson, Sir John Sparrow David," *DCB*.
30. Thompson's Report, 5 November 1885, LAC RG 13, vol. 1423, File 207A.
31. Minutes of the North-West Council, 5 November 1885, North-West Territories Government, Record Books, Minutes of the Council, NWT, 1877–1886, vol. 2, 1879–1885, SAB-S.
32. Rouleau's Notes, LAC RG 13, vol. 1423, File 207A.
33. Testimony of François Dufresne, Rouleau's Notes, LAC RG 13, vol. 1423, File 207A.

34. Testimony of Paskwy Ak, Rouleau's Notes, LAC RG 13, vol. 1423, File 207A.
35. Basil Johnston, *The Manitous: The Spiritual World of the Ojibway*, 1st ed. (New York: HarperCollins, 1995), xxii.
36. Johnston, *The Manitous,* 221.
37. Brightman, "The Windigo in the Material World."
38. For a small selection of scholarly works describing nineteenth-century wendigo cases, see: Sidney L. Harring, *White Man's Law: Native People in Nineteenth-Century Canadian Jurisprudence* (Toronto: University of Toronto Press, 1998); Hadley Louise Friedland, "The Wetiko (Windigo) Legal Principles: Responding to Harmful People in Cree, Anishnabek and Saulteaux Societies—Past, Present and Future Uses, with a Focus on Contemporary Violence and Child Victimization Concerns" (LL.M. thesis, University of Alberta, 2009); John Borrows, *Canada's Indigenous Constitution* (Toronto: University of Toronto Press, 2010); Shawn Smallman, "Spirit Beings, Mental Illness, and Murder: Fur Traders and the Windigo in Canada's Boreal Forest, 1774 to 1935," *Ethnohistory* 57, no. 4 (21 September 2010): 571–96. The wendigo was important to the mythologies of many Algonkian-speaking peoples, including the Cree, Ojibwe, Anishinabek, and Saulteaux. See: Borrows, *Canada's Indigenous Constitution,* 77. Scholars have noticed a concentration of wendigo cases in the late-nineteenth century, and a rapid tailing off of wendigos in the colonial archive in the first half of the twentieth century. See: Smallman, "Spirit Beings, Mental Illness, and Murder," 587–88.
39. Johnston, *The Manitous,* 235; Borrows, *Canada's Indigenous Constitution,* 84; Friedland, "The Wetiko (Windigo) Legal Principles," 39.
40. Brightman, "The Windigo in the Material World," 337.
41. Brightman, "The Windigo in the Material World," 337.
42. Charles A. Bishop, "Northern Algonkian Cannibalism and the Windigo Psychosis," in *Psychological Anthropology*, ed. Thomas R. Williams (The Hague: Mouton, 1975), 237–48.
43. Lou Marano, "Windigo Psychosis: The Anatomy of an Emic-Etic Confusion," *Current Anthropology* 23, no. 4 (1 August 1982): 385–97.
44. Brightman, "The Windigo in the Material World," 346.
45. Smallman, "Spirit Beings, Mental Illness, and Murder," 587–88.
46. "Richardson, Hugh (1826–1913)," *DCB.*
47. Hugh Richardson to Minister of Justice, 20 August 1879, LAC RG 13, vol. 1417, File 138A, Swift Runner Capital Case File.
48. Notes of Evidence, 6 August 1879, LAC RG 13, vol. 1417, File 138A.
49. Testimony of Kis-Sie-Ko-Way, Notes of Evidence, 6 August 1879, LAC RG 13, vol. 1417, File 138A.
50. Smallman, "Spirit Beings, Mental Illness, and Murder," 572.
51. Testimony of Kis-Sie-Ko-Way, Notes of Evidence, 6 August 1879, LAC RG 13, vol. 1417, File 138A.
52. Testimony of George Washington Brazian, Notes of Evidence, 6 August 1879, LAC RG 13, vol. 1417, File 138A.
53. Testimony of Kis-Sie-Ko-Way, Notes of Evidence, 6 August 1879, LAC RG 13, vol. 1417, File 138A.

54. Testimony of George Washington Brazian, Notes of Evidence, 6 August 1879, LAC RG 13, vol. 1417, File 138A.
55. Testimony of Inspector Gagnon, Notes of Evidence, 6 August 1879, LAC RG 13, vol. 1417, File 138A.
56. Testimony of George Herchmer, Notes of Evidence, 6 August 1879, LAC RG 13, vol. 1417, File 138A.
57. Kakisikutchin's Confession, Notes of Evidence, 6 August 1879, LAC RG 13, vol. 1417, File 138A.
58. Notes of Evidence, 6 August 1879, LAC RG 13, vol. 1417, File 138A.
59. Richardson to Deputy Minister of Justice, 20 August 1879, LAC RG 13, vol. 1417, File 138A.
60. Report of Governor-General-in-Council, 27 October 1879, LAC RG 13, vol. 1417, File 138A.
61. Edward Richard to the Minister of Justice, 4 February 1880, LAC RG 13, vol. 1417, File 138A.
62. Campbell to Sir John A. Macdonald, 24 October 1879, LAC RG 13, vol. 1417, File 138A.
63. Friedland is referring especially to the work of Sidney Harring, although she praises his sensitive engagement with the wendigo as part of the Cree, Ojibwe, and Saulteaux spiritual order. See: Harring, *White Man's Law*.
64. Friedland, "The Wetiko (Windigo) Legal Principles," 42. See also: Hadley Friedland, *The "Wetiko" Legal Principles: Cree and Anishinabek Responses to Violence and Victimization* (Toronto: University of Toronto Press, 2018).
65. Borrows, *Canada's Indigenous Constitution*, 83.
66. *Saskatchewan Herald* 7, no. 36, 28 September 1885, in *Battleford Beleaguered: 1885, The Story of the Riel Uprising from the Columns of the Saskatchewan Herald*, ed. William L. Clink (Willowdale, Ontario: W.L. Clink, 1984), 57–58.
67. Sharpe to Thompson, 24 November 1885, LAC RG 13, vol. 1423, File 207A.
68. Sharpe to A. Power, 24 November 1885, LAC RG 13, vol. 1423, File 207A.
69. Testimony of François Dufresne, LAC RG 13, vol. 1423, File 207A.
70. Testimony of François Dufresne, LAC RG 13, vol. 1423, File 207A.
71. Sharpe to Thompson, 24 November 1885, LAC RG 13, vol. 1423, File 207A.
72. Testimony of Thomas Mackay, *The Queen vs. Louis Riel: Accused and Convicted of the Crime of High Treason: Report of Trial at Regina, Appeal to the Court of Queen's Bench, Manitoba, Appeal to the Privy Council, England, Petition for Medical Examination of the Convict, List of Petitions for Commutation of Sentence, Ottawa* (Ottawa: Queen's Printer, 1886), 17–18.
73. Testimony of Thomas Mackay, *The Queen vs. Louis Riel: Accused and Convicted of the Crime of High Treason*, 19.
74. Testimony of Thomas Mackay, *The Queen vs. Louis Riel: Accused and Convicted of the Crime of High Treason*, 25.
75. Riel claimed in a letter to J. W. Taylor, the U.S. consul in Winnipeg, that he had, in fact, been eating stewed blood all winter because he was unable to digest anything else. Riel to J. W. Taylor, Regina, 1 August 1885, in *The Collected Writings of Louis Riel*, ed. George F. G. Stanley (Edmonton: University of Alberta Press, 1985), 157.

76. On Louis Riel and his trial, see Jennifer Reid, *Louis Riel and the Creation of Modern Canada: Mythic Discourse and the Postcolonial State* (Albuquerque: University of New Mexico Press, 2008); George R. D. Goulet, *The Trial of Louis Riel: Justice and Mercy Denied, a Critical, Legal and Political Analysis* (Calgary: Tellwell, 2005); Dan Asfar and Tim Chodan, *Louis Riel* (Edmonton: Folklore, 2003); Stanley, *The Collected Writings of Louis Riel*; J. M. Bumsted, *Louis Riel v. Canada: The Making of a Rebel* (Winnipeg: Great Plains, 2001); Maggie Siggins, *Riel: A Life of Revolution* (Toronto: HarperCollins, 1994); Joseph Kinsey Howard, *The Strange Empire of Louis Riel* (Toronto: Swan, 1970). For Riel in international context, see: Reid, *Louis Riel and the Creation of Modern Canada*; Thomas Flanagan, *Louis "David" Riel: Prophet of the New World* (Toronto: University of Toronto Press, 1996).
77. Riel's Certificate of Admission to Beauport Asylum, 11 May 1876, LAC, C-1228, 217–18.
78. Report of Dr. Jukes, 6 November 1885, John A. Macdonald Papers, LAC MG 26A, vol. 106.
79. Untitled poem by Louis Riel, BAnQ-M, Beauport Asylum Patient File of Louis Riel, P115, S2, SS6, SSS4, D2.
80. Riel to Taschereau, 18 June 1876, BAnQ-M, P115, S2, SS6, SSS4, D2.
81. Petition on behalf of Louis Riel, 24 October 1885, LAC RG 13, vol. 1421, part 1.
82. Riel to the Saskatchewan Delegation, 5 June 1884, LAC C-1228, 461–62.
83. Report of Dr. Jukes, 6 November 1885, John A. Macdonald Papers, LAC MG 26A, vol. 106.
84. Resolution Declaring Riel a Prophet, undated, LAC C-1228, 105.
85. "Batoche: A Comprehensive Survey of the Field," *Globe* (Toronto), 13 July 1885, 5.
86. Riel to Lemieux, Fitzpatrick and Dr. Frist, 16 June 1885, LAC C-1228, 1042.
87. Statutes of Canada, An Act for the Better Security of the Crown and of the Government (1868), c. 69, s. 5.
88. Burbidge to Campbell, 10 August 1885, LAC RG 13, vol. 2132, part 15.
89. Burbidge to Campbell, 10 August 1885, LAC RG 13, vol. 2132, part 15.
90. "Treason Felony in the North-West," *Canada Law Journal* 21, no. 11 (1 June 1885): 205–7.
91. Rouleau to Alexander Campbell, 4 December 1884, LAC RG 13-A-2, vol. 61, File 1315.
92. "Riel's Trial: The Rebel Ringleader Brought Before a Jury," *Globe* (Toronto), 21 July 1885, 2.
93. Hayter Reed to Superintendent of Indian Affairs, 3 November 1888, LAC, RG 13, vol. 1423, File 207A.
94. "Chase-Casgrain, Thomas," *DCB*.
95. *The Queen vs. Louis Riel: Accused and Convicted of the Crime of High Treason*, 8.
96. Louis Riel to Lemieux and Fitzpatrick, 18 June 1885, LAC C-1228, 1034.
97. Affidavit filed by Fitzpatrick, *The Queen vs. Louis Riel: Accused and Convicted of the Crime of High Treason*, 9–10.
98. "Riel's Diary," *The Globe* (Toronto), Wednesday, 15 July 1885, 4.
99. Testimony of Henry Walters, *The Queen vs. Louis Riel: Accused and Convicted of the Crime of High Treason*, 70.

100. See Testimony of Charles Nolin, *The Queen vs. Louis Riel: Accused and Convicted of the Crime of High Treason*, 99.
101. Testimony of Thomas Jackson, *The Queen vs. Louis Riel: Accused and Convicted of the Crime of High Treason*, 83.
102. Testimony of John W. Astley, *The Queen vs. Louis Riel: Accused and Convicted of the Crime of High Treason*, 27.
103. See: Testimony of John Astley, *The Queen vs. Louis Riel: Accused and Convicted of the Crime of High Treason*, 33.
104. Testimony of Thomas Jackson, *The Queen vs. Louis Riel: Accused and Convicted of the Crime of High Treason*, 84.
105. Testimony of Charles Nolin, *The Queen vs. Louis Riel: Accused and Convicted of the Crime of High Treason*, 99–100.
106. Testimony of Father Alexis André, *The Queen vs. Louis Riel: Accused and Convicted of the Crime of High Treason*, 114.
107. Testimony of Father Alexis André, *The Queen vs. Louis Riel: Accused and Convicted of the Crime of High Treason*, 112–14.
108. Testimony of François Roy, *The Queen vs. Louis Riel: Accused and Convicted of the Crime of High Treason*, 120–25.
109. Testimony of Daniel Clark, *The Queen vs. Louis Riel: Accused and Convicted of the Crime of High Treason*, 128; "Clark, Daniel," *DCB*.
110. Testimony of Daniel Clark, *The Queen vs. Louis Riel: Accused and Convicted of the Crime of High Treason*, 128.
111. Testimony of Daniel Clark, *The Queen vs. Louis Riel: Accused and Convicted of the Crime of High Treason*, 129–30. See also: Daniel Clark, "A Psycho-Medical History of Louise Riel," *American Journal of Insanity* 44, no. 88 (1887): 38–51; Daniel Clark, "A Few Canadian Cases in Criminal Courts in Which the Plea of Insanity Was Presented," *Proceedings of the American Medico-Psychological Association* 2 (1895): 171–91.
112. "The Louis Riel Case," *Observer* (London), 11 October 1885, 3.
113. *Louis Riel v The Queen* (Manitoba) [1885] UKPC 37 (22 October 1885).
114. "The Louis Riel Case," *Observer* (London), 11 October 1885, 3.
115. *Louis Riel v The Queen* [1885].
116. *Louis Riel v The Queen* [1885].
117. "Herbert, Henry Howard Molyneux, fourth earl of Carnarvon (1831–1890)," *ODNB*.
118. Carnarvon to Salisbury, 22 October 1885, PRO/30/6/130.
119. Carnarvon to Frederick Arthur Stanley, 25 October 1885, PRO/30/6/130.
120. R. Herbert to Carnarvon, 23 October 1885, PRO/30/6/130.
121. "Case of Louis Riel: Reasons for Non-Commutation of His Sentence," Lansdowne to Stanley, 13 November 1885, TNA, PRO/30/6/130.
122. Report of Dr. Jukes, 6 November 1885, John A. Macdonald Papers, LAC MG 26A, vol. 106.
123. "Kapapamahchakwew," *DCB*.
124. Testimony of Osisawehow, 9 October 1885, Iron Body Capital Case File, LAC RG 13, vol. 1421, File 194A.
125. "Dickens, Francis Jeffrey," *DCB*.

126. Francis Dickens to the Commanding or Indian Agent, Battleford, 3 April 1885, LAC RG 18-C-1, vol. 3778.
127. Fort Pitt Historical Society, *Fort Pitt History Unfolding*, 3.
128. Fort Pitt Historical Society, *Fort Pitt History Unfolding*, 43.
129. Hildebrandt, *Views from Fort Battleford*, 73.
130. Fort Pitt Historical Society, *Fort Pitt History Unfolding*, 47–48.
131. D. L. Scott to the Officer Commissioner NWMP, 26 January 1887 (copy), LAC RG 18, vol. 1075, *R v Dressy Man.*
132. Report of the Privy Council of Canada, John J. Magee, Clerk, 6 November 1885, LAC RG 13, vol. 1423, File 207A.
133. See: Man Without Blood Capital Case File, LAC RG 13, vol. 1421, File 198A; Ikta Capital Case File, LAC RG 13, vol. 1421, File 195A.
134. Bowker, "Stipendiary Magistrates," 169; Louis A. Knafla and Richard Klumpenhouwer, *Lords of the Western Bench: A Biographical History of the Supreme Court and District Courts of Alberta, 1876–1990* (Calgary: Legal Archives Society of Alberta, 1997), 161.
135. Rouleau to Campbell, 21 September 1885, R-996, Attorney General's Files, 283 L, SAB-R.
136. "Rouleau, Charles-Borromée," *DCB*; Knafla and Klumpenhouwer, *Lords of the Western Bench*, 161.
137. Rouleau to Campbell, 21 September 1885, R-996, Attorney General's Files, 283 L, SAB-R.
138. Rouleau to Thompson, 5 October 1885, Bad Arrow Capital Case File, LAC RG 13, vol. 1421, file 197A.
139. Witgen argues that a "political imaginary" that divided humanity into savage and civilized categories was "foundational to the colonial project in North America." See: Michael Witgen, "Seeing Red: Race, Citizenship, and Indigeneity in the Old Northwest," *Journal of the Early Republic* 38, no. 4 (3 December 2018): 606–7.
140. Osler to Burbidge, 16 August 1885, LAC RG 13, vol. 2132, part 11.
141. Osler to Burbidge, 16 August 1885, LAC RG 13, vol. 2132, part 11.
142. Ministry of Justice to W. Prescott Sharp and A. D. Stewart, 18 August 1885, LAC RG 13, vol. 2132, part 6.
143. Rouleau's Notes of Evidence, 3 October 1885, LAC RG 13, vol. 1421, File 197A.
144. *Saskatchewan Herald* 7, no. 36, 28 September 1885, in *Battleford Beleaguered*, ed. Clink, 58.
145. Sharp to Power, 24 November 1885, LAC RG 13, vol. 1423, File 207A.
146. Louison Mongrain Capital Case File, LAC RG 13, vol. 1421, File 200A.
147. Statement of W. B. Cameron, 11 March 1886, LAC RG 13, vol. 1421, File 200A.
148. Official Complaint of A. H. Stewart, Chief of Police in Hamilton, 23 September 1885, LAC RG 13, vol. 1421, File 200A.
149. Arraignment of Mongrain and Wawasehowein, 23 September 1885, LAC RG 13, vol. 1421, File 200A.
150. Rouleau's Notes, 25 September 1885, LAC RG 13, vol. 1421, File 200A.

151. Testimony of Clarence Loasby, Rouleau's Notes, 25 September 1885, LAC RG 13, vol. 1421, File 200A.
152. "McLean, William James," *DCB*.
153. Statement of W. B. Cameron, 11 March 1886, LAC RG 13, vol. 1421, File 200A.
154. Testimony of John Alfred Martin, Rouleau's Notes, 25 September 1885, LAC RG 13, vol. 1421, File 200A.
155. Testimony of Clarence Loasby, Rouleau's Notes, 25 September 1885, LAC RG 13, vol. 1421, file 200A.
156. Testimony of John Alfred Martin, Rouleau's Notes, 25 September 1885, LAC RG 13, vol. 1421, File 200A.
157. Testimony of Kasowakayo, Rouleau's Notes, 25 September 1885, LAC RG 13, vol. 1421, File 200A.
158. Testimony of Toussaint or Calling Bull and Kapesiweinokeo, Rouleau's Notes, 25 September 1885, LAC RG 13, vol. 1421, File 200A.
159. Testimony of Mesinachassayo, Rouleau's Notes, 25 September 1885, LAC RG 13, vol. 1421, File 200A.
160. "McLean, Amelia Anne (Paget)," *DCB*.
161. "McLean, Amelia Anne (Paget)," *DCB*.
162. Amelia McLean, 25 October 1885, LAC RG 13, vol. 1421, File 200A.
163. Statement of W. B. Cameron, 11 March 1886, LAC RG 13, vol. 1421, File 200A.
164. Amelia McLean, 25 October 1885, LAC RG 13, vol. 1421, File 200A.
165. Telegram for A. Power from Fort Qu'Apelle, 17 October 1885; Telegram for A. Power from Stony Mountain Penitentiary, 21 October 1885; Bedson to A. Power, 30 October 1885, LAC RG 13, vol. 1421, File 200A.
166. Bedson to A. Power, 24 October 1885, LAC RG 13, vol. 1421, File 200A; Statement of W. B. Cameron, 11 March 1886, LAC RG 13, vol. 1421, File 200A.
167. J. G. Moylan to A. Power, 28 October 1885, LAC RG 13, vol. 1421, File 200A.
168. S. L. Bedson to A. Power, 31 October 1885, LAC RG 13, vol. 1421, File 200A.
169. Statement of Anne Amelia McLean, 28 October 1885, LAC RG 13, vol. 1421, File 200A.
170. Statement of W. J. McLean, 28 October 1885, LAC RG 13, vol. 1421, File 200A.
171. J. S. D. Thompson to the Governor-General-in-Council, 5 November 1885 (copy), LAC RG 13, vol. 1421, File 200A.
172. Sharp to Thompson, 10 November 1885, LAC RG 13, vol. 1423, File 207A.
173. Thompson to Governor-General-in-Council, 16 November 1885, LAC RG 13, vol. 1423, File 207A.
174. Sharp to Thompson, 24 November 1885, LAC RG 13, vol. 1423, File 207A.
175. Testimony of Mooswar, Sharp's Trial Notes, LAC RG 13, vol. 1423, File 207A.
176. Rouleau to Thompson, 27 November 1885, LAC RG 13, vol. 1423, File 207A.
177. Report of the Privy Council of Canada, John J. Magee, Clerk, 9 December 1885, LAC RG 13, vol. 1423, File 207A.
178. Scott to Burbidge, 25 May 1886, LAC RG 13, vol. 2132, part 13.
179. Chapleau to Minister of Justice, 19 November 1886, LAC RG 13, vol. 2132, part 31.
180. NWMP Correspondence about *R v Wawasehowein*, LAC RG 18, vol. 1075.

181. Richardson's Notes on Wawasehowein's Second Trial, SAB-R, Richardson Trial Notebook, R-E3633.
182. Onion Lake Petition, 16 November 1887, LAC RG 13, vol. 1423, File 207A.
183. Père Merer to D. H. McDowall, 17 November 1887, LAC RG 13, vol. 1423, File 207A.
184. A. Lacombe to Thompson, 10 August 1889, LAC RG 13, vol. 1423, File 207A. Translation from the French my own.
185. Commissioner to Superintendent, 8 December 1887, LAC RG 13, vol. 1423, File 207A.
186. Burbidge to Campbell, 10 August 1885, LAC RG 13, vol. 2132, part 15.
187. Sutherland to Bedson, 15 July 1890, LAC RG 13, vol. 1423, File 207A.
188. Sutherland's Report on Ducharme's Death, 3 August 1890, LAC RG 13, vol. 1423, File 207A.
189. Stony Mountain Penitentiary Admissions Book, 1885, LAC RG 13, T-11095. Wahsahgamass was tried for a murder allegedly committed at the Saddle Lake Agency in 1918. See: Re-Trial of Wahsahgamass for Murder, LAC RG 10, vol. 7469, File 19118-3.
190. *The Queen v Machweekequonabe*, LAC, RG 13, vol. 2089. For the record of the case as it was appealed, see *R v Machekequonabe* (1897) 28 O.R. 309.
191. Trial transcript, *The Queen v Machweekequonabe*, LAC, RG 13, vol. 2089.
192. *R v Machekequonabe* (1897).
193. *R v Machekequonabe* (1897).
194. Sidney L. Harring, "The Liberal Treatment of Indians: Native People in Nineteenth Century Ontario Law," *Saskatchewan Law Review* 56 (1992): 322.
195. Lesley Erickson, *Westward Bound: Sex, Violence, the Law, and the Making of a Settler Society* (Vancouver: UBC Press, 2011), 53; Harring, *White Man's Law*.
196. Harring, "Liberal Treatment of Indians," 323.
197. Harring, "Liberal Treatment of Indians," 323.
198. Hay, "Property, Authority and the Criminal Law." See also: Ted McCoy, "Legal Ideology in the Aftermath of Rebellion: The Convicted First Nations Participants, 1885," *Histoire sociale/Social History* 42, no. 83 (2009): 175–201.

CONCLUSION

1. E. M. Forster, *A Passage to India*, ed. Oliver Stallybrass (New York: Rosetta Books, 2010), 214.
2. Forster, *A Passage to India,* 216.
3. Rex Ferguson, *Criminal Law and the Modernist Novel: Experience on Trial* (Cambridge: Cambridge University Press, 2013), 60.
4. Forster, *A Passage to India,* 164.
5. Forster, *A Passage to India,* 206.
6. Forster, *A Passage to India,* 248.
7. Forster, *A Passage to India,* 65, 165, 248, 270.
8. See: Green, *Freedom and Criminal Responsibility.*

9. R. B. Haldane, "The Work for the Empire of the Judicial Committee of the Privy Council," *Cambridge Law Journal* 14 (1921): 154.
10. André du Toit, "Victims of 'British Justice'? A Century of Wrong as Anti-Imperial Tract, Core Narrative of the Afrikaner 'Nation,' and Victim-Based Solidarity-Building Discourse," in *Ten Books That Shaped the British Empire: Creating an Imperial Commons*, ed. Antoinette Burton and Isabel Hofmeyr (Durham, NC: Duke University Press, 2015), 112–13.
11. Lyndsay Campbell, "Race, Upper Canadian Constitutionalism and British Justice," *LHR* 33 (2015): 41–92.
12. Truth and Reconciliation Commission of Canada, *A Knock on the Door: The Essential History of Residential Schools from the Truth and Reconciliation Commission of Canada, Edited and Abridged* (Winnipeg: University of Manitoba Press, 2015); Wolfe, "Settler Colonialism."
13. See: Alison Bashford and Philippa Levine, eds., *The Oxford Handbook of the History of Eugenics* (Oxford: Oxford University Press, 2010).
14. Maudsley, *Responsibility in Mental Disease*, 44.
15. Law Commission, *Criminal Liability: Insanity and Automatism*, Discussion Paper (23 July 2013), s. 1.4, p. 1, available at http://lawcommission.justice.gov.uk/areas/insanity.htm.
16. See, for example: N. J. Schweitzer and Michael J. Saks, "Neuroimage Evidence and the Insanity Defense," *Behavioral Sciences and the Law* 29 (2011): 592–607; Joseph R. Simpson, *Neuroimagining in Forensic Psychiatry: From the Clinic to the Courtroom* (Chichester, West Sussex: Wiley-Blackwell, 2010), and Steven R. Smith, "Neuroscience, Ethics and Legal Responsibility: The Problem of the Insanity Defense," *Science and Engineering Ethics* 18 (2012): 475–81.
17. See: Jennifer L. Skeem, Sarah Manchak, and Jillian K. Peterson, "Correctional Policy for Offenders with Mental Illness," *Law and Human Behavior* 35, no. 2 (2011): 110–26.
18. For example, John Gardner argues that the growing cosmopolitanism of British society means that we must grapple with the "moral consequences of human diversity"—but governing diversity is not a new problem for British criminal law. See: John Gardner, *Offences and Defences: Selected Essays in the Philosophy of Criminal Law* (Oxford: Oxford University Press, 2007), 156–57.
19. See: Deborah Woo, "Cultural 'Anomalies' and Cultural Defenses: Towards an Integrated Theory of Homicide and Suicide," *International Journal of the Sociology of Law* 32 (2004): 279–302; Taryn F. Goldstein, "Cultural Conflicts in Court: Should the American Criminal Justice System Formally Recognize a 'Cultural Defense'?" *Dickinson Law Review* 99 (Fall 1994): 141–68; Marie-Claire Foblets and Alison Dundes Renteln, eds., *Multicultural Jurisprudence: Comparative Perspectives on the Cultural Defense* (Portland, OR: Hart, 2009); Alison Dundes Renteln, *The Cultural Defense* (New York: Oxford University Press, 2004); Pascale Fournier, "The Ghettoisation of Difference in Canada: Rape by Culture and the Danger of a Cultural Defence in Criminal Law Trials," *Manitoba Law Journal* 29 (2002): 81; Will Kymlicka, Claes Lernestedt, and Matt Matravers, eds., *Criminal Law and Cultural Diversity* (Oxford: Oxford University Press, 2014).

20. See: Andrew Ashworth, "The Doctrine of Provocation," *Cambridge Law Journal* 35 (1976): 292–320, and Cynthia Lee, *Murder and the Reasonable Man: Passion and Fear in the Criminal Courtroom* (New York: NYU Press, 2003).
21. S. F. Moore, "Law and Social Change: The Semi-Autonomous Social Field as an Appropriate Subject of Study," *Law and Society Review* 7, no. 4 (1973): 734.
22. Maudsley, *Responsibility in Mental Disease*, 11.

Acknowledgments

This book has been with me, in one form or another, for ten years. It is a gift to get to thank the people and institutions that have made my work, and my life, possible.

First, thanks to the community of scholars at Princeton University. I miss cycling home from Firestone on warm nights through thick air that smelled of sweetgrass. My supervisor, Dirk Hartog, has shaped my understanding of what it means to be a scholar, a writer, an adviser, and a teacher. I admire his humane approach to this world and past ones. Heartfelt thanks also to Linda Colley and Keith Wailoo, whose intellectual guidance in my time at Princeton and beyond has been transformative. Thomas A. Green, though not in New Jersey, was the most perfect outside reader, providing witty, trenchant criticism on multiple dissertation drafts alongside invaluable insights into responsibility and legal thought.

My gratitude also to Margot Canaday, Regina Kunzel, Gyan Prakash, Bhavani Raman, and Kim Lane Scheppele. The Princeton Department of History, and its outstanding administrators, especially Kristy Novak, provided every kind of support. Thanks, too, to the Canadian Studies Program for its generous funding in this project's early stages. The friends and colleagues I met in New Jersey have taught me so much. Thanks to Michael Barany, Anna Bonnell-Freidin, Henry Cowles, Rohit De, William Deringer, Christopher Florio, Kellen Funk, Maeve Glass, Craig Green, Reut Harari, Evan Hepler-Smith, Zack Kagan-Guthrie, Jamie Kreiner, Radha Kumar, Kyrill Kunakovich, Hanna Lee, Molly Lester, Jane Manners, Mona Mady, Martín Marimón, Sarah Milov, Kalyani Ramnath, Marcia Schenck, Margaret Schotte, Sarah Seo, Chris Shannon, Melissa Texeira, Christina Welsch, and Fadzilah Yahaya. I am also grateful to Susanna Blumenthal, Howard Erlanger, and Mitra Sharafi for their intellectual and professional counsel. Mitra has been a model and an inspiration since our first meeting at Small World, both as a scholar and as a friend.

Many archives and libraries opened their collections to me, and I benefited from the patience and expertise of archive staff across the former British world. My thanks to the British Library, particularly Antonia Moon and Jonathan Sims; the National Archives (Kew); the Bethlem Hospital Archives and Museum and Colin Gale, who ceded his own desk to me when I worked there in 2014; Lincoln's Inn Library and Guy Holborn; the Berkshire Record Office; the London Metropolitan Archives; the Howard League for Penal Reform in London, particularly Anita Dockley; the Cambridge University Library; the Provincial Record Office of Victoria; the Old Melbourne Gaol, particularly Trish Rothville and Rosemary Hanscombe, at the National Trust of Australia (Victoria); the State Library of Victoria; the National Archives of Australia; Library and Archives Canada; Bibliothèque et Archives nationales du Québec (BAnQ) in Montreal and Québec City; the Saskatchewan Archives Board in Regina and Saskatoon; the Archives of Ontario, particularly Zoë Cliff; the Newberry Library; the Montana Historical Society; Widener Library at Harvard University; and Firestone Library at Princeton University.

Emma Rothschild and the Joint Centre for History and Economics at Harvard University and Magdalene College, Cambridge, welcomed me into a tremendously exciting transatlantic scholarly network, as intellectually ambitious as it is warm. At both Cambridges, my thanks to Sunil Amrith, Fahad Bishara, Allan Brandt, Rohit De, Megan Donaldson, Claire Edington, Bronwen Everill, Franziska Exeler, Jonnie Gorrie, Mathias Haeussler, Tim Harper, Diana Kim, Hannah Malone, Inga Huld Markan, Renaud Morieux, Louise Moschetta, Dan Navon, Jennifer Nickerson, Anne O'Donnell, Surabhi Ranganathan, Charles Rosenberg, Emma Rothschild, Kirsty Walker, Fei-Hsien Wang, Rowan Williams, and Fadzilah Yahaya.

The Centre for Criminology and Sociolegal Studies at the University of Toronto is a great place to work. Thanks to my community in Toronto, especially to Jacquie Briggs, Vincent Chiao, Rosemary Gartner, Philip Girard, Beatrice Jauregui, Tyler King, Matthew Light, Audrey Macklin, Wilhelmina Peters, Jim Phillips, Kristen Plys, Ashley Rubin, Margaret Schotte, Simon Stern, Mariana Valverde, William Watson, Rebecca Woods, and Scot Wortley. Thanks to the organizers and participants in the Sociolegal Workshop coordinated by Sida Liu, the History Writing Workshop coordinated by Yvon Wang, and the Criminal Theory Workshop coordinated by Vincent Chiao.

Through moves across three countries, the American Society for Legal History (ASLH) has been a beacon of scholarly engagement and personal connection. My participation in the Hurst Institute, led in 2015 by the inimitable Barbara Welke, changed how I think about the responsibilities of legal storytelling. My selection as a Kathryn T. Preyer Scholar in 2016 and Michael Witgen's incisive commentary on the paper that ultimately became this book's final chapter improved it immeasurably. Gautham Rao's editorial leadership and the anonymous reviewers for *Law and History Review* helped me to sharpen it into an article, which the society generously recognized with the Surrency Prize in 2019. This is typical of ASLH's sustained investment in junior scholars, and I plan to pay my many debts forward.

Six people read and commented on full drafts of this book, some multiple times. Sincere thanks to Pamela Haag, Dirk Hartog, Padraic Scanlan, Margaret Schotte, Mariana Valverde, and Rebecca Woods. Pamela Haag provided editorial assistance at a critical juncture. Rebecca and Margaret offered kind and critical perspectives from the histories of science and empire, shared parenting triumphs and foibles, and refilled wine glasses. Mariana gave her peerless theoretical insights as freely as she did her time and care, just as ready to take a three-year-old to a diner as to read a manuscript.

Portions of this book have appeared in article form and are reprinted here with permission. These include: "Heart of Ice: Indigenous Defendants and Colonial Law in the Canadian North-West," *Law and History Review* 36, no. 2 (2018): 199–234; "At Her Majesty's Pleasure: Criminal Insanity in 19th-Century Britain," *History Compass* 14, no. 10 (1 October 2016): 470–79; and "Wondrous Depths: Judging the Mind in Nineteenth-Century America," *Law and Social Inquiry* 44, no. 3 (2019): 828–49. At Yale University Press, my editor, Jaya Chatterjee, expertly guided the project through to publication. The anonymous reviewers were both generous and critical, and I appreciate their spirited engagement with the manuscript.

Thanks to my friends and family who have been regaled, sometimes despite their protests, with tales of nineteenth-century trials: Steve Aylward, Steve Birek, the Chan-Scanlans, Rosana Collepardo, Amy Coulterman, Leigh Evans, Samara Fox, Heather Fregeau, Laura French, Gabe Friedman, Megan Goldman-Petri, Jeff Goslan, Leon Grek, Sean Hayward, Sarina Isenberg, Thomas Lipton, Sophie MacIntyre, Alexandra Marchand, Amira Mekouar, Caela Moffet, Vinay Kumar Mysore, Palma Paciocco, James Phelan, Guillem Portella, Saro Setrakian, Warren Spruzenieks, Alex Swann, Elizabeth Therrien, Sarah Tischhauser, Mateusz Trybowski, Alice Tsier, Aria Umezawa, Clothilde Verdier, and Henry Weil. My grandmother, Jean Evans, and my father-in-law, Larry Scanlan, are sorely missed. My parents, Karen and Alan Evans, have been constant through it all, never quailing when I left Canada for England or law for history, even when they knew it would take me far away. They offered material and moral support at every turn, for which I am truly thankful.

Finally, thanks to Padraic Scanlan, who knows me and this book better than anyone. He has given me, and this work, so much. Our magical, magnetic, passionate son, Rafe, has cracked open new parts of what it means to be a person. Sharing my life with Padraic, whose skill and historical intuition I admire so deeply, has enriched how I think and write about the past, how I experience the present, and how I imagine my future. This book is for him.

Index